SALT,
LIGHT,
AND A CITY

Salt, Light, and a City

Introducing Missional Ecclesiology

GRAHAM HILL

WIPF & STOCK · Eugene, Oregon

SALT, LIGHT, AND A CITY
Introducing Missional Ecclesiology

Wipf & Stock
An Imprint of Wipf and Stock Publishers
199 W. 8th Ave., Suite 3
Eugene, OR 97401
www.wipfandstock.com

ISBN 13: 978-1-60899-756-5

Manufactured in the U.S.A.

For my wife Felicity and my daughters Madison, Grace, and Dakotah—
the women I adore and love more than words can express.
This book is only possible because of their love, belief, encouragement, and sacrifice.

Contents

Foreword

by Michael Frost

WHEN GRAHAM HILL BEMOANS the dearth of intentional and systematic ecclesiology in much of the missional conversation, I admit to feeling a pang of guilt. I suspect I may have played a part in stalling the discussion about missional forms of ecclesiology in certain circles. In my book, *The Shaping of Things to Come*, co-authored with Alan Hirsch, I proposed the formula that our Christology should determine our missiology, which in turn should determine our ecclesiology. Alan Hirsch reiterated this formula in his book *The Forgotten Ways* where he said,

> Not only our purpose is defined by the person and work of Jesus, but our methodology as well. These set the agenda of our missiology. Our missiology (our sense of purpose in the world) must then go on to inform the nature and functions, as well as the forms, of the church . . . [I]t is absolutely vital that we get the order right. It is Christ who determines our purpose and mission in the world, and then it is our mission that must drive our search for modes of being-in-the-world.[1]

I have heard that formula quoted back to me many times in the years since: Christology determines missiology, missiology determines ecclesiology.

We felt that it was an important way to break the fixation that many church growth experts had with "getting church right" in order to attract a disaffected or uninterested generation back to Sunday morning attendance. Without much reference to rigorous biblical scholarship or the missiological paradigm it proposes, church leaders were jumping straight into questions of ecclesiology, exploring the forms of church that would most likely appeal to the current generation. Whether it was Peter Wagner's homogenous unit principle or Kennon Callahan's keys to an effective church (competent programs, accessibility, visibility, adequate parking, landscaping, etc.)[2] or Rick Warren's purpose-driven approach (including seeker-sensitive services) or even Brian McLaren's early emphasis on engaging postmodern yearnings,[3] they were aimed at increasing the marketability of

---

1. Hirsch, *The Forgotten Ways*, 143.
2. Callahan, *Twelve Keys to an Effective Church*.
3. McLaren, *Reinventing Your Church*.

church services as the primary doorway to the Christian community and its message. As Warren said in *The Purpose-Driven Church*:

> Look beyond the hype of every growing church and you will find a common de-
> nominator: They have figured out a way to meet the real needs of people. A church
> will never grow beyond its capacity to meet needs. If your church is genuinely meet-
> ing needs, then attendance will be the least of your problems—you'll have to lock the
> doors to keep people out.[4]

This comes shortly after Warren anchored church growth in the ministry of Jesus himself, by saying, "One of the impressive characteristics of Jesus' ministry was that it attracted crowds. Large crowds. *Enormous* crowds."[5] There was no reflection on the fact that these crowds dissipated as soon as Jesus stopped meeting their needs by feeding or healing them and started demanding radical obedience to his kingdom (see John 6:60–66). This approach to beginning the missional enterprise by first tinkering with church forms, seemingly without reference to the Gospels, led many of us, Alan Hirsch and myself included, to go back to first principles. Surely, we said, if we re-encounter the ministry and teaching of Jesus this would necessarily shape our purpose in the world as his people. Our logic went: if we become students of the Scriptures, allowing our Christology to shape our missiology, then we can worry later about the forms of church that best serve that mission, depending on the context in which it is placed.

It has often bemused me that whenever I am conducting a seminar or teaching a class on the missional paradigm, the first question I always get relates to ecclesiology. Well, asks the first enquirer, what does this look like for a local church? I have always tried to resist answering this question too early. It betrays the enquirer's desire to picture the practical ecclesial model I'm presenting and then (presumably) to buy that model "off the shelf," so to speak. Instead, I would declare, let us focus on a trinitarian, Christ-centered missiology and we can worry about our ecclesiology later.

Well, clearly, later is upon us. Stalling the conversation about a missional ecclesiology can't go on continuously. As Graham Hill points out, the discussion regarding a missional reading of Scripture and its contribution to a mission-shaped paradigm for the church is well entrenched. It seems that the time is well and truly upon us for a thorough-going examination of the contribution the missional conversation can have on forms of ecclesiology. Usually, when this kind of work is attempted, however, the writer appears blind to his or her own church tradition, thus exploring missional ecclesiology from entirely within that framework. Their blind spot limits the scope of their work, but Graham resists the temptation to ignore the presumptions of his own tradition and takes a broad brush to this enterprise by beginning with a very handy treatment of twelve European and American theologians. By so doing, he ensures that Roman Catholic, Eastern Orthodox, Protestant, and specifically Free Church Protestant ecclesiologies are allowed to make a contribution to this discussion. Drawing on thinkers as diverse as Joseph Ratzinger, Hans Küng, John Zizioulas, Jürgen Moltmann, John Howard Yoder, and Miroslav Volf,

---

4. Warren, *The Purpose Driven Church*, 221.

5. Ibid., 207 (italics in original).

Graham insists that we not reduce the development of a genuinely missional ecclesiology to the ideas of a handful of popular evangelical church leaders and their practical books on the subject. This early section of *Salt, Light, and a City* might be the most challenging for some readers, but I think Graham makes an impressive contribution to this area. He is broadening the canvas widely and all the while providing a lens through which to view it, a lens informed by the great missional thinkers, David Bosch, Lesslie Newbigin, Darrell Guder, and others.

The second section of this book will appeal more obviously to students, leaders, and practitioners looking for a mission-shaped ecclesiology, but I would caution readers not to jump straight there. The work of engaging with great ecclesiologies contributes very directly to the conversation that occurs later in *Salt, Light, and a City*.

David Bosch wrote, "It is not the church that has a mission of salvation to fulfill in the world; it is the mission of the Son and the Spirit through the Father that includes the church."[6] In other words, the church does not create its own mission; it is the mission of God that creates the church. Ecclesiological concerns really should follow hot on the heels of any meaningful missiological exploration. Referencing Lesslie Newbigin, Graham points this out very clearly in *Salt, Light, and a City*, and thereby chastises me for seeking to delay this important work. It is a deserved though gentle rebuke, in spite of my anxieties about readers' inclinations to adopt inadequate, pre-fabricated models. *Salt, Light, and a City* is no cloying attempt at a simplistic universal model for the missional church. Graham insists we do the hard work of engaging trinitarian theology, contemporary missiology, and broad understandings of ecclesiology to find a way forward. In brief, it is an invaluable addition to any library of research into the missional paradigm.

In writing this I must declare that Graham Hill is a valued colleague of mine. I know him not only as an academic, but also as a friend and partner in the missional enterprise. A gifted scholar, he is also a missionary. This gives his work both theological weight and the energizing spark of passionate experience.

Michael Frost,
The Tinsley Institute,
Morling College, Sydney, Australia

6. Bosch, *Transforming Mission*, 389.

Introduction:
Forming a Missional Theology of the Church

You are the salt of the earth. But if the salt loses its saltiness, how can it be made salty again? It is no longer good for anything, except to be thrown out and trampled underfoot.

You are the light of the world. A city on a hill cannot be hidden. Neither do people light a lamp and put it under a bowl. Instead they put it on its stand, and it gives light to everyone in the house. In the same way, let your light shine before people, that they may see your good deeds and glorify your Father in heaven.

—MATTHEW 5:13–16

IN MATTHEW 5:13–16 JESUS provides three striking missional images of the church—salt, light, and a city.[1] Jesus confronts his listeners with a missional depiction of the church, seeking to reorient their understanding of their purpose in his redemptive plan. The church in mission is the salt of the earth, the light of the world, and a city set on a hill. As salt, light, and a city set on a hill, the church in mission is to let its "light shine before people, that they may see your good deeds and praise your Father in heaven." The purpose of the church's missional nature is the glorification and worship of the Father.

The church has always had to wrestle with what it means to have a missional nature and mandate, given by a missionary God. The contemporary church, of course, is no different, and is confronting new missional challenges and opportunities. Three stories illustrate this well—one each from Scotland, Australia, and South Korea.

Adelaide Place Church has worshiped in the city of Glasgow since 1829. Over time the city demographics changed, and the church found itself culturally irrelevant to people living in the inner city. The church had a large amount of debt and was beginning to empty out. The church took some risks, and began experimenting with ministries that might make sense to the cultures of inner-city Glasgow. These included ministries to in-

---

1. I am grateful to John Driver for helping me understand the importance of these three biblical images for the church's missional self-understanding. In a chapter on Matthew 5:13–16, called "Salt, Light, and a City," Driver provides a helpful analysis of these three biblical images for the church in mission: Driver, *Images of the Church*, 170–81. I draw my book title from Jesus's discourse in Matthew 5 and also from John Driver's chapter.

ternational students, migrant families, and homeless young women. In 1984 Adelaide Place gave some thought to the cultures and needs of their location—the ethnic, socio-economic, generational, and professional diversity of the inner city; the growing student population; the extent of homelessness; the tourist population, who swelled the numbers in the summer; and, the proximity of shoppers, entertainment seekers, and business people.

The church also required significant renovation, and Adelaide Place decided to use this as an opportunity for mission. Choosing not to merely renovate a worship space, the church decided to build for mission—a nursery, a café, and a guesthouse. During these last twenty-eight years the church has continued to monitor the needs of their community and the shifts in the surrounding cultures. Together with other churches they have formed an interdenominational Trust called Business in Glasgow (BiG), to reach out to the business community. This ministry offers support and encouragement programs to business people, and is the first step toward being missionary in that arena of the city's life. Working with the National Workplace Chaplaincy in Scotland, the church is seeking to develop a business model that will provide income support to small missionary initiatives, as well as offering opportunities for connecting with people through their workplace. They continue to seek God's guidance for how to genuinely reach the many cultures of Glasgow.

Over on the other side of the world Urban Seed is engaged in innovative missional experimentation. Urban Seed is a small, Christian, not-for-profit organization that engages faith, community, and culture in order to respond to poverty in Melbourne. Urban Seed was birthed out of the Collins Street Baptist Church fifteen years ago in the heart of the city of Melbourne, and presently runs street, food, hospitality, recreation, youth development, and school-based programs. These programs encourage and assist with connection to support services (e.g. mental health, drug treatment, health, and housing services) and create space for a Homeless Person's Legal Clinic. Urban Seed regularly connects with government, business, church, and local community groups as through advocacy and engagement they seek to address the underlying causes of disadvantage. Urban Seed's vision is to see communities of hope, healing, and justice. Urban Seed has chosen three impoverished priority neighborhoods in Melbourne to plant and renew local churches through contextual community mission groups—known as *Seeds Communities*.

The suburbs of Footscray, Norlane, and Long Gully are each renowned for their entrenched generational poverty, with the attendant symptoms of unemployment, addiction, violence, and disengagement from schooling. The suburbs also tend to have been under-resourced by larger church and mission groups. Many people regularly face material, practical, and spiritual struggles. Thus, Urban Seed has prioritized these communities. The Seeds communities form a network of groups who implement projects and mission initiatives that address pressing local needs in ways that creatively complement and connect traditional services. Some of the ways this is expressed is through accessible public *Word and Worship* gatherings, table-based hospitality events, and personal service to others with a particular focus on local schools. Their missional model is based on Jesus's instructions to his disciples when he sent them out: preaching, healing, and casting out evil—translating to their core areas of work: education, hospitality, and advocacy. They support local facilitators to work within communities to identify strengths, design action plans, and locate resources to solve basic needs, alleviate poverty, and strengthen community development.

Simultaneously, over in Seoul, South Korea, All Nations Church is pursuing a missional strategy soaked in prayer, discipleship, sacrifice, and a radical dream to see Asia won for Jesus Christ. Every day of the year, even in mid winter when it is snowing and bitterly cold, teams of evangelists go out into the streets and from home to home. From a church that started ten years ago in a home with seventeen people, it now has over one thousand worshipers, largely as a result of its missional endeavors. All Nations Church is convinced that God desires to bring revival to the nations, since he is a missionary God, and, therefore, the church is essentially a missionary community. After sending scores of full-time missionaries throughout Asia, they have decided to branch out further afield in their missionary efforts, including sending missionaries to nations that once sent missionaries to Korea. Instead of summer camps, young adults go on annual short-term mission trips and pray about whether God is calling them into full-time mission. All Nations Church has a vision to send another thousand full-time missionaries into these countries over the next decade—as many missionaries as people currently attending their Sunday worship services.[2]

Enormous challenges and opportunities face the Christian church in our globalized, rapidly changing world. In western cultures, these challenges include the institutional irrelevance and decline of the Christian church, the rapid changes within western cultures, and the demise of the status, influence, and privilege of Christianity. In what some have coined post-Christendom—Christendom being the period in western history in which Christianity was deeply wedded to the secular state and its institutions—Christianity in the West finds itself now on the margins of a culture in which it once enjoyed a central place.

This is not breaking news. It is becoming increasingly clear that Christianity needs to engage questions about how its traditions, theology, institutions, and gospel message might make sense to a secularized, consumer, globalized, technologically savvy, networked, highly individualistic, spiritually sensitive, and postmodern generation (just to name a few of the more common descriptors). With the rise of the Majority World churches and the globalized and networked realities of the younger generations across the planet, it is not only the church of the West that faces these challenges. The global church needs to consider how its worship, community, mission, governance, social engagement, theology, apologetics, and leadership forms might be relevant for the younger generations and might contribute to its missional mandate. This is true not only of the church in western contexts but also in the Majority World, where the church is experiencing exponential growth and fresh missional vitality, such as Africa, Asia, Eastern Europe, and South America.

---

2. From the stories of Adelaide Place, Urban Seed, and All Nations Church online: http://www.apbc.net, http://www.urbanseed.org, and http://yulbang.or.kr/. Used with permission.

In response to the particular expressions of these challenges in the West, the churches in western cultures have experienced an explosion of literature addressing questions about how the church might be more missional. Practitioners, church planters, and practical theologians explore, in this growing missional conversation, what it means for the church to be genuinely faithful to God's mission in the world. They investigate the implications of missional ecclesiology for the shape of church life, spirituality, outreach, community, and Christian ministry. This proliferation of missional literature can be traced back through the Gospel and Our Culture Network in the United States of America and the United Kingdom, through to such theologians as Lesslie Newbigin and David Bosch.[3] The perspectives of people like Lesslie Newbigin and David Bosch captivated the imaginations of a group of missionary ecclesiologists, such as George Hunsberger, Darrell Guder, and Alan Roxburgh. These, in turn, inspired a generation of missional thinkers such as Brian McLaren, Dan Kimball, Michael Frost, Alan Hirsch, and Erwin McManus. Many other authors might be mentioned as having influence on this missional stream of thought—and the number of people publishing on missional leadership and ecclesiology continues to grow. Missional ecclesiology is a movement of thought, rather than an organized movement, which is concerned with all cultures as missional fields, the missional nature and expressions of the church, the missional nature of God and Scripture, and the missional presence of God in the world.

The growth of the missional literature and conversation has been exponential, and its influence far-reaching, with many books, articles, websites, blogs, and missional plants produced each year. The consequences have included:

1. Shifts in local church, denominational, and para-church agency church planting strategies

2. The development of the alternative worship movement

3. Explorations in the intentional combination of businesses with missional plants, especially through social entrepreneurship

4. New expressions of church, evangelism, and mission

5. Changing emphases in ministerial and theological education

6. Missional discussions in cyberspace, especially through blogs and pod-casting

7. Whole denominations looking at fresh expressions of church—one example is the *Mission-Shaped Church* report[4]

8. The spread of missional thinking into mainstream ecclesial and leadership thought—many denominations and large churches are now exploring missional postures and practices.

It is not only churches, denominations, and Christian agencies that are seriously considering the implications of missional ecclesiology—many parishioners, pastors,

---

3. I first published some of this material in Hill, "Emerging-Missional Ecclesiology," 86–100, and dealt with many of the concepts at doctoral level in Hill, "Examination of Emerging-Missional."

4. Williams, et al., *Mission-Shaped Church.*

theologians, and other Christian leaders are wrestling with the consequences of missional ecclesiology for the mission, structure, and purpose of the church, and for their own missional orientation and practices. The church is essentially missional. It is missional at its very core—reflecting the missional nature and purposes of God. This realization is forcefully shaping the outlook and consciousness of many quarters of the global church.

It is clear from the wide-ranging challenges canvassed above that these are tumultuous times. Yet they are also thrilling times, as many pastors, academics, students, congregations, and Christian leaders explore, with fresh eyes, the missional nature of the church.

The proverbial "elephant in the room" seems to me, however, to be the lack of systematic or intentional ecclesiology in much of this missional conversation—or lack of theology for that matter. This is not only a shame but is deeply problematic, if we agree with Lesslie Newbigin that congregations are the "only hermeneutic of the gospel," and that all other missionary efforts "have power to accomplish their purpose only as they are rooted in and lead back to a believing community."

> I have come to feel that the primary reality of which we have to take account in seeking for a Christian impact on public life is the Christian congregation. How is it possible that the gospel should be credible, that people should come to believe that the power that has the last word in human affairs is represented by a man hanging on a cross?
>
> I am suggesting that the only answer, the only hermeneutic of the gospel, is a congregation of men and women who believe it and live by it. I am, of course, not denying the importance of the many activities by which we seek to challenge public life with the gospel—evangelistic campaigns, distribution of Bibles and Christian literature, conferences, and even books such as this one.
>
> But I am saying that these are all secondary, and that they have power to accomplish their purpose only as they are rooted in and lead back to a believing community.[5]

David Bosch makes similar assertions, claiming that the missional nature of the church is grounded in the doctrine of the Trinity, and that mission is to be "incarnated in the witness of a community, for the sake of the world."

> The missio Dei purifies the church. It sets it under the cross—the only place where it is ever safe . . . Looked at from this perspective mission is, quite simply, the participation of Christians in the liberating mission of Jesus, wagering on a future that verifiable experience seems to belie. It is the good news of God's love, incarnated in the witness of a community, for the sake of the world.[6]

My purposes for writing this book are:

1. To outline the thought of twelve Euro-American ecclesiologists from the Catholic, Orthodox, Free Church, and other Protestant traditions, and, thereby, present a useful, mostly descriptive, college-level introduction to the ecclesiologies of these theologians.

---

5. Newbigin, *Gospel in a Pluralist Society*, 227.
6. Bosch, *Transforming Mission*, 390, 519.

2. To present some concise and preliminary theological themes in missional ecclesiology, in conversation with those twelve theologians and with other sources.

3. To offer the first volume in a larger project on missional ecclesiology, and on the implications of such ecclesiology for churches and Christian leaders in western cultures.

As noted above, this book is the first stage in a broader writing project. In this first volume, I am self-consciously dealing with twelve Euro-American theologians, in an attempt to introduce some basic theological themes in missional ecclesiology—in the context of ecumenical conversation—and in an attempt to make ecclesiology more missional. This is an introductory theology (or ecclesiology) for the missional church, which addresses missional ecclesiology from a Euro-American perspective.

Why have I chosen to dedicate the first volume to twelve Euro-American theologians, from the four main streams of Christianity? The churches of western cultures are mostly experiencing decline, marginality, and liminality, and need to explore ecclesiology and missiology afresh—including the connections between these disciplines. This first volume provides a window into how Euro-American theologians, from four broad Christian traditions, are making sense of the nature and mission of the church, in their western cultural context. Their cultural context is now a turbulent, pluralistic, post-Christendom mission field. I have chosen these twelve ecclesiologists because of their influence within the western segments of their respective theological traditions (it might be argued that other thinkers should have been included, or are more important, but I had to limit myself to three theologians from each of the four broad Christian traditions). This first volume, then, is dedicated to constructing an introductory missional ecclesiology, in conversation with the perspectives of those in the midst of such western ecclesial decline and missiological renegotiation. I do not assume that the local and contextually framed theologies of these twelve have a universal validity. But I do think that their perspectives are worth wrestling with, especially as we seek to develop a missional ecclesiology in the light of western theological conversations—the conversations of those who are in the midst of ecclesial upheaval.[7] This first volume is a self-consciously western (Australian, for that matter!) missional theology.

The second, forthcoming volume will take a different approach. It will step away from Euro-American voices, and ask what those in the Majority World have to say to the missional nature and practices of the church. The quality and quantity of existing and historical ecclesiologies from the Majority World are so substantial, that they merit a dedicated volume. These include the theologies of people such as Kwame Bediako, Leonardo Boff, Samuel Escobar, John Mbiti, Oliver Onwubiko, René Padilla, Peter Phan, Juan Luis Segundo, Jon Sobrino, and Tite Tiénou—to name a few. While there is value in constructing some dimensions of a missional ecclesiology through conversation with Euro-American thinkers who are writing in the experience of western ecclesial decline, it is clear that any missional ecclesiology which ignores the ecclesiological insights of

---

7. For a good discussion of how local ecclesiologies may contribute to a global theological conversation and to missional understandings of the church, see Tizon, *Transformation after Lausanne*.

Majority World thinkers will be deficient, impoverished, and found sorely wanting. My hope is that the second volume will complement and complete this one.

My approach in this first volume is to dedicate the first twelve chapters to twelve important theologians from each of the major Christian traditions. The progression from Roman Catholic to Free Church ecclesiology is intentional. It moves from the theological tradition most distant from my own, to those closer to my position—that is, from Joseph Ratzinger's Catholic ecclesiology to Miroslav Volf's Free Church vision of the church.

The twelve chapters in *Part One* are primarily descriptive, as I provide an overview of the thought of each ecclesiologist. This is deliberate. While I have tried to provide an account of the ecclesiological thought of each of the twelve thinkers on their own terms, my desire to affirm my dialogue partners, to present them fairly and yet to remain true to my own Protestant evangelical convictions, no doubt comes through. I mostly try to present these twelve ecclesiologists on their own terms, with little commentary or evaluation (while recognizing the influence of my own epistemological outlook on what I see). I offer a summary of each ecclesiologist's thought, outlining his or her ecclesiology as contextually and fairly as possible. Readers can make their own theological and ecclesiological assessments of the twelve ecclesiologists as, no doubt, they will make of the missional ecclesiology I construct in the later part of the book. Only at the end of each chapter, in a section called Contributions to Missional Ecclesiology, do I present some thoughts on where I believe the ecclesiologist contributes to missional ecclesiology. I suggest what I find helpful about his or her ecclesiology, and where I have some reservations, especially in the light of the theological first principles I outline later in this introduction.

For those ecclesiologies distant from my own (especially Catholic and Orthodox ecclesiologies), I might have listed many theological reservations that emerge from my own ecclesiological tradition, but have resisted doing that. Instead, I have only provided brief reflections on the ecclesiologists at the end of each chapter, through the lens of the eight theological (or ecclesiological) first principles I hold dear. Students and classes can use the chapters of Part One as an introduction to the thinking of twelve leading ecclesiologists from four theological streams. I hope this work may serve as a useful text for pastors and college classes studying ecclesiology. I footnote where each ecclesiologist features in the missional ecclesiology of Part Two, so that readers can see how his or her ecclesiology is contributing to the brief ecumenical conversation developed later in the book. I hope that this will provide readers with a useful introduction to the thought of these twelve ecclesiologists, and also some initial reflections on how each of these twelve might enrich a missional understanding of the church.

Some of these ecclesiologists employ gender-specific language, since they are "of their time," and hence are quoted as such. Rather than use the mechanism *sic* on each of these occasions, I am affirming here the important contemporary shift away from such gender-specific language to that which is gender-inclusive.

In *Part Two*, I construct an introductory missional ecclesiology in conversation with the twelve ecclesiologists examined in the first half of the book. Most of the missional literature of the past twenty years is practical, telling us *how* to be a missional church, rather than *why* certain theological themes compel the church toward a missional self-understanding and existence. This book takes a different approach as I outline a basic missional understanding of the church. It examines some of the key theological themes that are foundational for missional ecclesiology, and does this in conversation with twelve ecclesiologists, in an effort to shape a missional theology of the church. These theological themes include theologizing-in-community, missiology, Christology, pneumatology, and trinitarian thought. In other words, I simply ask, "What do the theologizing community, Jesus, mission, the Spirit, and the Trinity have to do with a missional view of the church?" I do this in dialogue with the twelve ecclesiologists examined in the first half of this book and in conversation with other sources. I am not trying to develop a complete Christology, missiology, and so forth, but rather to show how some dimensions of these theological areas serve to build a missional ecclesiology. It is my contention that certain aspects of these interlocking areas of theology provide indispensible foundations for the development of a worthwhile, dialogical, theologically informed, and systematic missional ecclesiology.

The dialogical, ecumenical nature of this project is important. As a direct consequence of their developing perspectives on the nature of the church, the younger missional leaders are seeking to engage those from other expressions of Christianity (Evangelical, Orthodox, Protestant, Catholic, Free Church, Pentecostal, and the like) in fresh, relational, and more organic ways. Some of the older forums of ecumenical and interfaith dialogue are being less emphasized, and are being replaced by a more authentic, grass-roots relationship. This is an ecumenical and interfaith communion. It is found in cafes, around meals, in relationship, and in combined, marketplace-located enterprises and prayer.

There is a new generation of younger leaders and young adults, from throughout the various Christian traditions, who are meeting each other deeply in these ways, while exploring the benefits, convictions, and theological distinctives of their own theological and denominational traditions. Leading figures within the various institutionalized expressions of Christianity are having their tradition's views challenged by a younger, networked, globalized generation of Christians—especially in the realms of ecclesiology, social justice, and the church's mission in the world (this is one of the reasons why a subsequent volume will be offered to this one, which looks at Majority World ecclesiologists—but I will first seek to anchor missional ecclesiology in the existing traditions of theological reflection, before moving onto the contributions of newer theological movements). The perspectives of the distinct Christian traditions that I am dealing with in this book, and of their notable proponents, are not being disregarded in an offhanded manner, nor are they being rejected as completely irrelevant. However, they are being merged, reshaped, and incorporated into fresh, missional forms of ecclesiology, spirituality, and belief within Christianity. Dialogue and emergence are happening between the great Christian traditions whether we like it or not, because of the core values in postmodern culture. This is not the time to bury our head in the sand and hope our young people will embrace our theological position in an unquestioning way. Instead, they will (and should be encouraged to) explore and develop their own convictions in conversation with voices from their own and other Christian traditions—and, in the process, help their churches and theological traditions discover a renewed missional dynamism and passion.

Each chapter has *Questions for Reflection* at the end, which might prove useful for students, small groups, classroom settings, and individual study. The chapters also contain stories of local churches and Christian organizations that are involved in the challenging task of local mission. There are six Australian, two North American, one South Korean, one Malaysian, and one Scottish story. These are not "case studies" so much as simple illustrations of groups seeking a down-to-earth, no-nonsense missional ecclesiology. I have not chosen these churches, groups, and missional initiatives because they have reached some kind of missional perfection. These groups and individuals are passionate about mission and are just giving it an honest, concerted, and sacrificial go. The majority of the stories are Australian because they emerge out of relationships I have built with missional communities, and most of my relationships at this stage are in the Australian context. These groups have been gracious with me as they have provided their stories, and given me a glimpse into their hopes, struggles, passions, and raw missional endeavors. They try some things and succeed—they try other things and fail. None of them is presented as some kind of ideal, and you will note that I am not committed to one model of church or missional enterprise as though there is some ideal missional or ecclesiological form. All kinds of people and groups are experimenting with mission in their local setting—rural and urban, large church and small, local church and para-church, mono-cultural and multicultural, age-specific and intergeneration, and the like. I have chosen these stories to illustrate how Christians in a variety of contexts are experimenting with mission, and are seeking to ground missional ecclesiology in their local setting. I think these stories provide good conversation partners in my effort to build an introductory, intentional, theologically informed, and earthed missional ecclesiology.

As already mentioned, most of the missional literature is practical, while this book is intentionally theological. Some readers will rightly ask, "So what does this mean for my church? What does it mean for my missional practice?" I deal with those questions from time to time in the chapters in *Part Two*. I also see no point, however, in duplicating the works of others. To that end, I have provided a section immediately prior to the bibliography called *Resources: Practicing Missional Ecclesiology*, which shows where the theological themes articulated in this book are grounded practically in certain articles, texts, and websites.

From the outset, I should declare that my views of the church emerge from my biblical, Reformed evangelical, Christ-centered, Free Church, charismatic, trinitarian, ecumenical, and missional convictions. While we might debate the ontological or hierarchical relationships between these ecclesiological concepts, I am not presenting them here in any such order. These are theological first principles, which inform and determine:

1. The convictions I hold about the nature and mission of the church.

2. The brief assessments of the twelve ecclesiologists in *Part One* (such assessments are in the sections called *Contributions to Missional Ecclesiology*, at the end of each of the twelve chapters).

3. The aspects of the twelve ecclesiologies I choose to use, develop, and converse with in the construction of my own missional ecclesiology in *Part Two*, and which aspects I choose to ignore or exclude.

4. The missional ecclesiology I construct in this and future volumes.[8]

I outline here what these theological first principles mean for me (with explicit reference to ecclesiology) and, in a few sentences, why I am convinced about their importance. This is a list of criteria by which each of those convictions informs my judgments about how we ought to understand the church—they are the first principles I use in my evaluation of the ecclesiologies presented in this book and in my construction of a missional ecclesiology. For each I provide some description of the key theological reasons underpinning those convictions.

1. Biblical: While there is no one ideal or universal model of the church presented in Scripture, our ecclesiology is to be grounded in, and measured by, the commands, witness, and revelation of Scripture. The Scriptures are the infallible, authoritative word of God, inspired by the Holy Spirit. They have absolute and final authority in all aspects of corporate and individual faith, ethics, conduct, and witness.

2. Reformed Evangelical: To quote Michael Horton, and broaden out his definition to include our theology of the church, our ecclesiology is evangelical when it is "committed to the sufficiency of Scripture, the priesthood of all believers, the total lostness of humans, the sole mediation of Christ, the gracious efficacy and finality of God's redemptive work in Christ through election, propitiation, calling, and keeping. The linchpin for all of this was the doctrine of justification by grace alone, through faith alone, because of Christ alone."[9] It is my conviction that such Reformed evangelical, gospel convictions are necessary if we are to be faithful to the biblical vision for the church. The gospel defines God's purposes not only for humanity and cosmic history but also for the church. God controls the church, is completely sovereign over its nature, affairs, mission, and history, and is the church's only source of grace, election, atonement, salvation, and perseverance. The church's justification and eschatological hope are by grace alone, through faith alone, by Christ alone.

3. Christ-centered: Our ecclesiology must be centered on Jesus Christ, the Lord of the church. The church needs to reflect deeply on the person and work of Christ, be gathered and sent in the name and power of Christ, and allow the Spirit of the Lord Jesus Christ to shape its nature and mission. The early church developed its Christology and ecclesiology in a concurrent, integrated way, and the contemporary church best explores its self-understanding, structure, mission, and hope through the prism of the centrality and the Lordship of Christ.

---

8. I do not deal with each of the eight ecclesiological convictions in Part Two of this book in a systematic or consecutive way, but they do shape the missional ecclesiology presented in this and future volumes.

9. Horton, "Evangelical Arminians," 17.

4. Free Church: The church is to be separate from government control or the control of other secular institutions, and is to avoid the pursuit of societal status, privilege, or control.[10] Free Church ecclesiology affirms that Christians should be free to practice personal and non-coerced faith, believer's baptism, and freedom of conscience, and that churches should be free to cultivate the priesthood of all believers, congregational government, the autonomy of the local church, and interdependence with other Free Churches. Free Church ecclesiology maintains that this is New Testament Christianity, and that it is for our time as well.

5. Charismatic: Missional ecclesiology is inadequate without significant pneumatological foundations. The Spirit creates and animates the church, empowering it to witness to the gospel of Jesus Christ, enabling it to be a missional, transformational community, and forming it into an alternative, eschatological society embodying the reign of God. The church in the power and presence of the Spirit exists for the mission of Christ. The Spirit pours out gifts on the church "for the common good," and "to prepare God's people for works of service, so that the body of Christ may be built up."[11] This includes, but is not limited to, what are commonly called the ministry gifts, manifestation gifts, and motivational gifts.[12] At once the Spirit constitutes the church, empowers it for service and witness, fills it with Christ's empowering presence, and leads it into the eschatological mission of the triune God.

6. Trinitarian: There are clear limitations to the analogy between the church and the Trinity. However, the church is at its best when it reflects the interior life of the Trinity *and* the missionary passion and actions of the trinitarian persons in history and in the economy of salvation. The missionary nature and actions of the triune God are the source and the inspiration of the church's mission. It is important that our ecclesiology appreciates the *correspondence* and *difference* between God's divine, triune perfection—as demonstrated in both the divine communion and mission—and the creaturely, communing, sent nature of the church. Having said that, missional ecclesiology views the church through the light of the Father sending the Son, the Father and Son sending the Spirit, and the Trinity sending the church in mission into the world.

10. The Free Church ecclesiological vision also decouples the church from any forms of unhealthy pursuit or exercise of societal power. By this I do not mean that power is intrinsically evil or that Free Church equates to quietist. I footnote this point about societal power, because there is a real complexity to the theology of power and whether or how it ought to be sought and exercised by the church. If "societal power" means "power granted by society's elites on the condition of complicity with the injustices and abuses that benefit them," then the church ought to avoid and reject such societal power. But if "societal power" means "power granted by God, through various means, and exercised in the social sphere through various forms of influence and authority" then Free Church ecclesiology does not absolutely preclude the exercise—or even the pursuit—of societal power. A good account of these matters can be found in the 2011 John Saunders Annual Lecture, presented by Andrew Sloane, in which Sloane presents "a biblical and theological framework that justifies advocacy as a legitimate component of Christian involvement in the world, calling on 'power' to be used justly for the poor and disadvantaged." Sloane, "Justifying Advocacy—Speaking Truth to Power." Online: http://www.ea.org.au/Ethos/FaithCommunity/Justifying-Advocacy-Speaking-Truth-to-Power.aspx.

11. 1 Cor 12:7 and Eph 4:12.

12. Eph 4:11–12, 1 Cor 12:7–10, and Rom 12:6–8.

7. Ecumenical: Ecclesiology should be formed in an environment of critical yet authentic dialogue. This involves critical dialogue with those traditionally marginalized by the church, with other ethnicities and cultures, with persons representing all ages and both genders, and with other theological and confessing traditions. It also includes attentive, critical listening to the voices of the past, alongside (or perhaps preceding) the kind of dialogue I have described with the voices of the present. It is possible, in a qualified way, to say that God is present in the various theological, ecclesiological, socio-cultural, historical, and other permutations of the church (in one way or another), and that our ecclesiology is best served through critical dialogue, and through attention to the Spirit in various expressions of the church. As I have suggested, such an assertion demands qualification. On the one hand, there is a sense in which God is present everywhere, outside as well as within the church. On the other hand, there is the terrible possibility that some forms of the church can become apostate structures in which the form of godliness is present but the power has departed, and the Spirit of Christ is no more present than he is at a football game or the shopping mall. In the 2011 New College lectures, David Starling put it this way: "For all the discontinuities and differences within the history of the last 2000 years of Christianity, the New Testament nevertheless reminds us that our identity as the church is created by our union with Christ, a union that we possess in common with believers of all times and places."[13]

8. Missional: The church is fundamentally missional, because it serves and is formed by a missionary God. I agree unreservedly with David Bosch, when he writes that "the church's mission is not secondary to its being; the church exists in being sent and in building up itself for its mission . . . Ecclesiology does not precede missiology; there cannot be church without an intrinsic missionary dimension."[14] The mission of God determines and constitutes the nature, purposes, structures, ministries, and activities of the church in and of mission.

I teach at Morling Baptist Theological College in Sydney and, while teaching is my primary gift, I am a missionary at heart. While I love teaching and engaging students as they come alive to theology, Scripture, mission, and ministry, at times I feel frustrated by the administrative burden of tertiary education, and by how this can draw me away from mission in my local neighborhood. I feel deeply committed to personal and local church mission, discipleship, and community, and have sought all of my Christian life to do mission in my local community. My family is committed to building relationships with our neighbors, including hosting barbecues in our cul-de-sac, opening up our home, being involved in the issues that affect our local neighborhood, and sharing faith with friends, family, colleagues, and acquaintances. My wife Felicity is an especially effective missionary in her workplace, caring deeply for her staff and clients, expressing her love for Jesus and those she works with in word and action. Recently I have been involved

13. Starling, "Theology and the Future of the Church." Available for order online: http://www.case.edu .au/index.php/case_magazine/case_28_2011_theology_the_future/.

14. Bosch, *Believing in the Future*, 32.

with a group establishing a community center for immigrants to Sydney, which offers language, financial, family, and social support services. Like most Christians, Felicity and I have had mixed success with our missional efforts! Most missions seem to me to be unglamorous, local, relational, and, aside from the applause of the heavenly host, unnoticed. Much of it seems to fall on hard soil, or if the soil was receptive, this receptivity escaped my notice. However, I remain passionately committed to mission, to sharing the love of Christ in word and deed, and especially to witness through the local church and in the local community.

I am thoroughly convinced that a Christ-centered, gospel-shaped, earthy, and intentional ecclesiology should undergird all missional activity. Missional writings have tended to be long on missiology and short on ecclesiology or theology, but I think this is an unnecessary and artificial separation. My hope is that this book will begin to pull the two streams of missiology and ecclesiology together, into a reflective, if introductory, missional ecclesiology—and that others who are passionate about missional ecclesiology will continue this work in a more substantial way in the future.

PART ONE

Surveying the Euro-American Landscape

Roman Catholic

1

Joseph Ratzinger (Pope Emeritus, Benedict XVI): The Church as Communion

The Church is much more than an organization: it is the organism of the Holy Spirit, something that is alive, that takes hold of our inmost being. This consciousness found verbal expression with the concept of the "Mystical Body of Christ," a phrase describing a new and liberating experience of the Church. At the very end of his life, in the same year the Constitution on the Church was published by the Council, Guardini wrote: the Church "is not an institution devised and built by people . . . but a living reality . . . It lives still throughout the course of time. Like all living realities it develops, it changes . . . and yet in the very depths of its being it remains the same; its inmost nucleus is Christ . . . To the extent that we look upon the Church as organization . . . like an association . . . we have not yet arrived at a proper understanding of it. Instead, it is a living reality and our relationship with it ought to be—life."[1]

—Joseph Ratzinger

---

1. Ratzinger, "Ecclesiology of Vatican II," 5. Joseph Ratzinger was appointed Cardinal of Munich in 1977, Prefect for the Congregation for the Doctrine of the Faith in 1981, Dean of the College of Cardinals in 2002, and Bishop of Rome on April 19, 2005 (when he took on the name Pope Benedict XVI). He was the 265th Pope of the Roman Catholic Church, and his resignation from the office became effective on February 28, 2013.

A LIVING REALITY

WHILE SOME THEOLOGIANS, LIKE Miroslav Volf for example, have neatly summarized their ecclesiology in one or two books, the ecclesiology of Joseph Ratzinger needs to be extracted from a wide range of his writing. Ratzinger is sympathetic to the impulse to reform or change the church. However, he is convinced that questions about the nature and essence of the church precede such efforts and, indeed, provide the foundation for all such contemplation and activity. He believes that one must understand the essence of an organism in order to heal it and in order to avoid the negative consequences inherent in theologically unreflective reform. Rigorous ecclesiological debates and conversations about the nature and essence of the church also aid in bringing "clarity and help in the crisis of ecclesial consciousness through which we are now living."[2]

For Ratzinger, the New Testament witnesses to the origin and essence of the church through the message of Jesus Christ and through the church's self-description as *ecclesia*. The essence of the church is also to be derived from the Pauline doctrine of the church as the body of Christ and from the vision of the church in the Acts of the Apostles.[3] The message of Christ emphasized the kingdom of God. However, an overview of Christ's teachings, images, parables, prayers, ministry practices, and gathering of a community of disciples reveals that the Eucharist (or Lord's Supper as some call it) is an act of covenant, and the concrete creation of a new people who come into being through their covenant relation to God.[4] Christ's eucharistic action draws people into relationship with God and into his mission to reach all of humanity. It also draws people into unity with each other as a *people* through their mutual communion with the body and blood of Jesus. Therefore, the Eucharist is the center and permanent origin of the new covenant and of the church, and the many celebrations of the Eucharist are participations in the one body of Jesus Christ.[5]

"Election is not a privilege of the elected but a call to live for others"; therefore the community of faith is elected (chosen by and for God) not for its own exclusivity but for the sake of others. Thus, election and mission are richly connected in Ratzinger's writing.[6]

The church's self-description as *ecclesia* is used, according to Ratzinger, to indicate its self-perception as the final gathering of God's people. This is a perception that links it with the continuity of God's work in and through his people in human history, and with the mystery of the person, work, and coming of Christ. These relationships with Christ and God's work in human history include all of the diverse expressions of the church— from the local community of faith to the one all-encompassing church of Jesus Christ. It enlivens the church through the ultimate goal of perfect unity and is grounded in the christological center "that is made concrete in the gathering of believers for the Lord's Supper. It is always the Lord who in his one sacrifice gathers his one and only people. In all places it is the gathering of this one."[7]

2. Ratzinger, *Called to Communion*, 11.

3. Ibid., 21–45.

4. See Ibid., 21–28; Ratzinger, *Church, Ecumenism, and Politics*, 7–11.

5. Ratzinger, *Called to Communion*, 28–29.

6. Ratzinger, *Introduction to Christianity*, 174.

7. Ratzinger, *Called to Communion*, 32; Ratzinger, *Church, Ecumenism, and Politics*, 18.

According to the Apostle Paul, writes Ratzinger, ecclesiology is impossible without the rich Christology made concrete in the sacraments of baptism and the Eucharist. These sacraments open up into the deep community embodied in the Trinity.[8] Paul's description of the church being the *body of Christ* is rooted in biblical ideas, including the idea of the *corporate personality* (that we are all Adam). It is also rooted in the words and intent of Christ when he instituted the Eucharist, and the biblical concept of nuptiality (that all Christians are unified as they cleave to the Lord through participation in the sacrament of the Eucharist). The church "must constantly become what she is through unitive love and resist the temptation to fall from her vocation into the infidelity of self-willed autonomy."[9]

Furthermore, the narrative ecclesiology found in the Acts of the Apostles contains "interplay of multiplicity and unity, universality and particularity" and gives us a guide to how the early church dealt with questions about diversity and difference in their own context.[10] It is without doubt, however, that Ratzinger's description of "legitimately organized communities" is far from the autonomy of congregations described in Free Church and missional ecclesiologies. It rests heavily on the priestly administering of the sacraments and on recognition by the Catholic Church itself. This is because "the Church is not something one can make but only something one can receive, and indeed receive from where it already is and where it really is: from the sacramental community of his body that progresses through history."[11]

Ratzinger believes that the church is the *mystical body of Christ*. This is because Christ is continually founding it, and his presence is most clearly articulated to the world in the church. The church is the presence of Christ—contemporaneous with him while he is contemporaneous with us. Being the presence of Christ it grows from the inside outwards, through prayer, love, community, the sacraments, and hope. It is a living reality, being continually renewed and transforming the world. All Christians are in fact corporately *the church*, since *we are the church*. We are called to be the presence of Christ in the world, both individually and in community. All Christians are corporately *the church* through their co-responsibility for the health of the church and through engagement with the social and political realities of the world. They are also the church through participating in the church's development and historical dynamism, since all living things are in a process of continual renewal and the church is no exception.[12] Yet even in renewal the church remains a eucharistic community, and the body of the Lord binds together churches scattered throughout the world into *one* church.[13]

8. Ratzinger, *Called to Communion*, 33.

9. Ibid., 39–40.

10. Ibid., 40–45.

11. Ratzinger, *Church, Ecumenism, and Politics*, 10.

12. Ibid., 7.

13. Ratzinger, *Introduction to Christianity*, 257.

COMMUNIO AND THE CHURCH'S SUBSTANCE

In his analysis of the ecclesiology of Ratzinger, Volf argues that *communio* is the central and pivotal notion in his ecclesiology.[14] The Latin word *communio* means "communion, fellowship, and mutual participation and sharing" and, therefore, there will be times in this book when I use *communio* and *communion* interchangeably. This concept of *communio* influences and guides Ratzinger's views on faith, sacrament, Eucharist, the word of God, Christian leadership, and his positioning of the *communio fidelium* in liturgy.[15] It also shapes the relationship he draws between trinitarian and ecclesial communion.[16]

Volf correctly locates the concept of *communio* as the heart of Ratzinger's ecclesiology; and at times he is positive about this theme. Yet Volf's extrapolations of the negative consequences of this central idea seem to emerge more from his Free Church presuppositions than from an open examination of Ratzinger's writings or a qualitative investigation of Catholic communities.

In this section I proceed to outline briefly Ratzinger's understanding of the concept of *communio* and its implications for his ecclesiology. The concept of *koinonia* in Ratzinger's ecclesiology (Christian fellowship—communion with God and other Christians) expresses "the core of the mystery of the Church, and can certainly be a key for the renewal of Catholic ecclesiology."[17] In the same paragraph as this quotation, Ratzinger asserts that the church is a "mystery of communion." This central understanding of the church needs to be integrated adequately into ecclesiology, such that it shapes the concepts of the *people of God*, the *body of Christ*, and the church as *sacrament*.[18] Ratzinger maintains, "The Church by her inmost nature is *communio*, fellowship with and in the body of the Lord."[19]

Human beings may choose to unite with the Trinity and the rest of humankind through faith and immersion in the church. They look forward with eschatological hope to the fulfillment of this communion with the Father and the heavenly church when Christ returns. This communion is a grace from God that "involves a double dimension: the *vertical* (communion with God) and the *horizontal* (communion with men)."[20] Ecclesial communion is simultaneously both invisible and visible, and is grounded and located in the Eucharist. It is a communion of the saints through the Holy Spirit, prayer, shared mission, giving and receiving of one's goods, and the sacraments. It is a mutual relationship between the present earthly church and the heavenly church.[21] Christ enables the depth of this communion since Christians, "fellowship with the Word of God who became flesh, who through his death lets us share in his life and intends thereby to lead us also toward service to one another, to visible fellowship in living our lives."[22]

14. Volf, *After Our Likeness*, 32.

15. *Communio fidelium* means *the communion of believers*.

16. Volf, *After Our Likeness*, 29–72.

17. Ratzinger, *Some Aspects of the Church*, 1.

18. Ibid.

19. Ratzinger and Rahner, *Episcopate and the Primacy*, 45.

20. Ratzinger, *Some Aspects of the Church*, 2.

21. Ibid., 2–4; Ratzinger, *Pilgrim Fellowship of Faith*, 69.

22. Ratzinger, *Pilgrim Fellowship of Faith*, 70.

The one, holy, catholic, and apostolic church is *"ontologically and temporally* prior to every *individual* particular church." Therefore, the universal church is far more than a gathering of like-minded churches. Every local community of faith exists through a *mutual interiority* with the whole and receives its ecclesiality joined with it and out of it.[23] The Eucharist and the office of the bishop provide the substance of the communion between the churches. This is because the celebration of the Eucharist is never merely an act involving one particular church. It is a participation in the image and life of the one, holy, catholic, and apostolic church. It is also because the bishops, and especially the Pope, are the *perpetual and visible source and foundation* of this communion. Individual Christians are immersed in this universal church through faith and baptism. Their communion with each other is another expression of the same reality that is the communion between local and regional churches. They belong to the universal church as much as they belong to particular churches.[24]

The communion that shapes the life of the churches is expressed both through the solid unity found in the universal church and through the plurality and diversity of liturgies. It is expressed through the cultures, ministries, institutes, societies, spiritual gifts, and forms of discipleship and leadership found among the churches. Communion with churches outside the Roman Catholic Church is sought vigorously and is especially enjoyed with the Eastern Orthodox Church; however, it is imperfect with those churches that do not recognize communion with the universal church represented by the Pope. In addition, Ratzinger proposes, "The Blessed Virgin Mary is the model of ecclesial communion in faith, in charity and in union with Christ." This is because she is in communion with the earthly and heavenly churches, the apostles, and the church throughout the ages.[25]

Volf summarizes the influence of the concept of *communio* and its presence in Ratzinger's ecclesiology, with reference to the following ideas:[26]

1. Human beings enter Christian community through the act of faith, and such community simultaneously sustains this same faith. The act of faith is essentially ecclesiological and communal, since people exist *from* and *toward* each other. This idea is based on Ratzinger's understanding of the nature of conversion, the church, and trinitarian communion. Inclusion in ecclesial and trinitarian communion corresponds. This communality is expressed in the appropriation and acceptance of faith in the sacraments.

2. Through faith and baptism, human beings enter into ecclesial community. Once they are in the community, however, the Eucharist sustains them spiritually and ecclesially. Only a valid Eucharist achieves these results in individual Christians and in Christian communities.

3. The communal embracing and mediation of Scripture complement these sacraments of baptism and the Eucharist. The universal church has a sacramental role

---

23. Ratzinger, *Some Aspects of the Church*, 5; Ratzinger, "Local Church," 8.

24. Ratzinger, *Some Aspects of the Church*, 7–10.

25. Ibid., 11–13.

26. Volf, *After Our Likeness*, 29–72.

in sustaining this dynamic through the constitution of the office. This office is the hierarchical order (priests and bishops) and universal manifestation (universal church) of the church willed and manifest by God and his grace. The ecclesiality of the local church is derived from communion with the whole.

4. The laity, as the assembled community of the people of God, are not passive subjects in liturgical or eucharistic events. They are the *communio fidelium*. They are the active bearers of the word, the Spirit, and the presence of Christ. Communality, then, characterizes liturgical and Christian spirituality, leadership, worship, mission, and prayer.

5. Trinitarian communion shapes the church's understandings of ecclesial communion and human personhood.

Communio, then, along with his eucharistic theology, is clearly at the center of Ratzinger's ecclesiology.

EUCHARISTIC ECCLESIOLOGY AND ITS PRACTICAL IMPLICATIONS

Ratzinger's ecclesiology not only centers on the concept of *communio*, it is also essentially eucharistic in nature. This idea has already been touched on in the above descriptions of his ecclesiology. In other words, Ratzinger's ecclesiology is a *eucharistic ecclesiology*, as is illustrated in this quotation from his book *God Is Near Us*:

> The Eucharist is instrumental in the process by which Christ builds himself a Body and makes us into a single Bread, one single Body. The content of the Eucharist, what happens in it, is the uniting of Christians, bringing them from their state of separation into the unity of the one Bread and the one Body. The Eucharist is thus understood entirely in a dynamic ecclesiological perspective . . . The Church is eucharistic fellowship . . . The Church is, so to speak, a network of eucharistic fellowships, and she is united, ever and again, through the *one* Body we all receive.[27]

As noted earlier, the eucharistic nature of Ratzinger's ecclesiology has repercussions for his understandings of authority, community, service, and organization in the church. One consequence is that the observance of the Eucharist is never merely an act concerning one local church community. It is an involvement in the overarching dynamics of the one, holy, catholic, and apostolic church. As such, the Eucharist testifies to, and ultimately unites one with, the reality and importance of the broader structures and articulations of the universal church. According to Ratzinger, Eucharist, when rightly observed, especially unifies with the Roman Catholic Church and its leadership, as expressed through its bishops and pontiff. Therefore, local communities have an organic unity with the Catholic Church, if they are to be authentic, through their eucharistic bond to it, each other, and Christ.

Furthermore, Ratzinger's understanding of ministerial patterns and office emerges from his concept of *communio* and from his eucharistic ecclesiology. The rationale for this in Ratzinger's theology is that the administration of the Eucharist, which gives form to the vertical (humans with God) and horizontal (between human beings) dynamics of

27. Ratzinger, *God is Near Us*, 114–15.

communion requires priesthood and ordained offices. Community, the mandate of mission, and the apostolicity and presence of the Spirit in the *successio apostolica* (apostolic succession) characterize the priesthood that administers the celebration of the Eucharist. It is also characterized by the sacrament of the laying on of hands and by the expression of the traditional structure of the church. It is distinguished by the binding of "apostolicity and Catholicity together in the unity of Christ and the Spirit, which is represented and completed in the eucharistic community."[28] This is not to discount the ministry of the laity, according to Ratzinger, but to establish the leadership and ministry of the eucharistic priesthood who lead the laity to perfection in Christ.

Ratzinger says that he is in agreement with the first-century theologian Ignatius, when he writes about the significant connection between Eucharist and the office of bishop. Ratzinger then extrapolates that idea to include the priesthood in general, including a demarcation of the various roles of pope, bishop, priest, and laity. He unites his theology of the Eucharist with his understanding of the structures of the universal church and comes up with various consequences for the office and mission of the bishop:[29]

> The figure of the bishop is the expression at once of the unity and of the public character of the Eucharist . . . The bishop guarantees not only the unity of each individual community but also the unity of the individual community with the one Church of God in this world . . . If the Church *is* Eucharist, then the ecclesial office of overseer (*episkopos*) is essentially responsibility for the "coming together" that is identical with the Church.[30]

Therefore, eucharistic ecclesiology has profound consequences for Ratzinger's ideas about church structure and leadership.

THE RELATIONSHIP BETWEEN STRUCTURE AND CONTENT

According to Ratzinger, it is through repentance, faith, and baptism that one enters the Christian community. The church local and universal sustains this faith in Jesus as the Lord whom God raised from the dead inextricably and simultaneously, however. Faith is communal in its structure. The content of faith cannot be divorced from the mediation of faith supplied in the church's structure.

> Now at last we have reached the inmost core of the concept "Church" and the deepest meaning of the designation "sacrament of unity." The Church is *communion*; she is God's communing with men in Christ and hence the communing of men with one another—and, in consequence, sacrament, sign, instrument of salvation.[31]

Faith and Christian experience, therefore, are mediated through the church, which they encounter as sacrament, sign, and instrument of salvation. The faith that human beings experience and articulate in the confession of the Apostles Creed longs for unity and communion with other believers. This is because it is fundamentally and intricately

---

28. Ratzinger, *Principles of Catholic Theology*, 242–47.

29. Ratzinger, *Called to Communion*, 82–103.

30. Ratzinger, *Principles of Catholic Theology*, 253.

31. Ibid., 53.

related to the church, and its "significance lies in the interplay of common confession and worship."[32] This faith embraces community and is far more than intellectual assent to propositions about the nature and work of Christ. It is liberated from selfish independence through obedience and service in and to the whole. Ratzinger is referring here to immersion in, and sacrificial service to, the church instituted by Christ.[33]

Quoting De Lubac, Ratzinger agrees that "the mystery of the Trinity has opened to us a very new perspective: the ground of being is *communio*."[34] Therefore, for Ratzinger, when one professes faith in Jesus Christ a trinitarian understanding of the Godhead compels one to be immersed in community. Fellowship with other Christians is not just "an external circumstance of salvation, but virtually enters into its metaphysical existence."[35] The individual "I", then, finds fulfillment in entering into this trinitarian community (the ecclesial "I"). Such community is only discovered through the church, since the church, and especially its tradition and memory, is the "seat of faith." It exists throughout human history as the unceasing "common *situs* of faith."[36] Without the church, faith is merely a catalogue of ideas or experiences. With the church, it is made complete, one, and authentic. Faith is a gift of the church. The church is the place where faith is given substance, unity, and meaning. The church is a single subject *with* Christ, and is therefore the mediator of faith and Christian experience.[37]

On the subject of ecumenical and interfaith dialogue, Ratzinger asserts that ecumenism (and especially conversation between Christian traditions) holds many possibilities for dialogue, while being beset with a range of theological and practical problems. There exists a type of communion that is imperfect, but which is most hopefully and presently to be found between the Catholic Churches and the Eastern Orthodox Churches. The Orthodox Church, though separated from the See of Peter, shares a common "apostolic succession and a valid Eucharist" with the Catholic Church.[38]

Ratzinger claims that the type of communion experienced by those churches that deny the papal (Petrine) apostolic succession is *wounded*. This wound is most profoundly realized in the Protestant churches that do not share a valid Eucharist or the apostolic succession.[39] "This in turn also injures the Catholic Church . . . in that it hinders the complete fulfillment of its universality in history."[40] For Ratzinger, ecumenical dialogue is possible but complete unity is only achievable when all other churches recognize "the Primacy of Peter in his successors, the Bishops of Rome."[41]

---

32. Ratzinger, *Introduction to Christianity*, 63.

33. Ibid., 64.

34. Ratzinger, *Principles of Catholic Theology*, 22–23.

35. Ratzinger, *Das Neue Volk Gottes*, 245.

36. Ratzinger, *Principles of Catholic Theology*, 23.

37. Ibid., 51.

38. Ratzinger, *Some Aspects of the Church*, 12. See Ratzinger, "Proper Meaning of 'Sister Churches.'"

39. Ratzinger and Messori, *Ratzinger Report*, 163–64.

40. Ratzinger, *Some Aspects of the Church*, 12.

41. Ibid., 13.

CONTRIBUTIONS TO MISSIONAL ECCLESIOLOGY

Ratzinger fashions his ecclesiology around a wide range of sources and theological concepts. These include the New Testament teachings, from the Gospels through to Pauline ecclesiology, and the tradition of the church and the teachings of the church Fathers. In a typically Roman Catholic fashion, Ratzinger sees them as mutually informed co-authorities. Ratzinger's ecclesiology is profitable for missional ecclesiology, especially through its perspectives on the church's self-description as *ecclesia*, the concepts of *communio* and *koinonia*, some of the eucharistic and sacramental dimensions of his ecclesiology, and his thoughts on the Trinity and the church.[42] Trinitarian understandings of the nature of God and relations within the Godhead are important to Ratzinger and emerge regularly in his ecclesiology. For Ratzinger, Christology is made concrete in the sacraments of baptism and the Eucharist, and the church is the *mystical body of Christ*. Ecclesiology and the critical role of the church in God's eschatological and redemptive purposes are central to Ratzinger's theology. This ecclesiology is shaped by a panoramic and multifaceted theological landscape, and is focused on the interlocking notions of *communio* and Eucharist.

Ratzinger's ecclesiology does not feature prominently in *Part Two* of this book, compared with some of the other ecclesiologists. The notable exceptions are, firstly, his views on the pitfalls and reservations on the possibilities of interfaith and ecumenical dialogue; secondly, his thoughts on the importance of theological foundations for ecclesial reforms; and, thirdly, the practical ecclesial consequences of his theology of *communio*.

According to Ratzinger, the universal church takes priority over the local church. In his opinion, the universal church, especially as the institution of Roman Catholicism represents it, is "*ontologically and temporally* prior to every *individual* particular church." This union with the broader Catholic Church is such that local churches and individual Christians exist through a *mutual interiority* with the whole, that is, a union of dependency, submission, and grafting.[43] This union is embodied in the Eucharist and the office of the bishop, and especially the Pope. Free Church, evangelical ecclesiology, which is where my ecclesiological convictions rest, has some difficulties with these assertions. Firstly, as Miroslav Volf puts it, "Although the New Testament does indeed attest the phenomenon of personal interiority, it is no accident that *only the divine persons* dwell in human beings, or human beings in the divine persons . . . never human beings—neither as individuals nor as community—in other human beings."[44] Secondly, Free Church ecclesiology understands the relationship between the local and universal churches in a different order of priority, and constructs the relationship between the local and universal in a spirit of mutual interdependence rather than hierarchical precedence. Thirdly, Reformed evangelical ecclesiology believes that the individual Christian is saved by grace and faith alone, through the person and work of Christ alone, whereas Ratzinger affords the larger, universal church, as well as the local church, a defining place in the sacramental mediation of faith. Fourthly, Ratzinger's hierarchical

---

42. He features in chapters 14 and 17 in *Part Two* of this book.

43. Ratzinger, *Some Aspects of the Church*, 5; Ratzinger, "Local Church," 8.

44. Volf, *After Our Likeness*, 37.

construction of the trinitarian relations leads to the hierarchical precedence of the whole over the individual, hence Roman Catholicism's ecclesial structures. Miroslav Volf has demonstrated this in his analysis of Ratzinger, and shown that other trinitarian theologies lead to vastly different ecclesiological conclusions.[45]

It is not surprising that Ratzinger defines his Roman Catholic ecclesiology over against other ecclesiologies, from time to time.[46] For instance, Ratzinger believes that only a "valid" Eucharist, as defined by Catholicism, achieves ecclesial communion and individual spiritual maturation—defining this over against other theological traditions and celebrations of the Lord's Supper. He also asserts that denial of the papal (Petrine) apostolic succession is unacceptable, and that all Christian traditions must recognize "the Primacy of Peter in his successors, the Bishops of Rome."[47] This is not a surprising claim by Ratzinger, but it is very Roman Catholic, and it does tend to make Protestants and other non-Catholics recoil.

In the following quote Ratzinger summarizes the heart of his understanding of *communio* and its role in relationship to the spiritual dynamics, offices, sacraments, and structure of the church:

> Ecclesial communion is at the same time both visible and invisible. As an invisible reality, it is the communion of each human being with the Father through Christ in the Holy Spirit, and with the others who are fellow sharers in the divine nature, in the passion of Christ, in the same faith and in the same Spirit. In the Church on earth there is a relationship between the invisible communion and the visible communion in the teaching of the Apostles, in the sacraments and in the hierarchical order. By means of these divine gifts, which are very visible realities, Christ carries out in different ways his prophetical, priestly and kingly function for the salvation of mankind. This link between the invisible and visible elements of ecclesial communion constitutes the Church as the Universal Sacrament of Salvation.[48]

Because Ratzinger's ecclesiology is eucharistic he asserts that it is especially in the Eucharist that the church experiences the fullness of *communio*. In the celebration of the Eucharist the church knows the intimate penetration of God with humankind, and of humans with humans. In joining in this sacrament, the church experiences the mystical and extraordinary reality of "being made one among them—*one* body. In this way Communion makes the Church by breaching an opening in the walls of subjectivity and gathering us into a deep communion of existence."[49] Ratzinger believes that it is in the Eucharist that the church experiences communion most profoundly. This is where the church is generated, encounters Christ afresh, and is most truly the body of Christ. It is possible, in my opinion, for non-Catholic churches and ecclesiologists to explore the possibilities of communion that are present within the Lord's Supper, without necessarily embracing every dimension and conviction present in a eucharistic and sacramental

---

45. Ibid., 29–72.

46. We all do this and, of course, I am doing it in my ecclesiological assessments.

47. Ratzinger, *Some Aspects of the Church*, 13.

48. Ratzinger, "Letter to the Bishops," art. 4; Rowland, *Ratzinger's Faith*, 85.

49. Ratzinger, *Called to Communion*, 37.

ecclesiology like the one developed by Ratzinger. The move to make this occasion a mere observance or symbol may, at times, have robbed some churches from plumbing the depths of communion and fellowship resident within the congregation's participation in the Lord's Supper.

QUESTIONS FOR REFLECTION

1. Why does Ratzinger place *communio* at the heart of his ecclesiology (communion, fellowship, mutuality, and *koinonia*)?

2. What are the implications of *communio* for our understanding and experience of church?

3. Ratzinger's ecclesiology is a *eucharistic ecclesiology*. Why is the Eucharist central to Ratzinger's ecclesiology? What are the implications for his view of church and ministry?

2

Karl Rahner: The Church as Community of Witness

In this world of God, of Jesus Christ, and of incomprehensibility there is to be a community to bear witness to Jesus; to attest God's vouchsafing of himself to the world, and its inevitable victory . . . This community of witness comes from Jesus for the salvation of the world (not merely for their own salvation), attests him, points back in faith to him, his death, and his resurrection, and forward in hope to the revealing of his victory.[1]

—KARL RAHNER

THE NATURE OF THE CHURCH

FOR KARL RAHNER, THE local community of faith, no less than the universal church of Jesus Christ, is the place in which "Christ himself, his gospel, his love and the unity of believers are present."[2] In his portrayal of the nature, essence, and future of the church, Rahner places emphasis on the importance of the local church. For Rahner, the conclusions of Vatican II will be ultimately embodied in the local congregation, and the dynamics that make local congregations unique will play a critical role in the future mission and form of the church. Through attention to word, sacrament, and unity with other churches, through willing submission to received church tradition and structure, and through embodying "everything which is stated in this constitution on the Church with regard to the universal Church," the local church is able to be a "vital force" in the world.[3] This is especially true as the local church surrenders to Christ and his Spirit.

Rahner's ecclesiology is cemented on the conviction that the church is "the sacrament of salvation for the world," realizing Christ's presence in history, and is witness,

---

1. Rahner, *Servants of the Lord*, 21. Karl Rahner (1904 to 1984) was one of the most influential Catholic theologians of the twentieth century. His academic roles included teaching theology at Pullach and Innsbruck, Chair for Christianity and the Philosophy of Religion at Munich, and Professor of Dogmatic Theology at Munster.

2. Rahner, "New Image of the Church," 10.

3. Ibid., 11–12.

result, and bearer of his generous grace. The church is the basic sacrament of salvation in the sense that it manifests God's grace concretely, sociologically, institutionally, and visibly in history. Conversely, "it is a sacramental sign of the grace that is offered to the world and history as a whole."[4] This means that it is a sacramental sign of grace wherever and whenever the grace of Christ has been manifested to human beings, past, present, and future. When the people of God gather for worship, word, Eucharist, baptism, and community, this sacramental sign of salvation and grace is manifested. Yet the sacramental significance of the church is not limited to these obvious contexts. Whenever the grace of Christ is present in the world, not only in the institutional and sociological settings that constitute the visible church, this "grace is already visibly being signified as an element in saving history as realized in this world in virtue of the fact that the Church herself has this force of being a basic sacrament."[5] As the basic sacrament of salvation, this sacramental nature is not confined to particular institutional, ideological, or cultural settings, but is correctly understood as the "vanguard" manifesting the "grace of salvation" in an active, dynamic way, "far beyond the confines of the 'visible' Church as sociologically definable."[6]

Elsewhere, Rahner defines the church in the following way:

> The Church is the community, legitimately constituted in a social structure; in which through faith, hope and love God's eschatologically definitive revelation (his self-communication) in Christ remains present for the world as reality and truth.[7]

For Rahner, God's divine self-communication throughout human history "reaches its eschatological culmination in Christ," and consequently the church "is the historical and social presence of God's self-communication to the world in Christ."[8] God's gracious self-communication and self-giving in Christ are both embodied and exemplified in the church's nature and actions. This is especially true when it imitates Christ in proclamation, worship, Eucharistic celebration, mission, and love. It is the "eschatologically perfect self-giving of God to humanity in the historical and social domain."[9] Rahner goes on to write that even though the church is often lured into falsely behaving as though it is God, it is nevertheless true that it is the presence of God in the world and the "concrete embodiment" of the grace and salvation of God. The church, as a "permanent revolution," glorifies and points to Jesus Christ, demolishing the idols of institutional pride, egocentricity, control, power, and polytheism in its manifold forms.[10] Its self-criticism is an offspring of its own nature, of its realization that its nature is a grace, and of God's gracious presence in the church. Consequently, its self-criticism is "a form of grace."[11]

Rahner is interested in liberating trinitarian discussions from cold, Neo-Scholastic inquiry, helping Christians and churches experience the trinitarian dimensions of their

4. Ibid., 14.

5. Ibid., 15.

6. Ibid., 16.

7. Rahner, *Theology of Pastoral Action*, 26–27.

8. Ibid., 29.

9. Ibid., 30.

10. Ibid., 31–32.

11. Ibid., 32.

faith anew, and applying trinitarian theology to church, mission, pastoral theology, and the believer.[12] This has direct consequence for his pastoral theology and ecclesiology. God reaches out to humanity through gracious, divine self-communication in word and Spirit, and truth and love. This movement reflects, is a product of, inner-trinitarian processions. Incarnation and grace, word and Spirit, and truth and love are expressed in God's divine self-communication in history, "the economy of redemption," the Christ-event. This expresses the "very duality of the inner-trinitarian processions."[13] "The 'economic' Trinity is the 'immanent' Trinity and the 'immanent' Trinity is the 'economic' Trinity," declares Rahner's *grundaxiom*.[14] When applied to the church, this means:

> The Trinity of the economy of redemption is the immanent Trinity. The duality of the inner-trinitarian processions forms the basis of the presence of God in the Church and is therefore the basis of the nature of the Church. If the nature of the Church is to be elucidated, nothing more "intelligible" or simpler will suffice.[15]

This trinitarian theology proposes that the church is the "presence of God's truth and love," reflecting and expressing "the duality of the inner-trinitarian processions."[16] It is the presence of God's truth through its acceptance of the word of God, faithful confession and embodiment of that word, and truth-filled worship, fellowship, mission, and charismatic and diaconal forms. It is the presence of God's love through its love of God and neighbor, ministry offices and structure, joyful celebration of the sacraments, and so forth. Rahner avoids getting caught up in specifically differentiating between the activities that are the presence of God's truth versus activities that are the presence of God's love. He believes the relationship between these two is complex and interdependent, just as the inner-trinitarian processions cannot be simply differentiated.[17]

The church has a range of characteristics that are important to its nature, suggests Rahner.[18]

1. *Mystery:* The church reflects and represents the mystery of God and of Christ.

2. *Primal Sacrament:* While Christ is the arch-sacrament, the "primordial sacrament, God's fundamental, original sign" (*Ursakrament*), the church is the "primal sacrament," symbol, and sign (*Grundsakrament*).

> In everything it is and does the Church is a sign which functions by pointing away from itself to God, to God alone . . . The Church is the efficacious manifest sign of the presence of God, its real symbol, containing what it signifies; by grasping the sign man experiences what it signifies . . . Its saving, missionary significance is not solely

---

12. Rahner, *Trinity*, 10–15, 28–38, 117–20.
13. Rahner, *Theology of Pastoral Action*, 33.
14. Rahner, *Trinity*, 22.
15. Rahner, *Theology of Pastoral Action*, 33–34.
16. Ibid., 29, 33.
17. Ibid., 34–43.
18. Ibid., 43–63.

dependent on the number of its members. The Church's missionary zeal must be based on its awareness that it conveys salvation to the world (as its necessary sign).[19]

3. *New Law of the Gospel:* The church is characterized by gospel, and the self-giving love and grace of God, not by law.

4. *Eschatological Presence:* Even though the sociological institution of the church will not be necessary in the eschaton, the church is "eschatologically permanent" in the historical, contemporary, and eschatological realms, and consequently enjoys an assurance and immeasurable significance during each and every settled and troubled time.

5. *Ever New Actual Presence:* In every age and generation the church has an "ever new actual presence" as it participates in and symbolizes the "*history* of the final covenant."

6. *Reconciliation of the Permanent and the Historical:* The church has a permanent nature but this nature is always expressed in fresh, emerging, contextual, and historical forms, and the church must remain attentive to the Spirit, church leadership, and collective discernment as it seeks to navigate the tension between the old and the new.

Rahner believes that the local congregation, and the wider church for that matter, should not position itself in a sectarian or defensive way in relation to the world, nor should it be understood as a local branch of an institutional giant. He suggests that in a world where many people find themselves isolated, lonely, and objectified, the local church is to be a loving and authentic community of free belief, personal decision, and faithful and enthusiastic witness and unity. Moreover, instead of pursuing power in their roles, the leaders of the churches are to exercise their spiritual authority in the love of Christ, since their authority "stems from the mission of *Christ himself.*" Rahner, however, is realistic about our understanding of the shape churches will take when they are "formed by love." The practical outworking of love of God and neighbor in the local church remains to be explored in the fullest possible way, yet it will certainly be an antidote to individualistic, sectarian, superficial, or consumerist expressions of church that are sometimes observed.[20]

In the final stages of his theological engagement with the conclusions of Vatican II, in the document "The New Image of the Church," Rahner writes that it was necessary and proper for the Council to deliberate on the institutional structure of the church and the theological foundations of such structure. Nevertheless, he asserts that this discussion about form and institution is "subsumed and made subordinate to a more basic understanding of the Church" as "the people of God gathered together by God's grace," as "the outcome of God's grace, as the fruit of salvation."[21] The church is the people who are moved by the grace of God to declare in their witness, community, and love the message and salvation of Jesus Christ. He affirms the Council's conclusions that the church is the

19. Ibid., 44–49.
20. Rahner, "New Image of the Church," 25–27.
21. Ibid., 27.

church of faith, hope, and love, the church of the Trinity, the church of martyrdom, the church of the poor and oppressed, and the pilgrim, temporal institution in the "eschatological phase of saving history."[22]

CHANGEABLE AND UNCHANGEABLE DIMENSIONS

When treating Rahner's fundamental views on the nature of the church, it is worth considering his understanding of the "changeable and unchangeable factors in the Church."[23] He begins his treatment of this subject by appealing to those things that the church has agreed are unchangeable and bedrock for the Christian faith and church (even though they are often the source, content, and problem of much modern debate). These three things are:

> the abiding corpus of dogma in the Church, an interpretation of basic moral attitudes which has a permanent validity in Christian life (in other words an abiding Christian ethic), and a valid and permanent constitutional law of the Church.[24]

The church cannot alter these unchangeable dimensions of its doctrine, ethic, and ecclesiastical life. Those who deny these unchangeable things are outside the church.[25] Distinguishing these things from other changeable aspects of the theology, worship, and expressions of the church allows the people of God and its leaders to discern correctly what may and may not be reformed, and what may and may not be questioned.

Rahner, however, recognizes the complexity involved in discerning in these three arenas those things that are unchangeable or changeable. Unchangeable things have come to take shape in a historical and institutional form that symbolizes, but is not itself, the unchangeable thing. "The changeable and the unchangeable are not two entities simply existing side by side as immediately empirically apprehensible each in its own right."[26] Instead, that which is unchangeable resides, and is sometimes hidden, in the changeable, historical, contextual form.[27] In the process of seeking to be faithful to the received unchangeable dimensions of the doctrinal, ethical, and ecclesial life of the church, the church and the individual must pursue change, reform, and renewal. In astonishment, as a grace, the church and the individual Christian discover "faithfulness to the unchangeable factor" through obedient, Spirit-led change. Changeable and unchangeable are interwoven in life-giving ways by the Spirit of Christ and the grace of God.

THE ANONYMOUS CHRISTIAN

When outlining his response to Vatican II, Rahner describes the concept of the *anonymous Christian*, and the relationship of such a person to grace, salvation, mission, and the

22. Ibid., 28–29.

23. Rahner, *Ecclesiology*, 3–23.

24. Ibid., 5.

25. One can easily imagine the Protestant response to such a suggestion.

26. Rahner, *Ecclesiology*, 7.

27. Rahner et al., *Content of Faith*, 406–8.

church.[28] Maurice Boutin notes that there is "still great divergence on the interpretation of this notion."[29] For Rahner, non-believers should not be understood as fundamentally divorced or separated from the grace of Christ. Christ's grace and truth are active in their lives since he is at the center of all things. People who do not yet confess Christ may still be *anonymous Christians* since God's grace is at work in their lives, goes before the gospel, and prepares hearts to receive it; and, although it is at times hidden and unperceived, it is nonetheless present and prevenient. He describes, in some detail, his understanding of the intricate relationship between the idea of the *anonymous Christian* and professed Christianity, the church, and missionary zeal. This relationship encompasses the attitude of the Christian to the world and the non-believer, the reality of God's grace and salvation extended to the world, and the assurance the professing believer can know. An optimistic view of salvation and the world is seen as compatible with missionary zeal and ecclesial participation.[30] Christians do not need to view other religions or non-believers in a harsh or negative light but, rather, as recipients of God's grace. Rahner's views reflect the conclusions of Vatican II while developing them according to his own theological convictions.

There has been much debate about the validity and meaning of the notion of the *anonymous Christian*.[31] Rahner does not believe that every human being is an *anonymous Christian*. He only includes people who are oriented toward God, his glory, and his grace, and who allow themselves to be "taken hold of by this grace."[32] Within Rahner's writings there is the clear conviction that the concepts of the *anonymous Christian* and the "Church as the sacrament of salvation for the world" do not diminish the necessity or passion for preaching the gospel or for missionary zeal. He hopes that they might help Christians understand the relationship between the prevenient grace of God, the sacramental nature of the church, the missionary impulse of the gospel, the "assurance that this world will increasingly come to belong to the Church," and,

> the real hope that it will be possible for the world to be redeemed through the Church even in those areas of it where its inclusion in the Church has not acquired the status of a palpable fact in history.[33]

Elsewhere he writes of the relationship between the concept of the *anonymous Christian* and the missionary zeal of the church,

> Such a theory in no way cripples the missionary impulse of the Church but rather puts before it the person to whom it addresses itself in his true hopeful condition so that it can approach him with confidence.[34]

28. Rahner, "New Image of the Church," 16–24.

29. Boutin, "Anonymous Christianity," 602–29.

30. Rahner, *Anonymous Christianity*.

31. D'Costa, "Karl Rahner's Anonymous Christian."

32. Rahner, *Concerning Vatican Council II*, 395.

33. Rahner, "New Image of the Church," 24.

34. Rahner, *Concerning Vatican Council II*, 398.

THE CHURCH OF SINNERS AND GRACE

A theme that permeates Rahner's ecclesiology throughout the various stages of his life is the presence of grace in the church and the world, and the relationship between God's grace and the church of sinners. The church, writes Rahner, is the church of sinners.[35] While the church declares itself as holy through the grace of Jesus Christ, so often it appears as anything but holy and countless efforts have been made theologically, sociologically, and institutionally to reconcile this dilemma. The individual's struggle with sin and holiness is mirrored in the experience of the church as a whole, and the struggle of the corporate church seems to enhance the struggle of the individual.[36]

Rahner deals with the question of sin in the church in two parts, being *the church of sinners*, and sinful people before *the holy church of sinners*. Firstly, Rahner considers the church of sinners. There are sinners in the church who deny the grace and transforming power of God and who do not belong to the body of Christ in the same way as those who walk in humble submission, obedience, and discipleship to Christ. However, others struggle with sin and holiness while seeking full submission to the Lordship of Christ. Moreover, in its real, concrete, visible life, even among those in positions of responsibility and leadership, the church itself is sinful. This "is the truth of faith, not an elementary fact of experience. And it is a shattering truth." However, at the same time the church is genuinely holy. Its holiness comes from its union with Christ, its participation in his eschatological and ultimate purposes, and the grace of God poured out upon it. Its holiness is an inherent part of its essence, sign, and nature and an "expression of what it is and will remain infallibly and indestructibly until the end of time: the presence in the world of God and of his grace." While sin and its consequences can be devastating in the life of the church, the grace of God, so wonderfully demonstrated in the cross of Jesus Christ, is sufficient to make the church holy, to quicken our passion for this holiness, and to cause us to be humble when we see the failings and weaknesses of others and of institutions.[37]

Rahner's treatment of the relationship between sin in the church and the grace of God then turns to the question of sinful people "before the holy Church of sinners." He is dealing here with the question of how Christians come to practical and authentic terms with sinfulness in the church. The answer is not found in fleeing from the church, in isolated sectarianism, in romantic idealism, in illusive and Gnostic-like distinctions between the divine and the concrete, in fanatical and egocentric efforts of reform, nor in covering up or minimizing sin. The attitude of the Christian when faced with the reality of sinfulness in the church should be humility in the light of their own sin, personal ownership of the failings of the church, and dependency on the abundant and immeasurable grace of God. Out of this grace, God bestows mercy, forgiveness, and holiness. Out of that posture of humility and grace-dependency reform, repentance, and change are possible—for individuals and for the church. All of this resides in, and is dependent upon, the grace of God.[38]

---

35. Rahner, "Church of Sinners," 64–74; Rahner, *Concerning Vatican Council II*, 253–69.

36. Rahner, *Trinity*, 253–56.

37. Ibid., 256–65.

38. Ibid., 265–69.

MINISTRY OFFICE, LAITY, AND PASTORAL ACTION

The differentiations between hierarchy and laity, office and function, and formal and charismatic structure are important to Rahner's ecclesiology. While wanting to encourage the whole body of Christ to ministry and service, that is, to contribute to the growth, health, and vitality of the church, he is unapologetic for these distinctions since, in the perspective of the Roman Catholic Church, the hierarchical structures and ministries have been instituted by God and must be passed on through each successive generation.[39]

The whole of the body of Christ is the church, not just the hierarchy or the structures. Every person in the body of Christ has a charism of grace and ministry to be used for edification and service, to the glory of Christ. Ecclesiastical office is an expression of that broader charismatic structure, yet those who hold office have certain powers, rights, charisms, and obligations that come with their office. Those who hold office in the hierarchical, ecclesiastical structure are to respect and foster the charismatic life of the community of faith, cultivating the giftedness and ministries of the whole body of Christ. Those who hold office must recognize that among the laity there are "grace-given vocations and endowments" given "from above" which are to be cultivated but which, nonetheless, are accountable to the formal structures and offices of the church.[40]

The distinction between office and function is important. Office-bearers are not to rest in the authority of their formal status but are to exercise ministry graces and functions through the charisms that they have been given for the benefit of the church and the world. "The best situation is, of course, when office and free spiritual gifts are combined in one person." It is then that official, formal offices are fused with charismatic gifts and, consequently, the church is built up through the ministry office and the laity.[41]

Rahner defends the traditional structure of the Roman Catholic Church, with authority and "power of order and jurisdiction" located sacramentally in the Petrine office, the Curia, the colleges of cardinals and bishops, the diaconal and presbyteral bodies, and the ministry offices in the local churches. According to Rahner, the church's founder has handed the church this structure. Furthermore, it reflects the inner-trinitarian relations and best serves the church as the basic sacrament of salvation for the world. He is careful to locate this articulation of the Roman Catholic structure and the distinction between ministries and offices in the context of a theology of the whole church, and in a clear call for every individual Christian to be released to service, ministry, vocation, mission, and use of their charisms.[42] Geoffrey Kelly suggests that Rahner draws the connections between ecclesial structures, ministry offices, and charismatic graces to "promote a commitment" to pastoral action in the world and to explore "both the nature of the Church as the basis of pastoral action and the interrelationship of individuals and officeholders."[43] Rahner certainly considers the ecclesial nature of the

---

39. Rahner, *Theology of Pastoral Action*, 59–60, 64–70.

40. Ibid., 60–62, 70–77; Rahner, *Spirit in the Church*, 35–73; Rahner, *Nature and Grace*, 83–113.

41. Rahner, *Theology of Pastoral Action*, 62–63.

42. Ibid., 64–133.

43. Kelly, *Karl Rahner*, 257.

Christian and the importance of ecclesial structure, law, and order in the church to be directly related to fruitful and vital love of God and of neighbor, and faithful profession of the gospel in a pluralistic, secular world.[44]

THE SHAPE OF THE CHURCH TO COME

In 1972 Rahner published his small but spirited critique of the church and its future, *The Shape of the Church to Come.* In that work he wrestled with three questions he deemed fundamental for the future, mission, and wellbeing of the church: Where do we stand? What are we to do? How can the church of the future be conceived or envisioned?

The concerns expressed and the solutions offered in *The Shape of the Church to Come* are inspired by Rahner's missiological impulse. He is enthusiastic about seeing the church and its ecclesiology put into lively conversation with contemporary western culture and its problems, as well as exploring the missiological potential of the church's future. In order to understand the church's future, its people must wrestle with their understanding of the mission of the church, their sense of the history and traditions of the church, and their conceptions of the gospel message and its implications. Retreat into past habits, ecclesial patterns, and timidity is an inadequate response to the challenges that face the church and its future. The church requires the courage of an "ultimately charismatically inspired, creative imagination."[45]

Long before the popularity of theories about post-Christendom and the mission of the church, Rahner explored the transition the church was going through from privilege, homogeneity, and cultural dominance to a new position of marginality, smallness, peculiarity, and individual decision for Christ amidst mounting cultural pressure to pursue alternative worldviews. As a *little flock* churches are to demonstrate faithful witness to Christ and his mission to redeem the world. Appreciating the grace that is possible as a *little flock* is not the same as adopting the mentality of a sectarian group. The proper response to the transition the church is going through is a *missionary offensive* that reflects the missiological passion of God. "We are a little flock in society and we shall become a much smaller flock, since the erosion of the preconditions of a Christian society within the secular society still continues and thus takes away the ground more and more from a traditional Christianity."[46] The best defense in this environment is the *missionary offensive.*[47]

While Rahner remains supportive of the *magisterium* and its authority in the life of the church, he believes that the future of the church will require church leadership to explicitly ground its decision-making in Scripture and the gospel. Church leaders need to be willing to relinquish positions and postures that are not germane to the essence of the church. There will be times when church leaders will need to guide and even direct the people of God without resorting to artificial claims of divine inspiration. Rahner is not denying divine inspiration but is challenging the manner and frequency of such claims

44. Rahner, *Foundations of Christian Faith*, 389–401.

45. Rahner, *Shape of the Church*, 46–47.

46. Ibid., 31.

47. Ibid., 32.

in the future of the church. There must be a willingness to withdraw decisions, admit mistakes, and receive criticism. The church of the future will be *a servant church.*[48]

The church of the future will be *a declericalized church.* While priests and other office-bearers will have a continuing role to play in the future of the church, that role will become increasingly about cultivating the charismatic gifts and graces in the church. As more people come to faith in a secular and pluralistic society through free and personal decision, the church will grow *from below.* According to Rahner, basic communities of free association are the future of the church (these should not be confused with parishes—instead, they are fresh, spontaneous, informal, relational, and contextually appropriate gatherings of believers). He asserts that this cultural and ecclesial transition will mean that the priest will need to become more proactive in identifying, equipping, and releasing the whole body of Christ for ministry and service. In the *declericalized church* of the future, priests may come to the ministry married, fulfilling all the usual priestly functions as a married person, and women might be admitted to priestly office. The church will also be more intentionally *a sociocritical church* speaking into the societal systems and powers of the day and, often through basic, local communities, contributing to the needs of society and pursuing societal change.[49]

The new cultural challenges facing the Roman Catholic Church also confront the other Christian traditions, writes Rahner. This will demand that the church of the future is ecumenically oriented and willing to pursue unity even before theological and confessional differences have been sorted out. Rahner proposes an institutional unity among the major Christian traditions that precedes and fosters a richer unity of faith in the future. *Institutional unification* should not require dogmatic, structural, or practical uniformity. The sticking point, for Rahner, is the role of the pope in this institutional unification. For Rahner, this would involve the papal office having the primary function of developing unity among the churches and the *constituent churches* having reasonable autonomy from that office. The Catholic churches would grant the papal office more authority in their structure than would be expected in the constituent churches; however, these other Christian traditions would still honor and accept limited papal function. Rahner's concern in this discussion on ecumenism is the unity of the churches before the world as a testimony to the grace and gospel of Jesus Christ.[50]

CONTRIBUTIONS TO MISSIONAL ECCLESIOLOGY

Leo O'Donovan has contributed significantly to the study of Rahner's theology and ecclesiology.[51] In 1977 he facilitated a symposium on the development of ecclesiological

48. Ibid., 46–55, 61–63, 93–98, 119–21.

49. Ibid., 56–60, 110–14.

50. Ibid., 53–54, 102–6; Fries and Rahner, *Unity of the Churches,* 7–10; Rahner, *Confrontations 1,* 33–40; Rahner, *Concern for the Church,* 154–72. Rahner's suggestions did not win him friends in the Curia, and no doubt irritated many Catholics and non Catholics alike.

51. O'Donovan, *World of Grace*; O'Donovan, "Rahner: In Memoriam"; O'Donovan, "Final Harvest"; O'Donovan, "Journey into Time"; O'Donovan, "Karl Rahner and Ignatian Spirituality"; O'Donovan, "Karl Rahner"; O'Donovan, "On Reading Rahner."

themes during what he considered the three distinct periods of Rahner's life and writing. In the published findings three scholars, each competent in Rahner's thought, traced and expounded these three periods in Rahner's ecclesiological development:[52]

1. Peter Schineller considered Rahner's writings *before Vatican II*, where Rahner's ecclesiology emphasized the relationship between the church and the freedom and responsibility of the individual. During that period, his ecclesiology also focused on the relationship between the church and God's grace, and the church and the sinful nature of people and institutions.

2. John Galvin explored Rahner's writings *during the period of Vatican II*, where his ecclesiology dealt with the nature of the church, ministry, and office in the church and the limitations of the church.

3. Michael Fahey examined Rahner's ecclesiology *during the decade after Vatican II*, where Rahner wrestled with the conclusions and implications of the Council. Rahner also developed an ecclesiology for the concrete, visible church in contemporary culture (moving from his previous abstract ecclesiological considerations to more concrete concerns). He wrote about the tasks of the church in the world and wrestled with the shape of structural and pastoral changes for the post-Vatican II church. The church in the world and the missiological impulse of the church also figure highly in his later writings.

In this chapter I have given some attention to most of these Rahnerian themes, some receiving more attention than others have, paying most attention to his later, post-Vatican II ecclesiological concerns. Rahner's ecclesiology contributes to *Part Two* of this book through its missiological, eschatological, and trinitarian themes.[53] Rahner articulates a clear vision of the church as *the sacrament of salvation for the world* that realizes Christ's presence and eschatological mission and purpose in history. As the basic sacrament of salvation, the church "is a sacramental sign of the grace that is offered to the world and history as a whole."[54] William Dych notes that in Rahner's ecclesiology the church is sacramental in two senses: a sacrament of the salvation of its members and "the basic sacrament of the salvation of the world."[55] As communities of faith gather for worship, participate in God's mission, proclaim Scripture, and celebrate the Eucharist, this sacramental sign of salvation and grace is manifested. This sacramental nature is also present and active "far beyond the confines of the 'visible' Church as sociologically definable."[56] The church "is the historical and social presence of God's self-communication to the world in Christ."[57] Furthermore, the church mirrors and expresses in concrete form the inner-trinitarian processions of incarnation and grace, word and Spirit, truth and love. It is "at once mystery, primal sacrament, new law of the gospel, eschatological sign, God's ever-renewed

52. O'Donovan, "Changing Ecclesiology," 736–62.
53. He features in chapters 15 and 17 in *Part Two* of this book.
54. Rahner, "New Image of the Church," 14.
55. Dych, *Karl Rahner*, 85–86.
56. Rahner, "New Image of the Church," 16.
57. Rahner, *Theology of Pastoral Action*, 29.

presence in history," and the community that lives with the dynamic tension between the changeable and unchangeable, the permanent and the constantly renewed.[58]

Rahner's ecclesiology also enhances missional ecclesiology, through its attention to the reciprocal relationships between laity, offices, hierarchy, service, and charism in the church. He builds a theology of the church that inevitably leads to *a theology of pastoral action* in which all the participants in the life of the local and whole church contribute in significant, life-giving ways. Rahner describes the church as a church of sinners and a church that wrestles with its own sinfulness. The grace of God, however, makes it holy, reformed, repentant, and Christ honoring.[59] As the church responds to the secularization and societal changes around it, and transitions into a fresh position of self-understanding and societal relations, it requires the courage of an "ultimately charismatically inspired, creative imagination" in order to be faithful to the gospel, its nature, and its God-given missiological impulse.[60] Rahner's ecclesiology is also conducive to missional ecclesiology through some of its reflections on the role of the church in the world, on the availability of the peace of God to an anxious world, and on the presence of Christ in gathered and dispersed worship. He also writes lucidly on the possibilities and processes of dialogue within the dynamic and often confrontational systems of church life, and on the nature of ecumenical and interfaith discussion. The question of *anonymous Christians* is also fairly important for a missional ecclesiology, for the reasons I have described earlier in this chapter, and warrants further investigation.

Roman Catholic theological tradition, Christian ethics, and "valid and permanent constitutional law,"[61] are all unchangeable dimensions of the church, according to Rahner. Denying this places one outside the church. Protestants and others naturally shudder at such assertions. Evangelicals, for instance, place a much greater emphasis on the infallible, authoritative word of God, its final authority in matters of corporate and individual faith and conduct, and its ability to critique, renew, and change those things that Rahner considers unchangeable. Ecumenical dialogue, which is critical while authentic, will also require revision of such dimensions articulated by Rahner, in the light of the conversations had, the Scriptures examined, the theologies developed, and the Spirit discerned.

Rahner is not an easy read. His writing style is dense, his theological breadth and capacity are intimidating, and he seems to have little interest in providing easy or readily accessible answers. Yet his theological genius and passion, his relentless pursuit of theological answers supported by logical evidence, his fearless interrogation of theological solutions to challenging secular and ecclesial questions, and his obvious love for Christ, the church, and the pastoral and missional dimensions of the church's existence, make reading Rahner a rewarding, if difficult, experience. Rahner never enjoyed the popular following and acclaim experienced by Hans Küng, yet he dealt courageously, systematically, and insightfully with many of the same pressing questions that are entertained in

---

58. Kelly, *Karl Rahner*, 257–58; Rahner, *Theology of Pastoral Action*, 29–49.

59. Rahner, *Concerning Vatican Council II*, 265–69.

60. Rahner, *Shape of the Church*, 46–47.

61. Rahner, *Ecclesiology*, 5.

Küng's popular works. Rahner was arguably the leading Catholic theologian of his time and contemporary students of ecclesiology would gain much by reading his works.

QUESTIONS FOR REFLECTION

1. How might the church's self-criticism be *a form of grace*? Why don't we usually receive it this way and how might we change?

2. Discuss each of Rahner's six characteristics of the church. What does each one mean and how might each one shape our understanding of our own particular, local church?

3. Rahner regards the formal leadership structures in the church as a dimension and expression of the broader *charismatic structure of the church*. What does this mean? How can the appointed leaders in the local church cultivate and release the charismatic structure and energies of their congregation?

3

Hans Küng: The Church as Eschatological Community of Salvation

The Church, therefore, is the pilgrim fellowship of believers, not of those who already see and know. The Church must ever and again wander through the desert, through the darkness of sin and error. For the Church can also err and for this reason must always be prepared to orientate itself anew, to renew itself. It must always be prepared to seek out a new path, a way that might be just as difficult to find as a desert track, or a path through darkness. There is, however, one guiding light it is never without, just as God's people in the desert always had a guide: God's word is always there to lead the Church. Through Jesus, the Christ, it has been definitely revealed to us.[1]

—Hans Küng

ESSENCE AND FORM, NATURE AND UN-NATURE

Hans Küng is a prolific writer, and the scope and depth of his theology are difficult to summarize in a brief chapter such as this. Consequently, I focus almost exclusively on his views about the nature, structures, dimensions, and offices of the church. I do this by intentionally structuring this chapter around the sections of his majestic work on ecclesiology, *The Church*. The other work that I regularly refer to is *Structures of the Church*, which is a prolegomenon to *The Church*.[2] I have attempted a synopsis of Küng's ecclesiology by working especially with these two texts, adding insights from his other writings as needed, and referring to secondary sources occasionally.

In *The Church*, Küng attempts to develop a biblical theology of the church, subjecting systematic theology to the rigors of biblical exegesis. His goal is to examine the biblical themes relating to the church, and to analyze those themes in the order they are presented

---

1. Küng, *Church*, xi. Hans Küng has been President of the Foundation for a Global Ethic since 1995. He was formerly the Professor of Ecumenical Theology at the University of Tübingen, and has served there as an emeritus professor since 1996.

2. Küng, *Structures of the Church*; Küng, *Church*, xiii.

in Scripture. He attempts to build an ecclesiology grounded in the whole of the scriptural canon, engaging the latest historical-critical methods, with awareness of the influence of his own preconceptions, and with attention to addressing the present distortions in ecclesiology.[3] An ambitious set of aims indeed! For Küng it is possible to uncover the *essence* of the church, and to "distinguish permanent and continuing elements from changing and transient features."[4] While *essence* and *form* cannot be separated, they are also not identical. The first is rooted in the origins of the church, and the second contains the historical forms and expressions of the church. "The essence of the Church is therefore always to be found in its historical form, and the historical form must always be understood in the light of and with reference to the essence."[5] The essential nature of the church is not some abstract ideal that is divorced from the real and concrete church. It is always located in the historical church, finding expression in fresh ways as the church responds to the challenges, opportunities, and contexts it faces. The church needs to be loyal to the nature that God has entrusted to it, by embracing change and being "constantly willing to reform, to renew, to rethink."[6] Therefore, Küng writes of ecclesiology:

> Ecclesiology is a response and a call to constantly changing historical situations. This requires repeated and determined attempts to mould, form and differentiate in freedom, unless ecclesiologists give up in despair at each new situation, close their eyes to them and simply drift. The Church's doctrine of the Church, like the Church itself, is necessarily subject to continual change and must constantly be undertaken anew.[7]

Those dimensions of the church that are expressions of evil—shadowy, perverse, and illegitimate—are contradictions or pollutions of the *essence* or authentic *nature* of the church. For Küng, this is the church's *un-nature*, that is, unnatural historical manifestations, which can be critiqued, challenged, and repudiated, without assaulting the real or legitimate nature of the church.[8] The church is broken, bruised, wounded, and on pilgrimage; yet it is through the church that we receive faith as a gracious gift from God. Through the church, in full exposure to its *nature* and its *un-nature*, we hear the gospel, are called to respond, have our faith cultivated and enriched, and enter into a community of pilgrim believers. "Faith and the Church are interrelated and react fruitfully upon one another in mutual service." Yet "neither faith nor the Church should be made absolute," since they are both preceded by and dependent upon God's saving grace and action.[9] We must not idealize the church, nor become despondent about the frailties of the church. The Spirit invites us into realistic, concrete, present, and even joyful fellowship with the people of God. Both our admiration and criticism of the church are to be expressed through faith.

3. Küng, *Church*, 15–24.

4. Ibid., 4–6.

5. Ibid., 6.

6. Ibid., 13.

7. Ibid., 13.

8. Ibid., 27–29.

9. Ibid., 30–34.

THE ESCHATOLOGICAL COMMUNITY AND GOD'S REIGN

In *The Church*, Küng spends considerable time describing what Jesus might have meant when he proclaimed the reign of God. He also analyses the various arguments put forward on the question of immediate expectation for the reign of God verse distant expectation. Küng argues, along with Bultmann, Käsemann, and others, for *presentist-futurist* eschatology, that is, a present-future reign of God. He believes that this is the thoroughly biblical position that has implications for individual discipleship as well as Jesus's hopes and expectations for the church that he founded. Küng asserts that "the present points to the future: the final period of history begins with Jesus," and so we have eschatological hope and the certainty of faith that are grounded in historical realities and God's present reign. Conversely, "the future points back to the present: man's decision must not simply be a consolation for the future, and an excuse for neglecting the present world; it is rather a reason for changing it."[10] This *presentist-futurist* eschatology, present in Christ's message about the kingdom and reign of God, is critical for understanding Jesus's purposes for the church. It is also important for our understanding of the way the early church saw itself, and how we might understand the church today.[11]

Küng writes that, while it is clear that the kingdom and reign of God were central to Jesus's earthly preaching and teaching, he did not focus his attention on founding a church. His message of redemption and God's reign was inclusive and broad, rather than separatist, exclusive, or institutional. His pre-Easter life, ministry, and teaching cultivated the soil upon which the church would flourish. This church really came into being post-Easter, however, as the fruit "of the entire action of God in Jesus Christ, from his birth, his ministry and the calling of the disciples, through to his death and resurrection and the sending of the Spirit to the witnesses of his resurrection."[12]

It is possible to discern the link or continuity between Jesus's *presentist-futurist* message of the reign of God, and the post-Easter emergence of the church. Christ preached the coming reign of God, and demonstrated that inaugurated reign through his words, life, presence, death, and resurrection. The present-future kingdom had come to the world, being most clearly seen in the person and ministry of Christ. After the resurrection, the church was entrusted with the mandate to proclaim and embody this present-future reign of God, by reflecting and manifesting the love, sacrifice, mission, and passion of her Lord.[13] The church continues the ministry and proclamation of the pre-Easter and resurrection Christ in the present world, with eschatological implication, vision, hope, and certainty. Therefore, Küng describes the church as the *eschatological community of salvation*, called into existence through the eschatological event of the life, message, death, resurrection, and reign of Christ.[14]

10. Ibid., 68–69.
11. Ibid., 43–70.
12. Ibid., 70–76.
13. Ibid., 78.
14. Ibid., 81.

Each individual church is not the whole church, "but nonetheless fully represents it." The gathered church is much more than "a free association of individuals": it is a people called together through the action and Spirit of Christ, as *an ekklesia of God*. The church is not meant to be a solidified, rigid institution, preserving its existence for its own sake: it, ideally, lives with a sense of its eschatological mission as God shapes the world and human history toward his final purpose. The church has always been called to understand itself as *an eschatological community of salvation*.[15]

The kingdom of God should not be identified with the church, nor dissociated from it. The church is provisional, organized institutionally by human beings, and always developing, emerging, and changing. The kingdom of God is experienced in the present, yet belonging "fundamentally to the future": the definitive work of God, the goal of creation, and the realm of the absolute reign and sovereignty of God. However, the church as the *eschatological community of salvation* is an *anticipatory sign* of the final and already present reign of God: announcing and serving the reign of God in its mission, ministries, structures, and nature, in a provisional, frail, yet real way.

Küng goes on to describe the consequences of the church living in the service of the reign of God. (a) Its preaching, efforts, and self-understanding are eschatological, with a view to the "decisive, future, final" reign of God. It does not exist for itself, nor expend its energies trying to preserve itself. (b) It understands that "the reign of God is *an all-powerful act of God himself*," and so it trusts in the power and sovereignty of God, not in its own resources, ingenuity, or efforts. (c) It refuses to identify itself with or embrace the power systems, structures, ideologies, or honors of this world: instead, it takes on the form of a servant. (d) It appreciates its own frailties, weaknesses, temptations, and delusions, and, consequently, approaches the world and individual sinners with compassion, service, and empathy. (e) It will not elevate its own regulations, traditions, institutions, or offices above the demands and message of Christ. (f) Through the power and presence of the Spirit, and in an attitude of humble prayer and service, it will seek to live in faithful service to the reign of God proclaimed by its Lord Jesus Christ.[16]

THE CHARISMATIC STRUCTURE OF THE CHURCH

While recognizing the validity of ministry functions and charisms, Küng rejects what he considers an unhealthy clericalization and hierarchy in church structure.[17] Here he and Rahner are clearly at odds with Ratzinger. All members of the body of Christ have been called, sanctified, and united with Christ and his ecclesia, and any elitist distinction between those who hold or do not hold certain offices is foreign to Scripture and the authentic nature of the church. "The holding of an office in the Church, of whatever kind, is unimportant compared to whether, in exercising that office" a person is "truly one of the 'faithful,'" living "in faith and obedience, in hope and love."[18] Moreover, Küng

15. Ibid., 87.

16. Ibid., 96–103.

17. Küng, *Reforming the Church Today*, 52–63.

18. Küng, *Church*, 126.

asserts that the church is far more than a privatized, individualized, "free association of like-minded religious" and pious people. God gathers the ecclesia together by his mercy, grace, choosing, and God-initiated covenant with us. It is he who initiates salvation for the whole people of God, not merely as redeemed, separate, individualized persons, but as a community of believers who have been saved through God's action on behalf of them all, as one body.[19] God draws them into meaningful, concrete, historical, localized fellowship and, in doing so, establishes the only true and essential structure of the church.

> It is right to distinguish between the "structure" and the "life" of the Church, but wrong to assign to "structure" faith, sacraments and offices, and endow them with a particular importance as spiritual riches, while we pigeonhole the fellowship of believers under "life." There can be no faith, sacraments and offices, nothing of any institutional nature, without men, they cannot precede or be superior to men. All these things only exist in the fellowship of believers, who *are* the Church; it is this fellowship, which is identical with the new people of God, which constitutes the *basic structure* of the Church.[20]

While injustice, sinful passion, oppression, anxiety, self-reliance, and the like, are sometimes experienced as bondage in the assembly of believers, just as they are experienced in the world, the church is nonetheless called by Christ to live in freedom and to reflect the freedom that he offers. This freedom is offered to the individual believer and to the church as a grace through the Spirit.[21] For Küng, the church and its structures must be understood as the creation of the Spirit. This pneumatology is critical to Küng's ecclesiology. For him, the fundamental structure of the church is charismatic. The Spirit is an "eschatological gift" from God, who shapes the structure, orientation, ministries, community, and mission of the church.[22]

> Through the giving of the Holy Spirit the community recognized itself and testified to itself as the eschatological community. Thus the time of the Church, for Luke an essentially missional Church, is the time of the Spirit. The Spirit bestows power, authority and legitimacy . . . [23] God has revealed himself in his entire living power . . . There are no limits to his self-giving power, which has been revealed to his people and has transformed its whole existence, indeed creating it anew. His power sustains it and leads it towards its goal.[24]

The church, therefore, has a *charismatic structure*. Küng notes that in Scripture the charisms are not usually exceptional, and are never uniform, elitist, dysfunctionally enthusiastic, divisive, in opposition to biblical values, or bestowed by the Spirit in order to surpass or replace the revelation of Jesus Christ and his gospel. Charisms given to the church and to local communities as they gather for worship, fellowship, and mission, are

19. Ibid., 125–28.
20. Ibid., 130.
21. Ibid., 150–62.
22. Ibid., 162–203.
23. Ibid., 165.
24. Ibid., 168.

often rather everyday, and are edifying, serving, loving, diverse yet unifying, community-building, Christ-honoring, and widely distributed among the people of God. People in formal positions or offices are not the only ones who serve with such gifts. The gifts are distributed to the many for the benefit and edification of the whole. This charismatic life reveals the continuing and essential charismatic nature and structure of the church. Therefore, "one can speak of a *charismatic structure of the Church*, which *includes but goes far beyond the hierarchical* structure of the Church." This charismatic structure is revealed as God's people in community and on mission experience the authentic interconnectedness of "charism, vocation and service."[25]

According to Küng, the church can be understood as both *the people of God* and *the body of Christ*, since these concepts are not contradictory and since both "seek to express the union of the Church with Christ and the union of its members among themselves."[26] Paul addresses the charismatic structure of the church in 1 Corinthians 12 and Romans 12, and links the charismata, and the charismatics, clearly with the concept of the body of Christ. Individual charismatics do not arrive at the churches and choose, in an isolated and individualistic fashion, to use their gifts at will and according to their own tastes and interests—not even if such acts are done with the best of intentions. Küng notes that, according to Scripture, Christ, through his Spirit, graciously and sovereignly pours out the charismata.[27]

Christ calls and forms human beings into his body and his people—locally, regionally, and globally. It is he, through his Spirit, who enables Christian communities to live in love and unity, and who demands these of his disciples. He is present in the local and worldwide church, and especially in the worshipping congregation. Each gathered community is the "fullest sense of God's ecclesia" and yet cannot know this fullness in isolation from other communities of faith. Furthermore, while Christ is in union with his church, he is never "wholly contained in the Church." He embraces the church as his bride and body but, according to Küng, we must not make the mistake of identifying him with the church. The church can never wholly contain his majesty, uniqueness, Lordship, divinity, and so forth. "This relationship exists not ontologically and statically, but historically and dynamically."[28] The church exists and develops healthily when it orients itself in a posture of obedience, intimacy, and service to Christ. It does not have an independent authority, existence, commission, or power apart from its master, head, and husband. It is called to submit willingly to his word and Spirit.[29]

ONE, CATHOLIC, HOLY, AND APOSTOLIC

Küng gives substantial treatment to the *signs* or *dimensions* of the church, in his thorough treatment of ecclesiology, *The Church*. He begins by noting the Reformation and Protestant emphasis on the gospel rightly preached and the sacraments rightly administered, and the

25. Ibid., 181–203.

26. Ibid., 224–25.

27. Ibid., 227–29.

28. Ibid., 237–38.

29. Ibid., 230–41.

Catholic emphasis on the four attributes of unity, holiness, catholicity, and apostolicity. Without denying the validity of these constructs, he proposes that rigid, static, lifeless assent to these things is not enough for us to answer the question, "Where is the true Church?"[30] The dimensions of the church, which are often described apologetically or polemically by Protestant and Catholic theologians, are useful for discerning the presence of the true church and for shaping the life of the local, regional, and worldwide church, if they are vibrant, practiced, used, and life-giving.

While the church is noticeably separated into various groupings, such as Catholic, Orthodox, Protestant, and so forth, Küng maintains that Christians are to view the church, locally and universally, as "really and positively *one* Church, one people of God, one body of Christ, one spiritual creation."[31] For Küng, this is the picture of the church that emerges decisively from the New Testament. This oneness is not primarily a sociological, institutional, or external oneness. It is the spiritual work of Christ. Diversity in the church is not necessarily a negative thing, as long as the churches, in a spirit of unity, treat each other with respect, hold fast to the same gospel, and work together in mission, service, perseverance, and mutuality for the sake of Christ. "It is not the differences themselves that are harmful, but only excluding and exclusive differences." Küng is passionate about the reconciliation of the various groupings within the worldwide church, so that one, unified church might again be visible to the world. He recognizes the political, cultural, theological, and linguistic challenges to such unification but still believes that it is possible if the churches are willing, if common ground can be found, if churches begin the program of unification in their own context, and if the gospel of Jesus Christ, taken as a whole, becomes the standard for unity.[32]

When we speak of the catholicity of the church, we are referring to the fact that all the churches are not only made one through the Spirit and activity of Christ, but they are also "directed towards the whole, general," universal, total, all-embracing Church of Jesus Christ.[33] Oneness and catholicity are concepts that are closely related: the proverbial two sides of one coin.[34] The first is about unity and the second is about totality. Again, Küng views unity in catholicity as a distinct possibility for the church, but understands that concrete, theological, and ecclesiological differences abound. "We need to replace a short-sighted and exclusive 'Protestantism' and a diffuse and confused 'Catholicism' with an 'evangelical catholicity,' based and centered on the gospel."[35] Küng takes *evangelical* to mean *gospel driven* rather than the way Protestant evangelicals might usually understand the word (for example, the way David Bebbington has defined *evangelical*).[36] Küng's vision for unity is ambitious. Moreover, for Küng, while it is possible for some outside Christianity to experience Christ's grace and salvation through his sovereign action and

30. Ibid., 263–69.

31. Ibid., 272; Küng, *Structures of the Church*, 28–29.

32. Küng, *Church*, 273–96.

33. Ibid., 296.

34. Ibid., 303.

35. Ibid., 312–13.

36. Bebbington, *Evangelicalism in Modern Britain*.

will, without a voluntary decision on their part they should not be considered part of the one, catholic church.[37]

The church contains aspects that are sinful, broken, unnatural, and far from holy. However, "the Church is holy by being called by God in Christ to be the communion of the faithful, by accepting the call to his service, by being separated from the world and at the same time embraced and supported by his grace."[38] God's Spirit sanctifies and makes the church holy.[39] Despite the unnatural presence of sin in the life of the church, God makes the church holy through his sovereign will, activity, power, grace, and Spirit. Christ offers forgiveness and renewal to the church, so that through faith and the power of the Spirit it can embrace the holiness that is natural to its being.[40]

Finally, for Küng the criterion for gauging the unity, catholicity, and holiness of the church is apostolicity. The church is apostolic when it continues to witness to, proclaim, and faithfully adhere to the gospel message of Christ, handed to it by the original apostles. The church is apostolic in the sense that it is founded on "this apostolic witness and ministry, which is older than the Church itself."[41] Apostolic succession exists only in the sense that the apostolic mission is given to the whole people of God. The church carries on the apostolic mission throughout successive generations, providing an authentic link with the apostles, "when it preserves in all its members continuing agreement with the witness of the apostles, and also preserves a vital continuity with the ministry of the apostles."[42]

ROYAL PRIESTHOOD AND MINISTRY OFFICES

In his effort to outline the role and significance of offices in the church, Küng takes as his starting point the notion of the priesthood of all believers.[43] While, according to Scripture, Christ is the only high priest and mediator, all Christians have been set apart to be a royal priesthood. All Christians have direct access to God through faith, can offer spiritual sacrifices of worship, faith, and prayer, and are entrusted with the faithful preaching of the gospel and truths of Jesus Christ. Furthermore, every Christian can baptize, forgive sins, partake of the Lord's Supper (only those in particular offices may preside over it in Küng's ecclesiology), and reach out in service and mission to the world. Fellowship and worship among this priesthood move inevitably to mission and service. There is "no longer a priesthood in contrast to an unpriestly laity."[44] Küng believes that notions like priest, clergy, laity, and spiritual person (pneumatic) need to be examined afresh in the

---

37. Küng, *Church*, 317. See Küng, *Global Responsibility*; Küng, "Towards a Universal Civilization"; Küng, "Christianity and World Religions: The Dialogue"; Küng, "Global Ethics"; Küng, *Yes to a Global Ethic*; Küng and Moltmann, *Ethics of World Religions*; Küng, "Christian Scholar's Dialogue"; Küng, "What is the True Religion?"

38. Küng, *Church*, 325.

39. Küng, *Structures of the Church*, 48–49.

40. Küng, *Church*, 330–44.

41. Ibid., 353.

42. Ibid., 356.

43. Ibid., 363–87.

44. Ibid., 382.

light of the New Testament, so that our understanding of the priesthood of all believers and of ministry offices is truly biblical.[45] Küng extends the rights and functions of the laity into decision-making in the life of the churches and into church elections. He rejects any unbiblical "duality between clergy and laity," preferring to understand them as collaborating in the healthy functioning of the church. People in particular offices have "undeniable special authority" that should be exercised only "within, for, and in collaboration with the Church or congregation. Certainly then decision-making is a joint procedure."[46] Such decision-making includes ordinary Christian men and women involved in participation, considerations, and elections at all levels of church life, including electing "pastors, bishops, and popes."[47]

Küng understands formal ministry offices and other charismatic expressions of ministry, whether formal or informal, as essentially service in "the imitation of Christ." Instead of seeing ministry positions through a hierarchical lens, Küng prefers to see ministry office as fundamentally *diakonia*: self-abasement, service, living for others, and giving oneself away for the sake of others, the church, and Christ.[48] As we have already noted, Küng believes that the church has a *charismatic structure*. Its *diaconal structure*, of formal or appointed ministries, services, and offices, is a "specific aspect of this charismatic structure." He writes,

> The Church, being a fellowship of gifts of the Spirit, is also a fellowship of different ministries. Charisma and diakonia are correlative concepts. Diakonia is rooted in charisma, since every diakonia in the Church presupposes the call of God. Charisma leads to diakonia since every charisma in the Church only finds fulfillment in service. Where there is a real charisma, there will be responsible service for the edification and benefit of the community: "To each is given the manifestation of the Spirit for the common good" (1 Cor. 12:7).[49]

Recognizing the great diversity of gifts among the body of Christ, Küng notes that some, like apostles, prophets, evangelists, pastors, and teachers, have a particular function of service. Yet these are not greater than gifts that are less prominent. These ministry charisms, which are set apart as diakonia, are located and perform their functions within the overall *charismatic structure*, spiritual giftedness, and free ministries exercised in the broader life of the church.[50] They are embedded in the charismatic life of the priesthood of all believers. Nonetheless, pastors in churches have a special commission and authority to preach, administer the sacraments, and conduct their pastoral functions, in a spirit of obedience to Christ, humility, love, and service.[51]

---

45. Ibid., 382–87.

46. Küng, "Participation of the Laity," 511.

47. Ibid., 525–33; Küng, *Structures of the Church*, 83–94.

48. Küng, *Church*, 388–92; Küng, "Participation of the Laity," 518–20; Küng, *On Being a Christian*, 486–94.

49. Küng, *Church*, 393–94.

50. Küng, *Church—Maintained in Truth*, 19–32.

51. Küng, *Church*, 394, 436–41; Küng, *Structures of the Church*, 177–98.

Küng has some distinct views on the role and future of the Papal office. For him, the Papal office is at its best when it is about ministry and service, not domination or isolated authority. It is a ministry that should *pastor* the whole church, rather than *head* the church, that should share responsibility for governing the church in a collegial manner, and that should be continually open to review and reform. Küng recognizes that the existence of the Petrine primacy is an ongoing point of contention between the Catholic Church and other Christian groups, and that not everyone will be convinced by the justifications presented for such a primacy. He believes that this ministry role, which was designed for service, stability, and unity, has now become a massive and seemingly insurmountable obstacle to such unity and mutual understanding. His answer to this dilemma is that the Petrine ministry needs to relinquish power and authentically present itself as *a primacy of service*. It needs to become a primacy of pastoral care, service, ministry, humility, imitation of Christ, and reconciliation.[52] Given his views on the papacy and ministry, it is no surprise that his license to teach was withdrawn by an increasingly conservative Curia.

CONTRIBUTIONS TO MISSIONAL ECCLESIOLOGY

Küng's ecclesiology is a realistic one, recognizing the actual shape and condition of the church on the one hand, and challenging this church prophetically and with pastoral compassion and eschatological hope, on the other. Küng's ecclesiology contributes to *Part Two* of this book through its christological, missiological, eschatological, and pneumatological perspectives.[53] For example, the Spirit of God and the message of Christ convince him that the church needs to be reformed, renewed, and opened afresh to the changes possible and demanded by the Spirit and gospel. This requires courageous action and theological reflection. For Küng, this theological reflection and courageous action are crucial for genuine reform, and must be grounded in the person of Christ, directed toward Christ's eschatological mission in the world, and empowered by the Spirit. It involves the church discerning the presence of both nature and un-nature in its life and structures, living in the service of the reign of God, renewing its charismatic and diaconal structures, practicing its unity, holiness, catholicity, and apostolicity in life-giving ways, and embracing with confidence the priesthood of all believers. As the body of Christ, the church is called to imitate Christ, pursuing his missionary purposes, and to live faithfully as the creation of the Spirit, in eschatological expectation.

Küng is a passionate advocate for ecclesial reform. His ecclesiology is attentive to the various ways the church can embrace and distinguish between renovation and innovation, the charismatic structure of the church, the practical expressions of the core dimensions of the church (one, catholic, holy, and apostolic), and the servant nature of Christian ministry, leadership, and office. Küng eloquently describes the royal priesthood of all believers, the inadequacy of ecclesiologies that artificially separate clergy and laity, the ways in which the diaconal and charismatic structures of the church can be aligned, and the respective pitfalls of Catholic and Protestant theological method. Shared

52. Küng, *Church*, 444–80; Küng, *Structures of the Church*, 218–23.

53. He features in chapters 15 and 16 in *Part Two* of this book.

decision-making by the laity, free election of bishops, rediscovering the concrete dynamics of a church-from-below, and radically revisiting the role of women in the church and the current shape of pastoral care and worship, are all dimensions of Küng's agenda for reform in the church. Küng has detailed these proposals in *Reforming the Church Today*. He asserts that his ecclesiology and demands for reform "are not based on an adaptation to a *Zeitgeist* or sociological and practical considerations, but on the key document of Christianity."[54] They have their origins in Scripture, are supported by tradition, take into account the contemporary needs of the church, and align with the impulses of the Second Vatican Council. They are coherent with each other, the gospel, and Vatican II. In order to see Küng's vision of the church in a larger context than *The Church*, one has to read *Disputed Truth*, which is the second volume of his memoirs. This later work provides further reflections on the present problems in the Catholic Church and in the ecumene.[55]

It is encouraging to see the ways in which Küng has utilized biblical theology and contemporary New Testament scholarship in his ecclesiological portrait. However, there are some areas where Küng and I differ ecclesiologically. While much of his writing is resonant with the concerns of the Protestant Reformation, he continues, as one might imagine he would as a Catholic theologian, to assign primacy to the Pope. Küng is honest about the possibilities and pitfalls of the Papal office, he questions a theology of conciliar and Papal infallibility, and he helpfully shapes his discussion about the future role of the Pope around the idea of service—yet Protestant readers will most likely not share his conviction about the necessity of the continuation of the Papal office.[56] One does not have to share this conclusion to admire the courage of Küng's convictions in the face of such substantial opposition.[57] On another matter, George Tavard and others have questioned whether Küng's biblical exegesis is put at the service of non-biblical categories and philosophical assumptions, for instance, his use of the terms *nature* and *un-nature* to describe the holy and sinful elements in the church.[58]

Küng's ecclesiological vision of reform is not limited in his writings to an internal program. Its success is closely linked with the missionary heart of the church and with its ministry relationship with the world. This ministry relationship is not to be aggressive, power-hungry, secular, defensive, or domineering. It is to be one of loving service, compassionate discernment, ministry presence, active and committed engagement, the imitation of Christ, and faithful witness. The grace of God sustains the church and helps it truly be the church, even in the face of its frailties, anxieties, and sinfulness.

54. Küng, *Reforming the Church Today*, 3.

55. Küng and Bowden, *Disputed Truth*.

56. Oden, "Church," 117.

57. Küng's views on the Papal office caused him to be stripped of his license to teach Catholic theology, and he continues to be critical of the Catholic Church's stance on such issues as clergy sexual abuse. For his own account of these matters, of his conflicts with church hierarchy, and on why he remains a Catholic, see Küng and Bowden, *Disputed Truth*; Küng, "Why I Remain a Catholic"; Küng, "Abuse Rooted in Clerical Celibacy."

58. Tavard, "Church," 107.

The Church has a future because it has a present in the world. On its journey out into the world it has a mission, a commission, a task, a ministry that it must fulfill ... Indeed, the Church has a future; it has *the* future. This is the eighth day that passes description and cannot be foreseen, the day on which God will complete his work of creation, the Church will reach the goal of its pilgrimage and the world will recognize its Lord.[59]

QUESTIONS FOR REFLECTION

1. Küng writes, "One can speak of a *charismatic structure of the Church*, which includes but goes far beyond the *hierarchical structure of the Church*." How is the charismatic structure of churches different from, but connected with, formal leadership in churches?

2. What things can Christians do to identify, develop, and release the spiritual gifts of others? What will you do during the next twelve months?

3. In the concluding section, I outline Küng's vision for reforming the church today. What needs reforming in the local and wider church that you are involved in? Do you feel that you are able to be a constructive part of that reform? If so, what can you do?

59. Küng, *Church*, 488–89.

Eastern Orthodox

4

Thomas Hopko:
The Church as Fullness of God

In the Orthodox tradition, the Church is defined as "life in the Holy Spirit" and the "Kingdom of God on earth" not in any purely "interior" and "mystical" way in the hidden life of the soul, but concretely and objectively in the sacramental and doctrinal life of the covenant community which is incarnate in space and time, locatable in human history, and living in this present age.[1]

—THOMAS HOPKO

THE CHURCH AS SALVATION AND LIFE

THOMAS HOPKO'S THEOLOGY PASSIONATELY acclaims the nature and mission of the church. As much as any other theologian examined in this book (or possibly more so), Hopko places the church at the center of God's mission in the world and God's plan of salvation for humanity. His theology has ecclesiology at its core, and his descriptions of the nature and role of the church are exuberant. In the following paragraphs, I summarize some of the key assertions in Hopko's ecclesiology. These eight central ecclesiological affirmations are discernible within chapter 1 of Hopko's book, *All the Fulness of God*, and

---

1. Hopko, *All the Fulness of God*, 29–30. Thomas Hopko was the Professor of Theology at Saint Vladimir's Orthodox Theological Seminary from 1968 to 2002, the Dean of that seminary from 1992 to 2002, and is now their Dean Emeritus. He served as President of the Orthodox Theological Society in America from 1992 to 1995.

surface regularly in his writings. The last two claims are mostly developed from works other than the above-mentioned chapter.

1. *The church is the fullness of God:* The church as the *fullness* of God in Jesus Christ is the main idea in Hopko's ecclesiology. His ecclesiology centers on the conviction that fullness of life is possible through relationship with Christ, who himself is the fullness of God. Such fullness is expressed most clearly, and made accessible, through the church. Human beings are invited into a relationship with God that releases them to fullness of life. They are invited to know God, not abstractly or merely conceptually, but personally, and, in that relationship, to know fullness of life. Such fullness has been made possible through the life, death, and resurrection of Jesus Christ, and is offered to the world through the church, in the power of the Spirit.[2] The church presents humanity with fullness of life in Christ, with a way of life that is full, and with life's essential meaning. The church "is God's own life given in abundance in Christ and the Spirit as the life of the world."[3] Hopko contends, "The fulness of God in His Son and Spirit is in the Church which is Christ's body and bride."[4]

2. *The church is salvation and life:* Not only is fullness of life only possible in communion with God through the church but, moreover, salvation is only possible through the church. "For without the Church there is no complete access to God in Christ and the Holy Spirit, no abundant fulness of life as it has been lavished upon the world by the tri-personal God."[5] People enter God's salvation as they enter into communion with God and Christ through the church. Salvation is the experience of the whole covenantal community, and people enter this salvation through participation in the salvific experience and blessing of this community. This is different than saying that being a *member* of the church guarantees salvation, for it does not—the grace of Christ and obedience and discipleship to him are still necessary, if one is to fully participate in the saving life the church offers.[6]

Hopko writes that this soteriology and ecclesiology are grounded in trinitarian thought. As God lives in "perfect inter-personal communion," so he calls men and women to find salvation and life through the Son and the Spirit in covenantal community. This community, the church, reflects the divine communion within the Trinity, and draws people into this communion, into this life and salvation, which is the fundamental shape, meaning, and purpose of their lives.[7] Hopko writes the following about the relationship between salvation and the church:

---

2. Ibid., 13–29; Hopko, *Orthodox Faith—Spirituality*, 23.

3. Hopko, *All the Fulness of God*, 7.

4. Ibid., 9.

5. Ibid., 8.

6. Ibid., 43; Hopko, *Orthodox Faith—Spirituality*, 24.

7. Hopko, *All the Fulness of God*, 31–34, 39.

Salvation is the Church, and the Church is salvation, the gift of eternal life in the knowledge of God through communion with Him in His Son and His Spirit. This is the Orthodox faith.[8]

3. *"The Church is the mystical presence of the Kingdom of God on earth":*[9] The kingdom of God has broken into the world through the person and ministry of Jesus Christ, and the church is the mystical presence of that kingdom. For Hopko, the church is *the Kingdom of God on earth*, and attempts to separate church and kingdom ontologically are misleading and theologically deficient. The church makes God's kingdom known in the earth, as the mystical presence, embodiment, and tangible, incarnate community of love. The church not only witnesses to the kingdom, it *is* the kingdom. Hopko is not always clear whether he means the church is the sum total of the kingdom, or whether he means that while the church *is* the kingdom, it is not the *entire* kingdom.[10]

4. *The church is the world transfigured and the new creation:* The church and the world are not ontologically distinct, even though they are, at times, in disagreement or conflict with each other. The church is not an isolated entity existing in contrast to the world, even when it exists in antipathy to the world. "She is rather the world itself, the whole of creation as fashioned, redeemed, sanctified and restored by the power of God."[11] The church does not just show the world what it really is, and what it is destined to become—it *is* the world in its transfigured, renewed, sanctified state. "The Church is the new creation."[12] While it is certainly a foretaste of the renewal of all things, it is not merely a foretaste—it *is* the new creation, extending the invitation of God to all of humanity to enter this covenantal community of "total newness" and "total fulness."[13]

5. *The church is a eucharistic and sacramental community: one, holy, catholic, and apostolic:* Christians enter the community of faith sacramentally, through baptism and the Eucharist. What they need to realize, however, is that the church itself is the primary sacrament of salvation, the eucharistic and eschatological community that opens up the way for trinitarian fellowship with each other and with God.[14]

The church's oneness, holiness, catholicity, and apostolicity are sacramental, since these dimensions of its nature are derived from the nature of God, and from his divine unity, holiness, fullness, and mission.[15] Drilling these four marks of the

---

8. Ibid., 30.

9. Ibid., 9; Hopko, *Orthodox Faith—Spirituality*, 23.

10. Hopko, *All the Fulness of God*, 37.

11. Ibid.; Hopko, *Orthodox Faith—Spirituality*, 23; Hopko, *All the Fulness of God*, 66.

12. Hopko, *All the Fulness of God*, 34, 40.

13. Ibid., 35.

14. Hopko, "Tasks Facing the Orthodox," 240–41.

15. Hopko, *All the Fulness of God*, 36–39; Hopko, *Orthodox Faith—Doctrine*, 123–28.

church down to the local level, Hopko writes that every local church is the "one and only Church of Christ," that is, every parish is completely united with and expressive of *the* one church. Every dimension of the local church's life is holy, even the mundane, administrative, or structural aspects, because God has made it holy. The local church is catholic, since in communion with God it is "full complete and whole." Finally, the local church is apostolic because it is rooted in apostolic doctrine and tradition, and characterized by the missionary heart of God.[16]

6. *The church is a community of co-suffering love:* The spirituality of Orthodoxy emphasizes an individual and corporate participation in the humility, suffering, and love of Christ. However, corporate participation in Christ is emphasized. There is no such thing as a healthy spirituality that is isolated or individuated. Participation in Christ is experienced most fully in the community of faith.[17]

7. *The church is both trinitarian in nature and a theandric mystery:* Hopko writes, "Everything which is authentically of the Church is trinitarian in its essence and existence, in its content and life." The nature of the church is fundamentally *trinitarian*, and, consequently, its Scriptures, ecclesial structure, liturgy, sacraments, and so forth are all trinitarian.[18] The church is a *theandric mystery* because it is both human and divine at the same time. This is a mystery, but it is a mystery enacted by God. God's divinity is expressed through the church's humanity in a mysterious way that glorifies God.[19]

8. *The church is an object of faith:* Faith in the church, in what God is doing in and through the church, and in the eschatological significance and destiny of the church, is essential to Christian faith.[20] While the church is in constant need of reform and change, it nonetheless remains an object of faith—the people of God believe that the church is the fullness of God, the kingdom of God on earth, salvation and life, the new creation, the world transfigured, the co-suffering community of agapic love, and one, holy, catholic, and apostolic. There is no room in Hopko's ecclesiology for derision or dismissal of the church. The church is "God's gift to the world . . . the gift of communion with God through Christ and the Holy Spirit . . . invincible and indestructible."[21]

Why does Hopko write so energetically about the nature of the church and its role in offering human beings the salvation of Christ and the fullness of God's life in the Spirit? It is because he believes that both Christians and the world need to rediscover the true

---

16. Hopko, "Orthodox Parish in America," 2–4.

17. Hopko, *All the Fulness of God,* 42–47.

18. Ibid., 66–67. See Ibid., 22–29, 91–93.

19. Ibid., 93–95.

20. Ibid., 91.

21. Hopko, *Orthodox Faith—Doctrine,* 127–28.

nature of the church.[22] Ecclesiology "is the key issue of our time" and "the most critical issue facing Christians today," because what we believe about the church, *and* how we participate in the life of the church, have important, cosmic implications for the church, world, creation, and human history.[23]

WORSHIP, SACRAMENTS, LITURGY, AND SCRIPTURE

The most complete description of Hopko's convictions about worship in the life of the church can be found in his *Orthodox Faith* handbook, volume two, titled *Worship*. The topics considered in that book and the order in which they are presented are church buildings and symbols, the sacraments, the daily cycles of prayer, the church year, and the Divine Liturgy. The biblical and theological rationales for these dimensions of the church's worship are briefly presented in his book on worship, but are offered more fully in some of the other handbooks in his *Orthodox Faith* series, and in his other writings. According to Hopko, "the Orthodox Church is essentially a worshipping Church," so his perspectives on the worshipping life of the church are pivotal in his ecclesiology.[24] Instead of trying to summarize all of Hopko's thought on these elements of Christian worship, I concentrate here on his particular convictions about the sacraments, the Divine Liturgy, and the Scriptures.

In his book on worship, Hopko writes of the various theological meanings of the Orthodox buildings, altar tables, icons, symbols, and vestments, before moving on to describe the significance of the sacraments. Orthodoxy considers the sacraments as *holy mysteries*, and while there are seven recognizable sacraments—"baptism, chrismation (or confirmation), holy Eucharist, penance, matrimony, holy orders and the unction of the sick"—in truth, everything about the life of the church is sacramental.[25] The seven sacraments are, in fact, participation in the mysterious and sacramental life of the church—an immersion in the holy life of the church that we go through at various stages of our lives. The church itself is a sacrament, a mystery, the kingdom of God sacramentally revealed on this earth, and fullness of life is offered to men and women as they commune sacramentally with the church of Jesus Christ.[26] The Eucharist is particularly important in Orthodox sacramental, eucharistic worship.[27] Denying "intellectual or psychological" interpretations of the Eucharist, Hopko, in accordance with Orthodox sacramental theology, contends that the bread and the wine become the actual body and blood of Jesus Christ in the Eucharist.[28] Hopko sums up the importance of the Eucharist when he writes the following:

22. Hopko, *All the Fulness of God*, 35–36.

23. Ibid., 41.

24. Hopko, *Speaking the Truth in Love*, 178–81; Hopko, "Narrow Way of Orthodoxy," 8–11; Hopko, "Orthodox Parish in America," 5–6; Hopko, "Narrow Way of Orthodoxy: A Message," 296.

25. Hopko, *Orthodox Faith—Worship*, 25. See Hopko, *Orthodox Faith—Doctrine*, 129–32; Hopko, *Orthodox Faith—Spirituality*, 25–27.

26. Hopko, *Orthodox Faith—Worship*, 25–27.

27. Hopko, "Lima Statement," 59.

28. Hopko, *Orthodox Faith—Worship*, 36–37.

> The Holy Eucharist is called the "sacrament of sacraments" in the Orthodox tradition. It is also called the "sacrament of the Church." The Eucharist is the center of the Church's life. Everything in the Church leads to the Eucharist, and all things flow from it. It is the completion of all of the Church's sacraments—the source and the goal of all of the Church's doctrines and institutions.[29]

Before describing the Divine Liturgy in detail, in his book on worship Hopko writes at length about the daily cycles of prayer in Orthodoxy, and about particular times in the church's year that have theological and liturgical significance. In Orthodox ecclesiology, the Divine Liturgy is the "common work or common action" of the people of God, as they gather to worship and to have communion with each other and with God. Hopko underlines the case that in Orthodox ecclesiology the Divine Liturgy may only be celebrated on Sunday, under the leadership of the church, as *all* of the people of God gather together—"always everyone, always together . . . on behalf of all and for all."[30] The "narrow way of Orthodoxy" involves understanding the importance of the Divine Liturgy in the worshipping and missiological life of the church, without making the liturgy "an escape or else a cultural ornament."[31] In other words, faithful, Christ-centered liturgical worship should never be characterized by sectarianism or relativism, but, instead, by forms of openness, accessibility, and communication that avoid these two extremes.[32]

Appreciating the importance of the Eucharist and the Divine Liturgy in Hopko's ecclesiology enables one to see how and why his ecclesiology is both eucharistic and liturgical at its core (it would be interesting to see how this works missionally in Hopko's context). In the Divine Liturgy, the people of God experience the resurrectional, transfigured life offered through the person and work of Christ, through communion with the Holy Trinity, to the glory of the Father, in the power of the Spirit. The following quote, when placed beside Hopko's reflections on the Eucharist, demonstrates the eucharistic and liturgical nature of his ecclesiology:

> The Divine Liturgy is the one common sacrament of the very being of the Church Itself. It is the one sacramental manifestation of the essence of the Church as the Community of God in heaven and on earth. It is the one unique sacramental revelation of the Church as the mystical Body and Bride of Christ.[33]

Scriptures, and especially the Gospels, are read, and a sermon is offered, as part of the Divine Liturgy—just as Holy Communion is celebrated as part of the liturgical service. Scripture and homily are important in the liturgical worship in Orthodoxy, but they are not necessarily the centerpieces of gathered worship in the same way that they are in some other Christian traditions. The liturgical sermon, or preaching, is a sacramental and trinitarian act, firmly located within the Divine Liturgy.[34] It is "a sacramental act of

---

29. Ibid., 34.

30. Ibid., 154–55. See Hopko, *Orthodox Faith—Doctrine*, 18–19.

31. Hopko, "Narrow Way of Orthodoxy: A Message," 296–97.

32. Ibid., 299.

33. Hopko, *Orthodox Faith—Worship*, 155.

34. Ibid., 170, 180–95; Hopko, *Speaking the Truth in Love*, 49–50.

God's crucified and glorified Son Jesus Christ himself delivering the Word of his Father from heaven to those in his Church on earth."[35] The Bible is central to Orthodox tradition, holding "the first place." It is interpreted christologically, as symbolized by the primary place given to the Gospels in Orthodox liturgical worship. In terms of the Bible's authority and importance, it is part of the overall tradition of the church, rather than something that might be considered separate or distinct from that complete tradition. Hopko writes that the church's tradition is multifaceted, each part of it is "organically linked," and it continues to "grow and develop" until the age to come. There is a deep and indivisible connection between Scripture, tradition, and liturgy.[36]

According to Hopko, the Scriptures are "not over or apart from" the church, since their meaning, authority, vitality, and application are embedded in the church. There is a dynamic relationship between the Scriptures and the church, and the divine revelation of God.[37] The Scriptures are to be interpreted christologically.[38] Like the divine-human nature of Christ, and reflecting the theandric essence of the church, the Scriptures are theandric in character, being completely both divine and human.[39]

CATHOLICITY AND ECUMENICAL RELATIONSHIPS

Catholicity, in Hopko's writings, is essentially about the *fullness* of the church. In the church is to be found the fullness of God, the fullness of the kingdom of God, and the fullness of the abundant life offered in communion with God and his church. In the church is also found the fullness of the world in its transformed, redeemed, and sanctified condition. This fullness is one of unity and wholeness; otherwise, it is not fullness at all. Therefore, for Hopko, the church is *catholic in its fullness* as expressed in all of these dimensions, including its unity in Christ. The role of ecumenism is to move concretely toward such unity, as well as to enable conversations that lead toward a richer experience of that fullness. Such dialogue is warm and respectful, yet discerning and critical. Each party that participates in ecumenical discourse needs to examine openly their own faithfulness to the fullness of God as revealed in Christ, as well as the faithfulness of the other contributors.[40]

God alone makes the church catholic and, while ecumenical conversations and actions are worthwhile, the church must not misunderstand the Source and Author of its catholicity.[41] God fashions his church as catholic as an unchangeable grace, and the church responds by appropriating this gift in her communion, ecclesial life, and inter-confessional dialogue.[42]

---

35. Hopko, *Speaking the Truth in Love*, 56.

36. Hopko, *Orthodox Faith—Doctrine*, 12–17; Hopko, *All the Fulness of God*, 83–84.

37. Hopko, *All the Fulness of God*, 49–54, 90.

38. Hopko, *Orthodox Faith—Bible*, 7–9.

39. Hopko, *All the Fulness of God*, 8, 55–68.

40. Ibid., 8–9.

41. Ibid., 92.

42. Ibid., 96–97.

Hopko believes that the Eastern Orthodox Church is the true church, in contrast to other Christian traditions and confessions, and that only the Orthodox Church expresses the fullness of God and the genuine catholicity given by him.[43] Having said that, Hopko believes that the Orthodox Church should engage in ecumenical dialogue with other Christian groups, and with other religions. Even though other Christian traditions are in error, writes Hopko, there is "grace and truth" present in some groups that should be recognized and engaged.[44] There is also room for the Orthodox Church to engage in repentance and confession, as it seeks to lead other Christians back to the Orthodox faith, "the faith received, guarded, elaborated, and transmitted, without error or change, in the Orthodox Church."[45]

Hopko's approach to ecumenism is exemplified in an article he wrote examining Eastern Rite Catholicism, which are Christian churches in eastern cultures that come under the authority of Rome. Hopko argues that there are key issues that need to be considered before such churches can have real ecumenical relationship with the Eastern Orthodox churches. Hopko's concern is that some view the issues dividing these Eastern Catholic churches from the Eastern Orthodox churches as mostly about the authority of Rome, or about cultural or ritual preference. For Hopko, these are not the central questions to be worked through in ecumenical discussions. The main problems center on christological faithfulness, the validity of liturgical and sacramental forms, and commitment to certain biblical and theological truths, as understood by the different confessions.[46]

Hopko is convinced that the only true Church of Christ is the Orthodox Church, so the sole and final goal of all ecumenical participation, asserts Hopko, is to restore other Christian groups to the truth and catholicity of Eastern Orthodoxy. Therefore, Hopko rejects *denominationalism/religious relativism*—the idea that all churches, regardless of their denominational traditions and beliefs, are genuinely a part of the one, catholic church. However, he also rejects *religious sectarianism*—the idea that it is the human institutional forms and structures of Orthodoxy those other groups are essentially called to join. Other Christian groups must return to the truths of Orthodoxy, not because of the human, institutional expressions, but because of the divine, catholic *fullness* that Orthodoxy offers.[47]

According to Hopko, in the Orthodox Church the singular motivation for ecumenical involvement is the following:

> It is the goal of the Orthodox in the ecumenical movement, and the sole reason for their participation, to restore all Christian persons and groups to full and perfect unity with the catholic Church of history, with the victorious Church of the Kingdom of God, and we must add, with God Himself: Father, Son and Holy Spirit.[48]

43. Ibid., 98–100; See Hopko, *Speaking the Truth in Love*, 122.

44. Hopko, *All the Fulness of God*, 100–1.

45. Hopko, *Speaking the Truth in Love*, 122.

46. Hopko, *All the Fulness of God*, 9–10, 115–27.

47. Ibid., 105–13, 159–61; Hopko, *Speaking the Truth in Love*, 129–31, 181–84.

48. Hopko, *All the Fulness of God*, 101–2.

ECCLESIAL WITNESS, SERVICE, AND PRESENCE IN THE WORLD

Ecclesial witness and Christian presence in the world, in Hopko's opinion, are directly linked with some of the core dimensions of Christian spirituality. In his book on Christian spirituality, such individual witness and corporate witness are expressed in Christian virtues, agapic love, holding on to correct theological belief, practically living the beatitudes, and prayer and fasting. Such Christian presence and service are also expressed through generosity and contentment, marital love, sexual and familial relationships, the Christian's eschatological hope, and dependence on Christ in sickness, suffering, and death. In other words, the whole life of the Christian and the faith community is spiritual, and should be offered to the glory of God. This orientation, and its consequent actions, produces Christ-honoring witness, service, and presence in the world. If ecclesial spirituality and witness are to be authentic, they must be practical, action-oriented, and expressed through the entire life of the church.[49]

According to Hopko, the church's mission in the world emanates from its entire "eucharistic essence and experience," testifying to the church's and the world's nature, purpose, and future. The poverty of the church's witness demands a fresh examination of the same, and a willingness to reform the church in an effort to align its *rhetoric* and *reality*. This does not change the fact that the church confronts the world's *insanity*, and demonstrates to the world its redeemed, transfigured, and sanctified state. In Hopko's estimation, the world suffers from insanity because it has relinquished the truth of reality and the truth of the human condition that is offered by God, and embraced a multitude of delusions. Its insanity is also about the reduction of Christ to the images and tastes of a wide variety of religious traditions and political and social movements.[50] The church is often in trouble, and less than the church that it could be, because it participates in such insanity.[51] The mission of the church is to present and embody God's truth to the world— the truth of reality, the church and the world, the human condition and destiny, and of Christ. In a word, the mission of the church "is to serve man and the world by bearing witness to the fact that there is the Christ who saves, and that this Christ is present now in the midst of the earth in His Church."[52]

The mission of the church, then, is fundamentally christological and ecclesiological. Hopko writes that Christians "have nothing to offer people and the world but Christ and the Church."[53] Christians are to proclaim the fullness of God in Jesus Christ and in his church—no other mission or message is sufficient. Out of this commitment to presenting Christ and the church, the church can then engage in loving acts of mission, service, and presence. For Hopko, these include such activities as efforts for "social, political, and economic justice" and freedom, and leading individuals and groups toward genuine identity and community.[54]

49. Hopko, *Orthodox Faith—Spirituality*, 8.

50. Hopko, *All the Fulness of God*, 163–67.

51. Ibid., 184–88.

52. Ibid., 167.

53. Ibid., 172; Hopko, *Speaking the Truth in Love*, 57–59.

54. Hopko, *All the Fulness of God*, 172–84.

The church's mission can never be divorced from guiding people into a personal experience of Christ and his church. Confronting them with the truths of Scripture, leading them into liturgical worship, and offering them a spirituality that is grounded in the church's teachings and traditions enable this. It involves serving people by selflessly presenting the whole truth of the gospel, refusing to compromise the reality of Christ and his church, and allowing the missionary love and passion of Christ to grip people personally.[55] In Hopko's judgment, both *words* and *works* characterize all genuine mission. He writes that these words involve proclamation, teaching, apologetics, dialogue, and confession, while the works include sacrificial and charitable actions.[56]

ON THE MINISTRIES OF LAITY, CLERGY, AND MONASTIC

The clergy and laity together constitute the whole body of Christ. While some are set apart for specific ministries in the church—bishops, pastors, presbyters, and deacons, for example—Christ calls the whole community of believers to service.

Tracing the etymology and history of the words *clergy* and *laity*, and describing the relationship between these groups in the contemporary church, Hopko asserts that the laity, clergy, and monastic have distinct roles. The roles of the laity include offering themselves fully to Christ and his will, submitting to and supporting the leadership of the church, and using their charismatic gifts in mission and ministry. They involve exploring and using their "charism, calling, and competence" for the sake of Christ and the church, caring for their households, and living with integrity in the world.

The roles of the clergy are complementary to those of the laity, and incorporate providing guidance, governance, and direction to the church, and ministering through liturgy, Scripture, sacrament, and pastoralia. The roles of the monastic involve communion with God, wrestling with sinful desires, spiritual warfare, and keeping "silence, fasting, vigil, and prayer."

The laity, clergy, and monastic are indivisible, and mutually dependent and accountable. Yet the church is both hierarchical and conciliar, reflecting the nature of God, and all Christians are called to serve in their various God-given roles, "in communion with all the others, to the glory of God and for the good of all."[57]

CONTRIBUTIONS TO MISSIONAL ECCLESIOLOGY

Hopko's ecclesiology paints a multifaceted picture of the church, and in the missional ecclesiology of the second half of this book I converse briefly with some of his missiological, trinitarian, and eschatological perspectives on the church.[58] For Hopko, Christ and his church are at the center of God's purpose for humanity and history. The church is the *fullness* of God in Jesus Christ.

---

55. Hopko, *Speaking the Truth in Love*, 57–65.

56. Ibid., 67–84.

57. Ibid., 97–114; Hopko, "Ministry and the Unity of the Church," 273–75.

58. He features in chapters 14 and 17 in *Part Two* of this book.

While Hopko's portrait of the church can enrich missional ecclesiology in particular ways, I have some reservations (these naturally emerge from my Protestant, Free Church, and evangelical perspectives, articulated in this book's introduction):

1.   Hopko describes the church as salvation and life, a trinitarian, covenantal community. There is a tendency, at times, for Hopko to turn Christ's unique offer of salvation into the Orthodox Church's unique offer of salvation. While he undoubtedly does not intend this, it is easy for the reader to get this impression from his writings. Hopko's assertion that, "salvation is in the Church, and the Church is salvation, the gift of eternal life in the knowledge of God through communion with Him in His Son and His Spirit" is a radical departure from Protestant evangelical understandings of the nature of the gospel of Jesus Christ—salvation by grace alone, through faith alone, in Christ's saving and atoning work alone—and, I believe, from biblical portraits of the church and salvation. Salvation is in and through faith in Christ alone.

2.   He writes that the church is ontologically both the kingdom of God and the transfigured world. It is the kingdom of God on earth, the mystical presence of that kingdom, and the tangible, incarnate kingdom-community. Not only is the church the kingdom of God, it is also the world in its transfigured, renewed, and sanctified state. It is both a foretaste and more than a foretaste of the eschaton—it *is* the new creation, the redeemed community filled with all of the fullness of God. Hopko uses a wide range of other terms to describe this new creation. These include the one, holy, catholic, and apostolic community, the image of the Trinity, the theandric mystery, and the co-suffering community of agapic love. According to Hopko, even when the church is far less than it should be, we still believe all of these things about it. God fashions the church, and the church is an object of faith.

There is much to be embraced in these perspectives on the church, and they certainly provide a refreshing corrective to the criticisms one often hears directed at the church and its present condition. However, I do not agree that the church is the kingdom of God. The church is the fruit of, witness to, and prefiguring of the kingdom—but it is not itself the kingdom.

On the relationship between the kingdom and the church, I think that George Ladd (and Hans Küng, for that matter) is closer to the mark. Ladd writes:

> While there is an inseparable relationship between the Kingdom and the church, they are not to be identified . . . The Kingdom is God's reign and the realm in which the blessings of his reign are experienced; the church is the fellowship of those who have experienced God's reign and entered into the enjoyment of its blessings. The Kingdom creates the church, works through the church, and is proclaimed in the world by the church. There can be no Kingdom without a church—those who have acknowledged God's rule—and there can be no church without God's Kingdom; but they remain two distinguishable concepts: the rule of God and the fellowship of men and women.[59]

59. Ladd, *Theology of the New Testament*, 117.

3.   Hopko asserts that the issue of the church "is the key issue of our time" and "the most critical issue facing Christians today."[60] Ecclesiology is certainly *a* critical issue of our time, but is it really *the* key issue? The jury remains open in the deliberation of the arguments for and against this assertion.

4.   The Orthodox Divine Liturgy and the Eucharist have a vital place in Hopko's ecclesiology. Furthermore, he is open to ecumenical dialogue with other Christian groups and with other religions, denying religious relativism or sectarianism, but only on the terms of Orthodoxy. He is convinced that only Orthodoxy offers the fullness of God and the Christian faith "received, guarded, elaborated, and transmitted, without error or change."[61] There is no question that he is not alone in the conviction that *his* ecclesial tradition is the *true* Christian church. However, can ecumenical dialogue be meaningful when parties believe that their tradition exists without *error or change*?

5.   On the subject of ecclesial mission, Hopko asserts that the church's mission is derived from its entire "eucharistic essence and experience," and always leads "back to it, as the real presence in this age of God's coming kingdom."[62] In my opinion, mission is too often divorced from the church, and from the discipleship, community, and worship the church enjoys. Nevertheless, does Hopko overstate the case, and come close to saying that "the point of mission is to lead people into the Church"? Surely the overarching aim of mission is to lead people into an encounter with Christ and his gospel and then, as a consequence, into an encounter with the church (these things never occur in a linear manner, of course). All of the liturgical, ministerial, sacramental, ecumenical, and missiological life of the church should be centered on Jesus Christ and his gospel. As Hopko puts it, Christians "have nothing to offer people and the world but Christ and the Church."[63]

Hopko's vision of the church is, at times, refreshing. Some within the missional church movement have largely given up on the established or institutional church, to their own detriment, and Hopko confronts this attitude, reminding us of Christ's presence in the church, eschatological purpose for the church, and power within the liturgy, worship, ministry, and mission of the church. Missional ecclesiology should shape its prophetic and reforming impulse around such ecclesiological hope and faith.

60. Hopko, *All the Fulness of God*, 41.
61. Hopko, *Speaking the Truth in Love*, 122.
62. Hopko, "Tasks Facing the Orthodox," 241.
63. Hopko, *All the Fulness of God*, 172; Hopko, *Speaking the Truth in Love*, 57–59.

QUESTIONS FOR REFLECTION

1. How do you *feel* as you read Hopko's eight key assertions on the nature of the church (convinced, skeptical, troubled, enthusiastic, etc.)? Would you modify them?

2. Hopko writes that the issue of the church "is the key issue of our time" and "the most critical issue facing Christians today." Why does Hopko say this? Do you agree?

3. Are clergy and laity mutually dependent and accountable in your setting, and, if not, what practical areas of your church's life might need to change?

5

Vigen Guroian:
The Church as Peculiar, Ethical Community

The call of God is a call to form a special community. For the Christian understanding of calling, while it certainly includes the idea of individual vocation, is in its total conception one of a people. The Christian ethic is an ethic of a community . . . Christian ethics is the action of a whole people upon the world . . . (Our) reasons to act must be consistent with Christ's salvific mission.[1]

—VIGEN GUROIAN

THE NATURE OF THE CHURCH AND OF CHRISTIAN ETHICS

VIGEN GUROIAN IS COMMITTED to seeing the church rediscover its vocation as an ethical society. Aside from dealing with a variety of Orthodox scholars, Guroian consults the work of Yoder, Hauerwas, Schindler, Meilaender, MacIntyre, Lindbeck, Bonhoeffer, and Littell to describe the ecclesiological and ethical shifts in Christendom, and the challenges of the church in post-Christendom. Yoder and Hauerwas feature heavily in Guroian's works and their influence on his thought is clear.

Careful to be fair to the achievements of Christendom, Guroian is nevertheless aware of its failings, and that the Orthodox and other churches are facing threats and opportunities to their life and mission that are unique to the emerging, pluralistic, global culture. He believes that the ecclesial assumptions of Constantinianism need to be relinquished, and especially those about the relationship between the church and the world. Therefore, he writes the following,

---

1. Guroian, *Faith, Church, Mission,* 37. Since 2009 Vigen Guroian has served as Professor of Religious Studies at the University of Virginia. He formerly taught theology and ethics at the Ecumenical Institute of Theology at St. Mary's Seminary and University, Baltimore, and was the Professor of Theology and Ethics at Loyola College, Baltimore.

> Thus it seems to me that for the foreseeable future, the real bone of contention among Christian theologians and ethicists is going to be what constitutes an appropriate ecclesiology and *modus vivendi* for the churches *after Christendom*.[2]

For Guroian, Christian ethics, liturgy, and ecclesiology are tightly interwoven. His proposal is for an approach to Christian ethics that is fundamentally *ecclesially centered*, or, in other words, "an ethic of a community."[3] In their public witness and ethical outlook, Christians are joined together, to act ecclesially in ways that are "consistent with Christ's salvific mission." Contrasting his liturgical, Orthodox approach to ethics with that of his Catholic and Protestant contemporaries, Guroian writes that he is convinced that the rich liturgical tradition of the Eastern Orthodox Church contains wonderful resources and guides for Orthodox ethical reflection and action in post-Christendom societies.[4]

If post-Christendom Christian political and social ethics are genuinely *ecclesially centered*, then they must be grounded in an ecclesiology that is not sectarian, privatized, reactionary, or compromising.[5] Guroian is sympathetic to Schindler's and Meilaender's attempts to develop an ecclesial Christian ethic for post-Christendom societies. Along with Schindler, Guroian does not want to abandon natural law as a source of Christian ethics; instead, he wants to ground it in an ecclesial practice cemented in christological and trinitarian ontology. Following the lead of Meilaender, Guroian wants to navigate the middle ground between ethical sectarianism and accommodationism.[6] Building on these notions, Guroian's vision for the church as ethical society is fundamentally rooted in the conviction that communities of faith must express their ethical convictions practically, establishing "a singularly christic and trinitarian way of life."

> In striving to live moral lives, it has always been imperative—and it is especially imperative in our time—that Christians seek to invigorate those ecclesial forms of teaching, preaching, worship, and *diakonia* that constitute their special inheritance of faith and hope in Jesus Christ.[7]

> Unless Christian tradition and Christian ethics reside in the Church, they will have no integrity. The Church seeks not merely the salvation of individuals but the reclamation of the fallen social, political, and economic life of humankind.[8]

According to Guroian, liturgical worship (catechism, sacraments, and liturgy) provides the link between Christian tradition (Scripture, creeds, and doctrine) and Christian ethics. Christian ethics find their origin and wellspring in the church's liturgy, prayer, and worship.[9] Liturgy helps anchor Christian tradition in the moral imagination and in the

---

2. Guroian, *Ethics after Christendom*, 3. See Guroian, *Faith, Church, Mission*, 87–172.

3. Guroian, *Ethics after Christendom*; Guroian, *Faith, Church, Mission*, 37.

4. Guroian, *Ethics after Christendom*, 7.

5. Ibid., 14.

6. Ibid., 21–26; Guroian, *Incarnate Love*, 117–32; Guroian, "Tradition and Ethics," 207–22. See Schindler, *Introduction*; Meilaender, *Faith and Faithfulness*.

7. Guroian, *Ethics after Christendom*, 27.

8. Ibid., 52.

9. Guroian, *Incarnate Love*, 71; Guroian, "Seeing Worship as Ethics," 335–54.

character of individual Christians and faith communities alike.[10] It is important to pre-serve particular liturgical and worship practices, and especially baptism and eucharistic participation, because such practices shape the ethical outlook of God's people and help bring Christian tradition to life for each generation. Liturgy forms the moral imagination by directing it toward the age to come, that is, giving it an eschatological view, and by directing it toward the historical memory of the church as embodied in the sacraments. These eschatological and sacramental dimensions of Christian tradition are passed on through liturgy in such a way that they prune and mould the ethical sensibilities of the worshipping community.[11] While western culture attempts to make morality a private and secular affair, in Orthodoxy the liturgy of the Eucharist is the primary source and author-ity for Christian moral and ethical formation—the liturgy is Christian ethic's *ontological condition*.[12]

Guroian cautions his readers about the error of placing liturgy in the service of moral formation, the error of seeing morality as the sum total of the ethical life of the church, and the error of viewing the church as merely an ethical society. Each of these errors is tempting for the ethicist or for the person engaged in the moral formation of Christians. Christian ethics, however, are derived from the church's eucharistic nature, from its liturgical life, and from the traditional marks of the church. Christian ethics do not stand in isolation from the broader eucharistic nature, liturgical practices, or escha-tological orientation of the church. Instead, these things are interwoven in the church's ecclesiological tapestry.

> Ecclesiology is communion in being. Ethics is born out of that communion. Moral formation is a part of the process by which the members of the Church become what they are already by grace, the holy people of God. In Christian eucharistic liturgies and sacramental rites the entire meaning and substance of the marks of the Church are articulated in word and act; often these words and actions do imply or call into being moral conduct and ethics . . . Ecclesiology, eschatology and ethics are held together liturgically in one all-encompassing vision. And this is as it should be.[13]

Covenantal love, or *agape*, is at the heart of both Christian ethics and ecclesiology. It is the supreme virtue, given fullest expression in the person, life, and passion of Christ, who himself is the source of all virtue. The incarnation and the passion of Christ reveal such love. It is a love with trinitarian origins.[14] Guroian asserts that such covenantal love is not an abstract notion, but a concrete virtue and orientation, cultivated and realized in the faith community through mission, service, liturgy, worship, and other such prac-tices. Such love is an eschatological and eucharistic action, testifying to the age to come, connecting people with each other, and shaping the ethical imagination of the church.[15]

---

10. Guroian, *Ethics after Christendom*, 32–34.

11. Ibid., 34–47; Guroian, *Incarnate Love*, 51–78.

12. Guroian, "Moral Formation and Liturgy," 372.

13. Ibid., 374–75.

14. Guroian, "Notes toward an Eastern Orthodox Ethic," 232–36.

15. Guroian, *Incarnate Love*, 53–54; Guroian, "Love in Orthodox Ethics," 192–97.

Despite its divisions, Guroian maintains that the global church is one church, and should pursue ecumenical cooperation and fellowship. The church is united in Christ as one body, through the sacramental love and union of the Eucharist.

Eucharistic ecclesiology makes Christian ethics both *dialogic* and *iconic*, writes Guroian. That is, within the worshipping community there should be space for dialogical exploration of ethics and relations with the world. Furthermore, the church's icons, and the church itself as a primary icon, have an important role to play in shaping Christian ethics. This is because the "theology of the icon emphasizes imagination, perception, and interpretation," teaching individuals and faith communities the essential skills and theological understandings needed for ethical competency in post-Christendom.[16] He is not naïve, however, about the potential for perversions or misinterpretations of Christian liturgy to lead to "moral deformation."[17] Guroian is convinced that *a communal herme-neutic for Scripture* needs to be pursued.[18] Such a hermeneutic should appreciate the in-timate connection between eucharistic worship, eschatological vision, ethical formation, and scriptural interpretation. As churches actively read, respond, interpret, and apply Scripture in their contexts, and as they shape their identities, mission, goals, and com-munal life around the vision of Scripture, they might naturally cultivate applied ecclesial ethics. Guroian asserts that there is an undeniable link between liturgical worship, the cultivation of a communal hermeneutic for Scripture, and healthy, applied ecclesial ethics. When Scripture is socially embodied in a faith community, its ethical life and imagination flourish. Guroian locates this social embodiment in the Eucharist, since his ecclesiology is eucharistic in orientation.[19]

Guroian argues that much of today's public theology is unhelpful, since particular aspects of western culture's secular and pluralistic nature mitigate against such efforts. Public theology often has anemic and superficial ecclesiological foundations, and under-estimates the pervasive nature of secularism and the decline of the churches. Such public theology tends toward "flattened" or "overly functionalistic ecclesiologies that confuse the redemptive mission of the Church with the instrumentality of social reform or culture maintenance."[20] It is too often centered on society rather than the church. This view of contemporary public theology does not prevent Guroian from commenting on public, political, and societal issues—nationalism, medical and sexual ethics, and human rights, for example—but he approaches such issues from a particular theological and ecclesio-logical stance, which I outline here.

For Guroian, the answer to the church's inability to influence or be relevant to the broader culture is not found in the development of a public theology but, instead, in the church *being* the church.[21] Through liturgy and worship the church is strengthened and

16. Guroian, *Ethics after Christendom*, 48–50.

17. Guroian, "Moral Formation and Liturgy," 375–76.

18. Guroian, "Bible and Ethics," 133–35.

19. Guroian, *Ethics after Christendom*, 53–80.

20. Ibid., 4.

21. Guroian, *Incarnate Love*, 73; Guroian, *Rallying the Really Human Things*, 216. This proposition has a Hauerwasian ring to it.

discovers fresh ethical understanding and conviction. Simultaneously, it can then be a foretaste and exemplar of the kingdom of God. The church "moves simultaneously inward to strengthen ecclesial life and outward in dialogic and iconic fashion to draw others into its life and communicate its vision of the human good to the society at large."[22] Christians are not primarily called to renew and form the culture for the good of the culture. They are called to witness to Christ and his kingdom, to "make the Kingdom of God present," and to demonstrate to the wider culture the ethics and nature of the age to come.[23] They are called to be a Christ-like, kingdom-exemplifying, ethical, and peculiar community.

> The Church, if it is any kind of community at all, is a rather *peculiar* community. It is a community whose character . . . ought to contrast markedly with that of the world. Though it is a peculiar community, paradoxically it is one for all humanity. The Church is catholic. And it is catholic because it is an eschatological and sacramental manifestation of the Kingdom of God.[24]

The Orthodox Church is uniquely placed to examine post-Christendom mission, ecclesiology, and ethics, writes Guroian, because Orthodoxy has existed for quite some time in diaspora within western culture. Furthermore, he suggests that the Orthodox Church has not experienced, and consequently can analyze, the western "dualism of church and state" that connected "a unified Christendom and a unified secular culture." Whether one accepts the latter assertion, it is true that Orthodoxy is well placed to appreciate the opportunities and challenges of a diasporic experience within western culture (along with the Anabaptists, Mennonites, and other such dissenting movements). The Orthodox are well placed since this diasporic experience has been their historical location in many western contexts. It is interesting to note that Guroian often turns to Free Church and Anabaptist theologians as conversation partners in this endeavor.[25]

THE MORAL IMAGINATION AND APPLIED ECCLESIAL ETHICS

In addition to his reflections on political and social ethics, Guroian has written extensively in the broader field of applied ecclesial ethics and individual Christian morality. He is particularly interested in political and social ethics, sexual and medical ethics, ecological ethics, and the relationship between literature and ethical formation. In the section above, I briefly dealt with the core aspects of Guroian's political and social ethics. I turn now to some of the other main areas of his applied ecclesial ethics, and his desire to see the Christian moral imagination renewed.

In conversation with Kirk, Chesterton, and Eliot, Guroian writes of "the pressing need to cultivate the moral imagination in our day," and of the crucial role of the imagination in Christian moral formation.[26] He believes that the imagination helps people and communities make sense of their world and their beliefs, and apply those beliefs creatively

22. Guroian, *Ethics after Christendom*, 99.

23. Ibid., 83–101; Guroian, *Incarnate Love*, 66.

24. Guroian, *Incarnate Love*, 65.

25. Guroian, "Problem of an Orthodox Social Ethic," 721.

26. Guroian, "Moral Imagination," 10.

in their own setting. It "needs nurture and cultivation," since "if the moral imagination is not fed by religious sentiment and supported by reason it will be replaced by an idolatrous or diabolic imagination."[27] Imagination communicates with memory in the process of making sense of the world, and in the daily construction of personal ethical frameworks and decision-making. While Guroian does not say this, one might deduce that faith communities go through a similar process of ethical and moral imagination. Guroian writes that God breaks into the world in a way that enlarges the spiritual and moral imagination of his people, as evidenced in the incarnation and resurrection. When God's people respond imaginatively to him, the fruit is creativity in the ethical and ecclesiological realms (and innovation in other areas), as well as a more fully realized *humanitas*.[28]

For Guroian, the human imagination reflects our creation in the image of God. The church's ability (or inability) to cultivate the human imagination is strongly linked with its ability to develop the moral imagination of the individual and the faith community. Guroian defines imagination as "the self's process of finding direction and purpose in life by making metaphors from remembered experiences to understand present experience."[29] He describes "three forms of imagination" that are prevalent in western culture and which threaten the vitality of the moral imagination. These are "the idyllic imagination, the idolatrous imagination, and the diabolic imagination."[30] The first is hedonistic, sensual, escapist, and irresponsible. The second elevates things and people above God. Instead of seeking the peace that God offers, it seeks peace through the worship of idols. The third is often pursued when the first two are unsatisfying, and it is characterized by violence and perversion. These three forms of imagination are corruptions of the God-given, sanctified, moral imagination. Western culture faces a crisis of imagination, and the church and its liturgy play an indispensible role in cultivating and nurturing the moral imagination of the people of God.[31]

What does Guroian mean by this fourth form of the imagination—the *moral imagination*? He describes it in this way:

> The moral imagination is the distinctively human power to conceive of men and women as moral beings, that is, as persons, not as things or animals whose value to us is their usefulness. It is the process by which the self makes metaphors out of images recorded by the senses and stored in memory, which then are employed to find and suppose moral correspondence in experience.[32]

This moral imagination is also an eschatological imagination. The moral imagination depends on faith's eschatological vision. The eschatological hope of the church, nurtured in liturgical worship and the practices of the church, fuels and stimulates the church's

27. Ibid., 11.

28. Ibid., 14–15.

29. Guroian, *Rallying the Really Human Things*, 53.

30. Ibid., 50.

31. Ibid., 53–62.

32. Ibid., 55.

moral imagination.[33] It is a hope and a morality grounded in Christology—and Guroian advocates a Christology that emphasizes the resurrection, not only the incarnation and crucifixion.[34]

From the base of the theological foundations I have outlined so far in this chapter, Guroian considers specific issues in applied ecclesial ethics. These include sexual and medical ethics, and the role of literature in ethical development.[35] Often he relates these ethical considerations to ecclesiological perspectives. His reflections on the family are an example of this. Developing the thought of John Chrysostom, Guroian speaks of the "family as an ecclesial entity and mission of the Kingdom of God."[36] In a post-Christendom setting, an "ecclesial vision" of the family is a radical attempt to see the nuclear and extended family as a crucial dimension and a mission of the broader "ecclesial household." Examining the work of Chrysostom, the marriage and baptismal rites of the Orthodox Church, and Ephesians chapter 5, Guroian writes of the sacramental relationship between the Christian family and the church. The church's mission and vitality are deeply connected with the spiritual life and moral imagination of the family, and vice versa. The sacramental nature of the church is paralleled by the sacramental nature of marriage and family. The family is an ecclesial community imaging the Trinity and supporting the mission of the church. The family has a pedagogical role in discipling the next generation and in witnessing to the kingdom of God. The family is "a little church—the household of God (*oikonomia tou theou*) writ small."[37]

Guroian's ecological ethics are another example of the way in which he relates applied ethics to ecclesiology. The eucharistic ecclesiology of the Orthodox Church emphasizes blessing, especially in its sacramental rites and practices. Guroian contends that there is a rich thanksgiving in these rites and ecclesial practices for God's gracious gifts in creation. Furthermore, there is recognition of the priestly and stewardship roles of humanity and the church, especially with regard to the earth and the rest of the created order. The church has a real responsibility for the "cleansing and healing of creation." This task is emphasized in the eucharistic liturgy and the sacramental rites of the church. The inculturational nature of Christian faith demands that the people of God treat creation redemptively, and that the liturgical worship in the church move out into our care for the world.[38] Guroian concludes, "Ecology *is* an ecclesial concern . . . From an Orthodox perspective, ecclesiology and concern for the global ecology are virtually the same thing."[39]

33. Guroian, "Liturgy," 229.

34. Guroian, "I Confess the Cross," 345.

35. See Guroian, *Rallying the Really Human Things*, 83–176; Guroian, "Let No Man Join Together."

36. Guroian, *Ethics after Christendom*, 135.

37. Ibid., 154. See Guroian, "Family and Christian Virtue"; Guroian, *Faith, Church, Mission*, 45–55.

38. Guroian, "Christian Gardener," 229.

39. Guroian, *Ethics after Christendom*, 155–74; Guroian, "Cleansers of the Whole Earth," 274–76.

THE MISSION OF THE CHURCH

In Guroian's ecclesiology, the mission of the church is to see the world transformed by the kingdom of God. The church is to engage with the world politically, relationally, ethically, and so forth, in such a way that it sees the world transformed and restored to its rightful place in submission to the will and purposes of the Father. Therefore, Guroian contends that the church needs to recognize the fallen state of the world, but also the inbreaking presence of grace and the kingdom. The meaning of the world and of human history is understood through Christianity's christological, ecclesiological, and eschatological understandings. These understandings make sense of the world and its future, as well as making sense of the purpose of the church with regard to the world. According to Guroian, while the church is called to engage actively the political and social structures of its day, its vision should always be on the person of Christ, the age to come, and the kingdom of God. Furthermore, the church should not lose sight of the ministry it has to individuals in its effort to transform political and social institutions. The love of God should shape and be present in all the missiological actions of the church.[40]

Regarding the mission of the church, Guroian writes:

> It is the mission of the Church as the bearer of the Spirit to sanctify all things, making it known that there is no final polarity of nature and grace, state and Church, world and Kingdom of God . . . The mission of the Church is to make the Kingdom of God present by redeeming and transfiguring the world. This mission is not reserved solely to priestly and monastic vocations . . . It is the Church's mission to transform the human life of *persons*. The Church's primary although not exclusive concern is with persons.[41]

Guroian is critical of the separation of the church and the world which has developed in the Latin Church and in western culture. He writes that Orthodox ecclesiology will have none of this. In Orthodox ecclesiology, "the Church in its very essence contains the world and expresses its very fulfillment and destiny in eucharistic worship."[42] The church and the world might be at odds with each other on ethical issues, but Orthodox ecclesiology denies the dualism that exists in western theology, which claims that church and world are ontologically distinct. Ethical distinctions between church and world are possible in Orthodox ecclesiology, not ontological distinctions. The role of the church, through its agapic love, missiological actions, and liturgical worship, is to show the world what it really is and to transfigure the world. Through these dimensions of the church's existence, it calls the world back to its rightful place in submission to Jesus Christ and the Father. "Through worship Christians come to know themselves as agapic (powerless but charismatic) mission to the world."[43]

I have devoted a considerable amount of this chapter to describing Guroian's political, social, and applied ethics. It must be emphasized that Guroian's ethics are missiological.

40. Guroian, *Incarnate Love*, 22–26.

41. Ibid., 24–26.

42. Ibid., 157.

43. Ibid., 158–59.

All ethics that are faithful to Scripture and to Christ are necessarily missiologically shaped and grounded in the eucharistic worship of God's people. Guroian believes that there is an undeniable connection between the church's ethics, its missiological engagement with the world, and its ecclesiological wholeness and vitality.[44] A "crisis of mission" and a "dereliction of Christian ethics" go hand in hand.[45]

In an article called "Salvation as Divine Therapy," Guroian claims that western juridical notions of salvation may not serve the church in western culture well in its missiological endeavor. He contends that Orthodox images of Jesus as *divine physician*, and of salvation as *divine therapy*, are better missiological metaphors than those shaped around juridical notions. Juridical motifs are less accessible to contemporary culture than therapeutic ones, and do not necessarily reflect the biblical material any better. Therapeutic images are prevalent in western culture, including "therapeutic ideas about wellness, wholeness, and fulfillment."[46] The church can redeem and use these images in its mission, through the paradigms of Scripture, Eucharist, liturgy, and gospel.

CONTRIBUTIONS TO MISSIONAL ECCLESIOLOGY

Guroian does not present a systematic ecclesiology since he primarily writes in the field of moral theology. Yet his theological ethics are grounded in his eucharistic and liturgical ecclesiology, since, in his words, his ethics are *ecclesially centered*. In Guroian's ecclesiology, the church is a peculiar, ethical community. I draw on his missiological, ethical, ecumenical, and gospel-culture insights in the theological and practical sections of the missional ecclesiology I present in this book.[47]

In broad ecumenical conversation, Guroian presents a moral theology and an applied ecclesial ethic for post-Christendom. Rejecting ethical or ecclesiological sectarianism or accommodation, Guroian attempts to construct applied ecclesial ethics that are not characterized by retreat from the world or compromise with the culture. These applied ethics are not only about the church's articulated beliefs, theological positions, or self-understandings; they are also about the concrete ethical actions of local churches. Christian ethics are essentially about faith communities forging "a singularly christic and trinitarian way of life." Such ethics are about the church *being* the church in post-Christendom, without apology or corruption, and, therefore, missional ecclesiology is inadequate without an authentic and robust engagement with theological and public ethics.

It must be noted, however, that Guroian rightly questions forms of public theology that emerge less from Bible, theology, and concrete Christian community than from the historical marriage between Enlightenment liberalism and Christendom morality. Such public theology tends toward maintaining the status quo of Christendom, in both its reforming and conserving guises. If Christian ethics are to advance the cause of Christ and the mission of the church, they must be *ecclesially centered*. This means that the dynamic life of the faith community and the liturgical worship of the church (catechism, sacraments, prayer, and liturgy) play a central role in connecting Christian tradition (Scripture, creeds, and doctrine) with the moral imagination. The dynamic conversation between liturgy, tradition,

44. Guroian, *Faith, Church, Mission*, 40–42.

45. Ibid., 42.

46. Guroian, "Salvation," 310.

47. He features in chapter 15 in *Part Two* of this book.

missiology, ethics, and Christian practice must be rooted in covenantal, agapic love. This love is one that reflects the trinitarian, loving communion and the loving sacrifice of Christ. It is a love with eyes firmly fixed on the age to come. Churches are to cultivate an agapic approach to Scripture reading and worship, in a spirit of dialogue and participation. Worship, community, and prayer have the capacity to turn tepid, lifeless, conserving morality into transforming life and culture-changing Christian ethics. Guroian is convinced that such a community hermeneutic is only possible when churches appreciate the intimate connection between eucharistic worship, eschatological vision, ethical formation, missiological passion, and scriptural interpretation. I think that he is correct in his description of the interconnections between these ecclesiological dynamics. These things cannot be divorced from each other without doing damage to the church or distorting one of these dimensions of the church. This is precisely why Guroian's applied ecclesial ethics are so deeply shaped around ecclesiological convictions, and why they speak so clearly to the formation of the missionary actions and imagination of the church. While I would have liked Guroian to give more guidance on how to use Christian worship, prayer, and Scripture in the cultivation of the ethical imagination, he has raised important issues that local churches must explore in their own context and beyond Christendom.

Guroian's eucharistic ecclesiology has a substantial theology of the icon, which does not seem to be grounded in Scripture. For Guroian, it is not just that the church has icons—the church itself is a primary icon. His theology of the icon seems to me to be *post hoc*—attempting to justify theologically an established ecclesial practice rather than theologically critiquing it to see whether it has legitimacy. On this, I suppose, I am unashamedly Protestant evangelical, Baptist, and biblicist.

Guroian writes that the world does not define the church. On the contrary, he insists that the church defines the world, and that the church contains the world, since they are not ontologically separate. This is one of the theological and epistemological locations where Guroian and I differ. It seems to me that here he is assigning the work of the gospel to the church. It is the gospel of Jesus Christ that defines the world and its constitution, purpose, current state, and destiny. It is the gospel that does this work. At its best, when it is faithful to the gospel of Jesus Christ, the church testifies to the gospel and to the gospel's ability to sanctify and transfigure the world. The gospel of Jesus Christ, in the light of the perfection of God and the atoning work of Christ, shows the world what it really is, how it needs to respond, and what it is destined to be. A Christ-centered, gospel-shaped theology of the church locates the church in its rightful place.

QUESTIONS FOR REFLECTION

1. What does Guroian mean when he asserts that ethics should be *ecclesially centered*? Do we usually think of ethics in this way?

2. Guroian argues that Christian ethics find their origin and wellspring in the church's liturgy, prayer, and worship. Do you agree? Why or why not?

3. Guroian claims that "ecology *is* an ecclesial concern," and that "ecclesiology and concern for the global ecology are virtually the same thing." How might churches respond to this claim?

6

John Zizioulas:
The Church as Eucharistic Communion

Koinonia derives not from sociological experience, nor from ethics, but from faith. We are not called to koinonia because it is "good" for us and for the Church, but because we believe in a God who is in his very being koinonia.[1]

—JOHN ZIZIOULAS

COMMUNION AND HUMAN NATURE

IN *BEING AS COMMUNION*, John Zizioulas outlines his understanding of the nature and essence of the church. Ecclesiology is of central concern for all of theology and its considerations, and for human beings and cultures throughout each generation and age. Zizioulas asserts, "The Church is not simply an institution. She is a 'mode of existence,' *a way of being.* The mystery of the Church, even in its institutional dimension" is "deeply bound" to the nature and essence of human beings, the world, and God. Therefore, "ecclesiology assumes a marked importance" for all dimensions of theology and for the "existential needs" of human beings "in every age."[2]

Zizioulas's ecclesiology is deeply concerned with *hypostasis* and, more especially, *persona* (the substance, personhood, and nature of God, Christ, the church, and human beings).[3] In fact, his ecclesiology is saturated in this concept. He understands human nature to be richly connected with the nature of God, the church, and the redemptive and regenerative work and nature of Christ.[4] The nature of the church, and of human beings, is inextricably "bound to the very being of God." By immersion in the church, Christians

---

1. Zizioulas, *Church as Communion*, 104. John Zizioulas is the titular Eastern Orthodox Bishop of Pergamum, represents the Ecumenical Patriarchate of the Eastern Orthodox Church on international church bodies, is the Chair of the Academy of Athens, and was formerly Professor of Theology at Glasgow University and Kings College, London.

2. Zizioulas, *Being as Communion*, 15.

3. Elwell, *Concise Evangelical Dictionary*, 236; Zizioulas, "Contribution of Cappadocia," 23–25. Zizioulas understands *hypostasis* to mean *persona* instead of merely "essence."

4. Zizioulas, *Being as Communion*, 59.

become an "image of God" and assume "God's way of being."[5] They are connected with the relationality and communion of the Trinity. The church of Jesus Christ has the high calling of being conformed to God's own essence, in her theological vision, structure, ministries and ecclesiality.

God's being is essentially relational and communal, as is evidenced in the doctrine of the Trinity. God's being can only be known and experienced through love, relationship, and communion. "Ecclesiology must be situated within the context of trinitarian theology."[6] The Father wills the church into existence for his pleasure. The church will be presented to him at the climax of history. Her origins and destination are in the Father.

Trinitarian understandings of God are fundamental concepts in our understanding of the essence of God, the church, and human beings. This is because "the substance of God, 'God,' has no ontological content, no true being, apart from communion."[7] All individuality is abolished in this theological realization, since nothing exists aside from communion, not even God himself. The Father is the cause and origin of this communion in his being.[8] His communion is entwined with freedom, since God chooses this essential nature of his being.[9] The Father chooses to be the source of God.[10]

Zizioulas relates the nature of human beings, personal freedom, and the church, with the substance of divine-human communion. He asserts that freedom is indispensable for true being. This is a freedom to love and be in communion with other persons and God. He writes that his ecclesiology is founded upon the following notions, which were affirmed by the Patristics:

> (a) There is no true being without communion. Nothing exists as an "individual," conceivable in itself. Communion is an ontological category. (b) Communion which does not come from a "hypostasis," that is, a concrete and free person, and which does not lead to "hypostasis," that is concrete and free persons, is not an "image" of the being of God. The person cannot exist without communion; but every form of communion that denies or suppresses the person, is inadmissible.[11]

Human beings have a nature that is constrained and limited by our biological existence at conception and birth. Zizioulas calls this a *hypostasis of biological existence*. What this means is that we lack genuine freedom, full personhood, and rich interpersonal and divine-human communion. This is because biological existence only, at least initially, entails individuality and temporality. This mere biological existence is disintegrated at death.[12] Therefore, humans need a transformation of the essence of their being, through communion with God and the church. We need a transformation of the *constitutional*

---

5. Ibid., 15.

6. Zizioulas, "Mystery of the Church," 295.

7. Zizioulas, *Being as Communion*, 17.

8. Zizioulas, "Constantine Scouteris," 2.

9. Zizioulas, *Communion and Otherness*, 4.

10. Zizioulas, "Constantine Scouteris," 5.

11. Zizioulas, *Being as Communion*, 18.

12. Zizioulas, "Human Capacity," 430.

make-up of the hypostasis, and this is achieved through the *hypostasis of ecclesial nature*. Through regeneration and rebirth, at the point of baptism, human beings are transformed into God's manner of being. This is achieved through the mystery of the church, and the communion and change of our natures that it offers.[13] Human beings are brought into a new relationship with the world that transcends biology, familial ties, and the constraint of natural laws. They experience a unique and supernatural love, communion, change in their being, and relationship with self, others and God. Our natural biological essence is not eradicated, since Christians live in the body and are subject to death. However, our biological substance, and our transformed substance and nature, are bridged by the nature of the Eucharist, and by our communal participation in this sacrament (bridged by a *sacramental* or *eucharistic hypostasis*).[14] Our transformed nature contains the dialectic of "already but not yet," and draws its being from the being of God and from its eschatological future. It is ascetic in its denial of the biological limitations. These biological limitations and *hypostasis* are accepted, including eros and bodiliness, but realized, freed, and constituted in a regenerated way. We are freed from the dominion of egocentricity, individuality, and exclusiveness, and move irresistibly and freely into community, love, and ecclesiality.[15]

Zizioulas contends that the church comes into existence through the work of Christ and the Spirit in historical events. However, its goal and vision is meta-historical and eschatological. For Zizioulas, eucharistic worship and the institutional dimensions of the church aim to focus the community on the eschatological consummation of history and on the Trinity. They aim toward the impetus to live out the church's regenerated and life-giving essence in "this age and the age to come."[16]

In the Eucharist, the communal nature of the church is most fully realized. In the Eucharist the church remembers together the ministry and work of Christ. She accomplishes an eschatological act by reflecting on her eschatological nature and entering into the life of the Trinity. She is thereby constituted as the church.[17] The Eucharist constitutes the church's being, and manifests the historical form of God's relationship to the world. It leads or unites the people of God with the eschatological and eternal community.[18]

Zizioulas attempts in his ecclesiology to continue the Eastern Orthodox tradition of *eucharistic ecclesiology*. He particularly wants to develop the insights of the theologian Nicholas Afanasiev; however, he is keen to differentiate his theology from some of Afanasiev's work. This is especially true of his concern to expand his ecclesiology to embrace the rest of Orthodox theology, and to encompass ecclesiology's implications for human personhood, and the essential nature of the Father, Christ, and the church. His concern extends to examining whether a local church can be truly catholic by merely

13. Zizioulas, *Being as Communion*, 19, 50–53.

14. Ibid., 53–60.

15. Ibid., 61–65.

16. Ibid., 19–20.

17. It would be interesting to ask Zizioulas what this means, say, for those in the Salvation Army and other such Christian movements that do not normally celebrate the Eucharist.

18. Zizioulas, *Being as Communion*, 20–23.

celebrating the Eucharist. He endeavors to articulate the relationship between the local and the universal church, and to achieve a synthesis of the "dialogue between Eastern and Western theology."[19] These ideals are noble, but not achieved in any real depth in *Being as Communion* or his other ecclesiological writings to date.

TRUTH, COMMUNION, AND ECCLESIOLOGY

According to Zizioulas, truth may be identified with communion. If being is constituted as communion, then truth and communion may be "mutually identified."[20] Zizioulas demonstrates the development of this association and synthesis in Greek patristic thought by examining the various approaches to synthesizing truth, being, and history.[21] Fallen existence has caused a rupture between truth, being, and communion. This is evidenced in hypocrisy, individualization, and death. Truth can only be life and redemption from these consequences as communion. "Truth, once again, must be communion if it is to be life."[22] Human beings are a revelation of truth only when they are in authentic communion, a communion in which otherness and oneness coincide harmoniously.[23]

The Greek patristic synthesis between truth, being, and history has significant ecclesiological consequences, writes Zizioulas. Firstly, Christ's *whole personal existence*, as the truth, includes his communion with the church. This is achieved through the Spirit, who consecutively reveals Christ in history and constitutes Christ's "personal existence as a body or community. All separation between Christology and ecclesiology vanishes in the Spirit."[24] Therefore, Christ maintains personal particularity and union with the church and within the Trinity. He exists pneumatologically, giving birth to the church through the economy of the Trinity and the work of the Spirit.

Secondly, the church partakes in Christ's existence through community. Human beings partake in his existence through entrance into this community, by way of radical conversion and baptism. When we receive Christ's existence as our own, authentic community in the life of the church is realized. As the body of Christ, the church enjoys the same communion with the Trinity and with each other as the historical Christ. The church receives the eternal life that is identical with the life of God, and lives in the world in a transformational manner, anticipating the return and reign of Christ.[25]

Thirdly, it is in the celebration of the Eucharist that this is most clearly perceived and manifested. The Eucharist is the locus of truth,[26] the activity in which the church

---

19. Ibid., 23–26.

20. Ibid., 101.

21. Ibid., 72–100.

22. Ibid., 101–5.

23. Ibid., 106.

24. Ibid., 110–11.

25. Ibid., 113–14.

26. Such a proposition makes Protestant evangelicals recoil. For evangelicals, the Scriptures are the infallible, authoritative word of God, and have absolute and final authority in all aspects of corporate and individual faith.

incarnates and demonstrates its communion with the Trinity in this present place and time. It is the manifestation of the eschatological vision and hope of the community.

According to Zizioulas, the concept that the Eucharist is the locus of truth has further implications for the church:[27]

1. Christ's revelation as essential and foundational truth, is not Christ revealed so much *in* a community, but *as* a community. The Eucharist reveals and demonstrates this Christ-truth in history, creation, community, and experience, and in the grace and love of this Christ-truth springing up among us.

2. Conciliar infallibility, the authority of the bishop, and charismatic ministries among all the people of God owe their existence and irrefutability not merely to historical transmission. They are also indebted to the manner in which the eucharistic experience adds a transforming *vertical* and charismatic-pentecostal dimension to each of these ecclesial realities.

3. Dogmatic formulations of truth in the church are liberating and worshipful pronouncements, which serve to guard the Christ-truth revealed in the Eucharist from heresy. Such doctrines are incarnated in a particular time and culture, and they are cultivated in a spirit of acceptance of history and culture. They are also eschatologized, however, so that truth remains pre-eminent. In their inculturational nature they are relational while being prophetic, both transformational and critical. Doctrine and communion can no more be broken than can truth and communion.

4. The Eucharist demonstrates the cosmic dimensions of truth. This has pastoral and practical implications for ecology, humanity, and other contemporary social and global issues.

5. The people of God pronounce a celebratory, eucharistic, and worshipful Amen as they gather around the Eucharist. They are choosing to embrace truth, and in doing so embracing freedom. Truth is then eucharistically revealed as *freedom*. Human beings experience freedom only in this eucharistic communion, and "truth liberates by placing beings in communion."[28]

CHRISTOLOGY, PNEUMATOLOGY, AND THE CHURCH

Zizioulas is concerned that western ecclesiology, and theology in general, has been constructed from its Christology without due reference to a theology of the Spirit (pneumatology). He is not claiming that it is *christomonistic* as claimed by some Orthodox theologians (reducing everything to Christology).[29] For Zizioulas, while Christology has been central to western theology, a theology of the Spirit has been largely neglected in western ecclesiology.[30] He believes that this has had implications for western understandings of the structure

27. Zizioulas, *Being as Communion*, 114–22.

28. Ibid., 122.

29. Zizioulas, "Mystery of the Church," 295.

30. Zizioulas, *Implications Ecclésiologiques*, 141–54.

of the church, the sacraments, and ministry. He is also critical of eastern insufficiencies in this area and asserts the need for both western and eastern ecclesiology to demonstrate the critical relationships between Christology, pneumatology, and ecclesiology. Only a rich dialogue between the two theological traditions can lead to a fuller synthesis of these themes in theology.[31]

Neither Christology nor pneumatology should be primary in developing a healthy ecclesiology. Instead, they should be integrated theologically and in the liturgy of churches, since both have significant contributions to make to ecclesiology.[32]

For Zizioulas, "The Spirit is the Spirit of 'communion' and his primary work consists in opening up reality to become *relational*."[33] The Spirit is essential to communion in the Trinity and to ecclesial communion (*koinonia*).[34] The Spirit is also essential to the idea of Christ having a body, the church, and to the significance of the incarnation and the entire work of Christ. The Spirit prepares the church for the coming of Christ and the restoration of all things, and is thus essential to eschatology too. Therefore, the eschatological and communal aspects of pneumatology are "*constitutive* of ecclesiology" and the church. "Pneumatology is an ontological category in ecclesiology."[35] Zizioulas emphasizes pneumatology not because it is primary to Christology. He is convinced that it is constitutive of Christology rather than primary to it, and that it is neglected in most ecclesiological considerations.

The local churches are as important as the universal church since the Spirit constitutes the body of Christ simultaneously at both levels. To speak of the universal having priority over the local, or the other way around, is to deny an ecclesiology that is adequately formed by both Christology and pneumatology.

All forms of ministry need other ministries. All pyramidal ideas of church and leadership need to be dissolved in an ecclesiology shaped by Christology and pneumatology. This does not dissolve the necessity of ecclesial structures, but should rid the church of hierarchical or pyramidal understandings of their nature. "Christian spirituality . . . could not be experienced outside the community, which involved a multiplicity and variety of spiritual charisms."[36] Local churches, laity, synods, bishops, and the like, are all caught up in the communion of the body of Christ. All need each other's ministries and graces in order to function fully.

Institutions cannot take their reference, justification, or authority merely from history or tradition. It is the work of Christ through the Spirit that conditions these institutions, presenting them to God. They are dependent on prayer, and the presence of Christ and the Spirit. An eschatological perspective needs to shape ecclesial institutions.

While Christ *institutes* the church, the Spirit *constitutes* it. Partaking in the communal nature of the Spirit, the church becomes a part of our being, rather than merely an

31. Zizioulas, *Being as Communion*, 123–42.

32. Zizioulas, "Die Pneumatologische Dimension," 133–47.

33. Zizioulas, "Mystery of the Church," 299.

34. Zizioulas, *Communion and Otherness*, 5.

35. Zizioulas, *Being as Communion*, 132.

36. Zizioulas, "Early Christian Community," 27.

institution apart from us. This is especially the case because communion is innate to the essence, dynamism, and efficacy of the church, and to our connection with it. The notion of institution, then, is radically changed.

Rightly or wrongly, Zizioulas believes that pneumatology, especially in the liturgy, has mostly saved the Orthodox Church from many of the problems of the western church. He sees these problems as clericalism, anti-institutionalism, extreme forms of Pentecostalism, and anti-establishment tendencies. However, he understands that the global influence of western culture will add greater challenges that can only be solved by ecumenical cooperation and dialogue. Is it really the case that Orthodox churches have avoided clericalism and its associated problems? This assertion is open, no doubt, for considerable debate.

EUCHARISTIC COMMUNITY AND CATHOLICITY

Zizioulas considers that *"the Church constitutes the Eucharist while being constituted by it.* Church and Eucharist are interdependent; they coincide, and are even in some sense identical."[37] For Zizioulas, the concept of the catholicity of the church is inextricably linked to the idea of the church being a eucharistic community. Catholicity is a way of talking about the church as broad, inclusive, universal—the fellowship of Christians across all traditions, cultures, and times. While catholicity is ultimately made known at the end of the age, "its nature is revealed and realistically apprehended *here and now* in the Eucharist."[38]

Zizioulas's understanding of the catholicity and unity of diverse Christian communities that is formed by their common vision of the return of Christ, leads him to further convictions.[39] He is convinced that the catholicity of the church is achieved through her union and communion with Christ, as his body, especially in the Eucharist.[40] Therefore, catholicity is a present christological reality for the church, simultaneously given and demanded in her intimacy with Christ Jesus. Her catholicity is "neither an objective gift to be possessed nor an objective order to be fulfilled, but rather a *presence*."[41] This presence is Christ revealing her catholicity and communion with him. It is Christ demonstrating his presence in history, to all of creation, the world and humankind.

The catholicity of the church has a pneumatological dimension. In the celebration of the Eucharist the presence and ministry of the Holy Spirit are evident, revealing Christ in human history. Through humility, service, prayer, worship, and participation in the Eucharist, the church dynamically confronts the anti-catholic powers of the world.[42] Additionally, the eucharistic community reveals its catholicity to be grounded in the abolishment of all dualistic dichotomies, antagonisms, and divisions.[43] This, of course,

37. Zizioulas, "Ecclesiological Presuppositions," 333.

38. Zizioulas, *Being as Communion*, 143–45.

39. Ibid., 158–59.

40. Zizioulas, *Eucharist, Bishop, Church*, 117.

41. Zizioulas, *Being as Communion*, 159.

42. Ibid., 160–61.

43. Zizioulas, *Communion and Otherness*, 6; Zizioulas, "Early Christian Community," 30.

is an ideal based in his eucharistic ecclesiology, rather than what is often evidenced in the practices, theology, or history of the church. A long quotation from Zizioulas is warranted here, since it relates to one of the primary concerns of missional ecclesiology—the relationship of the church to the world.

> In such a catholic outlook, the entire problem of the relationship of the Church to the world receives a different perspective. The separation and juxtaposition of the two can have no essential meaning because there is no point where the limits of the Church can be objectively and finally drawn. There is a constant interrelation between the Church and the world, the world being God's creation and never ceasing to belong to Him and the Church being the community that through the descent of the Holy Spirit transcends in herself the world and offers it to God in the Eucharist.[44]

Ministry, writes Zizioulas, should be conceived of christologically and communally. In the Christian community, all ministries are *identical* to the ministries of Christ, since he has gifted the church with his own ministries. These ministries "transcend all categories of priority and separation," and are only possible in the context of community. Persons *in community*, rather than individuals *in absoluto*, possess them.[45] Even the apostolic succession of the bishops should be seen in this light. Each bishop is ordained within a community in order to serve such a community. Each bishop represents historically, along with the identification of each local community with the universal church, "a continuity of the apostolic presence in the *locus apostolicus*" of each community of faith.[46]

CHURCH STRUCTURE, APOSTOLICITY, AND MINISTRY

We turn now to the question of church structure in Zizioulas's ecclesiology. He writes, "The Church does not draw her identity from what she is but from what she will be. Eschatology is absolutely crucial to ecclesiology."[47] Consequently, apostolic continuity may be conceived of historically and eschatologically. From the historical point of view, those with apostolic gifts are sent missionally into the world to plant communities of faith, and as a collegium of apostolic figures. They are the foundation of the church, drawing the people of God together eschatologically in one place. In the second approach, and this is the one favored and emphasized by Zizioulas, historical succession throughout generations is not the primary emphasis in the subject of apostolic continuity. What is more important is the eschatological and eucharistic gathering of the church into a continuity of communities and churches, through the presence of the apostles and bishops. In the first approach, apostolicity comes to the church historically, with a special emphasis on Christology. In the second, it comes eschatologically, that is, from the future gathering of all of the people of God at the end of time, with a greater emphasis on pneumatology.[48]

---

44. Zizioulas, *Being as Communion*, 162.

45. Ibid., 163–66.

46. Ibid., 166–69.

47. Zizioulas, "Mystery of the Church," 296.

48. Zizioulas, *Being as Communion*, 172–81.

A theological synthesis of these two approaches is achieved when Christology is constituted historically, with reference to the present activity of the Spirit and in view of the coming eschatological communion with Christ, which defies the distance of time and space. The implications of this synthesis between the dimensions of past, present, and future are then carried over into ideas about our communion with the eschatological apostolic succession, and with the final gathering of all the people of God. The Eucharist is the clearest example of the synthesis between the historical and the eschatological, and the most common form of this synthesis in community life.[49]

Zizioulas vigorously contends that these understandings of apostolic continuity and succession shape our understanding of apostolic continuity as being both through the apostolic kerygma and through the apostolic ministry.[50] Scripture and doctrines are the apostolic kerygma, that is, the liturgical and concrete forms of dynamic communal faith, both historical and eschatological. They must be open to eucharistic renewal, the life-giving Spirit, communion with the "word made flesh," the future, and new forms of experience.

In the context of the Christian community, ministries and their associated structures have the following qualities:[51]

1. The ministry of the church is Christ's ministry outworked through the Spirit.

2. The structure of the church is relational, embracing both unity and diversity, and characterized by communion and *koinonia*.[52]

3. The territorial and geographical structure of the church is partially a consequence of the eschatological mystery of the church, and of the way in which it anticipates the ultimate salvation of all creation and the cosmos. She is a sign and foretaste of the coming kingdom in her geographical location and form.[53]

4. Bishops should image Christ and the apostles, and church leadership should govern and counsel collegially.[54] Everyone in a Christian community is indispensable for this Christian ministry and apostolic succession.

5. "Apostolic succession through episcopacy is essentially a succession of Church structure," which cannot be dismissed or neglected.[55]

6. Ministry and community are interdependent, and all ordinations need to be within a concrete local community.

---

49. Ibid., 181–88.
50. Ibid., 189–204.
51. Ibid., 196–246.
52. Zizioulas, *Church as Communion*, 106–8.
53. Zizioulas, "Mystery of the Church," 302.
54. Zizioulas, "Early Christian Community," 31.
55. Zizioulas, *Being as Communion*, 197.

7. All persons in the community are ordained to ministry within the life of the church, as laity, deacons, presbyters, or bishops. Ministry is essentially relational, interdependent, and communal.[56]

8. Church authority and structure are to be relationally hierarchical and relationally institutional. Hierarchy and institution are not done away with but reconceived relationally.

9. The church needs both the *one* (a central governing body and Patriarch) and the *many* (autonomy of local bishops and leaders) in its life, structure, and ministry. An ecclesiology of communion and diversity at the local level needs to be healthily balanced and complemented by the authority and leadership at the level of central authority.[57] Synodality and primacy must be maintained in such a way that local churches have freedom to be whole and catholic, with appropriate safeguards.[58]

10. In the experience of the church, the bishop is called to be *the image of Christ*, through relationship, spiritual leadership, and reflection of Christ and the Spirit. The bishop is also called to be the protector of the eschatological dimension of the church. The bishop connects the local community with the other communities of faith and the other bishops, past, present, and future. For Zizioulas, "there is nothing higher than the bishop in the Church."[59] The bishop makes the church catholic by,

    (a) expressing the fullness, unity and multiplicity of the eschatological community in each place; b) expressing the historical continuity of the Church in time; and c) expressing the communion and unity of the Church in space.[60]

11. The ministries of the church facilitate its *double movement* of separation from the world and mission within it.

12. The dilemma between ministry as either functional or part of a person's being is transcended when one conceives of ministry as: (i) relational and non-individualistic (the concepts of functionality or "a part of a person's being" are individualistic in nature); (ii) ambassadorial, that is, a gift for others; (iii) personally transforming, but mainly for the sake of the community; (iv) typological, in the sense of representing God in the midst of the community; (v) eschatologically oriented and significant, rather than temporal, and; (vi) of value for the ordained person, but never in isolation.

13. Communities are compelled by Christ to minister in communion and unity with other communities of faith in the world.

14. The recognition of ministries must happen within the full life of the Christian community, rather than by strict hierarchical or denominational arrangements or a rigid dispensational style.

56. Zizioulas, *Communion and Otherness*, 7.

57. Zizioulas, "Nature of the Unity," 344–46.

58. Zizioulas, *Church as Communion*, 108.

59. Zizioulas, "Bishop in the Theological Doctrine," 23–33.

60. Ibid., 35. See Zizioulas, "Episkope and Episkopos."

CONTRIBUTIONS TO MISSIONAL ECCLESIOLOGY

Zizioulas's ecclesiology emphasizes the interconnectedness between the essential nature of human beings (biological and transformed through Christ), and the nature of Christ, the Spirit, the Eucharist, and the church.[61] His ecclesiology furthers *Part Two* of this book through its christological, pneumatological, eschatological, and trinitarian frameworks, and its innovative treatment of personhood and *being*. All *being*, including the *being* of the church, is inextricably bound to the *being* of God. All *being* is communion; even God's *being*, since no true *being* can exist without communion. Personally, I am unconvinced by the philosophical and theological cogency of an ontology that appears to prioritize relationship over those who exist in and form (and are formed by) them.

Trinitarian thought is important to Zizioulas. His ecclesiology is situated within the context of trinitarian and eucharistic theology, and he attempts an active synthesis between communion, *koinonia*, truth, being, and history. Zizioulas laments the separation of Christ, the Spirit, and the Trinity in many western ecclesiological constructs, and attempts to demonstrate the relationships between these dimensions of God's *being*, the believer's regenerated *being*, and the *being* of the church. For Zizioulas it is vital that ecclesiology integrates Christology and pneumatology, not only in its considerations of the nature and shape of the church, but also in its mission and liturgy.

Zizioulas regards church structure, apostolicity, and ministry as living realities, most fully expressed in the eschatological visions, hopes, and activities of concrete local church communities. His ecclesiology furthers missional ecclesiology through its perspectives on ecumenical dialogue, on the nature of personal spiritual transformation (the ecclesiological significance of the person), on the relational character of ministry, on the faith community and catholicity, and on the relationship between the local churches and the wider body of Christ. In Zizioulas's eucharistic ecclesiology, the local church is of great importance. These local churches are made catholic through the presence of Christ in the Eucharist.[62] These local churches are rendered churches by their celebration of the Eucharist, and the presence of the whole Christ through the divine Eucharist. They are also rendered as such by their connection with the bishop,[63] and by their conformity to the truths of Christian faith in a concrete, local, geographical setting. Genuine Christian communities are characterized by diversity rather than conformity.[64]

For Protestant evangelicals, the notion that the Eucharist is the locus of truth, since *truth is communion* and the Eucharist is the ultimate expression of such communion, is unacceptable and unbiblical. Jesus Christ is the locus of truth, and it is the Scriptures (which reveal Jesus and his gospel of salvation) that are the infallible, authoritative word of God, and that have absolute and final authority in all aspects of corporate and individual faith. This issue demonstrates the difference between eucharistic and

---

61. He features in chapters 14, 15, 16, and 17 in *Part Two* of this book.

62. See the appraisals of Zizioulas's thinking in these areas by Kärkkäinen and Volf: Kärkkäinen, *Introduction to Ecclesiology*, 101; Volf, *After Our Likeness*, 103–4.

63. Zizioulas, *Eucharist, Bishop, Church*, 117.

64. Zizioulas, *Being as Communion*, 247–57.

evangelical ecclesiology. To be fair to Zizioulas, he does understand Christ and the Scriptures as truth—they are truth because they are *communion*, leading women and men into communion with the being of the triune God. Miroslav Volf notes that John Zizioulas does not exclude propositional, received, kerygmatic truth, but Zizioulas does (in contrast to evangelical understandings of truth) dramatically subordinate it "to the core personal dimension of truth." Hence Zizioulas's elevation of the Eucharist, since this "noncognitive interiority of the word in relation to the Church can only be secured sacramentally."[65] For Zizioulas, the Eucharist constitutes the church. Elsewhere he notes that the Spirit constitutes the church. The focus on the Spirit's work seems to me to be the biblical perspective. The Spirit of Jesus Christ constitutes the church, including, but by no means limited to, his presence and activity in the church's partaking of the Lord's Supper. The church is constituted by Christ alone—through his incarnation, sacrifice, death, resurrection, glorification, and eschatological mission, purposes, and will—to the glory of God the Father.

There is a strong concern for ecumenical relationships in Zizioulas's writings, and it is clear that he endeavors to cultivate ecumenical dialogue and understanding. For Zizioulas, the universality of the church complements its localized expressions and is an indispensable part of it.[66] When churches come together, a "network of communion of churches"[67] is the ideal, rather than a new form of church. Such networks commune through prayer and worship, and a shared vision of the gospel and the reign of Christ. Structures and gatherings are to be developed that facilitate such cooperation. Denominational groups (Orthodox, Catholic, Anglican, Baptist, etc.) are para-church entities and not truly churches. Confessional pluralism has unfortunately added a real problem to the complete ecclesiality of local churches in the present age. This problem, laments Zizioulas, is not easily solved; however, it is of "extreme importance to the ecumenical movement."[68] Zizioulas describes the inextricable relationship between local community and catholicity, and profoundly values Christian ministry and the role of the bishop. There is a discernable desire to heal confessional tension and to open fuller ecumenical dialogue. He acknowledges the interrelation between locality and universality in the expressions of the church. Relationality and community are underscored in all descriptions of missionary endeavor, ministry office, personal discipleship, and Christian community. Furthermore, Zizioulas's ecclesiology is deeply pneumatological. He strongly asserts that while Christ *institutes* the church, the Spirit *constitutes* it, and empowers it for mission and service.

While I find much of Zizioulas's ecclesiology compelling, I have two further reservations. The first, and this should not be surprising given my Free Church background, is with his hierarchical understandings of church governance, even if he frames these perspectives relationally. The second is the store he places in correctly comprehending the nature of God in order to appreciate the nature of human personhood and the church.

65. Volf, *After Our Likeness*, 92–94.

66. Jesson, "Orthodox Contributions," 18.

67. Zizioulas, *Being as Communion*, 258.

68. Ibid., 259–60.

While I am aware that such ontological arguments are critical to Zizioulas's ecclesiology, I am not persuaded it is possible to comprehend fully the nature or *being* of God. Jonathan Draper has similar reservations and writes, "I am not entirely convinced that it is possible to have, as a fundamental position, as Zizioulas insists we must have, 'a correct vision . . . (of) the being of God'. Perhaps I subscribe overmuch to Luther's prescriptions about the *Theologia gloriae*, and find the Thomist *via negativa* too compelling, to believe a 'correct vision' is attainable: perhaps 'more or less correct' would be more plausible."[69]

Ecclesiology and mission, in Zizioulas's writings, are interwoven. They are both built on the notion of *being as communion*. According to Miroslav Volf, Zizioulas's "*communio*-ecclesiology is based on an ontology of person acquired from a consideration of the nature of the Triune God."[70] Communion within the person of the Trinity is the paradigm for human communion and all possible communions within the church. Deindividualization and personalization are made possible within the communion of the church and through the salvific grace of God. Communion among the people of God is manifest in the Eucharist, which, according to Zizioulas, is the central point of all deindividualized and fully realized personhood. The Eucharist is the locus in which Christ constitutes the church, in a Spirit-mediated way. Zizioulas is convinced that the church can be found in all its completeness in the event of the Eucharist. This eucharistic ecclesiology determines Zizioulas's understandings of institution, bishop, laity, ministry, apostolicity, and other forms of church governance and structure.

QUESTIONS FOR REFLECTION

1. A key concept in Zizioulas's ecclesiology is *being as communion*. Why does Zizioulas believe that "there is no true being without communion"?

2. What difference would it make if Christology and pneumatology were treated equally in our understanding of the church?

3. Zizioulas writes that in the context of the Christian community, ministries and their associated structures have at least fourteen concrete qualities. Are there any ideas in this list that grab your attention, and why?

69. Draper, "Being as Communion," 401.

70. Volf, *After Our Likeness*, 75.

Protestant

7

Letty Russell:
The Church as Household of Freedom

*'Church in the Round' describes a community of faith and struggle working
to anticipate God's New Creation by becoming partners with those who are
at the margins of church and society. The metaphor (of the church as a round
table) speaks of people gathered around the table and in the world in order to
connect faith and life in action/reflection (the round table), work for justice
in solidarity with those at the margins of society (the kitchen table), and to
welcome everyone as partners in God's world house (the welcome table).[1]*

—Letty Russell

FEMINIST, LIBERATION ECCLESIOLOGY

Letty Russell's ecclesiology is a feminist, liberation ecclesiology, *from below.*
While her ecclesiological perspectives can be discerned in a wide range of her books
and articles, her most complete treatment of ecclesiology is in her book *Church in the
Round.* In that book, she uses the metaphor of a round table to describe the church. The
church, as round table, is a place of sharing, hospitality, and relationship. It is a table

---

1. Russell, *Church in the Round,* 12. Letty Russell (1929 to 2007) served the East Harlem Protestant
Parish in New York from 1952 to 1968, and pastored the Presbyterian church of the Ascension during much
of that time. She began teaching theology at Yale Divinity School, New Haven, Connecticut, in 1974, and was
Professor of Theology there from 1985 to 2001.

where the oppressed and the powerful, the female and the male, and the disregarded and the esteemed, can meet each other in a spirit of hospitality, mutuality, equality, and respect. It is a table where people participate in mutual learning through action/reflection methodology and through authentic human connection: connecting with each other's experience of faith and life, connecting with and reinterpreting theological, biblical, and church traditions, and connecting as genuine honor is given to those who have been marginalized because of gender, sexuality, socio-economic status, politics or ethnicity. It is a table where God is the host, and the great diversity of those gathered represent the extent of his invitation and hospitality, *and* the eschatological gathering of all of God's people to banquet at his table. It is a table that reflects the hospitality of Christ, as he reached out to the marginalized of his culture, and as he reaches out to humanity at the cross. Russell grounds the metaphor in the images of table in the New Testament and in Christology. She writes that,

> To speak of "the church in the round" is to provide a metaphorical description of a church struggling to become a household of freedom, a community where walls have been broken down so that God's welcome to those who hunger and thirst for justice is clear. This unknown reality is described in terms of what we have all experienced: gathering in the round, with or without tables, and experiencing the welcome of others.[2]

According to Russell, the church and its practices, structures, language, leadership, spirituality, and so forth, need to be interpreted through the lens of the marginalized and the excluded, not in a spirit of confrontation, but of dialogue, relationship, and mutual learning. The women's movement, for example, challenges the existing "patriarchal interpretation of ecclesiology" and offers "alternative ways of reconstructing tradition and church structures." Russell then proceeds to suggest that her primary concern is not gender issues per se, but the application of feminist theology to the contemporary interpretation and practices of the church, as a "constructive formulation of some of the changes needed in ecclesiology."[3] Feminist ecclesiology examines the church on its hospitality, its openness to the marginalized and excluded in society, and its commitment to justice and liberation. In a concise summary of feminist theological outlook, and relating this back to her guiding metaphor, Russell asserts that,

> *The critical principle of feminist ecclesiology is a table principle.* It looks for ways that God reaches out to include all those whom society and religion have declared outsiders and invites them to gather round God's table of hospitality.[4]

This argument is supported in Russell's writings with reference to feminist and liberation theologians, and she suggests that the church needs to reread its tradition and Scriptures from the margins and from particular contexts. Each marginal story will be unique, since it is located in a specific context, and so it will bring a particular contribution. The table talk that Russell describes occurs in a spiral of *commitment* to action, dia-

2. Ibid.
3. Ibid., 14.
4. Ibid., 25; Russell, "Hot-House Ecclesiology," 54–55.

logue, and learning, *sharing experiences* of struggle in particular contexts, *critical analysis* of the context and nature of those experiences, *questions* about established biblical and church traditions, and *further action, celebration, and reflection*. For Russell this process of action/reflection is a *"continuing theological spiral,"* since it does not merely happen once, but is a continual process of learning which, in turn, modifies the process. Russell believes that such action/reflection methodology is critical for robust ecclesiological reflection, for solidarity with the marginalized, for "talking back" to church tradition, and for the reinterpretation and renewal of church leadership, structures, and mission.[5] It is a form of *open ecclesiology* that begins with God's actions, mission, and eschatological purposes.[6] It then moves on to the implications of these things for our theological understandings of the church and for the practical structures of the church. This open stance toward God, the world, the other, the margins, the future, and to dialogue, has the potential to renew ecclesiological reflection and ministry models.[7] She calls her ecclesiology *feminist/liberation ecclesiology*, since it is committed to liberation for all those who are marginalized, including women.[8]

BIBLICAL INTERPRETATION AND INCLUSIVE LANGUAGE

In her introductions to two edited works on feminist biblical interpretation, Russell asserts that the Scriptures have the potential to liberate men and women, but that they first need to be liberated from established forms of "sexist interpretation" and their own "patriarchal bias."[9] Russell's feminist/liberation ecclesiology demands that the Scriptures be liberated from oppressive interpretations in the church, which she believes are as much about the domination of the marginal as they are about gender, and which she believes are endemic in the church. Employing and mining the experiences and insights of women throughout the world, and especially from the Majority World and other contexts where women suffer socio-economic, political, and gender domination, Russell writes that she has arrived at the following conclusion:

> From this perspective the Bible needs to be liberated from its captivity to one-sided white, middle-class, male interpretation. It needs liberation from privatized and spiritualized interpretations that avoid God's concern for justice, human wholeness, and ecological responsibility; it needs liberation from abstract, doctrinal interpretations that remove the biblical narrative from its concrete social and political context in order to change it into timeless truth.[10]

The statement and its context afford us some valuable insights into Russell's approach to biblical interpretation, that is, her feminist/liberation hermeneutics.[11] She is committed

5. Russell, *Church in the Round*, 29–45; Russell, "Hot-House Ecclesiology," 51–52.

6. Henson, "Letty Russell," 111.

7. Russell, *Human Liberation*, 155–82.

8. Russell, *Church in the Round*, 43.

9. Russell, *Feminist Interpretation*, 11; Russell, *Liberating Word*, 14.

10. Russell, *Feminist Interpretation*, 12. This is one of the reasons why I see the need for a subsequent volume dealing with Majority World perspectives.

11. Ibid., 13–17.

to interpretation of the Scriptures that is dialogical, particular and contextual, ethnically diverse, from below, unchained from the worst aspects of class and gender, practiced in community, related to real life issues, enabled by action/reflection processes, and concerned for justice, wholeness, and creation. There is a dual emphasis on the personal and particular on the one hand, and the broader context on the other (political, economic, gender, social, ethnic, and the like).

The challenges to such interpretation are significant, writes Russell, since the biblical texts have such evident patriarchal bias, and, therefore, "the issue continues to be whether the biblical message can continue to evoke consent in spite of its patriarchal captivity."[12] Such hermeneutics raise questions about the nature of biblical and ecclesial authority, and whether any Scripture that is deemed "sexist" can be acknowledged as authoritative. This hermeneutic is self-consciously establishing feminist and liberation criteria for authority in the Christian faith, and is pursuing a hermeneutical model "rooted in the concrete particularities of oppression and liberation, such as those expressed by Jewish feminist writers and writers from Black, Hispanic, and Asian perspectives." Russell proceeds to argue that "the Word of God is not identical with the biblical texts," that is, the biblical texts only become the word of God when they are experienced contextually as a living "witness to God's love for the world." Authority, contends Russell, should not be abstract or dominating, but relational, contextual, fluid, and partnering.[13] Evangelical readers will undoubtedly be troubled by Russell's location of interpretive authority in each individual community and their positive or negative experience of the Scriptures.[14] The essays by the contributors to the book *Feminist Interpretation of the Bible* seek to deal with such questions emerging from feminist/liberation hermeneutics.

Russell describes how feminist biblical interpretation is concerned with both *inclusive interpretation* and *inclusive language*. Inclusive biblical interpretation is complemented by research into inclusive biblical, theological, liturgical, pastoral, and homiletical language. Inclusive language affirms women "as fully human partners with men, sharing the image of God."[15] Such hospitality is partially aimed at confronting and refuting oppressive patriarchal power structures in society and church, which are often embodied in language. Russell suggests a wide range of practical ways the church and theological discourse can be more inclusive.[16]

A HOUSEHOLD OF FREEDOM: LEADERSHIP, STRUCTURE, AND PARTNERSHIP

The metaphor of the church as round table requires a style of leadership that is functional, contextual, and relational, rather than hierarchical, exclusivist, or gender-defined.

12. Ibid., 12.

13. Ibid., 137–46; Russell, *Imitators of God*, 11–13.

14. Russell, *Feminist Interpretation*, 16–17; Russell, "Beginning from the Other End," 98–101; Russell, "Feminist Critique," 68–71.

15. Russell, *Feminist Interpretation*, 13; Russell, *Liberating Word*, 16–18.

16. Russell, *Liberating Word*, 82–98; Russell, "Inclusive Language," 583–98. See Moore's response in "Inclusive Language and Power."

Russell challenges "theological doctrines of hierarchical divine order," which serve to justify patriarchal hierarchies through what Russell deems to be theologies of domination. She believes that traditional ordination practices reinforce aggressive and hierarchical structures of domination and exclusion.[17] Russell's ecclesiological vision is one of relational and functional leadership and structures that empower and commission all Christians for ministry, and that are characterized by a spirit of service. According to Russell, the antidote to structures of exclusion and hierarchy is not merely to have more women and other marginalized persons ordained; it is to reconceive and dismantle such oppressive structures altogether. She questioned her own ordination, because of her view that ordination is rooted in such power structures, her concern that it does not reflect the values of Scripture, and her acknowledgment that it has often harmed or disenfranchised those on the margins of the church. She remained ordained because of the effort it took her to overcome obstacles to ordination, and because of the opportunities she has to model a different kind of ministry and leadership. She also remained ordained because of the symbolic value. Her ordination represented her triumph over "the old patriarchal orders of ordination" and her solidarity with all those who have been denied ordination "because of their sex and sexual orientation . . . I do not view ordination as an indelible order, and whether to remain a clergyperson continues to be an open question for me and for many others."[18]

For Russell, leadership, ordination, and other ministerial structures and practices need to be reconceived as functional, flat, dynamic, changing, contextual, gift-oriented, and dedicated to humble service. She believes that such characteristics threaten existing power structures and models of ministry, and emerge both from Scripture as well as from women's emphasis on relationship, their "enculturation as nurturers", and greater concern for relationships rather than functions.[19] Feminist approaches to leadership emphasize partnership and mutuality, charismatic gifting, and contextual, empowering, functional, servanthood approaches.[20] For models of how such leadership would look in practice, Russell turns to Jesus's leadership style in the Gospels, to the example and inclusion of women leaders in Scripture, and to examples of contemporary women in ministry.[21]

Drawing hope from God's eschatological future, Russell's dream is for the church to be a *household of freedom* in which the present patriarchal structures, theologies, and languages of domination are replaced by God's eschatological freedom, equality, and partnership. Instead of Christian leadership and authority being used as patriarchal tools for domination, Russell's feminist/liberation ecclesiology demands a use of spiritual authority characterized by *partnership* and "*empowerment* for self-actualization together with others."[22]

---

17. Russell, *Church in the Round*, 46–54.

18. Ibid., 53–54.

19. Ibid., 52.

20. Russell, "Renewal in the Churches," 333–38; Russell, *Inheriting Our Mothers' Gardens*, 150–55.

21. Russell, *Church in the Round*, 58–74; Russell, *Becoming Human*, 23–26.

22. Russell, *Household of Freedom*, 21–41, 61; Russell, "Impossible-Possibility," 76.

Employing the New Testament idea of *oikos* (house), and the metaphor of the church as a *household of freedom*, Russell portrays God as the divine housekeeper who cultivates a household (the church) that is characterized by equality and a community of genuine partnership.[23] Occasionally using *partnership* and *koinonia* interchangeably, she defines partnership as "a new focus on relationship in Jesus Christ that sets us free for others . . . a two-sided relationship of giving or receiving, participation or community (1 Cor 10:16–17)."[24] This partnership with God transcends human sexuality. Christ demonstrates to us the possibilities of human partnership, as he partners with others as our Lord, servant, and liberator. A theology of partnership needs to be developed eschatologically, rooted in the life of Jesus, and grounded in the struggle for partnership in concrete, particular settings. The church goes through "advent shock or maladjustment with the present because of a longed-for future," and seeks ways to include all people "as full participants and welcomed into partnership in service."[25] Because of its eschatological vision the church must develop concrete expressions of partnership in light of "the other end"—God's new creation that is being revealed in the present. Taking her cues from Barth, Moltmann, and Johannes Metz, Russell's eschatology is *adventological*, understanding the future "as the *new* that is coming into history."[26] God's people live in the new creation now, in the now-but-not-yet dialectic of the new age, and, consequently, must embrace the fullness of *koinonia* in contrast to the present oppressive relationships or systems in the church and society.

When applied to leadership, church structures, and theological education, such partnership in God's *oikos* is characteristic of a *household of freedom*, where relationships are equal and dynamic, structures are functional and empowering, and authority is freely given and dispersed.[27] In *Growth in Partnership*, which was a follow-up work to *The Future of Partnership*, Russell focuses on educating for partnership—"a process of actualizing and modifying the development of the total person in and through dialogical relationships."[28] She asserts that such a holistic educational approach can break down the power structures in the church, provide an alternative to the professionalization of ministry, and cultivate authentic, transformative partnerships.[29]

Russell attempts to ground the concept of partnership in the cultivation of holistic educational and learning communities, in participatory forms of ministry, and in theological reflection as anticipation of God's great final reversal. She also discusses ways to encourage solidarity between oppressors and the oppressed, exploring how to foster the conscientization (critical consciousness) of the oppressed, and proposing how to enable churches and individual Christians to learn from and connect with the marginalized. In short, partnership in Christian leadership, ecclesial structures, and faith communities is encouraged through educational strategies, but, ultimately, "we learn through entering

23. Russell, *Household of Freedom*, 25–26.

24. Ibid., 92.

25. Russell, *Future of Partnership*, 103 (see the whole section 17–120).

26. Ibid., 170.

27. Russell, *Household of Freedom*, 82–99; Russell, "Good Housekeeping," 225–38; Russell, "Clerical Ministry," 126.

28. Russell, *Growth in Partnership*, 59.

29. Ibid.

into the process of partnership itself," and change happens when communities move forward courageously, sacrificially, and purposefully.[30]

SOLIDARITY, LIBERATION, AND POSTCOLONIAL MISSION

In Part Two of *Church in the Round*, Russell continues her metaphor of the church as round table and moves on to discuss what she calls *kitchen table solidarity*. Russell is especially concerned to see the church express solidarity and engage in dialogue with the marginalized and excluded in society and church. She describes how particular faith communities are taking up this challenge, working against oppressive social forces. She attends to the voices of those who are marginalized, as well as the voices of those who stand in solidarity with them, in order to ask penetrating questions of the church's theology and structures.[31]

Russell uses the themes of *kairos* (the right and opportune moment or place, or opportune time of crisis) and *jubilee* (liberation of those who are oppressed or burdened) to describe how liberating faith communities see themselves and their ministries.[32] Analyzing a number of forms of Protestantism in the United States, including the mega, mainstream, and mainline churches, Russell turns to particular marginal faith communities, and streams of liberation and renewal, for inspiration. These include liberation, mission, and feminist theologies, and renewed, basic, and feminist communities. She uses these as examples of churches and streams that are seeking to ground the biblical notions of kairos and jubilee in their ecclesiology and practice. They do this in their efforts toward justice and by embracing the marginalized, welcoming the stranger, practicing hospitality, flattening out their leadership and ecclesial structures, and joining with the oppressed in genuine acts of solidarity. The three central themes she draws out of these examples is the missionary and liberation nature of the church, the value of hospitality in creating welcoming communities, and the need to nurture spiritualities of connection.[33]

In Russell's writings it is clear that she is convinced that feminist and liberation ecclesiologies have the potential to reshape our traditional understandings of the nature of the church. She believes that the traditional notions of the church "as a place of salvation, as a sign of Christ's presence, and as a community of word and sacrament" can be reconceived through the perspective of "men and women who suffer from unjust structures related to their sexual orientation, race, gender, class, and so much more." The perspectives and struggles of these women and men witness to the Spirit of Christ as he forms the church, and calls the churches "to become communities of faith, compassion, and justice."[34] Russell modifies the saying "no salvation outside the church" to "no salvation outside the poor," and suggests that this is the case because this is where Christ promises to be present. Moreover, by separating issues of injustice from issues of personal sin, and

---

30. Ibid., 12.

31. Russell, *Church in the Round*, 76–77.

32. Ibid., 80–82.

33. Ibid., 75–111.

34. Ibid., 113.

by encouraging Christians to be "of, but not in, the world," many churches are committing a *double sin* that is eroding their witness and polluting their discipleship to Christ.[35] To the four signs of the church (one, holy, catholic, and apostolic), Russell adds a fifth, *just*, since for her it is impossible to conceive of the church without justice. She also qualifies the Reformation marks of the church in the light of feminist and liberation ecclesiology and argues that, when conceived rightly, these marks can contribute to justice.[36]

Postcolonial perspectives on mission also occupy Russell's theology. She examines colonial approaches and attitudes to mission, including the ways in which women and men participated in oppressive practices, but also postcolonial strategies of interpretation of mission and ecclesiology. Such postcolonial, cultural hermeneutics challenge the churches throughout the world to consider contextual forms of partnership, inclusion, and hospitality, and to consider how best to deal with the legacies or the remaining structures of domination in church life. Postcolonial interpretation engages in the tasks of *analysis* of the past and the present, *resistance* to ongoing forms of oppression, and *reconstruction* of a preferred, hopeful, indigenous future.[37] It provides a "critique and reconstruction" of existing theologies and practices of mission, ethics, and church, explores the "poetics of location," seeks to liberate those who suffer from ongoing oppression, listens to the voice of the other, and invites people to *God's welcome table*. Authentic liberation and mission are inseparable. "Evangelization is a *praxis* of liberation, for it is in the doing and telling of the Good News of Jesus Christ that we are set free."[38] Russell believes that the church has much to learn from postcolonial mission and theology.[39]

HOSPITALITY AND SPIRITUALITY

In the final two chapters of *Church in the Round* Russell turns her attention to the doctrine of election, the notion of Christian hospitality, and the development of a "spirituality of connection." As we have already seen, partnership is a primary theme in Russell's ecclesiology. In her opinion, authentic partnership in the church can act as an antidote to exclusivity and domination in the church. Contrary to such reconciling partnerships, the doctrine of election has been often used as a tool to support and justify oppression, exclusion, elitism, and patriarchy. Her feminist, liberation theology, however, views election as "situation-variable," that is, not only applied by God in a situationally variable manner, but also needing to be contextually interpreted. According to Russell, Scripture teaches us that God elects the oppressed, broken, and excluded. God's hospitality needs to be reflected in the church. God forms the church not based on an election of the privileged and powerful few, but as a richly diverse hospitable people who demonstrate authentic unity in diversity. Hospitality is the key to the formation of churches that are wonder-

35. Ibid., 119–27; Russell, "Justice," 18–19.

36. Russell, *Church with AIDS*, 135–45.

37. Russell, "Cultural Hermeneutics," 23–25.

38. Russell, "Liberation and Evangelization," 130.

39. Russell, "Cultural Hermeneutics," 25–40; Russell, "God, Gold, Glory and Gender"; Russell, "Affirming Cross-Cultural Diversity"; Russell, "Moving from Can't Do"; Russell et al., *Just Hospitality*, 23–51.

fully diverse yet deeply united. Instead of dominating others and demanding conformity, hospitality "creates a safe and welcoming space for persons to find their own sense of humanity and worth."[40]

Finally, Russell explores the ways in which feminist spirituality is about connection with the marginal, the broken, and the disdained. She discusses how such a spirituality of relationship can be sustained and nurtured through *synergy* with other people's gifts and personalities, through rediscovering *serendipity*, that is, joyful surprise when truly meeting, connecting, and standing in solidarity with another, and through *sharing* as an act of partnership with those near and far (literally and metaphorically). It is a spirituality of partnership, hospitality, and inclusivity, welcoming people into God's *household of freedom*.[41]

CONTRIBUTIONS TO MISSIONAL ECCLESIOLOGY

Russell's feminist/liberation ecclesiology contains many perspectives that benefit the maturation of missional ecclesiology. These include her insights into the nature of mission among the margins of society, the development of missionary and liberation structures, the ways in which the church can authentically express the priesthood of all believers, and the need for diversity and hospitality in the church's structures, language, cultures, and leadership.[42] Russell uses the metaphor of a *round table* to examine what it means for the church to be a community of partnership, hospitality, justice, equality, and welcome. The metaphor of the round table describes a table where all kinds of people meet as equals for fellowship, partnership, dialogue, and solidarity with each other, and especially with the marginalized. She also uses the metaphor of the church as a *household of freedom*, with God as the divine housekeeper who develops a church of genuine welcome and partnership (*koinonia*). Both of these metaphors provide fresh insight into the nature of the church, and the way in which the church can witness to the kingdom of God and engage in actions of solidarity and justice.

Russell's approach to ecclesial change is educational, and she particularly emphasizes dialogical learning through action/reflection methodology and through authentic interpersonal, interdependent partnership. While dealing with feminist issues, her focus is not only on gender matters per se, but on justice and liberation for all those who are excluded and treated inhospitably in church and society, including women. She challenges what she considers patriarchal and oppressive systems, structures, practices, and relationships in the church, and believes that the best way for these to be renewed is through dialogue and partnership, as these ecclesial dynamics are reinterpreted through the eyes of the marginalized. These challenges are prophetic for the church and afford us insight into how marginal groups, and many women for that matter, experience the church today, and might be more genuinely included. Some church planters or missionary innovators might

---

40. Russell, *Church in the Round*, 173; Russell, "Practicing Hospitality"; Russell, "Toward a Trinitarian Language."

41. Russell, *Church in the Round*, 182–208.

42. She features in chapter 14 in *Part Two* of this book.

consider themselves more progressive than the patriarchal systems Russell critiques—but it remains the case the most missional conferences and seminars in western countries are headlined by white, middle-aged, university educated, ecclesially employed males. Where are the voices from the margins of this dominant culture? Even in so-called progressive circles race, social status, gender, education, and theological and linguistic conformity are central to the culture and leadership of gatherings (even when the rhetoric suggests otherwise), and this form of structural complacency mitigates against the hospitality and diversity described in Russell's writings.

Issues of biblical interpretation, inclusive language, and sources of theological authority are also dealt with in Russell's writings. Feminist hermeneutics demands inclusive interpretation and inclusive language. Russell argues that the Scriptures can liberate people, but only if those Scriptures are freed from what she considers sexist interpretations and their own patriarchal bias. She suggests that when biblical texts are experienced contextually as a living "witness to God's love for the world," they become the word of God. According to Russell, biblical authority does not reside in timeless and abstract propositions and texts, but in the experience of those texts in particular locations and cultures, in a charismatic, relational, contextual, liberating encounter with God in the text. This understanding of authority as residing in the interpretation and *experience of the text by individual communities*, and especially those who struggle with oppression or impoverishment, is central to Russell's feminist hermeneutics. She rejects biblical texts that she considers patriarchal or reflective of patriarchal culture, and uses *liberation* and *partnership* as hermeneutical guides (or as hermeneutical sources of authority).[43] Russell's approach to hermeneutics and to sources of authority in the Christian life is problematic for evangelicals, for while the experiences of individual communities can afford fresh insights into Scripture and faith, surely interpretive and ethical authority cannot merely or exclusively reside in that realm. There must be a source of authority that is greater than the experience of particular communities, if their interpretations are to be meaningful or open to evaluation.

Russell challenges particular approaches to the doctrine of election. She also questions what she considers "theological doctrines of hierarchical divine order." For her, the former serve to exclude marginal groups from faith and participation, and the later reinforces hierarchical and patriarchal systems of leadership. While one cannot help but be sympathetic to the issues that Russell is dealing with, it is difficult not to conclude that she too readily, and too superficially, dismisses theological concepts or biblical texts that are contrary to her feminist theology. She seems to dismiss them as oppressive, without adequately dealing with their theological constructs or biblical supports. She calls for an approach to ministry that is functional, contextual, relational, open to both sexes, and inclusive of all groups, including various sexual orientations. Pastorally, it is easy to empathize with her demand for the inclusion of both genders and various sexual orientations in ministry, given the ostracization and aggression these groups have experienced. One needs to go back to the biblical text, however, as a source of authority that is greater

43. Köstenberger, *Jesus and the Feminists*, 69.

than the experience of these particular groups, to build a case for or against this demand. Russell's dismissal of texts that she deems patriarchal or oppressive makes it difficult for her to claim that she has done the substantial biblical analysis that is necessary to come to a valid or supportable conclusion. John Webster is rightly concerned about the approaches of such hermeneutics, and another critique of such theologies can be found in the work of Anthony Thiselton.[44] However, Letty Russell's passion for moving the church toward solidarity with the oppressed and the marginalized in society and church, lest it commit the *double sin* of separating issues of injustice from issues of personal sin, that is, of promoting faith that is "of, but not in, the world," is laudable.

QUESTIONS FOR REFLECTION

1. What does Russell mean by the metaphor of the church as a *round table*? Do you feel comfortable with this metaphor?

2. Why does Russell believe that the church's nature and practices should be interpreted through the eyes of the marginalized, oppressed, and excluded? How would these groups experience your church?

3. What is the *double sin* of the church? Why are some Christians "of, but not in, the world," and what do we do about this?

---

44. Webster, *Confessing God*; Webster, *Word and Church*; Thiselton, *New Horizons in Hermeneutics*.

8

Jürgen Moltmann:
The Church as Messianic, Relational *Koinonia*

The name the church gives itself—the church of Jesus Christ—requires us to see Christ as the subject of his church and to bring the church's life into alignment with him. Thus, ecclesiology can only be developed from Christology, as its consequence and in correspondence to it.[1]

—JÜRGEN MOLTMANN

MESSIANIC ECCLESIOLOGY

JÜRGEN MOLTMANN REFUSES TO call his works a *dogmatics* or a *dogmatic thesis*, since such terms indicate a closed or completed system of thought, no longer open to correction or dialogue. Instead, Moltmann sees his books as *contributions to theology*, developed in a spirit of theological and ecumenical dialogue, with a willingness to be assessed, rejected, or modified, and with a genuine recognition of the limitations of his personhood and position as a theologian. This open, dialogical, exploratory stance characterizes Moltmann's spirituality, ecumenical contributions, writing, and theological method. He views such a posture as necessary when placing oneself "beneath the cross."[2]

While Moltmann's ecclesiological thought is not limited to one book, his primary ecclesiological work is *The Church in the Power of the Spirit*. Moltmann recognizes that the church is in crisis as it seeks to relate to a changing cultural, global, pluralistic landscape. The church might respond by withdrawal and retreat from the world on the one hand, or unreflective opportunism and accommodation on the other. Neither of these responses is

---

1. Moltmann, *Church in the Power of the Spirit*, 66. Jürgen Moltmann was Professor of Systematic Theology at the University of Tübingen from 1967 to 1994, and while at Tübingen, he served as the Robert W. Woodruff Distinguished Visiting Professor of Systematic Theology at Chandler School of Theology, Emory University, Atlanta, Georgia (1983 to 1993).

2. Moltmann, *Trinity and the Kingdom*, xi–xvi. See Moltmann, "Ecumenism Beneath the Cross: I"; Moltmann, "Ecumenism Beneath the Cross: II."

satisfactory. In uncertain times the church needs to go back to its roots, writes Moltmann, taking its "bearings from its foundation, its future and the charge given to it."[3]

Moltmann calls his ecclesiology *messianic* and *relational*. He uses the terms messianic and christological interchangeably, and it is the christological aspects of his ecclesiology that we turn to first. While Hopko writes exuberantly about the church, Moltmann tends to reserve such adulation for Christ, and then move out from that christological praise and attention to ecclesiology. If there is an outstanding and dominant theological foundation in Moltmann's ecclesiology, it is the idea that the church's foundation, essence, power, mission, and future are built on and directed toward Jesus Christ. Christ alone is the defining source and Lord of the church. "Christ is his church's foundation, its power and its hope . . . The lordship of Christ is the church's sole, and hence all-embracing, determining factor. It can neither be shared nor restricted."[4] Moltmann asserts that not only must the church's ecclesiology cohere with its structure, practices, and politics (in other words, the *doctrina de ecclesia* must be consistent with the *politia ecclesiastica*); they must be interrelated in a spirit of submission, glorification, and witness to Christ. All worthwhile ecclesiology is formed christologically, and the church's essence depends "on its Christology."[5] The church's nature, theology, practical forms, and fellowships exist to glorify and testify to him, and to keep each other true to that purpose.[6]

Ecclesiology emerges from our understanding of who Christ is and our appreciation of his eschatological activities in human history, in the present state of the world, and in the world's eschatological future. The church exists within the ongoing drama of the tension between its social and cultural contexts on the one hand, and what Christ is doing in human history on the other. It is called to be attentive to both of these in its effort to submit to the Spirit of Christ, but there are times when it appears alien and foreign to the world, as it embraces "the strangeness of his mission, his cross and his promise." Moltmann writes,

> It is only when the church is alienated from its environment in Christ's way, that it can perceive and show in an alienated world that the kingdom of God which Christ has promised is our home . . . It will then be drawn into his mission: the messianic liberation of those who are imprisoned in its present day. It will then be drawn into his destiny of passion and bear its cross. It will then return to his future and answer for its hope.[7]

The church's identity and purpose is wrapped up in the messianic mission of Christ. It worships and takes its form as a reflection of the Christ of the Gospels and the broader Christian Scriptures, but it also witnesses to his eschatological mission. "The crucified and risen Christ represents this future of history in his person and in his whole suffering and

---

3. Moltmann, *Church in the Power of the Spirit*, xi–xii.

4. Ibid., 5.

5. Moltmann, "Crucified God: A Trinitarian Theology," 280.

6. Moltmann, *Church in the Power of the Spirit*, 6–7, 66.

7. Ibid., 68.

activity."[8] Moltmann contends that the church's mission is to pursue the mission of Christ, being caught up in his eschatological purposes for humanity and the universe, heralding and witnessing to his kingdom. This will inevitably lead it into conflict with the oppressive and opposing powers, as its conducts a ministry of liberation, and demonstrates to the world the world's transfigured, liberated form. The church is the *eschatological exodus* or the *exodus church*, demonstrating to the world what it means to depart from bondage into God's eschatological hope and future, that is, into the freedom and transformation of Christ. As "the social form of hope," the church reveals to the world what the world looks like when it submits to the gospel and kingdom of Christ, that is, the world in its unshackled, transformed, and redeemed condition.[9]

According to Moltmann, the church not only embraces the messianic mission, it is also defined by the passion of Christ and, therefore, is *the community of the Cross*. It is characterized by the cross and stands "beneath the cross."[10] In practice, this means that the church witnesses to Christ's reconciliation and liberation in its concrete engagement with the world, and especially with the oppressed, marginalized, poor, broken, handicapped, imprisoned, and the like. Following its Lord, the church will confront inhumanity and oppression, resist idolatry and power, and, in a spirit of hope, proclaim God's eschatological future.[11] Submission to Christ's lordship in this way, in the life of the church, is paralleled by the church's joyous, celebratory "feast without end."[12] Moltmann views this relationship between freedom through obedience to Christ's lordship and joyous celebration of the resurrection, freedom, and hope of Christ, as important. The individual and the church should know the wonder of submitting to the will and future of Christ's lordship, and the exuberant festivities of Christ's freedom, glory, friendship, and hope.[13] Both individuals and communities of faith should cultivate a messianic lifestyle, which is expressed through witnessing to Christ and his gospel in their eschatological hope, passionate prayer and contemplation, messianic peace and nonviolence, ecological and political action, christological ethics, and solidarity with the downtrodden.[14]

Moltmann claims that the correct way to discern *where* the church resides is to ask the question, "Where does Christ assure us that he can be found?" *Ubi Christus, ibi ecclesia* means, "Where Christ is, there is also the church," and is attributed to Ignatius of Antioch.[15] This approach, which is adopted by Moltmann, is an alternative to focusing on the traditional *marks of the church*, or on *ubi ecclesia, ibi Christus*, which means, "Where the church is, there is also Christ." Moltmann turns to the New Testament and demonstrates how Christ promises to be found in three arenas. Firstly, Christ promises to be found in the apostolate, sacraments, and community life of his people; secondly, among

8. Ibid., 74.

9. Ibid., 68–85; Moltmann, *Future of Creation*, 108.

10. Moltmann, *Church in the Power of the Spirit*, 85, 89; Moltmann, *Open Church*, 82–94.

11. Moltmann, *Church in the Power of the Spirit*, 97.

12. Moltmann, *Open Church*, 64–81.

13. Moltmann, *Church in the Power of the Spirit*, 108–21.

14. Moltmann, *Open Church*, 37–49; Moltmann, *Way of Jesus Christ*, 116–35.

15. Moltmann, *Church in the Power of the Spirit*, 122.

the poor, marginalized, rejected, broken, disregarded, and thirsty and hungry;[16] thirdly, in his Parousia, and, it should be noted, the first two arenas are shaped by this eschatological orientation. The church's nature, ministries, and location are united around "these three modes of [Christ's] promised presence. It will find the place of its truth in this field. If it omits any one of these promises of Christ's presence, its truth will be obscured."[17]

The church's messianic and relational theological foundations, its sole dependency on Jesus Christ, its eschatological hope, and its missiological mandate, anchor the church against the tide of change and set its course and bearings. Therefore, the church needs a dynamic ecclesiology, and Moltmann's primary *practical* goal in writing an ecclesiology is to encourage ecclesial reform. The transformation that is needed, according to Moltmann, is from an institutional, self-concerned organization, to a congregationally centered, spiritually alive, voluntary, charismatic, fellowshipping, missionary, messianic church. He is particularly interested in releasing the whole congregation to ministry and mission, and in seeing men and women participate equally in the renewal of the church.[18] The church belongs to God, and understands its past, present, and future in the light of the eschatological hope granted to it by God. The church is an *open church*, existing in dynamic relationship with God, humanity, and the future. Moltmann observes, "The church atrophies when it surrenders any one of these opennesses and closes itself up against God, men or the future."[19]

RELATIONAL, TRINITARIAN FOUNDATIONS

Moltmann's ecclesiology is *messianic, relational,* and *trinitarian.* When Moltmann describes the church as relational, he means that the church's nature, mission, functions, and future can only be understood in their relationship to other things. This includes the church's relationship to the eschatological history of Christ, the social and cultural contexts in which the church finds itself located, the trinitarian nature and mission of God, and the living connection and submission it has to Jesus Christ. The church's meaning and function, writes Moltmann, can only be understood in the light of such relational dynamics. Moreover, the church's essence is determined by its relationships with Christology, eschatology, and the mission and doctrine of God, "that is, from insight into the trinitarian history of God's dealings with the world." Moltmann is convinced of the value of such a relational ecclesiology, even if it does not afford "the nature or the concept of the church with a ready-made definition."[20]

The "church's mission and its meaning, existence and functions" can only be fully appreciated in light of the "trinitarian history of God," or, in other words, "the history of God's dealings with the world."[21] The church's relationship to God's reconciling movement in history forms its nature and purpose, writes Moltmann. The church stands within the

16. Moltmann, *Open Church,* 102–7.

17. Moltmann, *Church in the Power of the Spirit,* 121–32.

18. Ibid., xiii–xxiii.

19. Ibid., 2.

20. Ibid., 19–20.

21. Ibid., 50.

history of Christ, within the history of God's trinitarian movement in the world, and while it is an important dimension of God's eschatological purposes, it is only one historical agent in God's movement.[22] Moltmann describes the trinitarian mission of the redemption and reconciliation of humanity and creation, and shows how the church needs to understand itself in relationship to that mission. The church has a mission in the world, but it is not its mission—it is the mission of the Trinity, revealed in human history, breaking into the present and awaiting fulfillment in the future. The Spirit empowers the church to fulfill its nature and role in this trinitarian history of God's dealing with the world, by his transformative presence in word, sacrament, office, mission, worship, and witness to the gospel.[23] While the church's role is relativized in this perspective, it still has a vital purpose within the history of Christ. Its submission to the purposes and movement of God in history allows it to understand its complete dependence on Christ and then to realize its central and unique participation in God's trinitarian mission. Moltmann asserts,

> Thus the whole being of the church is marked by participation in the history of God's dealings with the world. The Apostles' Creed expresses this truth by integrating the *credo ecclesiam* in the *credo in deum triunum*. And no ecclesiology should sink below this level.[24]

Moltmann's ecclesiology, therefore, is not only *messianic* and *relational*, it is also *trinitarian*. His trinitarian ecclesiology honors the relational, interpersonal, charismatic nature of the church, since the church reflects the trinitarian community. "The church has a charismatic structure," discovering the source and model of its unity and reciprocity in the trinitarian fellowship. Moltmann believes that ecclesiology is fundamentally trinitarian, as the church reflects, participates in, and embodies this fellowship within the Godhead.[25] The church does not correspond to any one member of the Trinity, "but to the eternal perichoresis," that is, the unity and fellowship present within the trinitarian relations. Furthermore, Moltmann asserts that the church does not only correspond to the trinitarian unity, it also dwells and participates in this mystical triunity. The church is invited by God's grace into this unity and reflects or images this unity before the world, in its agapic fellowship, ministries and structures, sharing of possessions, pastoral compassion and care, and so forth. "The open space of the perichoretic sociality of the Triune God is the church's divine living space."[26] The church is about the liberation and freedom of men and women in Christ, and it goes about this mission and proclaims this eschatological hope through the cultivation of the "new sociality" of trinitarian community.[27]

One of the consequences of Moltmann's emphasis on the relational and trinitarian dimensions of the church is his attention to the depth of community in the congregation

22. Ibid., 53.

23. Ibid., 53–65.

24. Ibid., 65.

25. Moltmann, *History and the Triune God*, 63–64.

26. Moltmann, *Sun of Righteousness, Arise!*, 161–62.

27. Ibid., 164; Moltmann, *Experiences in Theology*, 328–33; Moltmann and Moltmann-Wendel, *Humanity in God*, 90–106.

and the release of men and women to ministry in the congregation. "The church with its structures, organizations, and powers exists exclusively for the sake of the *congregation*. There is in the church nothing higher than the congregation."[28] The renewal and reformation of the church "comes from below," as the congregation images the trinitarian unity and participates in the trinitarian mission, and as "a congregational church from below" brings revitalization. Moltmann maintains that the church is *for* and *of* the people in the local congregations. The role of Christian leaders and ecclesial structures is to support these congregations and release people to mission and ministry. Moltmann grounds this in three proposals: worship services led by the whole congregation, voluntary church membership, and the fostering of small, fellowshipping, missionary communities. Such congregations "from below" exemplify eschatological hope, nurture genuine relationships, witness to Christ, and demonstrate love for "the other one, the stranger and the enemy." In other words, they display trinitarian unity.[29] As this community life develops among the congregations and their leaders, and as every person's charismatic gifts are recognized and released, the churches might become communities "without above or below." Reform will also come from both above and below.[30] There is a discernible movement toward congregational and free church ecclesiology here. Moltmann is also concerned that both women and men are free to use their charismata in the mission and ministry of the congregation, and that male domination of women in ecclesial and secular life cease.[31]

THE TRANSFORMATIVE POWER AND PRESENCE OF THE SPIRIT

The title of Moltmann's major ecclesiological work, *The Church in the Power of the Spirit*, indicates the centrality of the Spirit in Moltmann's ecclesiology. He dedicates almost half of his ecclesiological treatise to the themes associated with the church in the power and presence of the Holy Spirit. According to Moltmann, the Spirit forms the church as the "messianic fellowship of service for the kingdom of God."[32] The Spirit is the primary shaper of the church's "means of salvation," and the church's charismatic ministries and structure. The Spirit forms the church through the "apostolic proclamation of the gospel," and by enabling correspondence between the gospel and the messianic community. The Spirit also forms the church through the eschatological and missiological practices of baptism, the Lord's Supper, worship, and personal Christian discipleship as "the messianic way of life." The Spirit leads the church to witness to and worship Christ, to embrace his messianic mission, to live in eschatological hope, and to pursue God's power and presence in all dimensions of its being.[33]

---

28. Moltmann, *The Passion for Life*, 115.

29. Ibid., 120–26; Moltmann, "Triune God," 5; Moltmann, "Crucified God," 27.

30. Moltmann, *Church in the Power of the Spirit*, 326–36.

31. Moltmann and Moltmann-Wendel, "Becoming Human," 364.

32. Moltmann, *Church in the Power of the Spirit*, 198.

33. Ibid., 197–288.

Moltmann grounds what it means for the church to live in the power of the Spirit in the practical ecclesial matters of congregational ministry and the distribution and use of the charismata. He also details the implications of his pneumatology for the commissioning of leaders and entire faith communities for service, for the structure and governance of the church, and for the relationships between clergy and laity in the church.[34] Yet these dimensions of the church's visible and tangible life are only appreciated fully and accurately as "manifestations of the church's life in the eschatological history of Christ and the trinitarian history of God."[35] Viewed in any other way corrupts our conception of them. Not only so, but unless they are viewed from this vantage point we run the risk of elevating them above the eschatological history and purposes of the Trinity, reducing their vitality or dislodging them from their proper location in the local congregation. It would also be wrong to assume that Moltmann merely apprehends or perceives the Spirit in the church's sacraments, ministries, missions, or any other forms and expressions. On the contrary, all of these ecclesial realities are "conceived in the movement and presence of the Spirit." The Spirit creates the church, shaping it for the glory and purposes of the triune God. This point is central in Moltmann's view of the relationship between the Spirit and the church, and so he writes:

> When we considered the sacraments, we did not see the Spirit in the sacraments, but the sacraments in the movement and the presence of the Spirit; and here too the Spirit is not apprehended in the ministries of the church, but the church, with its manifold ministries and tasks, is to be conceived in the movement and presence of the Spirit.[36]

The traditional attributes of the church—the one, holy, catholic, and apostolic church—are "only justified and comprehensible in the framework of the creative workings of the Spirit."[37] Moltmann proceeds to assert that these attributes are the result of Christ working in the church, through the power and the presence of the Spirit, for the eschatological purposes and glorification of the triune God and the extension of his kingdom. Supplemented by a range of other marks or attributes including, for instance, the *notae ecclesiae* of the Reformers, these characteristics witness to Christ and to the church's eschatological hope, in the power of the Spirit.[38] They are not merely internal attributes of the church, serving as a sign for where the true church exists; they are also used by the Spirit to proclaim and extend God's kingdom, to witness to the eschatological and trinitarian history of God, and to minister wherever brokenness, oppression, and conflict are present. The church witnesses to Christ in history as "unity in freedom, holiness in poverty, catholicity in partisan support for the weak, and apostolate in suffering."[39] In

34. Ibid., 289–336.
35. Ibid., 289.
36. Ibid.
37. Ibid., 337–38.
38. Ibid., 340–41.
39. Ibid., 361.

other words, the church in the power and presence of the Spirit participates in the mission of Christ.

In Moltmann's ecclesiology, the trinitarian experience of the Spirit in the church is the experience of *koinonia*. The Spirit enables the people of God to know free, reciprocal, liberating, meaningful fellowship with each other and with God. Through the ministry of the Spirit the trinitarian fellowship invites persons, the church, and the creation into its redemptive, agapic, eternal-life-giving *koinonia*. "It follows from this that 'the fellowship of the Holy Spirit' has to be understood in trinitarian terms as a *community of persons*, and not in a unitarian sense as a *community of essence*."[40]

Moltmann posits this *"trinitarian fellowship of the Spirit"* in contrast to unitarian ideas of the Spirit and human fellowship, and especially in contrast to Friedrich Schleiermacher. The trinitarian fellowship of the Spirit is about real fellowship with real divine and human persons. It is a fellowship characterized by unity and love, even in the midst of diversity and difference. Instead of emphasizing hierarchical, gender, ethnic, age, factional, theological, political, and other difference, and allowing these to be sources of division and misunderstanding, the church in the trinitarian fellowship of the Spirit is called to be inclusive. Those things that divide are to be relinquished for the sake of Christ, through the power and fellowship of the Spirit. Diversity is still respected but it does not erode unity. The social experience of this trinitarian fellowship is expressed through the practical and demonstrative love of neighbor, the effort to balance self-differentiation with immersion in community, and the fresh discovery of friendship. Erotic love is expressed as a free and generous gift, not merely in the sexual arena, since agapic love redefines other forms of love, including eros. Trinitarian fellowship in the Spirit is embodied and Christians express this fellowship physically, in such acts as the laying on of hands, the holy kiss, the shared meal, and so forth.[41] The Spirit breathes vitality into the faith community that energizes its mission, leadership, love, and compassion—this theme permeates all of Moltmann's ecclesiology.[42]

ESCHATOLOGICAL HOPE AND MISSIOLOGICAL ENGAGEMENT

This chapter on Moltmann's ecclesiology considers the five dominant themes that run through his thought. These are Christology, relationship, the Spirit, eschatological hope, and missiological witness. Each of these richly interconnects in his ecclesiology. His understanding of the church is built upon christological foundations. Those foundations inspire the church to explore how its vitality is realized in its eschatological, dynamic relationships. These relationships include those with the triune God, the world, nations and cultures, and other things that are not the church. The Spirit enables relational reciprocity. This relationality is characterized by hope for the future. It gives birth to relationally shaped missiological engagement. Moltmann declares that the church's eschatological hope is cemented in Christ, inspired by the Spirit, and framed within relationship. This is

40. Moltmann, *Spirit of Life*, 217–19.

41. Ibid., 221–67.

42. Moltmann, *Source of Life*, 55–69.

because the church not only witnesses to the eschatological history of the triune God—when it pursues or grasps its own eschatological hope it is compelled to hope for the future of Israel, the nations, and the world, since it is in reciprocal relationship with these. The church's future is connected deeply and inseparably with the future of Israel, the world, and creation. Its hope is not only for itself but also for the redemption and transformation of Israel, the world religions, and the economic, political, and cultural processes of the world. When the church speaks of its eschatological hope, it is never in isolation from its hope for these other things.[43]

Moltmann sums up the relational reciprocity and outward gaze that is native to Christian eschatological hope in the following way:

> Conversion, the new turn to the future which follows from the gospel of the kingdom, will prove itself in the new turn given to life's relationships in the direction of the other life. That is why 'the church of the kingdom of God' asks about Israel's hope, the hope of the world religions, the hope of human society, and the hope of nature. Christian eschatology is not merely eschatology for Christians; if it is to be the eschatology of the all-embracing kingdom, it must also be unfolded as the eschatology of Israel, of the religions, of human social systems and of nature.[44]

The kingdom breaks into human history "in the present, disputed and hidden rule of God" and "if we look in the opposite direction—this history of the rule of God is also to be understood eschatologically."[45] As a consequence of its desire to see God's reign extended and recognized upon the earth, the church not only prays in hopeful anticipation for the coming kingdom, it also participates in kingdom-oriented actions of justice, liberation, mercy, and the like, cooperating with God in his present rule in history. These actions are not done in isolation, but in cooperation with other groups whose deeds, whether they know it or not, result in and testify to the kingdom. The church is at its best when it understands the historical and the eschatological dimensions of the kingdom, and perceives it role in relationship to both of these realities.

> The church in the power of the Spirit is not yet the kingdom of God, but it is its anticipation in history . . . In provisional finality and in final provisionality the church, Christendom and Christianity witness to the kingdom of God as the goal of history in the midst of history. In this sense the church of Jesus Christ is *the people of the kingdom of God.*[46]

The church's eschatological hope, its expectation of the kingdom of God, shapes its mission and actions in the world. Moltmann writes that the church's service, mission, and ministries of social compassion and justice must "be determined by the open foreland of its hopes for the world."[47] As the *exodus church*, that is, the pilgrim people who show the world the redemption available in Christ, the church's nature and existence are

---

43. Moltmann, *Church in the Power of the Spirit*, 133–88.

44. Ibid., 135.

45. Ibid., 192.

46. Ibid., 196.

47. Moltmann, *Theology of Hope*, 326.

completely connected to its participation in the eschatological mission of the triune God in the world. Its service to the world and missiological engagement with the world must not be formed by the world's expectations of the church but by the eschatological expectation, mission, and will of God. The church's missiological presence in the world is for the kingdom of God and for the renewal and transfiguration of the world— "the church takes up the society in which it lives into its own horizon of expectation" of eschatological fulfillment.[48] Its mission is not merely about personal salvation or providing therapeutic, existential, or pastoral comfort—and it is certainly not about institutional service to the world on the world's terms. The church's mission is about both the redemption of the individual *and* "the realization of the eschatological *hope of justice*, the *humanizing* of man, the *socializing* of humanity, *peace* for creation."[49]

According to Moltmann, missiology, and especially mission to western culture, has confronted the church with an important inescapable truth—the church does not merely *have* a mission, "but the very reverse: that the mission of Christ creates its own church. Mission does not come from the church; it is from mission and in the light of mission that the church has to be understood."[50] Mission can only be fully understood through the *missio Dei* and includes, but is not limited to, evangelization and gospel proclamation. As the church focuses on the mission of Christ and the kingdom of God, the living church emerges—the church, then, can have extraordinary hope and purpose, even when its structures and ministries are under scrutiny. Its eyes are on broader, eternal, God-sized realities.

> We can say to the theologians and pastors and all the people who ask anxiously 'What's going to happen to the church?': forget the church—think about the kingdom of God, seek its justice and righteousness, and then the living church will be added to you, simply of itself.[51]

All ministries and actions that are oriented toward liberating people from "slavery in the presence of the coming God" are mission. The church's nature and purpose can only be comprehended in the context of the *missio Dei*, that is, in the context of the church's participation in the trinitarian history of the eschatological mission of God in the world.[52]

CONTRIBUTIONS TO MISSIONAL ECCLESIOLOGY

Permeating all of Moltmann's ecclesiology are messianic, eschatological, and relational themes, and these and other themes shape his contribution to my formation of a missional ecclesiology in Part Two of this book.[53] The church, writes Moltmann, has christological foundations that shape its nature, power, mission, and hope. Moltmann's ecclesiology is

---

48. Ibid., 328.

49. Ibid., 329.

50. Moltmann, *Church in the Power of the Spirit*, 10.

51. Moltmann, *Jesus Christ for Today's World*, 28.

52. Moltmann, *Church in the Power of the Spirit*, 7–11; Moltmann and Kuschel, *Pentecostal Movements*, 128–31.

53. He features in chapters 14, 15, 16, and 17 in *Part Two* of this book.

a *messianic ecclesiology*, grounded in his eschatological Christology. The church's distinctiveness, hope, and functions are found in the eschatological, messianic mission of Christ. As the *eschatological exodus,* the church is a herald, foretaste of, and witness to the world, showing the world its transformed and liberated condition in submission to the gospel and kingdom of Christ.

The church is not only compelled by the gospel to pursue the trinitarian purposes of God in history, it is also defined by the death and resurrection of Christ and is, therefore, *the community of the Cross.* Standing "beneath the cross," the church resides wherever Christ promises to be found: *ubi Christus—ibi ecclesia.* Christ promises to be found, firstly, in the apostolate, sacraments, and Christian community; secondly, among the poor, disregarded, and hungry and thirsty; and, finally, in his Parousia. This idea of the church being present not only in the contexts we usually assume but also among the poor and "the least of these" has probably been the most controversial aspect of Moltmann's ecclesiology—he builds this theology from his exegesis of Matthew 25:31–46. Whether Jesus is referring to the poor and needy in the world or to his own disciples in Matthew 25:31–46 is a subject of considerable debate, and Moltmann's claims hinge on a particular interpretation.[54] For Moltmann, Christ's presence in the church and among the marginalized is a result of Christ's Parousia, of the eschatological activities and purposes of God in creation, the church, and the world. The church's essence, structure, mission, and residence are united around "these three modes of [Christ's] promised presence. It will find the place of its truth in this field. If it omits any one of these promises of Christ's presence, its truth will be obscured."[55] This is a strong challenge to the church in general, but also to missionary theologians and practitioners, who might be tempted to emphasize one or two of these modes of Christ's presence to the exclusion or minimization of the others.

Moltmann's ecclesiology is also a *relational, trinitarian ecclesiology.* The church can only be comprehended in its relationship to other realities, organizations, and entities in the light of its inner relational dynamics and in its correspondence with the trinitarian relationships and the mission of the triune God. Furthermore, the church can only be conceived in its relationship to the eschatological history of Christ, the context in which it is specifically located, and the trinitarian actions and mission of God. Moltmann argues that while this makes definitions of the church complex and malleable and our understanding of the church provisional and open to correction, it is impossible to appreciate the church outside these and other relationships.

The Spirit forms the church and the Spirit is the primary actor in the church's charismatic ministries, proclamation, and structure. For Moltmann, the Spirit enables the church to worship Christ and participate in his messianic mission, to face the future with persistent eschatological hope, and to know God's gracious presence and matchless power throughout its life. As I assert elsewhere, missional ecclesiology is deficient without meaningful pneumatological underpinnings. Moltmann claims that the Spirit leads the church into the "*trinitarian fellowship* of the Spirit," and a richness of *koinonia*

54. For a discussion of the interpretation of this passage and the implications for Moltmann's ecclesiology, see Tripole, "Church for the Poor."

55. Moltmann, *Church in the Power of the Spirit,* 121–32.

and agapic love that witnesses to the world of God's eschatological redemption and history. Moltmann is concerned for the renewal and reformation of the church, including the establishment of *mature, responsible congregations, "messianic fellowships"* that witness to the eschatological Christ. His primary *practical* goal in writing an ecclesiology is to encourage ecclesial reform—from established, institutional, self-concerned structures to a church that is congregationally centered, spiritually alive, voluntary, charismatic, fellowshipping, participatory, missionary, and messianic. Reflecting his "open trinitarianism," Moltmann believes that the church should be an *open church*, existing in vibrant relationship with God, humanity, and the future.

The church's eschatological hope is not merely for itself but for all those it is in relationship with—Israel, the nations, other religions, creation, and the world—since the church is in reciprocal relationship with these in the trinitarian history of God. The church's mission is about both the redemption of the individual *and* "the realization of the eschatological *hope of justice,* the *humanizing* of man, the *socializing* of humanity, *peace* for creation."[56] It does not merely *have* a mission; instead, the church can only be fully comprehended as a missionary organism and community in the light of the Spirit's work, the eschaton, and the *missio Dei.*

QUESTIONS FOR REFLECTION

1. Why does Moltmann believe that Christology is the "dominant theme of ecclesiology" and that "ecclesiology can only be developed from Christology"?

2. Moltmann believes that the Spirit enables the people of God to know *koinonia*—free, reciprocal, liberating, meaningful fellowship with each other and with God. Does your church experience such *koinonia*? How can you help deepen your church's *koinonia*?

3. Moltmann says, "Mission does not come from the church; it is from mission and in the light of mission that the church has to be understood . . . The mission of Christ creates its own church." How would our churches change if they really believed that they were not merely to *do mission work* but *be missionary communities*?

---

56. Moltmann, *Theology of Hope,* 329.

9

John Webster: The Church as Communion of Saints

Evangelical Christians need an ecclesiology, and the ecclesiology they need is an evangelical ecclesiology, for the gospel is ecclesial. But an ecclesiology has to be a good deal more than a set of inchoate instincts which grab hold of whatever bits of doctrine float in their direction. A properly evangelical ecclesiology has to take its place within the scope of doctrinal affirmations which spell out the Christian confession of God, Christ, the Spirit, election, reconciliation, sanctification and the rest.[1]

—JOHN WEBSTER

INTERLOCKING DOCTRINES: GOD, CHRIST, GOSPEL, AND CHURCH

IN AN ESSAY TITLED "On Evangelical Ecclesiology," John Webster outlines what, in terms of the entire body of his work, is probably his most concise outline of an evangelical ecclesiology. His ecclesiology demonstrates the interlocking nature of the doctrines of God, the Christian gospel, and the church.[2] Evangelical ecclesiology, according to Webster, needs to be constructed upon evangelical convictions about such doctrines and, in doing so, avoid becoming an uncritical jumble of theological ideas, trends, and fancies. Webster welcomes the renewed interest in ecclesiology in western culture but laments the way many Protestant theologians and church leaders are developing ecclesiologies in a spirit of ecumenical eclecticism, and with little reference to evangelical theological convictions. He is disturbed by the trend, since evangelicals should be deeply concerned with the relationship between evangelical understandings of the gospel and the implications of this for ecclesiology. Suggesting that he risks becoming a "theological Ishmael" among his peers, Webster grieves the marked decline in "positive dogmatics" in contemporary

1. Webster, *Confessing God*, 192. John Webster taught systematic theology at Wycliffe College, a college of the University of Toronto, from 1986 to 1996, and was the Lady Margaret Professor of Divinity, Oxford University, from 1996 to 2003. He has served as the Chair of Systematic Theology at King's College, University of Aberdeen, since 2003.

2. Ibid., 153–93.

western Protestant theology, and the noticeable "shift from critical skepticism towards a soft correlationism chastened by a bit of Barth, a sparkling but Christianly not very specific conversation which has lost the rough edges of the gospel."[3]

Webster contends that the consequences of this theological drift have been problematic on a number of fronts, including ecclesiological fragmentation and imprecision. In contrast to this shift, he writes that evangelical ecclesiology must have the following purpose:

> The task of evangelical ecclesiology is to describe the relation between the gospel and the church. It is charged to investigate the sense in which the existence of a new human social order is a necessary implicate of the gospel of Jesus Christ—to ask whether the life of the Christian community is internal to the logic of the gospel or simply accessory and accidental. Are gospel and church extrinsically or internally related?[4]

Articulating the role of the gospel in constructing an evangelical ecclesiology and its role in measuring the quality of any ecclesiology, Webster quotes Edward Schillebeeckx as contending, "It is 'by the heart of the gospel message that any ecclesiology . . . can and must be measured.'"[5]

How is Webster using the term *evangelical*? In an article in which he develops an "evangelical theology of episcopacy," he writes that his use of the term *evangelical* is not as a "term of discrimination (over against, for example, 'catholic'), but in a more primary sense." He proceeds to describe his use of the term in the following way:

> An evangelical theology is one which is evoked, governed and judged by the gospel. In this sense, evangelical is simply equivalent to 'Christian': all Christian theology, whatever its tradition, is properly speaking evangelical in that it is determined by and responsible to the good news of Jesus Christ.[6]

According to Webster, while the doctrines of God, salvation, and ecclesiology are interconnected, an evangelical ecclesiology is a logical and necessary consequence of a biblical theology of the perfection of God—emphasizing the completeness, self-originating, otherness, and fullness of God's being. It is also a consequence of a theology of God's gracious, self-originating actions and offer of salvation to human beings. In his self-contained and self-originating perfection, God extends his grace and salvation to humankind, inviting us into relationship with him and each other in the image of the loving relations of the Trinity. This is made possible through the life, death, resurrection, and glorification of Jesus Christ, and through the power of the Spirit. In other words, God's perfect nature *and* the gospel of salvation call forth the church, shape the nature, purpose, and destiny of the church, and make the church "the communion of saints."[7]

---

3. Webster, *Word and Church*, 6.

4. Webster, "Church and the Perfection of God," 75.

5. Webster, "Self-Organizing Power," 70. See Schillebeeckx, *Church*, xiii.

6. Webster, "Self-Organizing Power," 69.

7. Webster, "Church and the Perfection of God," 76; Webster, "Self-Organizing Power," 72.

In his portrait of evangelical ecclesiology, Webster persuasively outlines the characteristics and consequences of interlocking the evangelical doctrines of God, salvation, and ecclesiology. It is clear that for Webster Christianity's evangelical nature produces and precedes its ecclesial nature. The church's essential nature is derived "solely from and is wholly dependent upon" the gospel of Jesus Christ, and is a logical and necessary consequence of that gospel. The gospel precedes the church—God's unilateral, asymmetrical, original, and paramount grace, especially as demonstrated in Christ's death and resurrection, precedes the response of the individual or the church and, moreover, shapes the church's nature, purpose, and future. The church's nature is not irrelevant to the gospel and should not be ignored as something unrelated to the gospel's faithful proclamation and embodiment, but neither should ecclesiology be inflated in such a way that it precedes or is set adrift from the gospel. All ecclesiological reflection, forms, and practice are to be shaped by an evangelical understanding of the gospel. God's perfection, his boundless grace, and the gospel of Jesus Christ all form and pave the way for ecclesiology, which is an important product of those things that go before it. Distinctions between Christ, gospel, and church must not be neglected or minimized.[8]

Webster makes a number of other notable assertions with regard to these themes, which he argues in some detail. Firstly, ecclesiology needs to be true to Christianity's entire doctrine of God and complete evangelical understanding of salvation and, furthermore, to begin with the evangelical understanding of God's perfection. Webster is critical of ecclesiological constructs that selectively draw from aspects of these doctrines, according to theological fashions or arbitrary preference, or that start from an inadequate theological base. He believes that starting with God's perfection and with his resulting unilateral, asymmetrical, salvific actions builds the right foundation for ecclesiology and ensures that such ecclesiology is encompassing rather than selective or jaundiced. The whole doctrine of God must be consulted, laying an adequate and firm footing for ecclesiology. Instead of convoluting the nature of God with the nature of the church, or the actions of God with the actions of the church, one is recognized as preceding and distinct from the other. God invites the church to reflect his nature and participate in his work, in response to who he already is and what he is already doing. God's movement toward the church is one of divine grace and love. The church's nature and response do not complete God since he is already perfect, self-contained, and the one who initiates all grace. He reaches out relationally, from his perfect being, toward the church, and this movement of God, which comes out of his nature, makes the church.[9]

Secondly, evangelical convictions about this complete doctrine of the perfection of God, including his self-initiating, salvific actions, must act as "the norm of ecclesiology," instead of some fashionable or isolated theological notion.[10] As examples, Webster singles out the terms *relation, communion ecclesiology,* and *koinonia.* Webster traces the influence of *communion ecclesiology* upon Roman Catholic, Eastern Orthodox, Mainline Protestant,

8. Webster, "Church and the Perfection of God," 76–78.

9. Ibid., 79–80, 88–89.

10. Ibid., 79.

Free Church, and inter-confessional thought over the last fifty years. Introducing his case with a rhetorical question to the reader, Webster's concern is that such ecclesiology, when separated from an adequate and biblical attention to God's complete revelation of himself, his perfection, and his salvific action at the cross, compromises "the imparticipable perfection of God's triune life" disturbing "the fundamental asymmetry of Christ and the church."[11] Christ and the church risk being conflated and evangelicals must deny such a theological move, emphasizing instead what Webster calls "relation-in-distinction." God reaches out relationally to human beings, as demonstrated supremely at the cross; but God remains distinct from the church.[12] God chooses the church, makes it holy, and enjoys relationship with it. Therefore, Webster would prefer to emphasize the church's *election* and *holiness*, as a consequence of God's choice, sanctification, grace, love, and action, rather than "using *communion* as an ecclesiological master concept."[13]

Thirdly, the church needs to be careful not to merge or uncritically blend "the reconciling work of God and those acts of the church in which that reconciliation is present."[14] Webster is convinced that some forms of contemporary ecclesiology confuse the unique, distinct, determinative, primary, divine, reconciling work of Christ, especially in his death and resurrection, with the important but derivative ministry of the church—in such areas as ecclesial practices, "ethics of reconciliation," moral action, and Christian service in the world. Against such confusion, evangelical ecclesiology maintains the biblical distance between the determinative reconciling work of Christ and the Christ-testifying, appointed, reconciling ministry of the church. For Webster, proclamation of the reconciling work of Christ (the gospel), that is, what Christ has already and completely done in human history as revealed to the church in his word, precedes and distinguishes Christian moral and ethical action, peacemaking, and ecclesial practices. In its derivative, limited mediating role, the church's reconciling work is primary about "indicating the gospel" as "the creature of the Word." To reverse the order of the action of Christ and the church is to lose the "fundamental asymmetry between divine and human action." Webster denies that such an ecclesiology leads to a passive or inactive church.[15]

Webster clearly articulates his ecclesiological case—the church is a *communion of saints* because God has elected and sanctified it (hence *saints*), and constituted it as an assembly, culture, polity, and people (hence *communion*). God has done this through his initiating action and as an expression of his perfect and complete nature. The church does not *participate* in God's being; instead, enjoying a union with him that does not flatten out distinctions, the church *fellowships* with God in response to his invitation, salvific action, and movement toward it that is characterized by love, grace, and communion.[16]

The christological implications of this, writes Webster, are important. They include the fact that theologians and church practitioners should not minimize or reduce the

11. Ibid., 84.

12. Ibid., 80–87; Webster, "Self-Organizing Power," 72–73.

13. Webster, "Church and the Perfection of God," 89.

14. Webster, *Word and Church*, 211–30.

15. Ibid., 228–29.

16. Webster, "Church and the Perfection of God," 90; Webster, *Confessing God*, 144.

uniqueness of the incarnation through ecclesiological language that equates the church's actions with it. The church's mission, worship, and fellowship are shaped by a theology of the incarnation, but this is not the same as suggesting that the church embodies "the same divine reality of which he (Jesus) is the supreme incarnation."[17] Neither should they mistakenly conclude that since the church is the body or fullness of Christ that he is to be ontologically identified with the church. Furthermore, all Christology must preserve both Christ's fellowship with the church on the one hand, and his distinction from it on the other.[18] The demise of a robust, evangelical, biblical Christology in western Protestantism has been problematic for western theology and has given rise to an inflated ecclesiology. Webster argues that such ecclesiology inflates "itself to do work which in a more orderly dogmatics would be appropriated directly to the risen Jesus in his offices as prophet, priest and king."[19] Putting Christology back in its rightful place also means restoring the church's confidence in the knowledge of Jesus Christ, in what he has done in and for the church and the world, in the timeless, transforming, non-contingent, graciously and divinely given gospel.[20]

Elevating Christology in such a way also has direct implications for Christian ministry and church forms. Drawing on the Heidelberg Catechism, Webster proposes the following "dogmatic rule for ecclesiology," and its consequence for an "evangelical theology of ministry":

> An adequate doctrine of the church will maximize Christology and Pneumatology (for it is Jesus Christ through Word and Spirit who 'gathers, protects and preserves') and relativize (but not minimize or abolish) ecclesial action and its ordered forms. Our next question is: how does this shape an evangelical theology of ministry? Jesus Christ is himself the minister of the church. He is himself prophet, priest and king; the ministry of revelation, reconciliation and rule by which the church is brought into being, restored to fellowship with God, and kept under God's governance is the action of Christ himself, the risen and ascended one who is now present and active, outgoing and communicative.[21]

Webster notes that while Christian ministry patterns itself after Christ, his ministry remains *distinct* and unique, he is the true and only head of the church, and all Christian ministries must point to him and the ministry that *he alone* can accomplish, and has already achieved. Christ and his gospel unify the church. An evangelical Christology, therefore, profoundly shapes Christian ministry and ecclesiology—otherwise, it is deficient and corrupt.[22]

Recognizing the centrality of the doctrine of God, of the gospel, and of dogmatic considerations about Christ and the Spirit helps the church construct an evangelical theology of Christian ministerial and church order, and ecclesial governance. Webster

17. Webster, *Word and Church*, 119–20.

18. Webster, "Church and the Perfection of God," 89–95; Webster, *Confessing God*, 142–44.

19. Webster, *Word and Church*, 2–3.

20. Webster, *Confessing God*, 144–45.

21. Webster, "Self-Organizing Power," 74.

22. Ibid., 74–79.

demonstrates this by constructing an "evangelical theology of episcopacy" that indicates "how episcopal ministry can be considered an ordered, institutional implication of the gospel."[23] Submitting the theology and practice of Christian ministry and church order to the scrutiny of the gospel, and to "critical and reformatory" evangelical dogmatics, Webster defends the role of the episcopacy. His defense is not for some timeless, inherited office, which is expressed the same way in every context, but rather for a form of Christian leadership and governance that is supported and scrutinized by the gospel.[24] Since Christian office is primarily about testifying to the gospel, person, and ministry of Christ, about ensuring that the church points beyond itself to Christ, and about safeguarding the true gospel, then *"episcope*, oversight, is the basic ministry of the church." While the episcopacy has a particular oversight role in this regard (teaching, leadership, church discipline, and so forth), the ground, function, and "primary task" of all office, including the episcopacy, are to "envisage, safeguard and unify the church's fulfillment of its gospel mandate."[25] Webster argues that all ministries are to be conducted in the searching light of the gospel, in submission to Christ, in the power of the Spirit, to the glory of God the Father.

The correct process for evaluating and sanctioning any ministerial office, leadership function, or ecclesial order is, according to Webster, the following: first, an understanding of the way evangelical ecclesiology is shaped and determined by the gospel; second, scrutinizing whether the current entire ministerial order, or a given particular ministry office, is a faithful, safeguarding, unifying expression of the gospel. The question, then, is how do these ecclesial ministries and forms honor the gospel and provide appropriate room for the primary, sovereign, matchless minister of the church, Jesus Christ?[26] In this area of church life, like all others, the interlocking nature of the doctrine of God, the gospel, Christology, and ecclesiology, comes to the fore.

HOLY SCRIPTURE, CHRISTIAN THEOLOGY, AND THE CHURCH

In a book examining an evangelical theology of Scripture, Webster describes why he prefers the term *Holy Scripture* to the more generic *Scripture*, in order "to indicate the place occupied by the biblical texts in the revealing, sanctifying and inspiring acts of the Triune God."[27] He grounds the doctrine of Scripture in the doctrine of God and his self-communication with human beings. Using the terms revelation, sanctification, and inspiration to provide insight into an evangelical understanding of the nature and function of the biblical text, Webster proceeds to outline his comprehension of each of these concepts. The triune God graciously, mysteriously, personally, and redemptively *reveals* himself in human history and uses Scripture as the medium of this self-communication. While Christians are called to glorify the triune God, this would be impossible to do

23. Ibid., 69–70.

24. Ibid., 81–82.

25. Ibid., 77.

26. Ibid., 69–82 (esp. 69, 76–77).

27. Webster, *Holy Scripture*, 8.

without God's self-communication in creation, election, human history, the cross, and the eschaton, as revealed in Scripture. God *sanctifies* "creaturely realities," especially in the incarnation, but also in the church and the biblical text, so that they become his means of self-communication. Inspiration is about God's "divine movement and therefore divine moving," as the Holy Spirit moves (*inspires*) people to present God's self-communication in human language, sanctifying and inspiring their text so that their words are uniform with the mind and heart of God.[28]

What are the implications of this doctrine of Scripture for the church? Webster writes of "the church as a 'hearing church,' as 'spiritually visible' and as 'apostolic.'"[29] He outlines his case for asserting that George Lindbeck and the post-critical theologians are in error when they conflate or blend the church's authority with that of Scripture. These theologians erroneously relocate authority from Scripture to church and end up with social moralism, virtue or immanentist ecclesiologies, elevated anthropological concepts in ecclesial practice, Scripture being subjected to tradition, and the location of Scripture as part of the doctrine of the church— when it is, in fact, part of the doctrine of revelation. Scripture, writes Webster, is far more than Lindbeck's "semiotic code" or "semiotic *positum* in the culture of the church."[30]

A clear description of the church, which presents itself regularly in Webster's writing, is that the church is *the creature of the word of God* or *the creature of the divine word*. The church receives God's self-communicative revelation in Scripture in an attentive, receptive spirit. Scripture shapes the church's self-identity, activities, theology, and so forth, and is used by Christ to rule over and form his church. The church's tradition is to be nothing more or less than "holy attentiveness" to Christ through Scripture. In an important sense, the church does not interpret or attribute meaning to Scripture. Scripture has its own clarity, which the church is required to respond to in attentive, willing, joyful submission.[31]

> The definitive act of the church is faithful hearing of the gospel of salvation announced by the risen Christ in the Spirit's power through the service of Holy Scripture. As the *creatura verbi divini*, the creature of the divine Word, the church is the hearing church.[32]

> The sphere of the clarity of Holy Scripture is the church, the creature of the Word of God; by the Word the church is generated and preserved, and by the Spirit the church sets forth the clear Word of God in traditions of holy attentiveness.[33]

The church is called to be a *hearing church*, attentive and submissive to the word, judged and scrutinized by it, submitting the church's beliefs, practices, structures, and traditions to the examination of Scripture. Webster describes how Scripture confronts

---

28. Ibid., 5–41. See Webster, "Biblical Reasoning," 738–42.

29. Webster, *Holy Scripture*, 42.

30. Ibid., 49.

31. Webster, *Confessing God*, 52–59.

32. Webster, *Holy Scripture*, 44.

33. Webster, *Confessing God*, 52.

and destabilizes the church, as well as unifies, comforts, and guides it. The church does not make Scripture authoritative; instead, it confesses the authority of Scripture, present in it by virtue of it being God's triune self-communication.[34] Because of the ministry of Christ and the presence of the Spirit, the church is more than a sociologically, politically, or historically natural community. It is much more than that—it is *spiritually visible* as it "receives the grace of God through the life-giving presence of Word and Spirit."[35] The church exists and submits to Christ who "commissions and sends" it into the world, into human history, solely by his grace and according to his will. Therefore, the church is *apostolic*, and its history is apostolic history.[36]

The church does not have power over Scripture but derives its authority, power, and identity from God's self-communication in Scripture. Scripture's authority is derived from Christ, its "authority *within* the church is a function of [its] authority *over* the church."[37] The formation of the canon was not the process by which Scripture was made authoritative. The church recognized, received, and submitted to the already present authority of Scripture, since Scripture is God's active, self-communicative, powerful word to all of creation.[38]

Contrasting the work of Arthur Schopenhauer with that of John Calvin and Dietrich Bonhoeffer, Webster develops a persuasive and affectionate account of the church as a *reading* community. By this, he means that the church is a community that reads Scripture for pastoral and spiritual nourishment, as "a *prayerful* activity," and as an expression of "communicative fellowship" firstly with God and then with each other.[39] Calvin and Bonhoeffer elevate the practices and purposes of hearing and expounding Scripture, and of putting Scripture into concrete and transformative practice. Spring-boarding off the thought of these two theologians and describing the approach to Scripture presented by them, Webster speaks of "faithful reading in the economy of grace."[40] This includes simple attentiveness to what Scripture is really saying, allowing Scripture to interpret itself, submitting in a teachable way to the Spirit of Christ in the word, and accepting God's gracious gift of loving self-communication.[41]

These thoughts extend into the prominence and purpose of Scripture in the theological seminary. Webster laments the decline in Scripture's centrality in theological education and ministerial formation. Scripture and the gospel of Jesus Christ must be at the heart of all such education and formation, and certainly at the heart of all theological reflection, both in the church and in the academy. "Christian theology is biblical reasoning."[42] Otherwise, the theological seminary is plagued by fragmented curriculum,

34. Webster, *Word and Church*, 38–42, 47–76.

35. Webster, *Holy Scripture*, 48.

36. Ibid., 50–52.

37. Ibid., 56.

38. Ibid., 42–67.

39. Webster, *Word and Church*, 76–86.

40. Webster, *Holy Scripture*, 86. See Webster, *Word and Church*, 87–110.

41. Webster, *Holy Scripture*, 68–106.

42. Webster, "Biblical Reasoning," 747–51; Webster, "Principles of Systematic Theology," 69–70.

"loss of positivity," speculative theology, theologically and spiritually malformed professors and students, and various other undesirable consequences.[43]

VISIBILITY AND INVISIBILITY

Webster is concerned to bring what he considers an appropriate correction to contemporary ecclesiology's emphasis on the visibility of the church, that is, its focus on the church's ecclesial and discipling practices, social forms, ethical and missiological engagement with the world, and the like. This is not a discussion about who is and is not a true believer—visibility here is about the concrete forms, practices, witness, words, rites, and assembly of the church, that is, what Webster calls it "phenomenal form." While recognizing the value of much of this discussion about the church's visibility, and showing how Bonhoeffer addressed the negative dimensions of the church that seeks invisibility, Webster wants to ground or orient this conversation in the invisible dimensions of the church that give life, meaning, scrutiny, and substance to its visibility. Building a theology of the church that begins and is founded on the perfection of God and on the sufficiency of Christ and his gospel does not diminish the importance of the visible life of the church, asserts Webster. It also does not lead to a "spiritualization" or "passivity" in the church. Rather, it gives fresh vitality to the church's activities and grounds them in realities that are deeper than their own forms.[44]

The church's visibility, its phenomenal forms, are expressions of the presence of the Spirit in its midst. Webster is clear on this point. The Spirit enlivens the church, moves it to glorify and witness to Christ, sanctifies its ecclesial forms, and inspires the church to testify not only to God's presence, but also to what he has already done and accomplished in Christ. Through faith, we discern the activity of the triune God within the visible life of the church, the presence of the Holy Spirit in its center and, therefore, "the visibility of the church is thus spiritual event, spiritually discerned." Furthermore, "the church is and is visible because God the Holy Spirit is and acts."[45]

In his attempt to construct a robust evangelical ecclesiology, Webster also wants the church to appreciate its visible actions as "attestations of God," witnessing and testifying to the all-sufficient and ongoing "Word and work of God," especially as articulated in the gospel and demonstrated in the cross and the resurrection of Jesus Christ. This theology of attestation is the focal point in which Webster connects "the fundamental norm of ecclesiology, namely the perfection of God in his works toward the saints," the divine election and sanctification of the church, and, finally, the visible forms, structure, and actions of the church.[46] Notice the progression of these three theological areas. Without the prior areas, that is, the doctrine of the perfection of the triune God and the doctrine of salvation, ecclesiological considerations about the church's visibility are at best deficient. In this regard, Webster singles out ethnographic, "practice," and over-realized ecclesiologies

43. Webster, *Holy Scripture*, 107–35.
44. Webster, "Visible Attests the Invisible," 96–100; Webster, *Confessing God*, 6.
45. Webster, "Visible Attests the Invisible," 101–4.
46. Ibid., 104.

for particular critique. In view of God's perfection and his sufficient, perfect, completed, self-communicative, gracious election and sanctification of the church, the only adequate response of the church is to attest or witness to him, his actions, and his gospel. Such witness or attestation is primarily given in the church's ministries of word and sacrament. In this regard, evangelical ecclesiology dare not neglect or minimize the importance of the proclamation of the word of God, as revealed in the Scriptures, and the church's complete submission to that word.[47]

CONTRIBUTIONS TO MISSIONAL ECCLESIOLOGY

Webster's evangelical ecclesiology is lucid, compelling, and ardent, while being biblically and theologically vigorous. Some have suggested, from time to time, that evangelical or Protestant ecclesiology is theologically thin, minimal, or jaundiced.[48] Such an accusation is countered with persuasive force in Webster's ecclesiology and rendered unsustainable, at least with respect to Webster's work. Mark Husbands and Daniel Treier pull together a range of evangelical thinkers in their edited book *The Community of the Word*, in order to construct an evangelical theology. It is Webster's chapters on the dogmatic foundations of an evangelical ecclesiology which make such an ecclesiology gripping, attractive, and sure-footed.

The evangelical ecclesiology articulated by Webster emphasizes the interconnected nature of the doctrines of God, salvation (especially election and sanctification), and ecclesiology, and this evangelical study of ecclesiology is instructive for the missional ecclesiology in the second half of my book.[49] Building an ecclesiology from the foundations of the doctrines of God and salvation helps prevent ecclesiology from becoming a muddle of ideas, vogues, whims, and fads. The gospel is the base for a faithful biblical and missional ecclesiology, defining and measuring any ecclesiology's value and concepts. Webster insists that evangelical ecclesiology is a necessary consequence of a biblical theology of the perfection of God, of his gracious, self-originating deeds, and of his election, sanctification, and salvation of individuals and the church. The perfect, triune, self-communicative God and his gospel of salvation determine the essence, goal, vocation, and future of the church (including its missionary substance and orientation), and assemble God's people as "the communion of saints."[50] The church's nature, vocation, forms, and practices are relevant to the gospel and should not be minimized. Yet they must be understood as derivative of the doctrines of God and salvation, since ecclesiology is built on, and scrutinized by, those prior theological foundations. The church is a *communion of saints*, since God has elected and sanctified it, and set it apart for communion with himself (by grace, not out of necessity, since he is self-sufficient). God has constituted it as "a chosen people, a royal priesthood, a holy nation, God's special possession, that you may declare the praises

---

47. Ibid., 105–12. See Webster, "Justification, Analogy and Action," 123–25.

48. Webster, "Church and the Perfection of God," 77.

49. He features in chapters 15, 16, and 17 in *Part Two* of this book.

50. Webster, "Church and the Perfection of God," 76.

of him who called you out of darkness into his wonderful light."[51] Webster's ecclesiology further establishes my conviction that to diminish the established church, or to portray it in a hopeless or jaundiced light (as some are in the habit of doing), is to miss the biblical depiction of the church and the hope for both the church and the world that is resident in the gospel of Jesus Christ.

Webster is also convinced that the church is *the creature of the word of God* or *the creature of the divine word.* God is self-communicative. He communicates to the church and the world in a variety of ways, but primarily through Scripture. The church is to be attentive and submissive to that word, formed, confronted, and scrutinized by it, in such a way that it cultivates a "holy attentiveness" to Christ. Scripture's "authority *within* the church is a function of (its) authority *over* the church."[52] Moreover, the church's phenomenal forms, its visible actions, are expressions of the presence of the Spirit. Since they are grounded in the doctrines of God and salvation, they are "attestations of God," witnessing and testifying to the all-sufficient and ongoing "Word and work of God" revealed in the gospel, at the cross and resurrection, and in Scripture. Missional ecclesiology needs to be grounded on solid biblical foundations. The confidence churches and pastors have in Scripture, in the gospel of Christ, and in the sufficiency of Christ's work, will have a direct impact on their missionary effectiveness, community formation, discipling capacities, and spiritual passion.

QUESTIONS FOR REFLECTION

1. "It is by the heart of the gospel message that any ecclesiology . . . can and must be measured." Why should the gospel message be so central to ecclesiology?

2. What happens when we shape our understanding and/or practice of church around ideas, trends, fads, and fancies that do not have well-considered, biblical foundations?

3. How could your church become a *hearing church*, cultivating holy attentiveness to Christ through attentive submission to Scripture?

51. 1 Pet 2:9.

52. Webster, *Holy Scripture*, 56.

10

John Howard Yoder:
The Church as New, Redeemed Community

Jesus made it clear that the nationalized hope of Israel had been a misunderstanding, and that God's true purpose was the creation of a new society, unidentifiable with any of the local, national, or ethnic solidarities of the time. This new body, the church, as aftertaste of God's loving triumph on the cross and foretaste of his ultimate loving triumph in his kingdom, has a task within history. History is the framework in which the church evangelizes, so that the true meaning of history is the fact that God has chosen to use it for such a "scaffolding" service.[1]

—JOHN HOWARD YODER

CONSTANTINIANISM AND THE CHURCH

JOHN HOWARD YODER LAMENTS that, while the Constantinian era has fortunately ended, the theological response to this reality has been inadequate. The church has tended to acquiesce to its historical situation, being shaped by the forces and whims of history

---

1. Yoder, *Christian Witness*, 10–11. John Howard Yoder (1927 to 1997) spent much of his teaching career at Goshen Biblical Seminary, now called the Associated Mennonite Biblical Seminary, and at the University of Notre Dame. On Yoder's quote here, the question might be asked, "Was the nationalized hope of Israel a *misunderstanding* or, rather, a *stage*?"

rather than seeing itself as a transformational, new community. What are needed are fresh interpretations and new, probing, theological questions.[2]

Theologically, the pre-Constantinian church understood the dichotomy between the fallen "form of the world," especially as typified in the state, and the redemptive, visible, transformational community of the church. While clearly understanding its distinction from the world (and each sphere of the world is, according to Yoder, "a demonic blend of order and revolt"), the pre-Constantinian church knew that Christ's ultimate lordship over the whole world gave them impetus and mandate for confronting the powers and for acting and speaking prophetically. The state's role was important but was essentially about governing responsibly, while the church's role was to be the contrast society in which "the true sense of history was to be sought."[3]

The heresy of Constantinianism is not primarily in social, architectural, political, or other structures. These were merely symbols of the deeper problem, that is, "that the two visible realities, church and world, were fused. There is no longer anything to call 'world'; state, economy, art, rhetoric, superstition, and war have all been baptized."[4] The confronting question moved from the distinction between and the purposes of the church and the world, to that of grace and nature. The doctrine of the invisibility of the church ensued, as a way of explaining why Christ's lordship could not always be perceived in the world, and the church's self-understanding in relation to the world, history, morality, eschatology, and so forth, was turned inside out.

For Yoder, the consequences of the fusion between world and church in the secular and ecclesial imagination included the superfluous role of discipleship in the church and the baptism of those dimensions of the world once understood as antithetical to, or at least distinct from, the church, while retaining "their former content." While the Reformation had potential for confronting this fusion, it misunderstood the roots of the structures and systems it confronted, devalued the expressions of distinctiveness present within the Middle Ages, and allowed the state to consider itself under no higher authority than those secular. Moreover, the church during the Reformation period continued to lose "the conviction that the center of the meaning of history is in the work of the church."[5]

Yoder does not intend here to devalue the Reformation or churches characterized by Constantinianism in their entirety. There are various dimensions of post-Constantine, Middle Age, and Reformation churches worth admiring. His concern with the Reformation is that it did not confront the essential Constantinian heretical view on the lordship of Christ over both the church and the world (Christ is Lord over both, but in distinct ways). Furthermore, the Reformation did not address the Constantinian distortion of the relationship between the church and the world, the meaning of human history, the two ages, and the rightful roles of church and state in eschatological perspective. The

2. Yoder, "Otherness of the Church," 54–55.

3. Ibid., 55–56.

4. Ibid., 57. See Carter on how Yoder understands Constantinianism in, Carter, *Politics of the Cross*, chapter 6.

5. Yoder, "Otherness of the Church," 57–60.

Reforms "created modern secularism . . . unintentionally, through the inner contradictions of their conservatism."[6]

This analysis of the pre-Constantinian church and its theological self-understandings, and of the paradigms and fruits of Constantinianism up to the present era, leads Yoder to draw some implications for the contemporary church.[7]

1. The church should believe and confess that "the meaning of history" lies in God's formation of a new redeemed community for his pleasure and purposes. Yoder asserts, then, that the critical and ultimate theological issue today is "between those for whom the church is a reality and those for whom it is the institutional reaction of the good and bad conscience, of the insights, the self-encouragement—in short, of the religion of a society."

2. Our theological concepts and contemporary notions of the world should conform to Scripture—the world is essentially "structured unbelief," in its various guises, forms, and expressions.

3. Christ/culture polarities and typologies, especially those created or patterned after H. Richard Niebuhr's constructs, are unbiblical and unhelpful for ethics, theology, discipleship, and the church's understanding of its authentic relationship with history and the world.[8]

4. The church needs to abandon striving for power, privilege, and effectiveness, and imitate "the foolish weakness of the cross" as "the city set on the hill. The true church is the *free* church."

5. The church is to "face deconstantinization" with attention to the Spirit, a rejection of the heretical eschatology of Constantinianism, and with a clear view of itself as an alternative, minority, missionary society, displaying God's eschatological purposes and the meaning of human history. In that spirit, deconstantinization can help uncover the distorted theological conceptions and practices that are rooted in Constantinianism, and assist the church authentically to be the church.

CHRISTOLOGY, THE CHURCH, AND THE MEANING OF HISTORY

For Yoder, the foundation of any adequate ecclesiology is a biblically faithful Christology, since the church was created and takes its reference from the death, resurrection, and glorification of Christ. The church lives in imitation of its suffering, prophetic, serving Lord. It is called to "readiness to let the form of the church's obedience to Christ be dictated by Christ rather than by how much the population or the authorities are ready to accept."[9] Through "conformity with the path of Christ," even when subjected to

6. Ibid., 60–61.

7. Ibid., 61–64.

8. For a summary and analysis of Yoder's critique of Niebuhr's *Christ and Culture*, see Carter, "Legacy of an Inadequate Christology," 387–401. Park has attempted to bridge the ecclesiologies of Yoder and Niebuhr through the work of Newbigin, in Park, *Missional Ecclesiologies*.

9. Yoder, "People in the World," 88–89.

persecution, suffering, and martyrdom, the believers' church preservers in faithful witness, surrender to God's will, "nonconformity to the world," and obedience in all things to Christ.[10]

Having established Christology as the starting point, Yoder develops his believers' church ecclesiology. Following the lead of Ernst Troeltsch and Franklin Littell, Yoder outlines a triangular typology to describe and distinguish the "three different streams of spiritual vitality" that emerged from the Reformation: the *theocratic*, the *spiritualist*, and the *believers' church*. It is worth noting that Yoder acknowledges the dangers of narrow caricatures, and the blunt nature of such typologies. Nevertheless, he suggests that these three streams, positioning themselves over against each other, essentially differ in their interpretation of the relationship between the church and the meaning of history, and in their understanding of ecclesiological systems and structures. The *theocratic* stream emphasizes God's redemptive work in the whole of society and human history, the *spiritualist* in the inward life of believers and Christian communities, and the *believers' church* in the formation of a new, transformed and transforming, covenantal community.[11]

The ecclesiology of the believers' church, in contrast to the other two streams and, according to Yoder, in keeping with the ecclesial vision of Scripture, can be articulated in the following way:

> The work of God is the calling of a people, whether in the Old Covenant or the New. The church is then not simply the bearer of the message of reconciliation, in the way a newspaper or a telephone company can bear any message with which it is entrusted. Nor is the church simply the result of a message, as an alumni association is the product of a school or the crowd in the theatre is the product of a reputation of the film. That men and women are called together to a new social wholeness is itself the work of God, which gives meaning to history, from which both personal conversion (whereby individuals are called into this meaning) and missionary instrumentalities are derived . . . In every direction we might follow in exposition, *the distinctiveness of the church of believers is prerequisite to the meaningfulness of the gospel message.*[12]

This quote gives a sense of how Yoder relates the mission and existence of the church with the meaning of history, and with the "meaningfulness of the gospel message." The church is the "aftertaste of God's loving triumph on the cross and foretaste of his ultimate loving triumph in his kingdom." It has a definite "task within history.

10. Ibid., 83–89. Weaver asserts, "Yoder's ecclesiology emerges from his Christology." Weaver, "John Howard Yoder Legacy," 459. Carter agrees: "Ultimately, Yoder's ecclesiology is grounded in his Christology insofar as the church is the community brought into existence by the resurrection of Christ and that is, therefore, incomprehensible apart from the resurrection . . . Thus, the church is, as Yoder and McClendon put it, 'an eschatological community grounded in Scripture." Carter, *Politics of the Cross*, 181. Carter is quoting from McClendon and Yoder, "Christian Identity," 571.

11. Yoder, "People in the World," 66–73. See Littell, "Church and Sect," 262–76. Carter provides a useful analysis of Yoder's "Three Types of Ecclesiology" in Carter, *Politics of the Cross*, 184–86, and in Carter, "Beyond Theocracy and Individualism," 177–80. Carter also notes the origins of the term *believers' church*, and the reasons why Yoder prefers the term *believers' church* to *Free Church* or *Anabaptist* (although, Carter remarks, Yoder does use each of these terms at times to "describe his position . . . depending on the context"), in Carter, *Politics of the Cross*, 182–84.

12. Yoder, "People in the World," 74–75. See Cartwright, *Royal Priesthood*, 66.

History is the framework in which the church evangelizes, so that the true meaning of history is the fact that God has chosen to use it for such a 'scaffolding' service."[13]

Furthermore, Yoder emphasizes both theologically and practically the interrelatedness of mission and community, and the need for an ecclesiology that refuses to separate the two. This is especially the case in the light of the task of the church within history.

> Peoplehood and mission, fellowship and witness, are not two desiderata, each capable of existing or of being missed independently of one another; each is the condition of the genuineness of the other.[14]

In "A People in the World," Yoder expounds the traditional Reformation *notae ecclesiae* (marks of the church), Menno Simons's *notae missionis* (marks of mission), and the taxonomies of Willem Visser 't Hooft and Stephen Neill. He does this in order to demonstrate the worth of believers' church ecclesiology, the superiority of this believers' church ecclesiology to the other two streams of Protestant ecclesiology mentioned above, and the unique ability of believers' church ecclesiology to integrate mission and community. He also wants to show how believers' church ecclesiology might be outworked in mission, discipleship, and community.[15] The believers' church is a community of disciples who live a distinctive "social existence" characterized by holiness, biblical ethics, and missionary presence enhanced by such holiness. Through genuine love, the grace of God, and free association, practices of discipline and "binding and loosing" are embraced.[16]

Continuing his triangular typology of Protestant ecclesiological streams, Yoder insists that notions of evangelism, human history, and the congregation can either be shaped by a faulty *theocratic* or *spiritualist* theological paradigm, or conceived biblically through *believers' church* ecclesiology. In believers' church ecclesiology, as the church serves and suffers, rejecting violence and power, it *is* the good news. "It is not merely the agent of mission or the constituency of a mission agency. This is the mission."[17] Within history, the church is called to be "a *discerning* community," examining human history and the present age through the New Testament ethic and the death and resurrection of Christ, and expressing "an ethic of social involvement as servants" in imitation of Christ.[18] Furthermore, the believers' church tradition elevates the "congregational structure of the mission," including, but not limited to, such spheres of the church's life as its liturgy, witness, leadership, and ecumenical relationships.[19]

13. Yoder, *Christian Witness*, 10–11.

14. Yoder, "People in the World," 78.

15. Yoder, "Otherness of the Church," 75–101. See Visser 't Hooft, *Pressure of Our Common Calling*; Neill, *Unfinished Task*; Simons, "Reply to Gellius Faber."

16. Yoder, "People in the World," 79–83.

17. Ibid., 91.

18. Ibid., 92–95.

19. Ibid., 96–101.

AN ECUMENICAL IMAGINATION AND DRIVE

A number of notable interpreters of Yoder have noted his ecumenical drive for unity and for unifying conversation. Michael Cartwright, for instance, groups two collections of Yoder's essays under the headings "ecumenical perspectives" and "ecumenical responses."[20] Mark Nation devotes part three of his work on Yoder to the theme of "faithful ecumenism," and Craig Carter sees ecumenism as a central Yoderian ecclesiological motif.[21] While I am only going to treat Yoder's ecumenical, unifying imagination here briefly, it is worth noting that this is not a mere openness or even pro-activity in ecumenical dialogue. It is much more than that. An ecumenical, unifying vision and imagination significantly permeate and shape Yoder's ecclesiology. As the eschatological community, the exemplar and foretaste of the kingdom, the church is called to strive for authentic unity. This deep unity is essential to the church's nature, witness, and purpose within history. The nature of the unity Yoder envisions is one characterized by conversation. These are conversations recognizing the final authority of Christ and Scripture—conversations pursued with a willingness to change positions. The conversations will be supranational, shaped by unity of ethical commitment, faith, and worship, and unwilling to retreat into ecumenical solutions that are superficial or merely institutional (such as ecumenical "mergers").[22]

The "ecumenical style" of the believers' church must prioritize the role of the local congregation, be firmly grounded in relationship, lead to genuine mission and hope, and be immersed in meaningful worship. It will ask probing questions about the relationship between the church and the world, the place of membership in community life and missionary endeavor, and the meaning of scriptural authority.[23] It will be ready to identify and reject the influence of Constantinianism, not only in its ecumenical efforts and conversations, but also in its interfaith encounters.[24]

ECCLESIOLOGY AS SOCIAL ETHICS, AND SOCIAL ETHICS AS GOSPEL

In "Why Ecclesiology is Social Ethics," Yoder engages with Karl Barth's discussion of "The Order of the Community" in *Church Dogmatics* IV/2. For Yoder, the church's engagement with social ethics is an expression of its essential nature as a "foretaste/model/herald of the kingdom." On the one hand, the church's worship and its political participation emerge from its nature, and, on the other hand, social ethics are not merely an expression of the essence of the church—ecclesiology *is* social ethics and social ethics *is* gospel. Gospel ethics, the church's nature as a foretaste, model, and herald of the kingdom, and the grounding of ecclesiology in the person, ethic, message, and redemptive work of Christ, are all interwoven dimensions of the same ecclesial and eschatological reality. The church is called to be an exemplification of the kingdom of God, and it is out of this

20. Cartwright, *Royal Priesthood*, 141–320.

21. Nation, *John Howard Yoder*, 77–108; Carter, *Politics of the Cross*, 186. Carter treats "the ecumenical character of Yoder's writings" in ibid., 188–90. See Yoder and McClendon, "Christian Identity," 561–80.

22. Yoder, "Nature of the Unity We Seek," 221–30.

23. Yoder, "Free Church Ecumenical Style," 231–41.

24. Yoder, "Disavowal of Constantine," 242–61.

exemplification that it has "access to social ethics." Yoder argues that he could demonstrate this from a variety of theological and scriptural standpoints. He chooses, however, "this particular Barthian innovation" as an entry point for analyzing the social ethics of Christendom since it allows him to "seek to enter the chink in the armor of the dominant Western tradition of social ethics at the point Barth has identified."[25]

Yoder explains the Barthian distinction between *Christengemeinde* (Christian community) and *Bürgergemeinde* (Civil community) as not a dualist distinction between spiritual and secular levels, dimensions, or realms, "but rather two different kinds of political and social identification." On one side are those who confess Christ as Lord, regardless of their vocation, denominational affiliations, ethnicity, and so forth, and on the other side are those who deny his lordship. The confessing church, rather than the non-confessing citizen of Christendom, is entrusted with the "gospel social ethics" especially through "telling the story of Jesus."[26] The church has a public role and much to say to the wider world, as was clearly demonstrated by the posture of the early church. This includes, but is not limited to,

1. Egalitarianism as implied by baptism into one body

2. Socialism as implied in the Eucharist

3. Forgiveness

4. The open meeting

5. The universality of giftedness.[27]

As a "liturgical or celebrating community," the church accepts its particularity, clings unashamedly to the scandalous message and vision of Jesus Christ, refuses to "relativize the claims of Christ," and embraces its embeddedness in a particular christological and eschatological narrative. The particularity of the incarnation of Jesus Christ is foundational, the source, for all Christian social ethics. While other sources might be consulted and their language might even be borrowed on occasion, Jesus' embodiment of kingdom ethics is the correct and only adequate source for Christian social ethics. "The particularity of incarnation" *is* "the universality of truth."[28] Refusing to base ethics in non-particular, "natural," or universal principles, Yoder grounds social ethics in the incarnation in a way that "would then call for and empower a *missionary ethic of incarnation*."[29]

Why is ecclesiology as social ethics in Yoder's perspective? Social ethics are a critical, indispensable dimension of ecclesiology, not because such ethics are universally applicable, irrefutably verifiable, or in harmony with the essentially relativizing "wider wisdom." Social ethics are an internally coherent and essentially demonstrative dimension of the new, eschatological community of faith; a community that has its origins, essence, and future hope in its participation and groundedness in the particular Christ-narrative. Such

25. Yoder, "Why Ecclesiology is Social Ethics," 106.

26. Ibid., 108–9.

27. Yoder, *For the Nations*, 33.

28. Yoder, *Priestly Kingdom*, 46–62.

29. Ibid., 44.

social ethics are safeguarded from "provinciality" because of the missionary nature of the faith community, and the outward-focused, affirming orientation of such ethics.[30]

Contrary to the impulse of Constantinianism to require all of human society to adhere to Christian social ethics, Yoder's believers' church ecclesiology emphatically asserts, "Christian ethics is for Christians," even if they need to be explained to the broader society. Yoder defends this approach to ecclesiology and social ethics against the charge of quietism, clericalism, or sectarian pride, and demonstrates why it is not a choice between attention to community or attention to mission and social engagement. For Yoder, these charges against his ecclesiology are caricatures—misunderstandings of his ecclesiological convictions and his view of ecclesiology as social ethics.[31] While convinced that the church is called to be an alternative community, he is not "against the nations." This is especially evident in his later work *For the Nations*, in which he argues, "that the very shape of the people of God in the world is a public witness, or is 'good news,' for the world, rather than first rejection or withdrawal."[32]

Moreover, if the church is to embrace the social ethics of Christ it must turn away from the "wider wisdom" that asserts that some ethical norms and perspectives are obvious, real, and common sense. It must pursue the ethics of Christ as an act of worship, as a "distinct consciousness," and as a celebration of the victory and reign of Jesus Christ. "The church does communicate to the world what God plans to do, because it shows that God is beginning to do it." When the church appreciates the inseparable relationship between ecclesiology, doxology, ethics, theology, and history, it "sees history doxologically." The consequences of seeing history in the light of eschatology, and with the worshipping vision demonstrated in apocalyptic literature, are many. The church's witness and ethic "explode the limits" established by the world; the church is able to discern what God is doing in history and where the powers and principalities have been at work. Yoder outlines a range of other consequences in "To Serve Our God and to Rule the World."[33]

In *The Christian Witness to the State*, Yoder writes that while Christ reigns and has overcome the state and other such powers or structures, the state exists in rebellion to his lordship. Christ's lordship is supreme, but Yoder speaks of delineation between how his lordship is expressed in the church and the state. He calls this the "order of providence," in which Christ reigns through the powers in a particular way, and the "order of redemption," in which he reigns in the church.[34] The church is called to witness to the state, because Christ has given the state a particular role in his purposes for history (to maintain order in society), and because of the cosmic, supreme, and eschatological lordship of Jesus Christ. The church witnesses to the state through its obedient discipleship to Christ; that is, through its existence as the eschatological community of hope.[35] In the light of that foundational principle, the church's witness, usually taking a critical form, will deal with

30. Yoder, "Why Ecclesiology is Social Ethics," 110–15.

31. Ibid., 118–20.

32. Yoder, *For the Nations*, 6.

33. Yoder, "To Serve Our God," 128–40.

34. Yoder, *Christian Witness*, 12.

35. Ibid., 13, 16–22.

societal issues as they arise, and will deal with them not merely through retort or proclamation, but through exemplification of the values and behaviors of the kingdom of God.[36] It will pattern its social ethics, its political actions, its efforts at facilitating reconciliation, and its community formation, around the message and life of Jesus, its "model of radical political action."[37]

As already demonstrated, in Yoder's ecclesiology the church is the eschatological community of faith that serves as herald, exemplar, and foretaste of the kingdom. Even in the face of its weaknesses, failings, and inadequacies, the church can rest in the grace that Christ is sovereignly in control, and is bringing all things to eschatological fulfillment. "But the church is responsible for the congruence between its ministry and that new world that is the church's way, because it is on the way."[38] The church is made up of people who have freely chosen to follow Jesus Christ. The responsibility of the church includes the need to interpret the social ethic of Jesus in each age and context, as informed by a careful reading of Scripture, and as exemplified by the efforts of the New Testament church to do this in a tumultuous, threatening, and constantly changing setting.[39]

"The alternative community discharges a modeling mission. The church is called to be now what the world is called to be ultimately."[40] It is called to seek peace,[41] cultivate a fresh way of seeing the world and reality, embrace and tell an "alternative narrative" (an eschatological and christological narrative), exemplify the hope and values of the kingdom, and be an alternative community characterized by a kingdom social ethic. For Yoder, orienting the church "back to true north" as an alternative, eschatological, kingdom-ethic community is to speak of "the peace church vision" as one of "worship and servanthood, reconciliation and creativity, *Gelassenheit* and the Power of Light, 'heartfelt religion' and transforming hope, and the person of Jesus."[42]

PRACTICES OF THE CHRISTIAN COMMUNITY

In an article called "Sacrament as Social Process," Yoder outlines five practices of the early church that require re-discovery and fresh interpretation in the contemporary context. He makes these practices accessible to a broader readership in his work *Body Politics*. For Yoder, the five practices are not only biblical, they also exemplify "a link between ecclesiastical practice and social ethics that is usually undervalued or ignored."[43] The church is political in the sense that it has a social organization, makes decisions, and deals with power, relationships, roles, other social groupings, and so forth. Yet it is also a dynamic human community, with connections, relationships, intimacies, and interdependencies,

---

36. Ibid., 38.
37. Yoder et al., *War of the Lamb*, 77–82.
38. Yoder, "Why Ecclesiology is Social Ethics," 123–26.
39. Yoder, *Priestly Kingdom*, 49–62, 85–88.
40. Ibid., 92.
41. Yoder et al., *Declaration on Peace*.
42. Yoder, *Priestly Kingdom*, 80–101.
43. Yoder, "Sacrament as Social Process," 34.

as indicated in the Pauline body metaphor.[44] The five practices, given slightly different names in the book and the article, are *binding and loosing, the fullness of Christ, the rule of Paul, disciples breaking bread together,* and *baptism and the new humanity.*[45] While they have rich meaning in the life of the Christian community and for the witness of the church, they can also exemplify social and political life to the wider society, especially when they are carried out with biblical faithfulness. Yoder attempts to present these practices ecumenically, which he defines as relevant and accessible to Christians across a broad range of denominational and confessional backgrounds.[46]

The five practices described by Yoder are,

1. *Binding and Loosing:* When an offence has been caused or taken, the people of God are to follow a process of confrontation, conversation, ethical and moral discernment, and, hopefully, forgiveness and reconciliation. *Binding* is about the obligation for ethical discernment, and *loosing* is about the freedom from this obligation that comes with reconciliation. Both God and people are involved. This process, "the law of Christ," begins with the particular relationship and moves outward into a congregational procedure of discernment and reconciliation. When done well it has the potential to enhance pastoral care, discipline, decision-making, and witness, and to serve as a model for society.[47]

2. *The Fullness of Christ:* The church needs to recognize and develop social processes that are coherent with the New Testament concept that every member of the body of Christ "has a distinctly identifiable, divinely validated, and empowered role." Yoder writes of the forces inhibiting full community life, ministry, and participation in the power of the Spirit. These include modern individualism, assuming we have "already arrived," Weberian distortions of charisma, labeling of a certain type of Christian piety as *charismatic,* modern use of the terms *gift* or *giftedness,* hierarchical *body images,* confusion between ministry roles and charisma, institutional rigidity, anti-structural stances, and so forth. What the New Testament calls for here, writes Yoder, is "counter-intuitive and counter-traditional." The church can witness to the wider culture as it identifies, develops, and releases all the giftings of the whole body of Christ.[48]

3. *The Rule of Paul:* While "prophecy" has a particular role when the people of God meet together, the gathered church is to be characterized by discernment and "dialogue under the Holy Spirit." This involves decentralization of power and of voice, attention to others, and real community discernment in the power of the Spirit.[49]

44. Yoder, *Body Politics*, ix.
45. Ibid., 1–70.
46. Ibid., x.
47. Ibid., 1–13; Yoder, "Sacrament as Social Process," 34–35. See Yoder, "Binding and Loosing," 323–58.
48. Yoder, *Body Politics*, 47–60.
49. Ibid., 61–70.

4.   *Disciples Breaking Bread Together:* According to Yoder, a faithful interpretation of the first "breaking of bread" in Scripture should lead us to conclude
that this was more than merely symbolic or mystical ritual or rite. It was actual,
concrete, economic sharing and solidarity. It was a sharing of resources, produc-
tive capital, jubilee values, identity, economic ethics, familial ties, vocation, charismata, and membership "of the historical community" of the age to come. This
willingness to enter into such sacrificial sharing and solidarity can be a witness
and model to the wider world.[50]

5.   *Baptism and the New Humanity:* Through baptism, people are inducted
"into a new humanity." This new humanity is one that explodes the distinctions
of class, ethnicity, and gender, and that removes "prior stratifications and classification" so that authentically egalitarian community can form. Yoder believes
that the church is called to exemplify such inclusiveness, especially in the light of
the contemporary tensions that exist with regard to ethnicity, gender, economic
distribution, and so forth. Baptism and the new humanity formed and heralded
by the church have political ramifications for inter-ethnic relations, non-violent
resistance to oppression, church planting and mission strategies, and religious
liberty. Culturally homogenous churches or missionary strategies are inappropri-
ate in the light of the biblical witness. The radical nature and the vast implications
of baptism are too often lost in the church's imagination of theology.[51]

Cartwright observes that Yoder attributes "eschatological significance" to these five
practices, since they show the world "its own calling and destiny."[52] These five practices
also have real implications for Christian social ethics and for witness and ministry in the
wider secular culture. Why does Yoder believe they are significant for ethics and witness?
They are earthy, human practices, yet God is actively involved. They are the practices of
the concrete, gathered, "believing community as a social body," that can exemplify social
processes and ethics for the wider world. Grounded in the ethic, life, and lordship of Jesus
Christ, they are not for an elite social group but for ordinary people. Not only are they
culturally appropriated in various times and settings, but they also posit the individual in
dynamic and healthy relationship to the community. They locate ethical reasoning and
behavior in the biblical narrative, apostolic model, and the New Testament church's frame
of reference. This "apostolic model" honors the relationship between reason, behavior,
community, and revelation. These five practices call the church to "respect the world's unbelief," while rejecting any social ethics characterized by a dualism that separates "Christ
from culture or law from gospel or creation from redemption." They are best practiced in
a spirit of service, and with attention to the church's formation as a new, eschatological
community of hope—a sign, model, herald, and foretaste of the kingdom of God.[53]

50.   Ibid., 14–27.

51.   Ibid., 28–46.

52.   Cartwright, *Royal Priesthood*, 360; Yoder, "Sacrament as Social Process," 44.

53.   Yoder, *Body Politics*, 71–80. See Husbands and Treir, *Community of the Word*, 182–87.

CONTRIBUTIONS TO MISSIONAL ECCLESIOLOGY

In his thorough examination of the theological and ethical thought of Yoder, Carter maps out "eight characteristics as keys to the proper interpretation" of Yoder. He suggests that Yoder's social ethics are characterized by post liberalism, Anabaptist thought, Barthian influence, ecumenism, and Christocentric and trinitarian themes, among other characteristics. Carter's criticisms of Yoder include the negative consequences of Yoder's refusal to systematize his thought, and the paucity of attention Yoder pays to the resurrection of Christ and to prayer.[54] Yoder's ecclesiology advances the missional ecclesiology in *Part Two* of this book through its christological, missiological, trinitarian, ecclesial, and gospel-culture frames of reference.[55] Yoder's ecclesiology is grounded in Christology and especially in the narratives of the Gospels. Christ's obedience, ethic, message, suffering, and death establish the spirit of Christian social ethics and shape the nature and eschatological vision of the church. Yoder's believers' church ecclesiology refuses to separate the purpose and essence of the church from the meaning of history, from the mission of God in the world, or from the "meaningfulness of the gospel message." The church of Jesus Christ is called to embrace a distinct "social existence," which includes reflecting trinitarian themes. This social existence and relationship to the broader culture involves rejecting violence and power, refusing to entertain any heretical Constantinian notions, pursuing holiness and biblical social ethics, cultivating both meaningful community and missionary presence, respecting free association, and imitating the servant nature of Christ. A faithful church abandons the reach for power, prestige, and effectiveness, and imitates "the foolish weakness of the cross" as "the city set on the hill. The true church is the *free* church." As we look at history, with discerning and eschatological eyes, we see God's sovereign purposes unfolding, including the formation of a new, redeemed, eschatological community.

Yoder's ecclesiology is consequential for the missional ecclesiology in this book and especially considerations about the priesthood of all believers, the missionary "marks" of the church, planting new missionary communities, interfaith and ecumenical dialogue, cultivating the practices of discipleship and Christ-centered community, and finally, of course, missional contextualization and public ethics. Ecclesiology for Yoder is social ethics and social ethics is gospel. Any attempt to extricate ecclesiology from social ethics, or from Christology or gospel, produces a deficient ecclesiological outcome. As I have already described, in Yoder's ecclesiology gospel ethics, the church's nature as a foretaste, model, and herald of the kingdom, and the grounding of ecclesiology in the person, ethic, gospel message, and redemptive work of Christ, are all interwoven dimensions of the same ecclesial and eschatological reality. As an exemplification and herald of the kingdom of God, the church has "access to social ethics." The incarnation provides a firm footing for social ethics, empowering a "missionary ethic of incarnation." Furthermore, as an alternative, eschatological, kingdom-ethic community, the church is to cultivate concrete practices linking the ecclesial life of the church with social ethics, and with the church's

54. Carter, *Politics of the Cross*, 22–37.
55. He features in chapters 14 and 15 in *Part Two* of this book.

presence in the world. Practices like the five that Yoder details in *Body Politics* can exemplify social and political life to the wider society. This is especially the case when these practices are characterized by biblical faithfulness and in the imitation of Christ.

I have flagged Carter's considerations on Yoder's ecclesiology and I agree with his concerns, and would supplement these with the issues raised by Peter Leithart, who has provided a recent sympathetic but critical analysis of Yoder's concept of Constantinianism. Drawing on the most recent scholarship in the field, Leithart is sympathetic to Yoder's theological portrait of Constantinianism. However, Leithart does contest three dimensions of Yoder's constructions of Constantinianism—firstly, Yoder's views on the historical Constantine; secondly, Yoder's possible convolution of ecclesiological and christological positions; and, thirdly, the way in which Yoder's anti-Constantinianism, especially in its eschatological shape, becomes a form of Constantinianism. He is also unconvinced by the biblical support Yoder provides for pacifism. Leithart's willingness to engage Yoder deeply and his appreciation for much of what Yoder is attempting to achieve theologically make this book an excellent foil and dialogue partner for Yoder's views on Constantinianism. The reader may not agree with all of Leithart's reflections on Yoderian theology—certainly much remains open for ongoing debate—but Leithart's work helps identify matters that are worth further consideration.[56]

An ecumenical, unifying imagination and vision permeate Yoder's ecclesiology. Yoder asserts that the unity that will characterize the eschaton should not be neglected in the church today. As "foretaste/model/herald of the kingdom," the church is to pursue visible, substantial, and genuine unity in the contemporary era. Such unity is essential to the church's nature, even though it presents some obvious challenges. Authentic conversations, characterized by a willingness to change positions when necessary, and located primarily in real relationship and local congregations, are the believers' church "ecumenical style."

QUESTIONS FOR REFLECTION

1. What does Yoder understand to be the "heresy of Constantinianism"? If it is not primarily about a person called Constantine, or even a period of history called Christendom, what are the key features of Constantinianism?

2. "Peoplehood and mission, fellowship and witness, are not two desiderata, each capable of existing or of being missed independently of each other; each is the condition of the genuineness of the other." What are the implications of this for our churches?

3. Discuss Yoder's five practices of the church. How would you apply them in your context? In what ways could they serve as a model for the world's social and ethical relations?

---

56. Leithart, *Defending Constantine*. See Buttrey on common ways in which people misinterpret or "prematurely write off Yoder": Buttrey, "Twelve Ways," 8–11.

11

Barry Harvey:
The Church as *Altera Civitas*

The first Christians consistently described themselves as citizens of an altera civitas, another city, with a population garnered from every tribe and language, people and nation . . . Although the church fostered its own political identity, thereby denying ultimate authority to Roman rule, it did not seek to isolate its members from the rest of the world . . . On the contrary . . . It cultivated its social existence as a distinct politeia within and for the sake of the world.[1]

—BARRY HARVEY

ECCLESIALLY GROUNDED HERMENEUTICS

BARRY HARVEY ATTEMPTS TO construct an "ecclesially based theological hermeneutics" in the introductory chapter of *Can These Bones Live?*[2] Harvey contends that the church's practices, forms, and existence as "the earthly-historical body of Christ," provide such a theological hermeneutic for the broader society and world.[3] By this he means that the visible church and its concrete, formative practices provide a theological hermeneutic about how human beings are meant to live in relationship with each other and with God, and about the current state of the world and its affairs. The church's life, language, and practices provide an ecclesially grounded hermeneutic "about the possibilities of human action, fulfillment, and happiness." This hermeneutic is also about the relationship between these things, human flourishing, the past, present, and future, and the "life, death, and resurrection of the man Jesus of Nazareth."[4]

---

1. Harvey, *Another City*, 23–25. Barry Harvey has served as Associate Professor of Theology in the Honors College of Baylor University, Waco, Texas, since 1988.

2. Harvey, *Can These Bones Live?*, 11.

3. Ibid., 12.

4. Ibid., 13.

For Harvey, this ecclesially based hermeneutic emphasizes the concrete, visible, earthy forms and practices of the church, handed down to each generation for them to adapt, preserve, and pass on to the next generation of believers. Such an ecclesiology emphasizes,

> . . . the constitutive practices of the church: Scripture reasoning, doctrine, baptism and Eucharist, and spiritual formation. I refer to these practices as constitutive because all Christians must engage in them in some fashion if we are to cultivate and sustain the distinctive form of life that characterizes the body of Christ in the world.[5]

The difficulty that naturally arises in such a church-based hermeneutic, confesses Harvey, is the obvious division and disorientation in the visible, earthly-historical church. This division is not merely along theological, confessional, or denominational lines but includes the fracturedness and uncertainty experienced by the people of God because of consumerism, individualism, humanistic materialism, and other dimensions of modern societies. The body of Christ has come "dismembered" because of these significant cultural shifts in modern societies and because of the failed social project of western Christendom.[6] Christians have become intrigued and captured by superficial consumeristic desires, privatized faith, individualistic choices, the workings of the modern nation-state, and the perspectives of liberal capitalism. These things have largely replaced the ecclesial "constitutive practices that made it possible for women and men, in the power of the Spirit, to participate in the economy of God's redemptive work in the world, with the capacity to imagine, reason, desire, feel, and act as members of Christ's true body."[7]

In Harvey's ecclesiology, the answer to the dilemma just described is not a return to Christendom, since many of the church's issues have their origin in the ecclesiological errors of Christendom. Instead, drawing on the imagery in Ezekiel's "valley of dry bones," Harvey proposes that the way forward involves a return to an ecclesial identity as *altera civitas*. *Altera civitas* means "another city," and is about the church's self-understanding as another, alternative, distinct community and social grouping from that of the world. This includes a renewed hermeneutic, witness, and community life grounded in the constitutive practices of the church. Harvey asserts that this involves examining our shared history and repenting and returning to spiritual passion in the church. It is also about cultivating an ecclesial identity around our christological convictions, our eschatological hope, and our sense of the place of the church within human history.[8] As the church shapes its constitutive practices and ecclesiological identity around the person, message, death, and resurrection of Christ, and around the eschatological, apocalyptic reign of God, the metaphorical "dry bones" of the church can live again. The church can then "interpret the persons, structures, and institutions that constitute the present world by comparing them to its own social practice that manifests (imperfectly to be sure) the form of community that alone truly deserves the title of peace: the City of God."[9]

5. Ibid., 14.
6. Ibid., 15–19.
7. Ibid., 17.
8. Ibid., 18–21.
9. Ibid., 31.

Harvey suggests that ecclesiology has the following role in post-Christendom.

> The principal aim of a post-Christendom ecclesiology, it seems to me, should be to help the church speak again in a self-consciously authoritative way, and thus let it reclaim itself as the church. This ecclesiology, however, will also provide a critical reading of a consumerist liberal society to the extent that it defines the body of Christ, in its practices and institutions, as in continuity and discontinuity with liberalism's social dispensation.[10]

A *modus vivendi* is an agreement between two parties, for instance, the post-Christendom church and the consumeristic postmodern society. Both parties work out a way to live together in the face of their disagreements and alternative ways of understanding reality. Harvey is concerned to see the church in post-Christendom understand itself, and especially its body politic and social ethic, as distinct from the world. The church provides a "critical reading" of the world and a contrasting dialogue partner for it. He believes that these tasks, which happen to be dimensions of the church as *altera civitas*, are the essential aims of ecclesiology in post-Christendom. In many of his writings, he draws on and extends the work of Dietrich Bonhoeffer to achieve these goals, along with various eastern Orthodox theologians.

Quoting John Zizioulas, Harvey writes that the "*raison d'être* of theology as an ecclesial activity" is located in the concrete, visible, and social practices of the church's worship, fellowship, mission, and obedience. Theology cannot be separated from ecclesiology or from the concrete practices of the church. Theology's *reason for being* "as an ecclesial activity" is, therefore,

> . . . tied to those practices and habits that enable us, in the power of the Spirit, to receive (by returning) the gift of God's own Triune way of being, a mode of life and of public service (the original meaning of liturgy) that "is not a moral attainment . . . (but) a way of *relationship* with the world, with other people and with God, an event of *communion*."[11]

Much has been written recently about theological hermeneutics, church effectiveness and health, missiological impetus, and trinitarian, interpersonal communion. Harvey suggests that these spheres of the church's life are interrelated, and that they can never really be achieved through mere abstract speculation. The visible, embodied, earthly-historical church explores and gives meaning to these dimensions of its life. This is especially the case in its constitutive practices: "Scripture reasoning, doctrine, baptism and Eucharist, and spiritual formation."[12] Through these constitutive practices the church has, and provides the world with, a hermeneutical lens. This lens is "a distinct way of interpreting the world, both as it has been and now is, and as it will be in the end."[13] Perceiving God's apocalyptic action in history, and especially in Jesus Christ, the church

---

10. Harvey, "Body Politic of Christ," 321; Guroian, *Ethics after Christendom*, 3.

11. Harvey, "Round and Round," 114; Zizioulas, *Being as Communion*, 15.

12. Harvey, *Can These Bones Live?*, 14.

13. Ibid., 50.

continues that action through its "life, worship, and witness." It provides an interpretation for all of human history.[14]

Using the Eucharist as an analogy, and in contrast to James McClendon's assertion that the contemporary church *is* the primitive church, Harvey argues that the contemporary church *is* and *is not* the primitive church. The church *is* the primitive church, since it is the primitive church's heir and continuation. The church *is not* the primitive church, since the church seeks to be faithful in a completely different world than that of the primitive church, and since the church is not yet unified across the ages in the eschaton. This dialectic of *is* and *is not* is the context in which the church seeks to faithfully be God's people in the present age, while recognizing its heritage, nature, and eschatological hope.[15]

As the early church found itself caught-up and transformed by the events surrounding Christ, that is, by the "*apocalypse* of the long-awaited eschatological reign of God," they embraced a "new set of allegiances, beliefs, dispositions, and loves." Proclaiming the gospel of Christ, they found themselves in conflict with the powers and principalities, and a part of a historical, apocalyptic narrative. Connected with the broader, historical story of the people of God, the early church pursued discipleship to Christ and shaped its ecclesial identity around its sense of location in this apocalyptic narrative. It saw itself as "under the apocalyptic shadow of the cross."[16] "God's apocalyptic reign in the ministry, passion, and triumph of Jesus Christ" so captured the early church's desires and allegiances, that their sense of identity was transformed. Their passion to preach and embody the message of Christ was fanned into flame and their confrontation with the world's powers was guaranteed. They found themselves "caught up in the apocalyptic action of God," not only called to communicate a gospel message, but also to put their lives and families at risk.[17]

It is clear that Harvey's desire is for a similar apocalyptic eschatology to fuel the passion of the contemporary western church. For Harvey, this apocalyptic eschatology, along with a sense of ecclesiological identity formed as a marginal, alternative community, holds the key to the contemporary church's renewal. The church needs to develop an ecclesially based theological hermeneutic for its own sake and for the world. Harvey contrasts the early church's apocalyptic conviction with the spirit of liberal capitalism, which he believes defines the modern western church's practices and identity. He is convinced that the roots of this demise are to be found in the fourth-century Constantinian shift and its associated theological vestiges.

ALTERA CIVITAS AND THE RISE OF CHRISTENDOM

Harvey devotes considerable attention to the church as *altera civitas*, an alternative *polis* with a distinct *politeia*, in his book *Another City*. As a minority religious group, viewed with suspicion by the broader society and the governing powers, the early church understood itself to be a distinct community. It viewed itself as an alternative political structure

14. Ibid., 50–51.

15. Ibid., 51–55.

16. Ibid., 57–59.

17. Ibid., 78–90.

within the broader culture. As a parallel and distinct community, it not only subverted the resident powers, it was also shaped by a desire to serve, heal, and restore the broader culture, in the light of the gospel of Jesus Christ. Therefore, Harvey concludes, the early church did not pursue an isolated sectarianism or introverted self-interest. The early church's ministry and mission within the broader culture were fashioned with a view to the servant leadership of Christ: that is, his triumphant death and resurrection, his eschatological vision, and the pilgrim but pivotal role he allocated the church within human history.[18]

> The church was therefore not merely the agency or the constituency of a mission program, the contents of which were essentially distinct from its practices and institutions. The community was the mission (Yoder 1994b:91).[19]

Describing further the early church's view of itself as *altera civitas*, Harvey writes that its "eschatological ecclesiology (or ecclesial eschatology)" was fashioned around the idea that it was called to be an alternative, distinct *polis* and community; that is, a city with a unique polity, politics, and identity. It saw itself as living in the age between Christ's resurrection and his glorious return, and "continuing Israel's story under new circumstances."[20]

Harvey traces the roots of this eschatological ecclesiology through the various twists and turns in the history of the people of Israel, including the eschatological self-understanding that unfolded in Israel's theology and political identity. For the early church, this drama reached its climax in the person, passion, and resurrection of Jesus Christ. Jesus was "nothing less or other than the presence of the kingdom in his person—the *autobasileia*."[21] Joseph Ratzinger describes the concept of the *autobasileia* well. Ratzinger writes, "Jesus himself is the Kingdom; the Kingdom is not a thing, it is not a geographical dominion like worldly kingdoms. It is a person; it is he."[22]

As not only ushering in a new kingdom, but himself the content and presence of that kingdom, Jesus continued on this ministry-of-kingdom-presence through the church. The early church considered itself the bearers of this christological and eschatological kingdom presence. Harvey is convinced that the early church's eschatological awareness and desire to make Christ's kingdom presence known were not merely theological constructs. Rather, these convictions were embodied in the early church's constitutive practices, missiological endeavors, and social forms as an *altera civitas*. For Harvey, while the early church was far from perfect in this regard, the Constantinian shift eroded much of this important eschatological ecclesiology. This included an erosion of this ecclesiology's associated practices.[23]

John Howard Yoder has significantly influenced Harvey's ecclesiology, as the bibliography to *Another City* demonstrates. Following the lead of Yoder and John Milbank,

18. Harvey, *Another City*, 21–26.

19. Ibid., 27.

20. Ibid., 34–35. Harvey is quoting Clapp here: Clapp, *Peculiar People*, 88.

21. Harvey, *Another City*, 55.

22. Ratzinger, *Jesus of Nazareth*, 49; Harvey et al., *Stormfront*, 11–27.

23. Harvey, *Another City*, 54–63; Harvey, *Can These Bones Live?*, 93–96.

Harvey explains the nature and effects of the Constantinian shift. He contrasts the "radically realized eschatology" of Constantinianism with the eschatology of the early church.[24] Whereas the pre-Constantinian church cultivated a clear distinction between itself and the world, after Constantine the church began to redefine its identity, ethic, vocation, and mission. The church began to see the meaning of history located in the structures and purposes of the broader culture. Church and world became blurred in the minds and concrete experience of Christians and those not committed to following Christ alike.[25]

Harvey argues that this Constantinian shift can be traced throughout western history to the present day and that it was not addressed in the Reformation.[26] The North American "social arrangement that sanctioned a moral and cultural identity between mainline Protestant Christianity and the liberal nation-state" is another form of Constantinianism. In contrast to the ecclesiological self-understandings of the early church, "another political vision" or "a radically realized eschatology" established itself in western Christendom. This vision and eschatology has been, and continues to be, difficult to dislodge. For Harvey, this process of erosion of the authentic, biblical vision of the church as *altera civitas* was further established by the Cartesian shift.[27]

THE CHURCH IN MODERN AND POSTMODERN CULTURE

With the Cartesian shift in western culture came the preeminence of reason, the spread of secular values, and the impulse to dominate nature. One might suggest that divinity was attributed to humanity and especially to human capacity, freedom, domination, and reason. In the Constantinian shift, writes Harvey, church and world were blurred in such a way that the church lost much of the ecclesiological vision of the early church. This included its role as a distinct *altera civitas* at the center of the eschatological meaning of history. In the Cartesian shift, the architects of this second philosophical and cultural shift sought to rid secular society of any of these eschatological or providential vestiges. Any notion of God's providential presence in, or purpose for, the natural or finite world, was rejected. Human reason, capacity, and will were elevated above all ideas of providence or fate. This type of thinking continues to dominate western culture today. It is expressed in secular humanism, the liberal nation-state, modern economics and science, and so forth. So-called "post-modern" changes have not dislodged the Cartesian shift, and some would suggest that it has only deepened.[28]

Harvey goes on to describe the current expressions of this Cartesian shift. These include modern human individualism, the pursuit of scientific progress, and the elevation of choice. To those we might add the notion of pluralism, the "invention of religion," the machinations of liberal capitalism, and the "role of the market."[29] In this

24. Harvey, *Another City*, 72–73.

25. Harvey, *Can These Bones Live?*, 99–110; Harvey, "Re-Membering the Body," 103.

26. Harvey, *Can These Bones Live?*, 110.

27. Harvey, *Another City*, 74–94; Harvey, "From the Heart of the Storm," 331.

28. Harvey, *Another City*, 95–111.

29. Ibid., 112–19; Harvey, *Can These Bones Live?*, 111–23.

setting, secularization and religion are not two competing forces. Instead, by designating a particular, private, separate sphere of experience and culture as "religion," this religious framework serves to support modern "cultural rationalization." Religion and secularization are "actually complementary artifacts of the modern world which together serve to weave the whole of creation into the rationalized fabric of Western culture."[30] Harvey especially laments how personal and corporate identities have shifted away from the "explicit harmonies of an intentional community." This identity is now "constructed within the vast (though often implicit) technical organizational of modernity."[31]

The result of these changes, in Harvey's estimation, is an "obvious spiritual, moral, and ecological poverty," and a paradoxical "risk culture." In this postmodern risk culture people attempt to manage the risk around them, while living unpredictable, particular lives themselves. The severance of people from their "communal roots and traditions . . . habits and customs," causes much of this impoverishment and risk-aversion.[32] Religion is compartmentalized, morality is eroded, and consumerism grips people's lives and imaginations. The modern enthusiasm for spirituality is Gnostic-like and therapeutic, and this includes much of contemporary western Christian spirituality. Harvey asserts that spirituality in much of the contemporary western church has greater similarities with Gnosticism than with biblical spirituality. The church, however, as *altera civitas*, must pursue a different path of self-understanding, spiritual formation as discipleship, and mission.[33]

RECOVERING *ALTERA CIVITAS* IN POST-CHRISTENDOM

Harvey recognizes the difficulties of recovering the ecclesiological notion of *altera civitas* in post-Christendom and in a postmodern culture. For Harvey, this is neither a sectarian isolation from the world nor an attempt to recover what has been lost since the Cartesian shift in modern culture. It is not an attempt to reproduce an identical community to the early church. Nor is it the pursuit of a fantasy, "a premature triumphalism, the illusion that a community can successfully avoid the ambiguities of power and so attain in the present world a perfection that in Scripture and tradition is reserved for the age to come."[34]

Regardless of the difficulties and of the temptations to practice isolation, nostalgia for Christendom, uncritical reproduction of early church forms, or other illusions, Harvey contends that the biblical mandate to recover *altera civitas* in our present context is undeniable. Drawing on the work of George Lindbeck and others, Harvey believes that the experience of Israel in diaspora can serve as a model or guide for the contemporary, pilgrim church in western culture.[35] He is cautious, however, about allowing this to be-

30. Harvey, "Post-Critical Approach," 39.

31. Harvey, *Another City*, 121.

32. Ibid., 127.

33. Ibid., 128–34; Harvey et al., *Stormfront*, 1–11; Harvey, "Post-Critical Approach," 45–48; Harvey, "Body Politic of Christ," 327–29; Harvey, "Eucharistic Idiom," 305–10.

34. Harvey, *Another City*, 12, and see the whole section on pages 9–20; Harvey, "Body Politic of Christ," 323; Harvey, "From the Heart of the Storm," 329–30.

35. Harvey, *Another City*, 138–45; Harvey, "Body Politic of Christ," 339–42; Harvey, "From the Heart of

come ecclesiological abstraction. Consequently, he endeavors to ground the connection between the church in postmodern culture and the diasporic experience of the Jewish people in the concrete, visible, historical experiences and expressions of the church. This includes, for instance, the way the social forms of the church continue the eschatological hopes of the Jewish people in diaspora. Harvey emphasizes the "genesis of the church from its roots in historic Judaism *and* its subsequent history." The constitutive, social practices of the church developed from their Jewish pedigree and the church, like the people of Israel in diaspora, needs to cultivate a sense of distinctive "orientation in time, rather than control over space."[36]

As I have suggested, Harvey works with the perspectives and language of Yoder, de Certeau, Bonhoeffer, Brueggemann, Lindbeck, and a few others, in order to demonstrate the implications of the Jewish diaspora for the church in postmodern culture. He also wants to contrast what he calls "postmodern risk culture" with "the diasporic politics of the church." He undertakes this comparison of the contemporary church with the Jewish diaspora, and this contrasting of secular culture and ecclesial politic, with particular reference to the church's "body politics." He notes how the church's historical memory, social dynamics, eucharistic practice, marginality, liturgy, and missiology can be understood in the light of the Jewish diaspora. Furthermore, the church's eucharistic worship, as an *altera civitas*, is, according to Harvey, deeply connected with its mission in postmodern culture. This eucharistic worship is not only about liturgy and about sacrament, not only about gathered worship and about partaking of the Lord's Supper. It is also about how the church does mission, justice, service, and presence in the world, *and* the concrete forms of its body politic.[37]

In a review of a book by Anton Houtepen, Harvey makes the point that it is "a bit arrogant" to suggest "all is lost for the church if Europe relapses into a postmodern form of paganism." This is especially true when we consider the expansion of the church in the Majority World contexts.[38] I agree with Harvey's point. However, it is a shame that he does not turn to Majority World churches for clues on how the post-Christendom church might exist as an alternative, dispersed community;[39] that is, as an *altera civitas*, immersed in the realities of marginality and misunderstanding. Many Christian communities in these Majority World contexts have been wrestling with these issues and others that Harvey raises, for generations.

Harvey writes that an ecclesiological identity that is adequate for the current postmodern context is shaped by the dynamic relationship between the church's self-understanding as *altera civitas* and as parallel *polis*, and its concrete constitutive practices and body politic. It is an identity characterized by a sense of being a pilgrim people. The church is in the center of the meaning of history. This identity results in the practice of

the Storm," 319–25. See Lindbeck, "Church."

36. Harvey, *Another City*, 146–48.

37. Ibid., 150–57; Harvey, *Can These Bones Live?*, 123–27.

38. Harvey, "God," 576.

39. I will address the question of theological voices from the Majority World in my forthcoming volume on missional ecclesiology.

a body politic that involves a form of "sanctified subversion." As an alternative community, the church exists as a contrast to the spirit of the world, and a threat to the powers and principalities. The church is a reflection of the loving service and sacrifice of Jesus Christ.[40] Rather than making peace with the established rulers and perspectives of this age, the church is to foster a body politic grounded in the ethics and constitutive practices of Scripture. The church is to be a clear and uncompromising alternative to the established order.[41] When the church truly appreciates its eschatological vocation in the present age and makes the costly but crucial decision to *be* the church, then it is serving Jesus Christ and his kingdom obediently and authentically.[42]

ECUMENICALLY SHAPED CONSTITUTIVE PRACTICES

In Part Two of *Can These Bones Live?* Harvey outlines four constitutive practices that might help the post-Christendom church explore fresh forms of biblical faithfulness, witness, and ecclesiological vitality. He is convinced that these core, constitutive ecclesial practices can help the contemporary western church discover fresh, earthly-historical ways to follow Christ, and to be *altera civitas*. These core practices include the imaginative interpretation and reading of Scripture, and the Christ-centered and community-formed development of sound doctrine. They also include the centrality of baptism and Eucharist in the formation of an eschatological body politic, and the practices of spiritual discipline that "incorporate the habits and skills of the church's interpretive art into our bodies."[43] Finally, Harvey locates these core ecclesial practices in "the cultivation of the church as a distinctive social body." His argument for these practices is developed ecumenically, that is, with reference to a wide and impressive range of theological and literary sources and personalities.

Harvey believes that imagination, fueled by the narratives of Scripture, can forge a conversation between the senses and the intellect. Reading Scripture imaginatively, and seeing the contemporary relevance and counter-cultural demands of Scripture's narratives, can help Christians move toward scriptural reasoning. Harvey is not convinced that factual/mechanical or experiential/symbolic approaches to reading Scripture serve the post-Christendom church well. Instead, Harvey advocates a reading of Scripture in community, in such a way that the ongoing connection between the narratives of Scripture, the shared history of the people of God, and the present experience of the church, becomes clear. This is also an eschatological reading, as the community understands itself continuing this narrative until the final return and glorification of Jesus Christ. The narratives of Scripture are the church's historical memory and can be a "travel itinerary" for the contemporary church.[44]

---

40. Harvey, *Another City*, 158–65; Harvey, "Body Politic of Christ," 336–38.

41. Harvey, "Re-Membering the Body," 96–116; Harvey, "Insanity, Theocracy," 51–52.

42. Harvey, "Post-Critical Approach," 50–52.

43. Harvey, *Can These Bones Live?*, 22–25.

44. Ibid., 131–64.

The role of sound doctrine is in danger of being marginalized in post-Christendom western Christianity. Harvey is concerned that doctrine's proper function is understood and that its relationship to scriptural reasoning is appreciated. Church doctrine should not be a mere system of abstract theological constructs. Instead, sound doctrine serves the church best when it is integrated "with the other practices and virtues of the church." Doctrine is meant to complement an imaginative community reading of Scripture and to center on Christ. Scriptural reasoning introduces us to the content of faith through a process of imaginative engagement with Scripture's narratives, and doctrinal theologizing helps us understand the meaning of that content. Such doctrine should shape, and be shaped by, the other core ecclesial practices of the church. This doctrinal discovery and articulation should be grounded in the ongoing missiological, liturgical, and community life of the church.[45]

The church's eucharistic worship is crucial to the formation of its "distinctive social idiom," its authentic unity, and its missiological passion. Harvey wants to avoid a Gnostic-like or otherworldly view of baptism and Eucharist, and to redress the divisions surrounding the sacramental practices that were originally designed to bring unity. He wants to highlight the role of these sacraments in the formation of a concrete, eschatologically witnessing social idiom. Eucharistic worship and baptism, according to Harvey, are fundamentally about the church's "body politic." They are about how the church expresses its mission, community life, *altera civitas*, and eschatological presence before a watching world. They are apocalyptic actions, testifying to the ultimate apocalyptic actions and reign of Jesus Christ.[46]

Combined with scriptural reasoning and sound doctrine, baptism and Eucharist provide a solid base of faith-community practices, upon which can be built practices of personal formation. These practices of spiritual formation enable Christians to embody the social idioms and values of the kingdom of God, of the age to come—not only individually, but also in their shared social life as an alternative, parallel community.

> The practices of spiritual formation—prayer, confession, the giving and receiving of counsel, forgiveness and reconciliation, fasting, hospitality, and the works of mercy —are a necessary complement to the work of these other constitutive activities of the church, enabling Jesus's followers to embody in their daily lives the ultimate meaning and destiny of creation.[47]

Finally, Harvey suggests that these constitutive practices provide Christians with the resources to be a pilgrim people in the present age; that is, the resources the church needs to be a city that is moving toward the age to come, and that understands its eschatological significance in history. The church is to provide a contrast to the prevailing culture's *libido dominandi*, that is, its "lust for mastery" over creation and others. The church witnesses to and embodies a "different economy" from that of liberal capitalism, cultivating associations and relationships that speak of an age to come. Its role is to establish "a new, universal society" that not only testifies to the age to come, but is in the center of the meaning of

45. Ibid., 165–98.

46. Ibid., 199–231; Harvey, "Eucharistic Idiom," 301–18; Harvey, "Post-Critical Approach," 52–56.

47. Harvey, *Can These Bones Live?*, 231–64.

history, setting the pace and standard for the rest of society.[48] In other words, "the church which participates in God's messianic suffering is the vanguard of the new humanity."[49]

CONTRIBUTIONS TO MISSIONAL ECCLESIOLOGY

Harvey's Free Church ecclesiology is developed ecumenically, through conversation with a wide range of theological, philosophical, and literary sources. Harvey's ecclesiology facilitates the shaping of a missional ecclesiology in *Part Two* of this book, through its ecclesial, gospel-culture, and hermeneutical observations.[50] For Harvey, the church and its constitutive practices provide a theological hermeneutic for the world, that is, for the world's present state, essential meaning, relationships, and future possibilities. The church is such a hermeneutic because of its relationship to Christ and his eschatological purposes for history and for humankind. The visible, earthly-historical church and its practices provide an ecclesially based theological hermeneutic.

The central ecclesiological motif in Harvey's writings is the nature of the church as *altera civitas*, an alternative *polis* with a distinct *politeia*. This understanding of the church as an alternative society influences his perspectives on the renewal of the church in a post-Christendom context, the possibilities of ecumenical dialogue with other systems of theological thought, the role of worship and liturgy in shaping the culture and imagination of this alternative society, and the nature of discipleship in a rapidly changing cultural context. The church is a parallel and distinct community, subverting the present powers and age, providing a standard and vanguard for the world as a foretaste of the age to come. As an alternative, distinct *polis*, the church needs to cultivate its unique constitutive practices, so that its "body politic," ethic, and social forms are counter-cultural, missiological, and Christ-glorifying.

While Harvey's ecclesiological insights have been applauded, especially in Free Church and Anabaptist contexts, some theologians have raised concerns, or at least some suggested modifications to his theological constructs. I think their reservations have merit:

1. J. Nelson Jennings suggests that western ecclesiologists should be careful not to develop a post-Christendom ecclesiology without consulting the theological and missionary voices of the Majority World.[51]

2. Dale Coulter cautions that while the social practices of particular faith communities can afford those communities real insight into truth, they need sources outside themselves to arbitrate or inform their findings (Harvey would not deny this). The Holy Spirit can break into the community's experience with fresh insight alongside, over-and-above, or within its social practices.[52]

---

48. Ibid., 265–87; Harvey, "Where, Then, Do We Stand?," 378–79; Harvey, *Politics of the Theological*, 2.

49. Harvey, "Post-Critical Approach," 56.

50. He features in chapters 14 and 15 in *Part Two* of this book.

51. Jennings, "Another City," 304.

52. Coulter, "Another City," 335–36.

3. Hans Boersma believes that Harvey needs to treat the issue of ecclesial authority in a substantive manner, and Edward Oakes is concerned that the eclectic, "homeless" character of Harvey's ecclesiology tends to convolute or muddy his proposals.[53]

John Howard Yoder and Dietrich Bonhoeffer heavily influence Harvey's post-Christendom, Free Church ecclesiology—an ecclesiology that is steeped in the thought of postliberalism and radical orthodoxy. Harvey asserts that the church's core, constitutive practices—Scripture reasoning, doctrine, baptism and Eucharist, and spiritual formation—can help the church *be* the church in the present age. They can also help the church *re-member* its distinct, visible social idioms, as a sign, foretaste, and herald of the kingdom of God. They provide the resources for the pilgrim city, which is journeying toward the age to come. Like the Jewish people in diaspora, the church can discover purpose and identity "as a distinct minority, remaining an uncompromising and faithful servant of God's final (though still future) triumph in the risen Christ."[54]

QUESTIONS FOR REFLECTION

1. Harvey asserts that the early church understood itself as *altera civitas*. What does he mean by this? What difference would it make to your church to see itself as *altera civitas*?

2. Sound doctrine serves the church best when it is integrated "with the other practices and virtues of the church." Is this true, and, if it is, what are the implications?

3. Discuss the practices of spiritual formation. Which of these are you using, and how would you expand this list?

53. Boersma, "Can These Bones Live?"; Oakes, "Can These Bones Live?"
54. Harvey, *Another City*, back cover.

12

Miroslav Volf:
The Church as Image of the Trinity

Life in the small Christian community in Novi Sad taught me two basic ecclesiological lessons . . . The first lesson: 'no church without the reign of God.' The church lives from something and toward something that is greater than the church itself. When the windows facing toward the reign of God get closed, darkness descends upon the church and the air gets heavy, when the windows facing toward the reign of God are opened, the life-giving breath and light of God give the churches fresh hope. The second lesson: 'no reign of God without the church.' Just as the life of the churches depends on the reign of God, so also does the vitality of the hope for the reign of God depend on the communities of faith.[1]

—MIROSLAV VOLF

WHERE TWO OR THREE ARE GATHERED

MIROSLAV VOLF GROUNDS HIS ecclesiology in the theological framework of "God's eschatological new creation," meaning that the church is the gathering of God's people in joyous and vigilant expectation of the final gathering of the entire people of God throughout the ages.[2] Moreover, in this age, there is "no church without the reign of God," and there is "no reign of God without the church." The church not only waits in hopeful expectation of the liberating indwelling of the triune God, but also experiences this presence in its present manifestation.[3] "Present participation in the trinitarian *communio* through faith in Jesus Christ anticipates in history the ecclesiological communion

---

1. Volf, *After Our Likeness*, x. The subtitle for this chapter on Volf's ecclesiology is the same as the subtitle for Volf's book *After Our Likeness*. Miroslav Volf was formerly Professor of Systematic Theology at Fuller Theological Seminary, California, and is a member of both the Presbyterian Church of the United States, and the Evangelical Church in Croatia. He is now Director of the Yale Centre for Faith and Culture, and Henry B. Wright Professor of Theology, Yale University Divinity School, New Haven, Connecticut.

2. Ibid., 128.

3. Volf and Lee, "Spirit and the Church," 29.

of the church with the Triune God."[4] Furthermore, this communion with God, expressed through the gathered community, is a relationship with the triune God enabled through the Spirit. It integrates the present church and particular local churches with the extended history of the people of God throughout the ages.[5] The internal and external processions of the Trinity are, ideally, instructive for and formative of the communion/mission poles of the church. Volf's ecclesiology, as indicated in the subtitle to *After Our Likeness*, portrays the church as the image of the Trinity.

For Volf, the presence of the church in the world is necessarily externally perceivable since the church is identifiable when, through a congregation, the presence of the Spirit is mediated or the effects of the Spirit's presence are evident.[6] Therefore the nature of the church cannot be separated from the evidence of the church. Whenever the church is present it has an eschatological and manifest impact on the world in which it resides. Volf tends to diminish the "mystery" or invisible aspect of the church in his ecclesiology, an aspect which certainly receives fuller treatment in the ecclesiologies of Ratzinger and Zizioulas.

In Free Church ecclesiology the constitutive presence of the Spirit of Christ in a church is manifested by the word, the sacraments, the presence of the people, obedience to Christ's commandments, and the biblical organization of the church.[7] In particular, church organizational life is shaped in such churches by the desire to invest power in the entire congregation. Volf suggests that the ecclesiality and theological credibility of such congregational structures are evidenced in the dynamism, proliferation, and orthodoxy of the Free Churches.[8] He is critical of the ecclesiological frameworks of the Catholic and Orthodox traditions.[9] Yet he is also critical of the Free Church tendencies toward individualism and a one-sided emphasis on "the subjective conditions of ecclesiality."[10] He believes this risks "grounding the church on the faith, holiness, and communal will of its members."[11]

As an alternative to the exclusivity and shortcomings of the Episcopal and early Free Church models, Volf proposes an ecclesial model "according to which the objective and subjective conditions of ecclesiality appear as two dimensions of a single process."[12] In other words, the objective conditions of ecclesiality in the Episcopal traditions are the liturgical and sacramental actions of the bishops, the churches, and the laity. The subjective conditions, in the early Free Church tradition, are genuine personal faith and obedience to God's revealed commandments. When we examine Volf's ecclesiology, we see an attempt to integrate these objective and subjective dimensions of church life, in a uniquely

---

4. Volf, *After Our Likeness*, 129.

5. Ibid.

6. Ibid., 130.

7. Ibid., 131–32.

8. Ibid., 133.

9. See Reimer, "Miroslav Volf," 16–19, for a critique of Volf's use of Free Church sources.

10. Volf, *After Our Likeness*, 135.

11. Ibid.

12. Ibid.

Free Church fashion, as a single process for developing healthy, missionary, and interdependent Free Churches.

In Volf's vision of the church, he takes Matthew 18:20 as the foundational biblical text that determines what the church is, and how the church is externally evidenced.[13] The text reads, "For where two or three come together in my name, there am I with them." In *After Our Likeness* he expounds this particular text theologically and exegetically in order to build his book on the nature and expression of the church. For Volf, the church is "first of all an *assembly*"[14] of God's redeemed people. In "a specific way" they "assemble at a specific place," that is, in a particular locale.[15] It is a concrete gathering of the people of God in a specific place. Volf quotes Otto Weber when he asserts that the church does not exist "*above* the locally assembled congregation, but rather 'in, with, and beneath' it."[16] Furthermore, the local church and the universal church are "partially overlapping entities."[17] This overlapping constitutes them both, through their common pneumatological immersion, as the church of Jesus Christ waits in anticipation of "the eschatological gathering of the entire people of God."[18] Christ is pneumatologically present in the local gathering of the people of God constituting it as the church "in a proleptic experience of the eschatological gathering of the entire people of God."[19]

The church is also a communion of persons who gather in the name of Christ, and who consent to the apostolic, confessional understandings of the nature of Jesus Christ. They are the church as they gather in personal identification with Christ as their source of salvation, faith, "freedom, orientation, and power."[20] Explicit faith is put in Christ as Savior and commitment is made to allow him to determine the lives of those gathered.[21] Sanctification is invited through the work of the Holy Spirit. Confession of Christ's Lordship is made public.[22] Charisms are expressed specific to each individual for the benefit of the entire community.[23] Cognitive assent to who Christ is and what he has done is paralleled by personal obedience and submission to his Lordship.[24]

According to Volf, the sacraments are essential to the life and essence of the church—baptism and the Lord's Supper. However, this is only in that they are a public representation and form of the confession of faith for the gathered people of God. They

13. Ibid., 136.

14. Ibid., 137.

15. Ibid.

16. Ibid., 138.

17. Ibid., 141.

18. Ibid.

19. Ibid., 145.

20. Ibid., 145–46. See Jesson, "Where Two or Three Are Gathered," 17; Volf, "Kirche Als Gemeinschaft," 52–76.

21. Volf, "Nature of the Church," 68. Volf writes, "It is the *presence of Christ* that makes the church to be the church."

22. Volf, *After Our Likeness*, 154.

23. Volf, "New Congregationalism," 232.

24. Volf, *After Our Likeness*, 151 (see 146–50). For an analysis of Volf's opinions on this matter, see Stewart, "Shape of the Church," 544.

are an expression of such faith.[25] In addition, churches are to be in inter-ecclesial relation with other churches. This is not because this communion is itself a church, but because it anticipates the coming together of the whole people of God at the end of the age.[26]

Volf concludes by defining a congregation as a "holy, catholic, and apostolic church"[27] in the following way:

> Every congregation that assembles around the one Jesus Christ as Savior and Lord in order to profess faith in him publicly in pluriform fashion, including through baptism and the Lord's Supper, and which is open to all churches of God and to all human beings, is a church in the full sense of the word, since Christ promised to be present in it through his Spirit as the first fruits of the gathering of the whole people of God in the eschatological reign of God.[28]

THE MEDIATION OF FAITH AND A THEOLOGY OF HUMAN PERSONHOOD

Volf begins his discussion in *After Our Likeness* on faith, person, and church by suggesting that "in the complex ecclesial reality of *all* churches, the relation of individuals to the church depends on their relation to Christ, just as their relation to Christ depends on their relation to the church; the two relations are mutually determinative."[29] In this assertion, he is suggesting that there is a level of complexity in the relations between human persons, Christ, and the church that cannot be captured in simplistic notions about the difference between Catholic collectivism and Protestant individualism.

Volf, in his explication of the ecclesial mediation of faith, goes on to propose, by expounding Matthew 18:20, that Christ's presence is promised to the entire congregation. Individuals, as part of such congregations, partake of this divine presence.[30] Therefore, "the transmission of faith occurs through interpersonal ecclesial interaction." "God's salvific activity always takes place through the multidimensional confession of faith of the *communio fidelium*."[31] It is in the community of faith that one is introduced to Christ and nurtured into maturity. In community, a person receives the sacraments and the content of faith, passes on the timeless truth of the gospel, and discovers how such faith is to be embraced and outworked.

The embrace of the church's role in the mediation of faith, however, is always in the context of the individual's personal commitment to God in faith, since "the goal of ecclesial mediation must be a person's own *fiducia*" (confidence, trust, and assurance in

---

25. Volf, *After Our Likeness*, 152–54.

26. Jesson, "Where Two or Three Are Gathered," 154–58.

27. Ibid., 158.

28. Ibid. Elsewhere Volf writes, "Here, then, you have a definition of the church that is capable of providing impetus for new and fruitful developments: *the church is the continuation of Christ's anointing by the Spirit*." Volf, "Nature of the Church," 69.

29. Volf, *After Our Likeness*, 159.

30. Ibid., 162.

31. Ibid., 163.

Christ).[32] Explicit personal acceptance of saving grace is essential for salvation through the person and work of Jesus Christ.[33] Moreover, since one receives faith *through* the church as a dynamic local community of gathered, worshipping, and believing persons, no special priestly office is required to mediate this faith. It is received, instead, as a gift among the general priesthood of all believers that constitutes the local church.[34] Once encountering the living God through faith, persons need to enter a community of believers since there is an ecclesial quality about salvation. Volf writes,

> The ecclesial mediation of faith serves to bring human beings into a direct (though not unmediated) relation to God; *they* must in faith accept salvation from *God*. These individual human beings, however, do not remain alone with their God. By entering into this relation to God, supported by the communion of believers, they are simultaneously constituted into the communion of believers.[35]

Volf proceeds then, in *After Our Likeness*, to develop a theological understanding of human nature, an anthropologically affirming trinitarian ecclesiology. This dissolves Christians neither into "an undifferentiated multiplicity," nor into "pure relationality." Rather, it portrays them as unified through the Spirit and in trinitarian fellowship, while respecting "the independence of communally determined persons."[36]

TRINITARIAN ECCLESIOLOGY

In his chapter "Trinity and Church" in *After Our Likeness*, Volf claims that no significant examination of the correspondence between the ecclesial communion and the trinitarian communion has been undertaken.[37] He proceeds therefore to discuss the correspondence between these concepts and the limitations of the analogy between the communions. His discussion addresses the nature of the divine communion and the implications of this communion within the Godhead for the church, personhood, and the structure of ecclesial relations.

For Volf, one's understanding of the Trinity ultimately shapes one's ecclesiology and, indeed, one's theology in general.[38] Reflecting on the correspondence between trinitarian and ecclesial communion serves to form how the church understands the paradoxes of unity and multiplicity in her ecclesial life. It also helps ground the church's self-understanding in its core experience and reality. He is writing here of the initiation through baptism into a trinitarian existence, event, and communion. "If Christian initiation is a trinitarian event, then the church must speak of the Trinity as its determining reality."[39] This determining reality must lead to the relationships between Christians and churches

32. Ibid.
33. Ibid., 164.
34. Ibid., 166.
35. Ibid., 172.
36. Ibid., 189.
37. Ibid., 191–220.
38. Ibid., 193.
39. Ibid., 194–95.

being characterized by love. This love reflects "the mutual *love* of the divine persons."[40] When Christians assemble in the name of Christ, even if their number is small, they can be an image "of the Trinity."[41]

There are limitations on the church's ability to image the Trinity. This includes our limited understanding of the full glorious nature of the triune God and our limited, creaturely ability to reflect the divine Creator. There are also the weaknesses inherent in a sojourning church moving toward eschatological consummation.[42] Ted Peters, for instance, provides a robust critique of the notion of the Trinity as a model for the church.[43] However, these limitations should not dissuade us from exploring the correspondence between the communions, as well as the practical implications for ecclesial life.[44]

There is, in Volf's ecclesiology, a real correspondence between the relationship and mutual interpenetration of the trinitarian persons and that of Christians and congregations.[45] Like the divine beings in the Godhead, Christians cannot live in independence and isolation. Christians express their ecclesial personhood in community, giving and receiving, and through interconnectedness. "A Christian lives from and toward others."[46] Disciples are designed to live in community. Such community is characterized by relationships corresponding to the trinitarian relations and held together by covenant. Such community demonstrates the love, mutual interpenetration (perichoresis), and communion of the Trinity. Churches do this in a real but imperfect fashion. Reflecting the Trinity will also involve churches embracing inter-ecclesially, that is, ecumenically being toward and seeking fellowship with other local churches.[47] Moreover, while "the indwelling of other persons is an exclusive prerogative of God,"[48] human beings in community have a unique opportunity to influence the formation of Christ-like characteristics in each other. Local churches in meaningful fellowship can enrich, broaden, and influence each other in a way corresponding to the "catholicity of the Triune God."[49]

Volf maintains that his understanding of the relations in the Trinity leaves no room for "pyramidal dominance of the one (so Ratzinger) nor a hierarchical bipolarity between the one and the many (so Zizioulas)." This, he suggests, is because he views these other positions as asymmetrical, monocentric, and monarchical. He sees his position as painting a portrait of a communion of divine persons that has more than one center of growth, procession, generation, and development. It is harmonious, exhibiting equivalence or correspondence among the divine constituents or persons of God,

40. Ibid., 195.

41. Ibid., 197.

42. Volf, "Trinity Is Our Social Program," 405.

43. Peters, *God as Trinity*.

44. Volf, *After Our Likeness*, 198–200.

45. Ibid., 204; Volf, "Community Formation," 213.

46. Volf, *After Our Likeness*, 206.

47. Ibid., 207–8.

48. Ibid., 211.

49. Ibid., 211–13.

since unity and multiplicity are equiprimal in God.[50] The ecclesiological implications of this view of the Trinity are non-hierarchical leadership in the churches, unity of spirit, and multiplicity. It also leads to equal valuing of gifting, services, and activities, and the granting of inalienable rights to ecclesial persons. These rights are grounded in deep love and anticipation of the submission and liberation of all things under Christ, at the end of the age.[51] These are

> [a] people whose social vision and social practices image the Triune God's coming down in self-emptying passion in order to take human beings into the perfect cycle of exchanges in which they give themselves to each other and receive themselves back ever anew in love.[52]

LEADERSHIP, PARTICIPATION, AND ECCLESIAL STRUCTURE

Volf emphasizes in chapter 6 of *After Our Likeness* that questions about ecclesial leadership, authority, office, and structure are built on more foundational and primary theological assumptions. These include the nature and essence of the church, the mediation of faith and salvation, and the correspondence between ecclesial and trinitarian realities. Once these foundations have been laid, questions about office are critical for forming ecclesiology, and especially ecclesiology shaped within the context of ecumenical dialogue. Therefore, Volf proceeds to build an ecclesiology that answers the problems of "the relationship between universal and particular priesthood, between Spirit and church law, and the understanding of ordination."[53]

The church, according to Volf, is a *polycentric community*, rather than episcopocentric. It is to be participative, characterized by the broad demonstration of the charismata, and a fellowship of interdependent persons mediating faith and salvation to each other. In other words, a confessional community constituted by the Holy Spirit, and an ecclesial reality in which people live for and toward each other.[54]

Volf's ecclesiology is essentially a *participatory ecclesiology*, emphasizing the active priesthood of all believers.[55] The outpourings of the charismata on particular persons within the life of the churches "are empowerments for pluriform service in the church and in the world, empowerments which come from God's grace, and which can change and overlap."[56] This assertion is consequential for the core values and practices of missional ecclesiology. This polycentric, participative understanding and model of church life is, according to Volf, firstly a re-interpretation of what is happening in churches already. This

---

50. Ibid., 193, 214–17. Reimer suggests that Volf projects his understanding of the nature of the church on his trinitarian theology, and then proceeds to use that theology to justify his ecclesiology. Reimer, "Miroslav Volf," 18.

51. Volf, *After Our Likeness*, 217–20.

52. Volf, "Trinity Is Our Social Program," 418–19.

53. Volf, *After Our Likeness*, 221–22.

54. Ibid., 224; Volf, "New Congregationalism," 235–37.

55. Kärkkäinen sees this as the core of Volf's ecclesiology: Kärkkäinen, "Miroslav Volf," 134–41.

56. Volf, *After Our Likeness*, 226.

is because the laity's participation in worship "must be acknowledged ecclesiologically as constitutive for the church."[57]

Other more episcopocentric models of church life are, in Volf's opinion, fertile ground for lay passivity.[58] They encourage neglect of the charismata and missionary disinterest. Therefore, the laity needs to be theologically elevated so that they perceive themselves to be the vehicle through which God constitutes the church. This constitution is evidenced and given expression through the distribution of the charismata. These charismata are centered on Christ, universally distributed, and fundamentally interdependent. They are guided by the sovereignty of God and synchronically and diachronically plural—among the people of God they are manifold, occurring at a specific time and place, and changing over time and in accordance with the gifts and graces of the community. They are a demonstration of the "priesthood of all believers."[59]

Institutions and institutionalized procedures are inevitable in church life, in Volf's ecclesiology.[60] Our understanding of the nature and relations of the Trinity, and the correspondence of these with the new natures and relations of the gifts of the Spirit among the gathered community of faith, should shape the kind of institution that the church is. Institutional formation is inevitable, yet the churches are able to shape themselves as institutions in trinitarian and Spirit-graced ways. They should aim to be empowering, participative, charismatic, community-centered, and symmetrical/polycentric. Formalization of rules of interaction is necessary even in love-dominated communities. Yet these must be flexible, adaptable, preliminary, and alterable. They are to be grace and love-filled, and, ultimately, a reflection of the relations within the Trinity.[61] Rather than resenting or resisting the institutional life of the church, or the church's boundaries concerning theology and behavior, Christians are to respect these and respond proactively. This is especially true because their "actions and relations *are* the institutional church."[62] They are to especially exercise the charismata, and form guidelines to protect the open expression of the charismata among all the people of God.

In the light of these ecclesiological perspectives, assigning people to certain roles within the life of churches "must always be viewed as provisional."[63] Other matters of procedure, practice, and principle among the communities of faith are also provisional in nature. Only the divine revelation of the gospel of Jesus Christ is not subject to revision, "even though this revelation, too, and certainly our own knowledge of it, is open to eschatological completion."[64]

Volf draws a number of implications for ordination. Firstly, the charismata of office are given exclusively by the Spirit, and the congregation and other leaders merely receive

57. Ibid., 227.

58. Volf, "New Congregationalism," 234–35.

59. Volf, *After Our Likeness*, 228–33.

60. See Volf, "Democracy and Charisma," 430–31.

61. Volf, *After Our Likeness*, 234–39.

62. Ibid., 241.

63. Ibid., 244.

64. Ibid., 245.

this charisma publicly through ordination. Secondly, entire local communities led by the Spirit of God confer ordination (rather than other officers perpetuating themselves through ordination). Thirdly, ordination is provisional, revocable, and based on ongoing use of the particular charisma given to the leader for the benefit of a concrete community of faith.[65]

While, unfortunately, some missional ecclesiology focuses on the institutional forms of the church, proposing that its current expressions tend to stifle creativity and missionary activity, Volf appreciates that, even more importantly,

> [t]he church needs the vivifying presence of the Spirit, and without this presence, even a church with a decentralized participative structure and culture will become sterile, and perhaps more sterile even than a hierarchical church . . . Successful participative church life must be sustained by deep spirituality. Only the person who lives from the Spirit of communion (2 Cor. 13:13) can participate authentically in the life of the ecclesial community.[66]

CATHOLICITY AND ECUMENICAL DIALOGUE

Volf considers the volatility over the issue of catholicity to be rooted in the nature of catholicity itself and in the differing viewpoints of the Episcopal churches and the Free Churches.[67] The paradox of catholicity is that all churches desire to be catholic, but only in accordance with their own ecclesiological stance.[68] This, however, is problematic, since catholicity is essential to the nature and to our understanding of the church. Catholicity demonstrates the church's "plurality in its unity" and its effort to "find in its plurality its unity."[69] Neither plurality nor unity can be compromised in the quest to form a church that is truly catholic, and that is engaged in issues about the relationship between unification and differentiation. Neither plurality nor unity can be sacrificed as the church seeks to demonstrate the grace and power of catholicity to a world that is itself becoming increasingly uniform yet pluralized. Catholicity is primarily an internal problem for the church. It contains, however, external questions that particularly revolve around issues of "exclusivity and inclusivity." This is evidenced, for instance, in the interfaith arena.[70]

Volf rejects a quantitative version of catholicity which focuses on the universal expansion of the church or on that which is universally believed. He prefers a qualitative understanding that emphasizes that "the church is catholic because the *fullness of salvation* is realized within it . . . *The catholicity of the entire people of God is the ecclesial dimension of the eschatological fullness of salvation for the entirety of created reality.*"[71] The catholicity of the church is defined eschatologically, since the sojourning church expresses the realities of the new creation with great anticipation. It is also defined this way because such catholicity of expression is birthed as the Spirit of God anticipates the

---

65. Ibid., 246–51; Volf, "Democracy and Charisma," 432–33; Volf, "Way of Life."

66. Volf, *After Our Likeness*, 257.

67. Volf, "Catholicity of Two or Three," 525–27; Volf, "Changing and Changeless."

68. Volf, "Catholicity of Two or Three," 525.

69. Ibid., 527–28.

70. Ibid., 528; Volf, *After Our Likeness*, 262.

71. Volf, *After Our Likeness*, 266–67.

coming together of the whole people of God in the new creation. This final eschatological consummation is the essential event in which the church is fully realized and completely catholic. In the meantime, churches are partially or relatively catholic.[72]

For Volf, the catholicity of the local church "arises from the 'manifold grace of God' (1 Pet. 4:10) and from its encounter with the richness of creation."[73] The catholicity of the local church is realized through its connection with the whole people of God, as within its concrete historical setting it anticipates the eschatological new creation. The ecclesiological whole that it is connected to, however, is not merely the existing church in this world, but rather the eschatological gathering of the people of God. It anticipates this gathering with great hope. This anticipatory catholicity is expressed as God graces local churches with the fullness of the charismata so that they might be constituted as a church. They live as a church through the power of the Spirit, the catholicity of salvific grace and charismata, and the ministerial giftedness of their members. Anticipatory catholicity is also expressed through open relations with other churches and loyalty to the apostolic tradition. It is articulated as churches and individual Christians embrace all others who confess faith in Christ, regardless of race, gender or social class, and through "positive integration (not assimilation!) of cultural plurality."[74]

A commitment to ecumenical dialogue, particularly with regard to ecclesiology, and to embrace and reconciliation is demonstrated in Volf's works *Exclusion and Embrace* and *After Our Likeness*.[75] Our understanding of ecclesiology, social justice, conflict resolution, peacemaking, embrace, the new creation, and Christian community must be enriched through ecumenical dialogue.[76]

The emergence of post-confessional Christianity, the decline of the societal and ecclesial significance of denominations, the deepening independence of local churches, and the critical evaluation of the traditional ecumenical movement, all contribute to the profound crisis the ecumenical movement finds itself in today.[77] Yet division impoverishes all Christians and ecclesiology is best shaped within ecumenical and interdenominational dialogue.[78]

A plurality of ecclesiological models is desirable and legitimate, demonstrating the vitality of Christianity within "multicultural, rapidly changing societies demanding diversification and flexibility."[79] Also, postmodern ecclesiology must necessarily be formed in dialogue with premodern traditions and the wisdom contained therein, especially as one seeks to build up the "*communio*-structures" of the vast expressions of Christianity and the local church.[80]

72. Ibid., 267–69.

73. Ibid., 270.

74. Ibid., 271–82.

75. See Volf, *Exclusion and Embrace*, 53–54; Volf, *After Our Likeness*, 19–25; Baum, "Church We Love," 13–14.

76. Volf, *Exclusion and Embrace*, 54.

77. Volf, "Ecumenical Quandary."

78. Volf, *After Our Likeness*, 21–22.

79. Ibid., 21.

80. Ibid., 23, 25.

CONTRIBUTIONS TO MISSIONAL ECCLESIOLOGY

Volf's ecclesiology enhances the missional ecclesiology in *Part Two* of this book through its missiological, eschatological, trinitarian, ecclesial, and gospel-culture outlook.[81] God's eschatological new creation, the missionary, ethical, and ecclesiological consequences of living in anticipation of that reality, and a rich theology of the Trinity form much of the theological framework for Volf's ecclesiology. The mutual personal indwelling of the triune God and his people is the eschatological future and hope of the church. The church is formed in the image of the Trinity and participates in the rich relationships of the triune God. Volf says that this is both a source of eschatological anticipation and present experience.[82] Such an eschatological expectation sits well with missional ecclesiology, which regularly articulates dissatisfaction with the marriage of contemporary western Christianity and the values of western capitalism and modernity, to the detriment of an eschatologically formed approach to discipleship, mission, and community.

As I have noted, the trinitarian analogy has possibilities, but also limitations and obscurities. At times the trinitarian language operates at a level of abstraction the New Testament texts on the church do not exemplify. The New Testament texts, as Ted Peters notes, focus on Christ's self-giving love as the model for our relationships, not trinitarian perichoresis. Perichoretic theological speculation is, furthermore, a high-level theological abstraction in contrast, say, to Paul's instructions on life in community (or Luke's theologically loaded description of it). While I describe my own ecclesiological convictions as trinitarian, and devote a whole chapter later to the importance of trinitarian theology for missional ecclesiology, I am aware of the real difficulties presented by the language's obscurities and abstractions, the distance of much of the thought from the New Testament texts, and the considerable objections to the trinitarian analogy. I wish to explore the possibilities of trinitarian theology for missional ecclesiology without minimizing these objections and while holding trinitarian and biblical ecclesiological convictions together.

Missional ecclesiology can learn much from the Free Church ecclesiology espoused by Volf. For example, Volf asserts that the presence of Christ amidst the gathered people of God is the sole condition for the ecclesiality of a congregation, constituting those gathered believers as a church, whether this church is healthy and whole or completely dysfunctional.[83] For small groups of believers gathered in basic, simple, or home churches, and for those engaged in missionary experimentations on the fringe of the established church, these ecclesiological perspectives are refreshing. The church is primarily, according to Volf, a specific and concrete gathering of people in Jesus's name. It remains a church when these same people are engaged in mission and service outside their gatherings.

Volf's ecclesiology also has implications for our understanding of the relationship between charismata and participation, the charismatic structure of the church, and the implications of trinitarian thought on ecclesial structures. He contributes to missional ecclesiology's appreciation of the catholicity of the local congregation, the need for the people of God to be engaged in acts reconciliation and forgiveness, and Free Church

---

81. He features in chapters 14, 15, 16, and 17 in *Part Two* of this book.

82. Volf, *After Our Likeness*, 128–30.

83. Ibid., 136.

perspectives on leadership, office, and ordination. For Volf, the church is constituted by the presence of Christ in the Spirit. This is mediated through the entire local community of faith, not primarily through ministers, priests, or other ordained persons. Each member of a congregation is to use the full range of their gifts for ministry and leadership, and is to participate in acts of catholicity, reconciliation, service, and ministry. They are to participate in the decision-making of the life of the community.[84] These issues are of real concern for missional ecclesiology, which emphasizes flat, fluid, and more grass-root leadership and governance structures in local communities of faith.

Volf suggests that God's people are to express their ecclesiality through such things as:

1. Cognitive specification and confessional affirmation of faith in Christ, his nature, and work;[85]

2. Holding to historical Christian belief and the Scriptures, although these need to be explored graciously and dialogically;[86]

3. Practicing the sacraments of the Lord's supper and baptism (in contrast to ordained ministry, these sacraments are a necessary condition of the church in that they are an expression of faith and of the confession of faith);[87]

4. Engaging in social concern and being intentionally missional.

Churches seeking creative ways to express their missionary essence need to take heed of such things, especially if they are going to maintain biblical faithfulness along with missionary experimentation. The active presence of the Holy Spirit gives evidence to the existence of a church. Volf writes that Christ acts within a congregation through the charismata, which are universally distributed, fundamentally interdependent, synchronically and diachronically plural, and given sovereignly by God himself.[88] Therefore, the laity and their charismatic gifting are critical in Volf's ecclesiology. This is an ecclesiology characterized by inclusion, mutuality, participation, commonality, and the priesthood of all believers. Not only so, but the church is also constituted by the Spirit of God through the medium of the laity. When this is recognized, lay passivity may be overcome, the division of persons into hierarchical positions may be avoided, and the charismata may be more widely used. Office-bearers may be valued in an appropriate manner, and mission and ministry may be extended.[89]

Some aspects of Volf's ecclesiology need further exploration if they are going to be applied contextually in a missionary setting. Volf's perspectives on the relationship between local and other churches are an example. Not merely a concrete expression of some abstract, universal church, the local church in Volf's ecclesiology is "the real anticition or proleptic re-

---

84. Ibid., 224–28.
85. Ibid., 148–49.
86. Ibid., 146.
87. Ibid., 152–54.
88. Ibid., 228–33.
89. Ibid., 221–57.

alization of the eschatological gathering of the entire people of God."[90] However, each local church is joined to all the others through "their common relation to the Spirit of Christ" who makes both the local and the universal church "into the anticipation of the eschatological gathering of the entire people of God."[91] They are also joined through their same confession of faith. Fellowship with other churches leads to "differentiated unity" and acknowledging other churches is an "interecclesial minimum."[92] This is a challenge for isolated forms of church life, especially in the missionary experimentations and church plants of a wide range of Protestant movements which, at times, may grasp at independence in unhealthy ways. This is an area of Volf's ecclesiology that helps us wrestle with the relationship between the local church and other Christian churches, denominations, and agencies, but his perspectives here certainly need to be contextualized and critically developed. Volf may be too optimistic about the willingness of local churches to engage genuinely with other churches, and about the ability of local churches to remain unshaped by their immediate ideological, political, and cultural contexts. He may place too much hope in the ability of burgeoning local "free-churches" throughout the globe to resist the class differentiation, materialistic tendencies, and entrepreneurial ideologies that surround them. Therefore, Volf's idealistic portrayal of interecclesial cooperation may not necessarily contain all the needed answers for the problems of isolated and cocooning independent Christian communities.

Volf writes the following, as he introduces the purpose and themes in his ecclesiology: "Today, the thesis that ecclesial communion should correspond to trinitarian communion enjoys the status of an almost self-evident proposition. Yet it is surprising that no one has carefully examined just where such correspondences are to be found, nor expended much effort determining where ecclesial communion reaches the limits of its capacity for such analogy."[93] This is exactly what Volf sets out to do in his Free Church ecclesiology, as he seeks to "clarify the limits of the church's ability to image the Trinity" and "concretize those insights at various points in the analysis of the actual correspondences between the Trinity and the church."[94] Missional ecclesiology must take trinitarian thought seriously if it is to genuinely ground the nature, structures, and ministries of the church on the centrifugal and centripetal dimensions of the eschatological mission of the triune God.

QUESTIONS FOR REFLECTION

1. How important is it to form our ecclesiology around our theology of the Trinity? What are the consequences of that approach for ecclesiology?

2. Why should our relationships reflect the relationships within the Trinity? How do we apply this idea in our church communities and our interpersonal relationships?

3. How can churches become *polycentric communities* with a *participatory ecclesiology*?

90. Ibid., 140.
91. Ibid., 141.
92. Ibid., 157.
93. Ibid., 191.
94. Ibid., 198.

PART TWO

Introducing Missional Ecclesiology—
Through Conversation

Intermission

13

The Thinking-in-Community Church: Encountering a Life-Giving Theology

How all-important it is that a vigorous spiritual life, in close association with the Holy Scriptures, and in the midst of the Christian community, be maintained as a background for theological work . . .

. . . insofar as we are determined to be true theologians, we think within the community of God's people, and for that community, and in the name of that community;—how shall I say?—we think as a part of the community itself . . .[1]

—HELMUT THIELICKE

WE THINK AS A PART OF THE COMMUNITY ITSELF

MINISTRY PRACTICE OPERATES, TOO often, without an adequate or reflective theology of the church, or a theology of mission. Theological reflection on the mission of God and the nature of the church is separated, in many instances, from concrete ministry practice. Although ecclesiology, missiology, worship, and ministry practice are deeply connected, Christian leaders and congregations can lose their enthusiasm for conducting a life-giving conversation between theological reflection and missional or ministerial practice. Fragmented ministry practices, personal conflict and dissatisfaction, retreat

---

1. Thielicke, *Little Exercise for Young Theologians*, 4–5, 37.

from difficult questions about programs and purposes, and unquestioning adoption of offshore solutions, are some of the results.

For these reasons, and more, a well-developed missional theology of the church, its nature, structures, and mission, is crucial for the health of churches, for faithfulness to the gospel, and for mission in the contemporary cultural context. Missional ecclesiology is also important for the longevity, integrity, and theological and personal conviction of Christian leaders and congregations. As Helmut Thielicke reminds us, such theological reflection, if it is to be life-giving, must be characterized by spiritual discipline and vitality, submission to the truth of Scripture, and participation in authentic Christian community. With this exhortation in mind, with a sense of dependence on God's grace, and with a real awareness that "we think as a part of the community itself," I deal with the following two questions in the rest of this book. "What do the mission of God and theologies of Jesus Christ, the Holy Spirit, and the Trinity, have to do with missional ecclesiology?" Moreover, "How can missional ecclesiology be *reframed*, or given fuller theological shape, through conversation, through *thinking-in-community*?" In the case of this book, that conversation is with twelve thinkers. I construct some introductory theological foundations for missional ecclesiology in conversation with these Roman Catholic, Eastern Orthodox, Free Church, and other Protestant ecclesiologists. The notion that "we think as part of the community itself" encourages us to develop an ecclesiology in conversation with a wide variety of theological traditions. We are part of a theologizing, worshipping, eschatological, and catholic community—one that spans diverse ethnic, theological, and institutional cultures and traditions, a wide variety of historical movements, and an array of intriguing personalities and thinkers. It is my hope that I can capture some of this in my construction of some introductory theological foundations for missional ecclesiology.

QUESTIONS FOR REFLECTION

1. Why do you think that theological reflection is often separated from ministry practice?

2. Adding to Thielicke's list, what do you think are the characteristics of life-giving theology?

3. Which area of theology most informs your understanding and practice of mission? Why is this area important to you?

14

The Mission-Forged Church:
Participating in the Mission of God

*Mission refers to a permanent and intrinsic dimension of the church's life.
The church "is missionary by its nature" . . . and it is impossible to talk
about church without at the same time talking about mission. Because
God is a missionary God, God's people are missionary people. The church's
mission is not secondary to its being; the church exists in being sent and
in building up itself for its mission . . . Ecclesiology does not precede missiology; there cannot be church without an intrinsic missionary dimension.
And Shenk (1991:107) quotes Emil Brunner's famous adage: "The church
exists by mission, just as fire exists by burning."*[1]

—David Bosch

CONTEMPORARY SOURCES OF MISSIONAL ECCLESIOLOGY

MUCH HAS BEEN WRITTEN recently about the relationship between the nature of God,
the missional essence of the church, and the Christian mission to contemporary
cultures. Some years ago I participated in a postgraduate class on forming missional leaders, taught by Alan Roxburgh. During a brainstorming session facilitated by Roxburgh,
the class came up with thirteen sources for this increasing interest in the missional nature
and practices of the church.[2] I list these here, with some brief description.[3]

- *Post-Christendom:* Churches in western cultures are often in post-Christendom settings, of various forms, and are trying to find meaning and direction in the context
of marginality and liminality.

1. Bosch, *Believing in the Future*, 32.

2. Roxburgh, A. *Issues in Forming Missional Leaders*—a postgraduate subject at Burleigh College,
Adelaide, 2005. See Roxburgh, *Missionary Congregation*; Roxburgh, *Crossing the Bridge*; Roxburgh and
Romanuk, *Missional Leader*; Roxburgh, *What Is Missional Church?*

3. The brevity of these descriptions runs the real risk of oversimplifying or caricaturing these move-
ments/phenomena. I encourage the reader to research each for a fuller understanding of their nuances and
major ideas.

- *Missiology at Home:* A realization that missiology begins at home, that all cultures are mission fields, and that the church must learn from missiology.

- *The Growth of the Majority World Churches:* Recognition that Christianity is burgeoning in Africa, Asia, and Latin America, and that western churches have much to learn from missions, theology, and church life in those regions.

- *Disenchantment with Abstract Rationalism and Unreflective Pragmatism:* Disillusionment with expressions of Christianity that are too abstract and cerebral on the one hand, or too unreflective, emotional, and pragmatic on the other.

- *Decentered Church:* Discussions about the forms of church that are less centralized, complicated, hierarchical, and solid.[4]

- *Modern/Postmodern Conversation:* A questioning of modernity's epistemology and its influence on the church's theological frameworks. An examination of the possibilities and pitfalls of postmodern (or hyper-modern) epistemology, apologetics, and cultural expressions.[5]

- *Globalization:* Globalization presents missional challenges for the church, such as pluralism, multiple narratives, social mobility, and the networking of societies.

- *New Testament Studies:* Particularly works dealing with the historical Jesus, broader christological themes, Pauline interpretation, and narrative theology (and the writings of N.T. "Tom" Wright).[6]

- *Insights from Communication, Network, and Change Theories:* Theologians and practitioners are considering the implications of communications theory, the networking of global cultures, the information age, and theories about how organizations move beyond technical forms of change to the skills and capacities required to negotiate radical, discontinuous, and adaptive change.[7]

- *Radical Orthodoxy:* A mainly British theological movement that mines the patristic, medieval, and renaissance material for contemporary theology. It asks, "What are the foundations of our theology, missional activity, and ecclesial life, and how can Christology be recovered as the source of these things?"[8]

- *Postliberal Theology (sometimes called Narrative Theology):* Focuses on the narrative structures of faith, doctrine, Scripture, hermeneutics, and theology, and argues for a recovery of narrative theology and readings in contemporary church life and mission.[9]

4. Ward, *Liquid Church*; Simson, *Houses That Change the World*. Ward adapts the work of Bauman's *Liquid Modernity*.

5. Gibbs and Bolger, *Emerging Churches*, 15–26.

6. Wright, *New Testament and the People of God*.

7. Castells, *Rise of the Network Society*; Heifetz, *Leadership without Easy Answers*; Bate, *Strategies for Cultural Change*.

8. Milbank et al., *Radical Orthodoxy*.

9. Hauerwas and Jones, *Why Narrative?*

- *Christology:* A renewed interest in the relationship between Christology, ecclesiology, missiology, and discipleship, including significant theological debates about "incarnation" as a motif for mission and ministry, and about theories of atonement.[10]

- *Missiologists:* Writers such as Lesslie Newbigin, David Bosch, Christopher Wright, and Jonathan Bonk have been read widely (and some less academic authors have popularized their missiologies). Such missiologists have substantially influenced missional ecclesiology.[11]

These and other sources have contributed to the development of missional ecclesiology and to conclusions about the relationship between the *missio Dei* and the church's missional nature.

THE CHURCH'S MISSIONAL NATURE: *MISSIO DEI*

How does mission relate to the nature of the church? The relationship between the missional nature of God and the missional essence of the church is such that mission is "a permanent and intrinsic dimension of the church's life."[12] The church is essentially missional. Mission is central, pivotal, and constitutive of its nature. As Michael Frost and Alan Hirsch say, "The church should define itself in terms of mission—to take the gospel to and incarnate the gospel within a specific context."[13] David Bosch writes that "the classical doctrine on the *missio Dei* as God the Father sending the Son, and God the Father and Son sending the Spirit was expanded to include yet another 'movement': Father, Son, and Holy Spirit sending the church into the world."[14] The church serves the mission of Christ and is caught up in the missional purposes and "movements" of the triune God. The church exists because of that mission—the eschatological mission of God's redemptive reign over all creation and history.

After the Willingen conference in 1952, Karl Hartenstein wrote a summary piece that catalyzed decades of ongoing conversation about the relationship between the *missio Dei* and the church. He also discussed how the *missio Dei* and the *missio ecclesia* relate to Christ's holistic, eschatological reign. According to Hartenstein, "Mission is not just the conversion of the individual, nor just obedience to the word of the Lord, nor just the obligation to gather the church. It is the taking part in the sending of the Son, the *missio Dei*, with the holistic aim of establishing Christ's rule over all redeemed creation."[15] In a

10. Guder, *Incarnation*; Frost and Hirsch, *Shaping of Things to Come*, 33–162.

11. Influential books include: Newbigin, *Gospel in a Pluralist Society*; Bosch, *Transforming Mission*; Bonk, *Missions and Money*; Wright, *Mission of God*; Newbigin, *Open Secret*; Winter et al., *Perspectives*; Shenk, *Transfiguration of Mission*; Cardoza-Orlandi, *Mission*; Bevans and Schroeder, *Constants in Context*; Williams, *Mission-Shaped Church*; Oborji, *Concepts of Mission*.

12. Bosch, *Believing in the Future*, 27–32.

13. Frost and Hirsch, *Shaping of Things to Come*, xi.

14. Bosch, *Transforming Mission*, 390.

15. Hartenstein, "Theologische Besinnung," 54, quoted in Engelsviken, "Missio Dei," 482. Bevans and Schroeder trace the origins and trinitarian dimensions of the *missio Dei* further back than Willingen, to the writings of Barth and the trinitarian "divine missions" outlined by Augustine, Bonaventure, Aquinas, and de Bérulle. Bevans and Schroeder, *Constants in Context*, 289–91. Bevans and Schroeder also examine how

thought-provoking article, Tormod Engelsviken traces the theological development of the notion of the *missio Dei*. He considers its trinitarian basis and the various understandings and misunderstandings that have arisen around it. In the following three points, I condense his main reflections. I believe they provide a helpful starting point for our understanding of the *missio Dei* and the missional nature of the church.

Missio Dei and the Kingdom of God

Our understanding of the nature and scope of the kingdom of God influences our understanding of the *missio Dei*. It also shapes our understanding of the nature of the church, salvation history, and God's eschatological actions and actors. In other words, is God's kingdom universal and "relatively independent of the church"? Alternatively, is God's kingdom "the present and final salvation that God offers in Christ," in which the church is an important actor?[16]

Missional Intention and Dimensions

As Lesslie Newbigin says, some aspects of the church have specific missional intention, while others do not. All aspects of the church, however, have missional dimensions. The church must put focused energy into areas that have concentrated missional *intention*, in response to the missional *nature* of the church and in order to preserve the missional *dimension* that resides in every aspect of the church. This is an important distinction (and caution) by Newbigin, especially in light of the popularity, and potential domestication, of the word "missional."[17]

> . . . there is a missionary dimension of everything the church does. But not everything the church does has a missionary intention. And unless there is in the life of the church a point of concentration for the missionary intention, the missionary dimension which is proper to the whole life of the Church will be lost.[18]

Trinitarian, Redemptive, and Ecclesiological Qualifications

Both Tormod Engelsviken and Andrew Kirk rightly argue for a qualified use of *missio Dei*, in line with "trinitarian and redemptive" notions. Our use of the idea of the *missio Dei* must not diminish the trinitarian mission (the *missio Trinitatis*), or the person and redemptive work of Jesus Christ. It must also not marginalize the important role of the church in the mission of God. "The church is the instrument or agent of the *missio Dei*." Our understanding of the *missio Dei* must distinguish and honor the unique persons and roles within the Trinity and be rooted in Scripture. A biblically grounded understanding

---

the *missio Dei* has developed in Catholicism, Orthodoxy, and Protestantism, including primary documents, theologians, and missiologists in each "stream of Christianity." Ibid., 296.

16. Engelsviken, "Missio Dei," 483.

17. Ibid., 484.

18. Newbigin, "One Body," 43.

of the *missio Dei* declares God the Father as "the only source of all mission, Jesus Christ the only Lord and Saviour, and the Holy Spirit the only divine lifegiver and power."[19]

David Bosch asserts that the *missio Dei* has "important consequences" for "the *missiones ecclesiae* (the missional activities of the church)."[20] This includes the need for the church to cease focusing merely on the *activities* of mission. Instead, it should recognize that gospel proclamation, church planting, works of justice and compassion, and so forth, are all grounded in and directed toward the *missio Dei*. They are not so much missional activities as expressions of the essential missional nature of the church. A missional view of the church supports Bosch's claim that the mission of the church is essentially about the *nature* and *essence* of the church. It is not merely about the *adiaphora* (that is, a thing not regarded as essential to faith or to the actual nature of the church) or *addresses* (that is, a message for proclamation) of the church. Rather than being a contingent, peripheral, optional activity of the church, the church "is missionary by its nature" and "exists by mission, just as fire exists by burning."[21] While it is possible to speak of the mission as a set of determining goals or aims (such as in a *mission statement*), or as *missional actions*, missional ecclesiology prioritizes the *missional nature of the church*. Missional ecclesiology proceeds from there to missional systems, strategies, and structures. It is a theological and ecclesiological vision, shaped by the messianic mission of Jesus Christ. Darrell Guder and Andrew Kirk put it this way:

> What would an understanding of the church (an ecclesiology) look like if it were truly missionary in design and definition?[22]

> All true theology is, by definition, missionary theology, for it has as its object the study of the ways of a God who is by nature missionary and a foundational text written by and for missionaries. Mission as a discipline is not, then, the roof of a buildi3ng that completes the whole structure, already constructed by blocks that stand on their own, but both the foundation and the mortar in the joints, which cements together everything else.[23]

A missional ecclesiology defines itself through the mission of God and the person and work of Jesus Christ. It locates the Messiah, and the church's participation in his messianic mission, at the center of the church's being, organization, and ministries. The messianic mission of Jesus Christ is central to the church's life and being, and the faithful pursuit of this mission is the essential character of the church that is faithfully participating in the redemptive work of the Father.[24] Craig Van Gelder says that "ecclesiology and missiology are not separate theological disciplines, but are, in fact, interrelated and

---

19. Engelsviken, "Missio Dei," 485–94; Kirk, *What Is Mission?*, 25.

20. Bosch, *Transforming Mission*, 391.

21. Bosch, *Believing in the Future*, 31–32. Bosch is making his case with support from the Vatican Decree on Mission (paragraph 9) and from a quote attributed to Emil Brunner.

22. Guder, *Missional Church*, 7.

23. Kirk, *Mission of Theology*, 50.

24. Barrett, *Treasure in Clay Jars*, ix–x.

complementary."[25] The *apostolic* characteristic of the church, mentioned in the Nicene-Constantinopolitan Creed, is critical to the church's foundation and missional commission in the world.[26] When we approach the Scriptures in the church's worship and study, a missional hermeneutic must complement and collaborate with a missional ecclesiology.[27] Biblical ecclesiology places mission at the center of the church's being and ministries, and develops a biblically faithful, community formed, missional hermeneutic.

Open Arms to the Mission of God

Northside Church is located near the heart of Sydney. It is a church that has been through radical change in three years. The change began with prayer, that God would bring new life into a 110-year-old church, to kick-start its mission into North Sydney. In 2008, the small and mainly elderly congregation at Northside invited a small group of young adults to plant a new congregation in the church. This re-potting of the church has led to an ongoing transformation of nearly every area of the church's life. Through intentional mission among their local community, and placing mission at the heart of their life together, the church has changed from a small, struggling fellowship to a growing, vibrant, intergenerational church—following the mission of Jesus, cheering each other on, and telling their stories of life-changing encounters with Jesus.

From the beginning, the hope was that Northside would be a transforming community to North Sydney and beyond. The urban setting of Northside means that many young professionals live around the church. To reach this busy but often isolated group, the church has focused on three movements. The first is arms open to God through worship, teaching, and prayer. The second is arms open to each other through lively, hospitable, and generous community. The third is arms open to the community. Northside is positioned in the center of 250 cafes and restaurants—so they use this visibility missionally, through regular outdoor events, advertising, and being in the community. New people have come to "Alpha", followed people off the streets into worship services, and been recipients of kindness, hospitality, and generosity. All of this is celebrated and cheered on. The church will continue to change and transform as they hope to affect their area by participating in the mission of God.[28]

---

25. Van Gelder, *Essence of the Church*, 30–31, 96–98.

26. Guder, *Missional Church*, 83; Van Gelder, *Essence of the Church*, 123–26.

27. Guder, *Missional Church*, 11.

28. Online: http://www.northsidebaptist.org.au. Used with permission.

THE COMMUNION-IN-MISSION: *MISSIO ECCLESIA*

The essential character of the church is missional. The church seeks to participate in God's redemptive activity in the world.[29] The church is "a communion-*in-mission* . . . missional by its very nature."[30] Our understanding of the church's *communion* and *mission* should be trinitarian, biblically shaped, historically informed, contextually relevant, eschatological-ly oriented, and practically applied in ordinary, concrete, local church settings. Our gaze is primarily toward the messianic mission of Christ and the trinitarian *missio Dei*—as well as the consequences of this Christ-centered missiology for the communion, nature, organization, mission, and ministries of the church.[31]

> Mission, then, in biblical terms, while it inescapably involves us in planning and action, is not *primarily* a matter of our activity or our initiative. Mission, from the point of view of our human endeavor, means the committed *participation* of God's people in the purposes of God for the redemption of the whole creation. The mis-sion is God's. The marvel is that God invites us to join in.[32]

The concept of the *missio Dei* draws our attention to "a profoundly theocentric reconceptualization of Christian mission" and theology. God is seen as healing and re-storing all of creation through the nature and "movements" of the Trinity, in the unique redemptive history of Christ. The church is drawn into missional participation.[33] On the one hand, the perichoretic nature of the Trinity reveals *the communal nature* of the church as "a temporal echo of all the eternal community that God is." On the other, the "sending that characterizes that divine communion" is reflected in *the missional essence*, structures, and endeavors of the church.[34] The trinitarian nature of God is richly connected with the substance of ecclesiology and missiology. Communion and mission, as trinitarian reali-ties, are central to our understanding of the church and its presence and purpose in the world. They are also fundamental to the role and destiny of the church in the eschatologi-cal history of Christ.

Craig Van Gelder is right to propose that an adequate missional view of the church embraces other ecclesiological perspectives and seeks to reconceive them missionally (while, of course, preserving a faithful interpretation of biblical texts). Such perspectives include the relationship between God's redemptive reign and the nature of the church, and historical descriptions, signs, and marks of the church. They also include New Testament theologies of the church and core biblical images of the church—such as the *people of God, body of Christ, communion of saints*, and *creation of the Spirit*. Van Gelder writes that missional ecclesiology also reformulates other conceptions of the church through a missional hermeneutic. These include its holiness and humanity, spirituality and sociality, catholicity and locality, universality and contextuality, diversity and unity,

---

29. Barrett, *Treasure in Clay Jars*, ix–x.
30. Bevans and Schroeder, *Constants in Context*, 298, quoting Flannery, *Ad Gentes*, 2.
31. Guder, *Missional Church*, 11–12.
32. Wright, *Mission of God*, 67.
33. Guder, *Missional Church*, 3; Bosch, *Transforming Mission*, 390.
34. Gunton, *Promise of Trinitarian Theology*, 79. Quoted in Guder, *Missional Church*, 82.

institutionality and missionality, and its apostolic-missional-sent dimensions.[35] Missional ecclesiology must be firmly grounded in an adequate, rich, and biblical understanding of the nature of the church. Michael Jinkins brings a word of caution, however. Drawing on Avery Dulles's *Models of the Church*, he says that an adequate ecclesiology must take into account the variety of ways the church has been understood throughout its history—missionally, institutionally, communally, sacramentally, and the like. Such an ecclesiology must be constructed through a critical engagement with the various ecclesiological taxonomies we have available. The church is a mystery and we need various models to try to understand it.[36]

Ecclesiology must have the mission of God, and the person and work of Jesus, at its core. Close to that center is a robust relationship between theology and ecclesial practice, a clear approach to Scripture and hermeneutics, and a discerning, worshipping, missional community. This is because there is a dynamic and inseparable relationship between the *missio Dei*, the centrality of Christ, biblical faithfulness, practices of discipleship, and the "ordinary" praying, discerning, fellowshipping, missional, gathered congregation. In the gathered and dispersed community, we see the trinitarian *communio* and *missio* most clearly demonstrated.

Furthermore, authentic ecclesiology and theology must be missiology. That is, they must be based in missiological hermeneutics, as seems to be the case in much Asian, African, and Latin American theology.[37] At the very least, all ecclesiology and theology must be missiologically and christologically oriented. There is a range of positions on this matter, for example:

1. For David Bosch, a missional theology is far more critical than a mere theology of mission. This is because "we are in need of a missiological agenda for theology, not just a theological agenda for mission; for theology, rightly understood, has no reason to exist other than critically to accompany the *missio Dei*."[38]

2. Christopher Wright begins his important work on the mission of God by asserting,

Mission is what the Bible is all about; we could as meaningfully talk of the missional basis of the Bible as of the biblical basis of mission . . . The proper way for disciples of the crucified and risen Jesus to read their Scriptures, is *messianically and missionally*.[39]

He goes on to construct a missional hermeneutic that respects, expands, and analyzes certain postmodern, contextual, or proof-texting approaches to the interpretation of Scripture. His hermeneutic builds on the biblical foundations of mission. It examines the ways in which biblical authority operates in Scripture, and in which the *missio Dei* moves out to become the mission of humanity, Israel,

35. Van Gelder, *Essence of the Church*, 101–26.

36. Dulles, *Models of the Church*; Jinkins, *Church Faces Death*, 50–68.

37. Erwin Raphael McManus, in Sweet, *Church in Emerging Culture*, 251; Bosch, *Believing in the Future*, 27–28.

38. Ibid., 32.

39. Wright, *Mission of God*, 29–30.

Jesus, and the church.[40] While recognizing the need for a "biblical basis of mission," he writes that,

> A *missional hermeneutic of the Bible*, however, explores the nature of biblical authority itself in relation to mission. Does a missional approach to the Bible help us in articulating what we mean by biblical authority?

3. Michael Frost and Alan Hirsch suggest that Christology should lead to missiology, which, in turn, should lead to ecclesiology. This way all ecclesiology is grounded in the prior christological and missiological agendas.[41] Christology informs, directs, and anchors all missiology and ecclesiology.[42]

4. Alan Kreider writes that missional theology reflects the paradigm of the early Christians.[43]

5. Erwin McManus proposes that Jesus employed a missional hermeneutic, as opposed to his detractor's theological interpretations. McManus says that Christians should move from a theological to a missiological view of the Scriptures.[44]

6. Robert Webber writes that all theological reflection needs to be embedded in the *missio Dei*, as the people of God together discern God's historical actions and their faithful, contextual response. He builds this argument on Martin Kaehler's declaration that, "mission is the mother of theology."[45]

7. Craig Van Gelder contends that every ecclesiology should be a missiological ecclesiology. Even more controversially, he suggests that every historical ecclesiology has performed as a missional ecclesiology.[46]

All agree that our view of the church's nature, theology, structures, fellowship, and presence in the world must be shaped by the *missio Dei*. Conversely, it is my conviction that clearly conceived, biblical notions of the Trinity, the kingdom of God, the person and work of Jesus Christ, and the gospel must qualify our understanding of the *missio Dei*. The *missio Dei* can enrich our understanding of the mission of the church (the *missio ecclesia*) and the communion of the church (the *communio ecclesia*) even further, if it is supported by the twelve "missionary paradigms" outlined by David Bosch.[47] Bosch also

---

40. Ibid., 29–69.

41. Frost and Hirsch, *Shaping of Things to Come*, 228.

42. Frost and Hirsch, *ReJesus*, 42–45.

43. Kreider, *Change of Conversion*, 106.

44. McManus, *Unstoppable Force*, 85, 94.

45. Webber, *Younger Evangelicals*, 241–42. Martin Kaehler quoted in Shenk, *Write the Vision*, 42–43.

46. Van Gelder proposes, therefore, that, "To some extent, every historical ecclesiology has functioned as a missiological ecclesiology, even if it has not defined itself as such. There are not multiple missions of God. God is one. His mission in the world is one. The church's understanding of its existence in the world, therefore, regardless of its presence in different contexts, should reflect an understanding of the mission of the Triune God." Van Gelder, *Essence of the Church*, 37–38.

47. Mission as church-with-others, mediating salvation, quest for justice, evangelism, contextualization, liberation, inculturation, common witness, ministry by the whole people of God, witness to people of other

warns against the temptation "to incarcerate the *missio Dei* in the narrow confines of our own predilections . . ." and against the temptation to use abstract theories to confine or delineate the mission of God. We can only appreciate the mission of God fully, and avoid defining it "too sharply," through "*poiesis* (which involves 'imaginative creation or representation of evocative images')."[48] Many of these images are presented to us through the narratives of Scripture. Bosch presents six interlocking biblical images/events (which serve as an antidote to merely relying on "logic or analysis")—the incarnation, the Cross, the resurrection, the ascension, Pentecost, and the parousia. Some images come to us as historical or contemporary stories of churches "in the missional mode,"[49] so let me offer an *evocative story*, as we consider the *missio Dei*—the story of City Tabernacle Church in Brisbane.

A Church Transformed by the Missio Dei

The City Tabernacle Church is an old cathedral-like church located in the heart of the city of Brisbane. After experiencing a period of decline, the challenge for the City Tabernacle was to retain a viable presence in the city center. Over the past seven years the church has sought to realign its missional identity by embracing a variety of strategies, which have all been designed to see it connecting and engaging with its growing residential community. Conversational English classes are held around meals, with people encouraged to get involved in "Christianity Explored" courses. A glossy magazine, containing a variety of general interest articles about inner-city life, is published by the church and posted directly to all of the residential addresses in the inner city. It always contains a lead article designed to encourage people to think about the deeper issues of life. Ministry among inner-city parents is thriving through playgroups. Friday mornings involve sausage sizzles and a coffee cart outside the front of the church. These initiatives have helped cultivate relationships with those who are walking from their high-rise residential units down into the city for work.

The church also launched the nationally televised Lord Mayor's Carols in the City. This high-class presentation attracts top-line Australian and international artists, and raised the church's profile and credibility in the wider community, providing a non-threatening opportunity for the sharing of the gospel message. Among the challenges has been the fact that, on average, inner-city residents move on every few years. New believers sometimes only remain with the church for a couple of years, before moving away. Nevertheless, the church has seen their calling as being faithful kingdom builders who follow the missio Dei, and they have experienced an extraordinary transformation in their church life, spiritual vitality, and mission.[50]

---

living faiths, theology, and action in hope. Bosch, *Transforming Mission*, 368–510. Bevans and Schroeder also offer some interesting paradigms in: Bevans and Schroeder, *Constants in Context*, 281–395.

48. Bosch, *Transforming Mission*, 512–18.

49. Frost and Hirsch, *Shaping of Things to Come*, 23.

50. Online: http://www.citytabernacle.com. Used with permission.

THE MISSIONAL MARKS OF THE CHURCH: *NOTAE MISSIONIS*

Since the Reformation, it has been common to speak of the *notae ecclesiae* (the "marks" of the true church). It is important that we question the validity and substance of any such list of "marks," and ask how they might be understood or reconceived missionally. How do the *notae ecclesiae* relate to the *notae missionis* (the "missional marks" of the church, or the marks of the church in mission)?

At the First Council of Constantinople (381AD), the church formulated the confession: "We believe (in) the one, holy, catholic, and apostolic church," and the Nicene Creed uses these four terms for the church.[51] In post-medieval theology, these four marks were used apologetically. This became especially the case as the Roman Catholic Church opposed John Wycliffe and groups in the fourteenth century, such as the Lollards and Hussites. The issue such groups were raising, among other things, was "How is the true church to be recognized? What are its marks? The answer came to be given in terms of these four: Unity, Holiness, Catholicity, and Apostolicity."[52] The Reformers did not deny these four attributes and, indeed, they emphasized their adherence to the creeds of the early church.[53] They especially applied the four dimensions of the creed to their developing theology of the invisible church.[54] Having clashed with Rome's ecclesiology, the issue of "What are the marks of the true church?" became of fundamental importance.[55] Max Davidson goes on to suggest that, in summary, the Reformers' answer was that the true church exists where the gospel of Jesus Christ is preached in its purity and entirety, and where the sacraments are administered properly (especially baptism and the Eucharist). Christians are both a part of the invisible church and the visible, earthly, gathered *ecclesia*.[56]

According to the Reformers, the church is known not by its relationship with Rome or by the apostolic succession of bishops, but by the *notae ecclesiae*—the "marks of the church." Max Davidson writes that there were two different streams of thought within the Reformation on how the *notae ecclesiae* should be articulated (the state churches of the Reformation and the churches of the Radical Reformation).[57]

John Calvin believed that the church is to be found where the word of God is preached, where church discipline is practiced, and where the sacraments are administered according to Christ's institution. He associated the marks with testing and verification, which is to say that whereas Martin Luther saw the marks as mere indicators of the visible church,

---

51. McGrath, *I Believe*.

52. Davidson, *Marks*, 1; George, *Theology of the Reformers*, 86.

53. Davidson, *Marks*, 1; George, *Theology of the Reformers*, 86; Avis, *Church in the Theology of the Reformers*.

54. Luther, *WAT*, 41.211; Masters, *Baptist Confession of Faith 1689*, 26.1.

55. Radmacher, *Nature of the Church*, 60.

56. Davidson, *Marks*, 1–2. Calvin, for instance, writes, "Just as we must believe, therefore, that the former church, invisible to us, is visible to the eyes of God alone, so we are commanded to revere and keep communion with the latter, which is called 'church' in respect to men." McNeill, *Calvin: Institutes*, 4.1.7.

57. Davidson, *Marks*, 2.

Calvin saw them as more important in authentication, verification, and testing.[58] Calvin considered church discipline as an important "mark of the church."[59]

For Martin Luther, organizational systems, bureaucracies, and approaches to church governance are not the core of what constitutes a church; rather it is the assembling of God's people together in such a way that *the gospel is taught purely and the sacraments administered rightly.* Thus, the word of God and the sacraments are the constitutive elements of the church, and in 1521 he wrote to Ambrosius Catherinus, "The entire life and substance of the church rest in the word of God." By way of explanation, he wrote, "I don't mean the written gospel, but the word that is proclaimed; neither do I mean every sermon preached in a church and from a pulpit, but the genuine word which proclaims faith in Christ."[60] This genuine proclamation of the gospel and right administration of the sacraments could be expressed in a variety of ways, according to the context of the gathered community.

Martin Luther disliked the German word *Kirche* because he considered it a term that might lead people to seeing buildings and structures as constitutive of the church. The true church, he asserted, is the people called together by the Holy Spirit through the gospel of Jesus Christ. For Luther, churches are not merely a place of dry preaching of the Scriptures and participation in the sacraments—even though faithfulness to these things is essential to the genuine church. Churches are called to be radical communities of service, prayer, social transformation, and good works. These are not "marks" of the church as such, but evidences of the transformational power of those marks (that is, of the authentic and passionate proclamation of the gospel and participation in the sacraments). Luther also emphasized the universality of the church, and the fact that people through cultures and times have been drawn together into one communion, this "communion of saints," under the supreme and sole lordship of Jesus Christ. "Wherever you hear the word and preaching of faith, and confessing and acting accordingly, you have, no doubt, the true *ecclesia sancta catholica ("the true holy, catholic church").*"[61] Luther defined the church as *communio sanctorum* ("the communion of saints").[62] He wrote that there are at least seven marks of an authentic church.[63] These are:

- *Scripture:* The preaching, profession and possession of, and obedience to, the word of God, characterize the true church. This is the primary evidence "that the true *ecclesia sancta catholica* must be there, even though their number is small."

- *Baptism:* The proper administration of baptism, in accordance with Christ's ordinance;

---

58. Calvin writes, "From this the face of the church comes forth and becomes visible to our eyes. Whenever we see the Word of God purely preached and heard, and the sacraments administered according to Christ's institution, there, it is not to be doubted, a church of God exists (see Eph 2:20)." McNeill, *Calvin: Institutes,* 4.1.9.

59. Calvin et al., *Reformation Debate.*

60. Luther, *WAT,* 7.721.

61. Ibid., 6.287; 7.219; 10.3.407; 50.629.

62. George, *Theology of the Reformers,* 87, 96.

63. See Klug, "Luther's Understanding of Church"; Luther, *WAT,* 41.

- *Communion:* The correct form of the Lord's Supper, administering, believing, and receiving it according to Christ's teaching;

- *Discipline:* The power of the keys, that is, binding and loosing as church discipline both publicly and privately;

- *Leadership:* The lawful vocation, consecration, and ordination of church leaders;

- *Worship:* Prayer, worship, thanksgiving, and the Lord's Prayer (or other spiritual songs) in the vernacular and in accordance with Scripture; the public use of the Apostle's Creed, intercession, the Ten Commandments, and catechisms;

- *Suffering:* Persecutions, sufferings, and trials due to faith in Jesus Christ, and because of steadfast adherence to him and his word.

Ulrich Zwingli described the genuine church as marked by a communion of all elect believers, by the fellowship of believers in a particular community, by the correct and unifying use of the sacraments, and by the unity produced through Scripture. Saturated in Augustine of Hippo and Erasmus of Rotterdam, Zwingli emphasizes unity as a major function of the sacraments and a vital "mark" of the true church.[64]

A robust missional ecclesiology does not take the presence of the true church for granted but, instead, seeks to clarify and examine the "marks" of the true church of Jesus Christ (the *notae ecclesiae*). While we might consider some of the Reformation "marks" to be trapped in their historical and institutional context (the "correct" distribution of the sacraments, for instance), this is no excuse for the missional church to avoid identifying the characteristics or "marks" of authentic Christian churches. The Nicene "marks" of the church (one, holy, catholic, and apostolic) and the various Reformation "marks" of the church (as treated briefly above) need to be honored and biblically scrutinized, if our missional plants and initiatives are going to last and truly glorify Christ. We may not define them all in the same way that John Calvin, Martin Luther, Ulrich Zwingli, and others do—indeed, each defined them in slightly different ways, according to their theology and context—but we must certainly take them seriously in our formation of missional churches. However, all of these "marks" must be conceived (or at least broadened) through the perspective of the *missio Dei.* The missional marks of the church (*notae missionis*) and the marks of the authentic church (*notae ecclesiae*) are inseparable and interdependent.

The *Gospel and Our Culture* movement, for example, reframes each of the four classic marks of the church through the lens of missional ecclesiology. They seek to be fair to the original intent of the marks, while emphasizing the missional dimensions and possibilities of each:[65]

1. *Unity* through baptism, unified in mission, and concretely demonstrating what it means for the people of God to be a unified and "unifying community;"

2. *Holiness* through separation to God and for his missional purposes; holiness through the church being a sanctified and "sanctifying community," especially in its transformational activities in the world;

64. Bromiley, *LCC*, II.56.29–30; II.61.22–62.13; III.226.16–228.28.
65. Williams, *Mission-Shaped Church*, 96–99; Guder, *Missional Church*, 254–64.

3. *Catholicity* through the inclusion of all who would believe in Christ, that comes through missional proclamation to all peoples, and through the church being a "reconciling and reconciled community;"

4. *Apostolicity* through continuing the original apostolic witness to the gospel of Jesus Christ, as contextualized and reinterpreted for each culture and time; apostolicity through the church being a "proclaiming community;" apostolicity as the foundation for the church's catholicity, holiness, and unity: "These marks express the sent-ness of the church; they describe what this sent community does and how it does it."[66]

We have already seen in our chapter on John Howard Yoder, that Yoder, developing the thought of Menno Simons, proposes four missional "marks" of the church. These are holy living, brotherly and sisterly love, witness, and suffering.[67] He also describes what might be considered the fruit of such *notae missionis*, the "five sample practices of the church before the watching world." These are healthy conflict transformation, releasing the whole body of Christ, listening to each other and to the Spirit, hospitality and the sharing of resources, and the transcendence of prejudices.[68] Barry Harvey also develops a list of constitutive practices: imaginative interpretation and reading of Scripture; Christ-centered and community-formed doctrine; the centrality of baptism and Eucharist in the formation of an eschatological body politic; embodied spiritual practice; and shaping the church as a distinct society.[69] Alan Roxburgh writes that the missional church has three primary themes: (1) western society as mission field; (2) mission is about the *missio Dei*; (3) missional church is about the church being a contrast society.[70]

I suggest here my own initial list of *notae missionis*. The four *notae missionis* are missional *foundations*, *ecclesiology*, *contrast*, and *outlook*. Missional practices and characteristics result from these four missional "marks." While these might intersect or overlap with the *notae ecclesia*, I present this list as additional and complementary to them, not as replacing them.[71]

Missional Foundations

The missional church has an *unswerving commitment to the gospel of Jesus Christ* and to the *reliability and authority of the Christian Scriptures*. It interprets its nature, hope, and mission, and builds its structures, forms, and ministries upon the historical and redemptive person, work, mission, and gospel of Jesus Christ. It unreservedly obeys and follows God's authoritative self-revelation in Scripture, as it seeks to worship, glorify, and witness to the Father, Son, and Holy Spirit.

66. Ibid., 256.

67. Yoder, *Royal Priesthood*, 75–89.

68. Yoder, "Sacrament as Social Process," 34–39.

69. Harvey, *Can These Bones Live?*, 22–25.

70. Roxburgh, *What Is Missional Church?*, 5–8. I discovered this article by my friend Alan Roxburgh after developing my *notae missionis*, and am delighted that he identifies similar themes.

71. I have found the following material helpful in deciding what to put in this preliminary list: Frost and Hirsch, *Shaping of Things to Come*, 11–12; Barrett, *Treasure in Clay Jars*, 162–72; Guder, *Missional Church*, 254–68.

Missional Ecclesiology

The missional church *embraces a thoroughgoing missional ecclesiology* in its theology, structures, mission, and ministry practices. It understands its *nature as essentially missional*—it is from that theological footing that it reflects on and pursues the missional nature of its practices, structures, systems, offices, ministries, and missions. The *missio Dei*, the trinitarian relations (communion and mission), the person and work of Jesus Christ, and an awareness of the power and presence of the Holy Spirit, shape this ecclesiology.

Missional Contrast

The missional church *engages specific cultures as a contrast society*—called out by God to give witness to his eschatological reign and kingdom in a particular cultural context. It demonstrates missional faithfulness in all cultural contexts (whether it finds itself in a position of cultural marginality and liminality, or cultural influence and prominence). It self-consciously examines the relationship between the gospel and the culture, and resists compromises that might arise from unhealthy church-state-culture relationships. The missional church understands the importance of missional relevance and critical contextualization, but it is also an alternative, distinct, eschatological society—aliens, sojourners, exiles, and pilgrims, formed into a counter-cultural, Spirit-empowered community, looking to Jesus Christ with eschatological hope.[72]

Missional Outlook

The missional church views all cultures as mission fields—this is its basic *outlook* and orientation. Its outlook is missiological in a way that shapes its theology, structures, offices, practices, and church-state-culture relations. While it recognizes particular missional needs in particular contexts, it does not fundamentally distinguish between *evangelism here* and *mission over there*. Every society, culture, people-group, and setting is a mission field.

Missional Practices and Characteristics

The four *notae missionis*—missional *foundations, ecclesiology, contrast,* and *outlook*—result in a diverse and contextual array of missional practices and characteristics. Missional churches practice a dynamic proclamation of the gospel in a variety of modes and forms. They practice a missional reading of Scripture, that is, a missional theology and hermeneutic. They also practice a missional strategy of presence, action, and word. These missional practices, just like its structures, are fluid, contextual, indigenous, gospel affirming, biblically based, and under constant renewal and reform. The expression and range of these practices will vary according to context, culture, and so forth, but they are always an expression of the missional nature of the church—the faith community actively examines their missionality and gospel-faithfulness through the lens of Scripture and the mission of God.

The missional church evidences many, but rarely all, of the following missional practices and characteristics (this is a provisional, indicative list):

72. Roxburgh, *What Is Missional Church?*, 5–8.

- Scriptural and gospel obedience, witness, and adherence;

- Concrete missional expressions of unity, holiness, catholicity, and apostolicity;

- Christ-centered and trinitarian spirituality;

- A sense of missional vocation;

- The presence of agapic love;

- Practices of forgiveness, conflict resolution, and reconciliation;

- Mutual accountability;

- Hospitality and the embrace of "difference";

- Participatory ministry and worship, and mission *of* and *by* the people;

- Commitment to practices of justice, peace, and mercy;

- A kingdom-sized, eschatological vision and purpose that includes, but is bigger than, the local church;

- An identity as a church "of sinners and of grace";

- Apostolic and five-fold ministry (Ephesians 4:11);

- Intentional discipleship practices;

- Missional approaches to Christian leadership;

- Innovative ways of being church in a rapidly changing, pluralistic society;

- Experimentation with ancient and contemporary worship traditions and styles;

- Narrative and creative gospel communication;

- Suffering for the sake of the gospel;

- Missiological ethics and values;

- An identity as a "community of the cross," the resurrection, and the eschaton;

- Continuation of the apostolic *kerygma* and mission;

- An authentic, relevant community.[73]

David Bosch writes of the Reformation views of the "marks of the true church," that the Reformers unintentionally bequeathed to Protestants an understanding of the church "as a place where certain things happen." Missional ecclesiology, however, views the church as essentially "a body of people sent on a mission."[74] While the above might be a limited characterization of the Reformers' understandings of the "marks of the true

73. This is just an indicative list and is not in order of importance. These characteristics emerge from the following, and other, texts: Guroian, *Faith, Church, Mission*, 99–108; Moltmann, *Theology of Hope*, 102–12; Moltmann, *Church in the Power of the Spirit*, 7–11, 64–65; Rahner et al., *Content of Faith*, 449–51, 592–97; Küng, *Church*, 354–59; Russell, *Church in the Round*, 87–96; Yoder, *Royal Priesthood*, 65–101, 114–15, 170, 350; Yoder, *Priestly Kingdom*, 118–19.

74. Hunsberger and Van Gelder, *Church between Gospel and Culture*, 337. Referring to lectures given by Bosch at Western Theological Seminary in Michigan in April 1991.

church," it does caution us to be careful when considering the *notae missionis* and the *notae ecclesiae*. We must not fall into the trap of emphasizing certain ecclesiological expressions or activities, in such a way that we minimize the importance of the church being caught up (and then participating) in God's mission in the world. Understanding the nature of the church as essentially and ontologically missional precedes questions about the expressions of such missionality.

A thorough examination of the classic and Reformation "marks" of the church enriches missional ecclesiology, and helps us distinguish between that which is necessary for the *esse* (being) of the church, and that which is appropriate for the *bene esse* (well being) of the church.[75] The "marks," practices, and characteristics of missional churches that I have proposed add a missional dimension and texture to the Reformation and classic marks of the church. They are to be viewed as complementary and enriching, rather than contradictory.

HOW DOES THE CHURCH PRACTICE THE MISSION OF GOD?

What are some of the features of a church practicing and shaped by the mission of God? I list some sample features here, following this progression: Cultivating *missional perspectives*; Cultivating *missional postures*, and; Cultivating *missional practices*.

CULTIVATING MISSIONAL PERSPECTIVES

There are a variety of ways to approach the question, "How does the church's mission relate to its nature and structures?" John Zizioulas, for example, suggests that the *ad extra* ministries of the church—its missional and social engagement with the world—are organically related to its existence and sacramental nature (he also says that they must be presided over by the bishop). However, while the *ad intra* ministries of the church are permanent and related to its eucharistic structure (ecclesial ministries directed toward building up the church), the *ad extra* ministries of the church are fluid, contextually responsive, and need-oriented.[76] While Zizioulas does attempt to place mission at the ontological core of the church, he ends up giving the impression that missional engagement is more peripheral than essential. On the other hand, Miroslav Volf views the mission of the church as innate to its essence and identity. He writes, "If the church is the image of the Trinity, then the church's being is a form of mission."[77] Joseph Ratzinger adds that the church's missional nature flows out of its being as *communion*—the triune God constitutes the church communally and mission flows from that communion. In other words, the processions of the three persons within the Trinity unfold as the *missio Dei* in salvation history—visibly in the incarnation and in the church's *communio* and *missio*, and invisibly in grace.[78]

---

75. McGrath, *Christianity's Dangerous Idea*, 471.

76. Zizioulas, *Being as Communion*, 225.

77. Volf and Lee, "Spirit and the Church," 35.

78. See Ratzinger, *God of Jesus Christ*.

While I do not want to minimize the variety of perspectives on offer, it should be clear by now that missional ecclesiology defines the church through the paradigms associated with the *missio Dei*. Jürgen Moltmann writes that "the more the Christian West disintegrates culturally and geographically," the more the church will need to look beyond the West to discover what it means to be a missional church that is defined by the *missio Dei*, in a marginal and uncertain setting. Drawing from the burgeoning missional, ecumenical, kingdom-oriented, and lay movements beyond the western cultures, the church needs to understand afresh that "the mission of Christ creates the church." Moltmann writes that the church is only understood "in the context of the *missio Dei*" since "mission comprehends the whole of the church"—he writes that mission comprehends the church's nature, its gospel proclamation, its spread of the kingdom, and its charitable and liberating ministries.[79] As the *community of the exodus,* the church departs from captivity and exile into the freedom of the kingdom of God. It follows the *messianic mission of Jesus,* spreading the freedom of the kingdom, embodying the "social form of hope," sharing in the "prophetic ministry of Christ" as "witnesses of the gospel."[80]

> The all-encompassing messianic mission of the whole church corresponds to Christ's messianic mission . . . The real point is not to spread the church but to spread the kingdom . . . The missionary concept of the church leads to a church that is open to the world in the divine mission, because it leads to a trinitarian interpretation of the church in the history of God's dealings with the world.[81]

CULTIVATING MISSIONAL POSTURES

John Howard Yoder asserts that, in the main, the pre-Constantinian church understood itself as a distinct, visible, and transformational community, called to demonstrate a polity and culture in redemptive contrast to the world. During the period of Christendom, "the two visible realities, church and world, were fused. There is no longer anything to call 'world'; state, economy, art, rhetoric, superstition, and war have all been baptized."[82] The consequences for the church included the superfluous role of discipleship, the validation of secular institutions and ambitions, the removal of the distinction between church and world, and a distortion of the meaning of human history.[83] As we have seen in the chapter on Yoder, he is convinced that the church should wrestle with the legacy of Constantinianism, rejecting its negative dimensions without throwing the proverbial baby out with the bathwater. The church should believe and confess that "the meaning of history" resides in God's eschatological and sovereign formation of a redeemed

79. Moltmann, *Church in the Power of the Spirit*, 7–11.

80. Ibid., 76–85.

81. Ibid., 11. Elsewhere Moltmann writes, "It is not the church that has a mission of salvation to fulfill to the world; it is the mission of the Son and the Spirit through the Father that includes the church, creating a church as it goes on its way . . . The church participates in Christ's messianic mission and in the creative mission of the Spirit." Ibid., 64–65.

82. Yoder, "Otherness of the Church," 57.

83. Ibid., 60–61.

community for the sake of his kingdom and glory, while establishing theological conceptions of church and world that are biblically based. Christ/culture polarities and typologies need to be evaluated in the light of Christian theology. The church should embrace the foolishness of the cross, rejecting all efforts after power or privilege, while facing the realities of deconstantinization with missional courage, enthusiasm, and innovation. The Spirit empowers the church to be an alternative, marginal, missional community, witnessing to God's eschatological purposes and meaning in history.

The church in the western world is in an age of post-Christendom, marginalization, and liminality.[84] The author who best captures the shape of this change is Stuart Murray.[85] Murray defines post-Christendom in the following way:

> Post-Christendom is the culture that emerges as the Christian faith loses coherence within a society that has been definitively shaped by the Christian story and as the institutions that have been developed to express Christian convictions decline in influence.[86]

While Christianity is expanding in Majority World contexts, and especially Africa, Asia, and Latin America, and the churches in those regions are experiencing their own kind of Christendom,[87] western cultures are facing quite a different phenomenon. Even renewal movements such as Pentecostalism have been unable to stem the decline or change the overall pattern of marginalization. Church attendance is diminishing and we observe little interest in denominations, the exodus of younger people, the rise of biblical illiteracy, the prevalence of irrelevant forms of worship and liturgy, and various other expressions of post-Christendom.[88] For many postmodern people, church has come to be seen as "ingrown, tired, petty, crotchety, and out of touch—or else manic, wild-eyed, and lunatic."[89] John Drane even goes as far as to suggest that "we are now faced with the serious possibility—likelihood, even—that the Christian faith might disappear entirely from our culture within the first half of this century."[90] A "clash of epistemologies" is occurring in the west, as secularism, religions, modernity, postmodernity, pluralism, the forces of globalism, and the revival of traditional and religious fundamentalism are engaged in a complex coexistence and struggle.[91] Wilbert Shenk writes that while institutional recognition and

---

84. Liminality is being used here as a term for the transitional state that groups go through when they are experiencing significant cultural and social change and, as such, it might be "regarded as a time and place of withdrawal from normal modes of social action, it can be seen as potentially a period of scrutinization of the central values or axioms of the culture in which it occurs." Turner, *Ritual Process*, 167. Liminality can be dangerous for a cultural or social group, but it is necessary for significant change to occur successfully. The status of those groups (of persons) going through such liminality "becomes ambiguous, neither here nor there, betwixt and between all fixed points of classification." Therefore, it is a period when much of the life and structure of the group is being redefined. Turner, *Dramas, Fields, and Metaphors*, 232.

85. Murray, *Post-Christendom*, 1–22, 178–88.

86. Ibid., 19.

87. See Jenkins, *Next Christendom*.

88. Guder, *Missional Church*, 2.

89. McLaren, *Church on the Other Side*, 14.

90. Drane and Drane, "Breaking into Dynamic Ways," 142. Quoted in Murray, *Post-Christendom*, 7.

91. Hiebert, *Missiological Implications*, 1.

numerical growth are poor "primary indicators of the church's health," these drastic symptoms of post-Christendom "point to an etiology to be found within the church itself."[92]

The cause or origin of such ecclesial decline is largely rooted in the theological paradigms, ecclesial expressions, and missional approaches of Constantinianism and Christendom—a legacy that needs radical and courageous examination. Shenk considers this etiology to be particularly expressed in Christendom's fostering of an ecclesial life where ethical and moral standards are noticeably lower than the gospel's expectation and vision. The church has conformed to the cultural systems of the world, and their attendant powers and principalities. Ecclesiastical structures are often archaic, lacking integrity, vitality, and a distinct identity. In order to understand what it means to be the church in a post-Christendom context, we need to understand Christendom and the Constantinian legacy, their history, vestiges, and inner and societal dynamics.[93]

Stuart Murray believes that post-Christendom moves the Christian church, congregations, and the Christian story into marginality and liminality, and, hopefully, a renewed missional self-understanding.[94] For western culture, "The fourth and twentieth centuries form bookends marking transition points in the history of the church . . . Christians must now struggle to understand the meaning of their social location in a decentered world."[95] Stanley Hauerwas and William Willimon insist that churches need to consider themselves "resident aliens, an adventurous colony in a society of unbelief."[96] The Christian church in western culture needs to rediscover its exilic nature as an alternative *polis* and a countercultural movement. It needs to become a discipling community that,

> again asserts that God, not nations, rules the world, that the boundaries of God's kingdom transcend those of Caesar, and that the main political task of the church is the formation of people who see clearly the cost of discipleship and are willing to pay the price.[97]

George Hunsberger suggests that this is concretely outworked as the church forms an alternative community, articulates a "wider rationality," heals people's fragmentary lives, and fans into flame a "subversive witness." In the same work, Craig Van Gelder proposes that the church not only needs to accept its changed status, it also needs to develop a public theology that can contextualize and communicate theology, Scripture, and the wider rationality of faith, to contemporary culture.[98] Disestablishment, then, may be a constructive way forward, as the church rediscovers its missional ecclesiology. According to Douglas Hall, intentional disestablishment is a work of theology.[99] Stuart Murray develops a helpful taxonomy of the choices the church can make about the Christendom

---

92. Shenk, *Write the Vision*, 5.

93. Ibid., 27–29.

94. Murray, *Post-Christendom*, 20.

95. Ibid., 187–88. See Harvey, *Another City*, x.

96. Hauerwas and Willimon, *Resident Aliens*, 44–49. Hauerwas continues the tradition developed by John Howard Yoder and his critique of the Constantinian church.

97. Ibid., 44.

98. Hunsberger and Van Gelder, *Church between Gospel and Culture*, 19, 41–43.

99. Hall, *End of Christendom*, 35–49.

ecclesiological legacy, now that it finds itself in postmodernity and post-Christendom: denying, defending, dismissing, dissociating, demonizing, disavowing, disentangling, deconstructing, and disembarking.[100]

Naturally, not everyone agrees with all the content of John Howard Yoder's Constantinian thesis, or the proposals of those who have followed his lead. There is no question, however, that the spirit of Constantinianism, and the various forms of western Christendom, had an effect on the church's self-understanding, view of its relationship with the world and history, and approaches to mission, discipleship, sacrament, worship, politics, and institution. Missional ecclesiology must deal with the legacy of Constantinianism, especially, but not exclusively, in western cultures, forming appropriate and brave responses. These responses must take into consideration Yoder's proposal that ecclesiology *is* social ethics and social ethics *is* gospel, since the church's social reality and ethic are to be a foretaste, model, and herald of the kingdom, and a reflection of the gospel of the redemptive person, ethic, message, and work of Jesus Christ. The church has a public role and voice in society and its social ethics must be rooted in the gospel and in the incarnation, in such a way that "would then call for and empower a *missionary ethic of incarnation.*"[101] "The alternative community discharges a modeling mission. The church is called to be now what the world is called to be ultimately."[102] Missional ecclesiology calls for a church that moves beyond the ecclesial confines, theological limitations, and missional anemia of Constantinianism. The church is to pursue a fresh faithfulness to the gospel of Jesus Christ, and the practices of peace, reconciliation, kingdom ethics, forgiveness, social processes and ethical commitments of the New Testament, decentralization of power, attention to the other, and community discernment.[103] Yoder also challenges the missional church to embrace hostility, economic sharing and solidarity, ethnic diversity, non-violent resistance, religious liberty, and culturally/ethnically/socially diverse approaches to church planting, congregational development, and mission.

Barry Harvey challenges the church to rediscover its biblical nature as an alternative society and city, as *altera civitas*. Because of the person and the final, eschatological work of Jesus Christ, the church is constituted as an alternative city that remembers and worships Jesus Christ, pursues the mission of God in the world, and demonstrates the eschatological purposes, kingdom, and presence of the missional, triune God in human history. Harvey draws parallels with the postexilic Jewish community in diaspora (while admitting the limitations of such an analogy). As an alternative city the church's worship, fellowship, and mission are characterized by kingdom ethics, eschatological outlook, counter-cultural values, and missiological passion, and by practices of justice, peace, mercy, compassion, humility, service, and presence in the world. These are the concrete forms of its body politic—a body politic grounded in the ethical commitments, social dimensions, and constitutive practices of Scripture. Harvey rightly asserts that the church in every age must make a decision to *be* the church.[104]

---

100. Murray, *Post-Christendom*, 150–60, 178–216.

101. Yoder, *Priestly Kingdom*, 44.

102. Ibid., 92.

103. Yoder, *Body Politics*, 61–70.

104. Harvey, *Another City*, 9–20, 150–57; Harvey, *Can These Bones Live?*, 123–27.

The Missional Church is Inculturational and Contextual

Following the messianic mission of Christ and the pattern of the *missio Dei* in God's redemptive work in history, the mission of the church is both contextual and inculturational. Stephen Bevans demonstrates how contextual theology and practice pay attention to the following: "(1) the spirit and message of the gospel; (2) the tradition of the Christian people; (3) the culture of a particular nation or region; and (4) social change in that culture, due both to technological advances on the one hand and struggles for justice and liberation on the other."[105]

A central theme that runs through much of Miroslav Volf's writing is the relationship between the church, reconciliation, mission, and contemporary cultures. Volf is concerned with the diversity of cultures colliding and communicating across a shrinking globe, as well as the rapid evolution of cultures.[106] Cultures are the substance from within which churches emerge and are immersed. These cultures have characteristics and expressions that churches can and do adopt, adapt, transform, discard, and replace.[107] Christian mission happens through inculturation and contextualization in a given culture or subculture, since churches and individual Christians are immersed *within* cultures.

> There is no single correct way to relate to a given culture as a whole, or even to its dominant thrust. There are only numerous ways of accepting, transforming, rejecting, or replacing various aspects of a given culture from within. This is what it means for Christian difference to be *internal* to a given culture.[108]

According to John Zizioulas, the relationship between the church and the world is complex. Theological ideas such as incarnation, contextualization, communion, and trinitarian relations may inform this dynamic interaction between church and culture, and lead to mutual enrichment. The existential longings and concerns of human beings and cultures must be put into a genuine conversation with Christian theology, community, and practice. This is because these expressions of Christian faith and belief relate to "whatever is human—and not only."[109] Mission is essentially relational, writes Zizioulas, being shaped by the concept of *being as communion*. Zizioulas contends that this relational shape of *being* and of mission takes up all human beings, all of creation, and, indeed, the entire cosmos. The church needs to radically and urgently reject past dichotomies in this area, since,

> Perhaps the most urgent mission of the Church today is to become conscious of, and proclaim in the strongest terms, the fact that there is an intrinsic koinonia between the human being and its natural environment, a koinonia that must be brought into the Church's being in order to receive its fullness.[110]

---

105. Bevans, "Models of Contextual Theology," 186.

106. Volf, "It Is Like Yeast," 12.

107. Volf, "Theology, Meaning, and Power," 100–2.

108. Volf, "It Is Like Yeast," 13–14.

109. Zizioulas, *Church as Communion*, 108–9.

110. Ibid., 109. There are certain ontological assumptions shaping Zizioulas's ecclesiology, of course.

John Zizioulas rejects any ontological distinction between the church and the world that emphasizes a *dichotomy* between the two, or that cultivates an ecclesial posture "*vis-à-vis* the world." Instead, he writes that the ontological relationship that exists between the church and the world and the "relational character of ministry" mean "that the only acceptable method of mission for the Church is the *inculturational* one: the Church relates to the world through and in her ministry by being involved existentially in the world."[111] Through participation in the eschatological mission of Christ in the world and in history, the church learns what it means to be inculturationally present in the world—in response to, and for the sake of, the *missio Dei*.

CULTIVATING MISSIONAL PRACTICES

Joseph Ratzinger is right when he says that authentic mission, proclamation, and *evangelium* should be expressed and experienced as "glad tidings," and as the joyous overflow of faith. The church has often been experienced as punctilious, joyless, and a place of cramped scrupulosity and narrowness of spirit. This is contrary to the heart of Christianity and true *evangelium*. The joyous announcement of "glad tidings" should be expressed in the community of faith in ways that are far deeper than external enthusiasm or entertainment. It might include the renewed celebration of holy days, the vanquishing of loneliness through genuine community, and *evangelium* that is deeply embedded in the hope of the gospel. Such *evangelium* comes from joyful submission to the Messiah. Mission is not a duty to be performed and neither is discipleship. The community of faith is to bear witness to the world of the one who has liberated them to joy and hope, in the midst of uncertainty, suffering, and opposition. It would be wrong, however, to focus exclusively on the subjective states coming from faith in the gospel. Mission is not centered on such subjectivity but on the communion with others and with God that is made possible through the person and work of Jesus Christ. It is centered on his redemptive work and on his kingdom message. Proclaiming the astonishing gospel of Jesus Christ, the church not only presents truth and hope to the watching world but also discovers that there are "glad tidings" in times of darkness and in times of celebration.[112]

The Missional Church Lives and Exists for Others

Joseph Ratzinger writes that election by God is a call to live for others. Christian identity, and communion with others and with God, is for the sake of mission to the world. John Thornhill quotes Joseph Ratzinger and builds on his thinking, when he writes:

> Election, being picked out by God, is not exclusive; it does not set those chosen apart, in a privileged position that contrasts with that of the others who have not received the call. "Election is not a privilege of the elected but a call to live for others." The election of Israel, the election of the Church, the election of Christ . . . does not mean being called forth from the rest to have the privilege of *being different*; it means being called forth from the rest to have the privilege of *existing for the rest*.

111. Zizioulas, *Being as Communion*, 224.

112. Ratzinger, *Principles of Catholic Theology*, 75–84.

This principle has an importance for the theology of the Church that will be immediately recognized.[113]

According to John Zizioulas, the church needs to "offer herself to the world for reception," rather than practice aggressive mission or evangelism. This is because *the church receives* much from the world, and *is received* by the world—she exists to give what she has *received from God*: the love of the Father incarnate in the Son, the good news of the gospel, and the *kerygma*. Reception always occurs through the power of the Spirit, through the love of God expressed in the faith community, and through the inculturation of the gospel.[114] In a spirit of hospitality and generosity, the missional church lives and exists for others, for the sake of the messianic mission of Christ, and in the power of the Holy Spirit.

The Missional Church has a "Modeling Mission"

The church participates in the mission of God by *being the church*. Soaked in the values of the kingdom, shaped by the trinitarian relations, characterized by agapic love, and united with its head and his messianic mission, the church is a missional organism. The *missio ecclesia* is the communion-*in-mission*. John Howard Yoder writes, "Peoplehood and mission, fellowship and witness, are not two desiderata, each capable of existing or of being missed independently of one another; each is the condition of the genuineness of the other." He goes on to suggest that the missional community is characterized by holiness, forgiveness, love, *koinonia*, witness, christological ethics, suffering, and willingness to allow Christ to direct its entire life. Such characteristics might be included in the *notae missionis* of the church (the "missional marks" of the church). For Yoder, Constantinianism diminishes the mission of the church, since, by deforming the church's relations, identity, and orientation, it compromises the church's mission and authentic nature. Instead of talking about the "missionary structure of the congregation," Yoder prefers to describe the "congregational structure of mission." The church has a "modeling mission," as it witnesses to the kingdom and mission of God.[115] Its "minority ethic" is a "*missionary ethic of incarnation*," confronting the kingdoms of this world and witnessing to Jesus Christ.[116] Yoder outlines five ecclesial practices that testify to the person, mission, and kingdom of Jesus Christ, "before the watching world."[117]

The missional congregation has a "modeling mission" that can be expressed in a wide range of forms—alternative churches, niche congregations, established parishes, cell and home churches, base communities, and so forth. The church's ability to model the ethics, lifestyle, and trinitarian relations of the kingdom of God are not limited by forms or styles. In the final analysis, all that really matters is that churches and their leaders willingly surrender to the mission of God in the world, and obediently surrender their entire life together to the Lord Jesus Christ. I am not pretending that this is easy!

113. Thornhill, *Sign and Promise*, 36, quoting Ratzinger, *Introduction to Christianity*, 174.

114. Zizioulas, "Theological Problem," 3–6.

115. Yoder, *Royal Priesthood*, 75–101, 350–52.

116. Yoder, *Priestly Kingdom*, 44, 118.

117. I outline these in my chapter on Yoder. See Yoder, *Body Politics*.

The Missional Church Practices Hospitality

Skye Jethani, the senior editor of *Leadership Journal*, recently wrote an on-line piece called *Special Needs Boy Removed from Church*. In that piece, he told of a twelve-year-old boy with cerebral palsy who was removed from a "seeker-sensitive" Easter service for being a "distraction." The mother complained, and the church's leadership rejected her request for a ministry for special needs children. After she took the story to the media, the church issued a statement that "this young man and his family were not removed from our church. They were escorted to a nearby section of our church where they watched the service in its entirety . . ." The church said that it is "our goal to offer a distraction free environment for all our guests. We look forward to resolving any misunderstanding that has occurred."[118]

Like Jethani, I do not want to unduly criticize this church or assume that this is typical of their ministry approach. However, it is my firm conviction that the congregation shaped by the mission of God practices a radical, Christ-like hospitality. The Christ-centered congregation embraces and celebrates difference and reaches out to the marginalized, forgotten, and fringes of the culture. It recognizes that it is in these places that the kingdom of God can be found, and that it is in this movement of embrace that it images the *missio Dei* and testifies to the cross of Christ.

Letty Russell, who writes much on these issues, says, "Hospitality calls us to be a community of faith and struggle that connects with those at the margin and celebrates the way God has called a diverse people, so that we may all share together at God's welcome table!"[119] Russell invites an ecclesiology that prioritizes *kairos* (the right and opportune moment) and *jubilee* (liberation of the marginalized, forgotten, oppressed, or burdened).[120] Missional churches examine their structures, practices, and attitudes toward others to see whether they are liberating and characterized by a concern for justice, the inclusion of the marginalized, the welcome of the stranger, practicing hospitality, flattening out of leadership and ecclesial structures, and, as Russell challenges us, joining with the oppressed in concrete, opportune moments of solidarity.[121] We must not succumb to the temptation to separate matters of justice, mercy, and compassion, from issues of personal sin. Nor can we afford to cultivate churches that commit the *double sin* of being "of, but not in, the world."[122] While we may not accept all of Russell's conclusions about the nature of Christian hospitality (each of us will need to determine whether the inclusivity she requests is biblically justified), her postcolonial theology has real implications for missional ecclesiology. Russell calls for an *analysis* of the past and the present, a *resistance* to ongoing forms of oppression, and a *reconstruction* of a preferred, hopeful, indigenous, hospitable, welcoming, and compassionate future.[123] As we have seen, Letty Russell asserts that genuine human liberation and authentic Christian mission are

118. Jethani, "Special Needs Boy Removed from Church."
119. Russell, *Church in the Round*, 181.
120. Ibid., 80–82.
121. Ibid., 75–111.
122. Ibid., 119–27.
123. Russell, "Cultural Hermeneutics," 23–25.

inseparable, and missional ecclesiology in western cultures has a great deal to learn from liberation thought and from postcolonial mission and theology.[124]

A Church of and for the Homeless

The mission of the Homeless Church in San Francisco is to bring the saving, life-changing power of Jesus Christ to the hurting people in that city. They believe that there is a solution for homelessness that does not lie in just outer changes but, more importantly, in inner transformation. They believe God can bring hope to the hopeless, healing to the sick, and confidence to those who have none left. They rely not on their own strength but in the power of God to transform lives through his church.

Evan and April Prosser received the vision for the Homeless Church while he was still pastoring in a church (with four walls!) in Orland, California. They moved out of their comfortable home, bought a motorhome, and use it as a base for mission among the homeless in San Francisco. The new church is not an outreach but a church of and for the homeless. There are four parts to the vision of the Homeless Church: 1. A church on the street, of and for homeless people; 2. A community made up of small "pocket bodies" wherever people live; 3. A ministry supported interdenominationally; and 4. Further down the line, a warehouse where worship and preaching will be constantly happening, with services available like food, showers, laundry, and shopping cart check-in. After 14 years of ministry among the homeless of San Francisco, the busses are gone, owing to police pressure on people living in vehicles, which resulted in no more "camps" of homeless people. So since 2009, they meet where people gather, holding services at one of the local piers and at a big intersection in their neighbourhood.[125]

The Missional Church Helps People Become Disciples of Jesus

There are many dimensions of western culture that work against genuine discipleship to Jesus—individualism, consumerism, pluralism, and relativism, to name a few. Helping Christians cultivate a "messianic spirituality" is one of the great challenges facing the contemporary church.[126] Thomas Hopko suggests that the church's missional witness is directly linked with Christian spirituality.[127] He writes that congregations enhance the church's mission through the cultivation of virtues and ethics, the modeling of agapic

---

124. Ibid., 25–40.

125. Online: http://www.homelesschurch.org, and at their Facebook site for the *Homeless Church of San Francisco*. Used with permission.

126. Frost and Hirsch, *Shaping of Things to Come*, 111–64.

127. Hopko, *Orthodox Faith—Spirituality*, 8.

love, encouraging people to live the beatitudes, and helping people foster meaningful practices of prayer and spiritual discipline. In other words, congregations that follow the mission of God are dedicated to helping people become devoted disciples of Jesus Christ. These congregations help to equip people with the resources, character, and support to follow Jesus in their unique cultural and personal setting. Some good works have been published recently on missional discipleship, and my sense is that this is a growing field of interest, particularly given the complexities of making disciples of Jesus in the contemporary global culture.[128] In addition, one cannot overlook the seminal work of Dallas Willard in the area of Christian discipleship, in our efforts to help people discover a form of discipleship sculpted by the mission of God and the person of Christ.[129]

The Missional Church Releases the Streams of its Missional Vocation

Scot McKnight notes that there are five streams "flowing into the emerging lake." These streams are not unique to missional ecclesiology, yet "together they crystallize" into a missiological movement.[130] These five streams are the prophetic (or provocative), postmodern, praxis-oriented, post-evangelical, and political. It seems to me that when these streams are interwoven they give contour or definition to some of the main perspectives of missional ecclesiology. Each stream needs to be chastened by Scripture and theology. Missional churches need to be intentional about releasing these streams in their ecclesial life, and in so doing, discover new expressions of their missional vocation.

The Missional Church Seeks Genuine Reform

The church is missional when it prophetically challenges the powers and principalities present in the world and within its own structures and life. This prophetic and apostolic role was too often forfeited in Christendom and especially in church-state relationships (most traditions of Christianity have suffered from this problem to a greater or lesser degree). A prophetic (or at least provocative) examination of ecclesial structures, leadership practices, and church-state or gospel-culture relationships is vital to a robust missional ecclesiology. Many questions surround this topic. How rigorously do we challenge the ecclesiological norms and givens in our traditions? How clear are we about the necessary criteria for such ecclesiological scrutiny? Why do we resist prophetic voices that challenge our structures, practices, and systems? What is the nature of true reform in the church?

While one would not always hold Joseph Ratzinger up as a model of the reforming spirit, he does have some useful insights into the nature of true reform in the church. He is enthusiastic about the church's responsibility for maintaining a prophetic witness in the world, especially in the arena of social compassion and justice. He reflects on the bitterness, anger, and disappointment that many people feel toward the church, on their sense of hope that the church might be different from the institutions of this world, and on the passion many have for reforming the church. Ratzinger writes, "In their heart of

---

128. See Frost, *Exiles*; Hirsch and Hirsch, *Untamed*; Putman and Stetzer, *Breaking the Discipleship Code*.

129. Willard, *Divine Conspiracy*; Willard, *Spirit of the Disciplines*; Willard, *Renovation of the Heart*; Willard, *Revolution of Character*; Willard, *Great Omission*.

130. McKnight, "Five Streams," 1–2.

hearts people expect more of her [the church] than of all worldly institutions . . . There, at least, one would hope to know the taste of freedom, of redeemed existence—to emerge from the cave . . .”[131] True reform in the church, writes Ratzinger, has certain distinguishing features.[132] These reflections can enrich missional ecclesiology's prophetic impulse; just as a missional ecclesiology's prophetic voice might enhance Catholic ecclesiology. According to Ratzinger:

- True reform is not driven by humans with personal agendas, nor shaped according to our tastes or inventiveness, but by the grace of the Lord of the church. This grace precedes us, leads us to pure freedom, and causes us to uncover and release what God has fashioned the church to be—not make the church ourselves.

- True reform is the realization of a double act of purification and renewal in the church.

- True reform entails human constructions, institutions, and accommodations to culture, place, and time. These become obsolete, however, and “risk setting themselves up as the essence of the Church, and thus prevent us from seeing through to what is truly essential.”[133] These are to be dismantled and revisited regularly in order for the church to reform. This reforming activity must be characterized by a removal or dismantling that is steeped in faith and that leads to *communion*.

- True reform is the expansive manifestation of faith itself, since in every age “faith itself in its full magnitude and breadth is the essential reform that we need.”[134] Such faith is the substance by which we view and engage the church that God is shaping in our midst.

- True reform involves mutual responsibility for the church and reciprocal service among its people. Office-bearers engage in ever greater self-dispossession, and the presence of the Spirit is preferred over administrative machinery.

- True reform ought to embrace an examination of conscience throughout the church, that releases the healing and removal of all that is not of God.

- True reform is expressed in the context of authentic and passionate worship and Christian spirituality, since Christian spirituality is expansive. True reform will also be expressed in such things as liturgy, a liturgical spirit, prayer, spiritual disciplines, and the like. In *The Spirit of the Liturgy* Ratzinger writes that the liturgical spirit is normative in the Christian life (his ecclesiology, of course, is both eucharistic and liturgical). The liturgical spirit is remedial and subversive, combating such things as individualism, religious bondage and formalism, pragmatism, cultual dilettantism, and worldliness in worship.[135]

131. Ratzinger, *Called to Communion*, 135.

132. Ibid., 140–56.

133. Ibid., 142.

134. Ibid., 145.

135. Ratzinger, *Spirit of the Liturgy*, 91–110. Ratzinger sees prayer, liturgy, worship, gospel, catechesis, and catechism as spiritually formative and renewing, as an antidote to the values of the world, and as the “feast of faith.” See Ratzinger, *Feast of Faith*; Ratzinger, *Gospel, Catechesis, Catechism*; Ratzinger and Messori,

- True reform has a personal center in morality, forgiveness, and expiation. This is because the church is a communion of those who need healing, grace and liberation, and who transmit these to others.

- True reform involves pain and possibly martyrdom, but is sustained by the joy of redemption and the hope of the eschatological gathering and communion of God's people.

Hans Küng, who has been a passionate advocate for ecclesial reform throughout his life, writes that the church is in a continual process of reform, by either discarding its deformations, or by pursuing a deeper faithfulness to Jesus Christ and to Christ's vision for the church. Genuine ecclesial reform "arises primarily from the demands made in the gospel by the Lord of the church, the call to metanoia, to new faith, to new righteousness, holiness, and freedom, to new life . . . Reform is a way in which the church fulfills the will of God, following in the footsteps of Christ with an eye on the coming kingdom."[136] Küng is certain that authentic reform is not revolution or innovation, not violent upheaval or abandonment of the past, and neither is it a restoration to the old, established, or sentimentalized past. He writes,

> Genuine church reform . . . does not aim at a contented continuation of an old system, but courageously breaks with old systems in order to find greater truth. Instead of restoring old forms, it looks for new forms fitted to the age; instead of insisting with fresh intensity on the rigid observations of laws and ordinances, canons and codes, it seeks to renew the inner life of institutions and constitutions. While retaining a sense of traditions, genuine reform is concerned with finding the new and creative forms demanded by the present time; it is not restoration, but again *renewal* . . . The only measure for renewal in the church is the original gospel of Jesus Christ himself; the only concrete guide is the apostolic church. The credibility of the church depends crucially on its constantly undertaking new reforms and renewing itself afresh.[137]

The reforming impulse and imagination are important dimensions of mission ecclesiology. As the church follows and participates in the mission of God it is subject to constant scrutiny by the gospel of Jesus Christ and the presence of the Spirit. The church is ever being renewed and reformed.

QUESTIONS FOR REFLECTION

1. How does the *missio Dei* shape your understanding of Christian ministry and leadership?

2. In what ways does your church need to be more hospitable and open to difference?

3. If you were to create a list of the "marks of the true church" (*notae ecclesiae*), and a list of the "missional marks of the church" (*notae missionis*), what would you include in each?

Ratzinger Report, 119–35.

136. Küng, *Church*, 340.

137. Ibid., 340–41.

15

The Christ-Centered Church: Following the Messiah and His Eschatological Mission

The messianic mission of Jesus is only fulfilled in his death and is put into full force through his resurrection. Through his history it becomes the church's gospel for the world. Through his death and resurrection the church participates in his mission, becoming the messianic church of the coming kingdom and man's liberation. In so far as the church participates in his mission, it is drawn into his fate and will experience the 'the power of his resurrection' in the 'fellowship of his sufferings.'[1]

—Jürgen Moltmann

LUKE TESTIFIES TO THE CHURCH'S MISSIONAL MESSIAH, THE CHRIST, THE SON OF GOD

It is my firm belief that Christology is foundational for ecclesiology in general, and for missional ecclesiology in particular. Before I make this case more fully, it is important that I direct our attention to the portrait of the person and work of Christ given to us in Scripture. Who was Jesus? What did his life, death, and resurrection accomplish? Moreover, what are the implications of his mission, and of our Christology, for ecclesiology? I will do this by guiding our focus briefly to the person and work of Jesus described in Luke-Acts. I focus solely on Luke-Acts, not because other books and passages of Scripture are unimportant, but because of scope and length constraints in this book, and because of the importance of the Christology of Luke-Acts in contemporary theological and exegetical debates.[2]

---

1. Moltmann, *Church in the Power*, 83.

2. These debates have recently centered on theories of the atonement. For an in-depth treatment of the debate, I recommend: Tidball et al., *Atonement Debate*; Beilby and Eddy, *Nature of the Atonement*. Another debate centers on whether Luke presents an obvious Christology. For opposing arguments, see Buckwalter, *Character and Purpose*; Schweizer, *Good News*. For a fuller treatment of the biblical basis of mission than I am able to provide here, see Bosch, *Transforming Mission*; Wright, *Mission of God's People*.

Furthermore, and most importantly for the purposes of this book, Luke brings a unique evangelistic, missional, and apologetic perspective. He was concerned to provide an apologetic for the Christian movement on the one hand, and a retelling of the gospel story in the light of Christ's concern for the outcast, underdog, and marginalized on the other. Luke had a missional heart, and described the mission of Christ and the early church. He recorded certain missionally oriented stories, stories that reveal the missional heart of God, such as the Prodigal Son and the Good Samaritan, which are only found in his gospel. He vividly described the mission of Jesus—including the despised and marginalized, commending the Samaritans, reaching out to the poor, broken, and spiritually desperate, and offering the gospel to the Gentiles—and then demonstrated how the early church pursued and understood that mission.

In these next few paragraphs, I will treat the gospel of Luke and the book of Acts as a two-volume work, with a predominantly Christian audience. Both writings probably had a common author, Luke the physician, who was principally a theologian of salvation history, with a particular interest in the missional purpose and works of Jesus Christ. The two works are continuous, so when I speak of Lucan theology I am referring to his theology as expressed in his two-volume work *Luke-Acts*.[3] It is reasonable to suggest that the formulation of a systematic Christology is not Luke's primary purpose for writing. However, the Christology that is developed in his writings plays an important role in achieving his main purposes, and affords us with an understanding of the person, work, and mission of Christ. An adequate comprehension of the person and mission of Christ should and must have dramatic consequences for the way we live and minister, and for our understanding of the nature, structures, and mission of the church.

Luke declares that Jesus is *the Christ*, using the title frequently. Luke considers the title *Christ* or *Messiah* as the major, if not central, christological title, and he regards it as the one that has the most significant role in depicting the nature of Jesus.[4] Jesus is the chosen Lord of the covenant, God's "anointed" agent. This truth is confirmed as early as his birth, and Peter announces it during his Pentecostal speech. Paul also confirms the importance of the title *Christ*. He is the *Christ* at his enthronement. After suffering as the *Christ,* he enters into the glory reserved for him. As *Messiah,* he is the *Son of David,* and the *King of Israel* or *King of the Jews.* In Lucan theology *Christ* especially means God's holy, authorized covenant leader. God's anointing of Jesus as *Messiah* established his uniqueness to be chosen, commissioned, and empowered. He is the *Christ* because he was specifically anointed as such by the Holy Spirit. Jesus identifies himself as the fulfillment of one of God's glorious promises—that is, God promised to anoint, by the Spirit, a *Messiah.* In a functional sense, as *Christ/Messiah* Jesus heralds the fulfillment of God's divine, redeeming purpose. Ideally, this eschatological mission of Christ in human history, this enthusiastic proclamation of him as God's Messiah, shapes the church's mission. God's mission in Christ directs the church's energies and vision so that they align with what he has done, is doing, and will do through Jesus the Messiah.

3. Richard, *Jesus*, 174.

4. Ibid., 179.

In the gospel of Luke Jesus himself only expresses the designation the *Son of Man*, which occurs on twenty-four occasions. On these occasions, Jesus is referring to the passion and the parousia. In Acts, however, Stephen uses the phrase immediately before he is martyred. In Luke's writings, Jesus is depicted as having present and future roles as the *Son of Man*.[5] When used in the present tense in the gospel of Luke, Jesus as the *Son of Man* can forgive sins, is Lord of the Sabbath, violates restrictive social and dietary norms, experiences the pain of rejection and betrayal, and has a mission to save the lost. When used in the future tense in Luke's gospel, Jesus's role as the *Son of Man* is to be the supreme and powerful judge beside God in the heavens. Similar to other designations, Jesus as the *Son of Man* fulfills God's eschatological, missional purposes in human history and walks in submission to the will of the Father. These dimensions of Jesus's life have a formative influence on the church's Christology, its understanding of suffering, its recognition that human history belongs to God and his eschatological purposes in Christ, and its appreciation of its mission to spread the gospel of Jesus Christ.

Luke-Acts presents an astounding picture of the humanity of Jesus. This is especially true in the gospel of Luke. Like all humans, Jesus knew the struggles of temptation, needed divine strengthening, knew the pain of rejection and grief, knew the pain of unfulfilled desires, experienced strong emotions, such as tenderness and compassion, and had a need for intimacy with God through prayer. At the moment of death on the cross, he commended his spirit into his Father's hands. In the developmental years of his earthly life, he "increased in wisdom and in favor with God and people."[6] The humanity of Jesus is plainly evident in Luke's theology. Luke connects this humanity with Jesus's broader eschatological mission, and also with his earthly mission among the poor, marginalized, and despised. In his humanity Jesus exemplified transformed human nature—compassionate, humble, forgiving, agapic, liberated, and submitted to the Father—and Luke came to understand these and other dimensions of Jesus's nature, ministry, and teachings as formative for Christian discipleship and community. In both Jesus's humanity and divinity the church is confronted with the extraordinary mission of God in the world and, consequently, forms an understanding of its nature and mission around this full appreciation of the divine/human nature of Jesus Christ. The mission of the early church in Acts, for instance, was shaped by their appreciation of the divinity of Christ—proclaiming the eschatological gospel of his death and resurrection—and also the humanity of Christ—engaging in missional acts of compassion, justice, healing, and the like.

The designation *Son of God* for Jesus is also significant in Luke's theology. On occasions, he adds the title *Son of God* to the equivalent narrative in Mark. In his gospel, Luke used the phrase on such occasions as his summation of Jesus's healings and exorcisms, the proclamation by the angel Gabriel of Jesus's birth, and during the trial of Jesus. These incidences depict Jesus as the *Son of God* in a unique relationship with God, which is evidenced by the miraculous and the extraordinary. God the Father announces, "This is my beloved Son, in whom I am well pleased" at the baptism of Jesus. Satan taunts him with

5. Kee, *Good News*, 13.

6. Luke 2:52.

the phrase "if you are the *Son of God*" during the temptation, and demons recognize his nature. As the *Son of God,* he extends the offer of repentance to his people. In the future, he will be the "judge of the living and the dead." He is the present model for humanity by which God will evaluate all on the appointed day. Lucan theology misses few opportunities to reflect upon the truth that Jesus is the fulfillment of God's design for humanity and his redemptive mission in the world. Through his person and work, God has intervened in human history. The Christ-event is founded in the salvation of God for all humankind. Luke gives saving significance to the whole Christ-event, including his incarnation, life, death, resurrection, ascension, exaltation, and enthronement. This revelation of God's saving purposes reaching their climax in Christ forged the missional imagination of the church—an imagination with distinct christological substance—and must shape the missional passion and commitment of the church today.

The birth narrative in Luke's gospel introduces vital themes for Luke, and it is in these crucial two chapters that Jesus's Davidic heritage is highlighted. Luke speaks further of Jesus as the Son of the Most High who will reign forever on the throne of his father David, the horn of salvation from David's house, one who has traceable Davidic ancestry, and one who was even born in the "city of David." Three important addresses in Acts are heavily royal-Davidic in perspective: Peter's Pentecost speech, Paul's sermon at Pisidian-Antioch, and James's decision at the Council of Jerusalem. While the concept occurs in Acts, however, the title *Son of David* does not. Lucan theology considers Jesus as the legitimate Davidic heir to the throne of Israel. His incarnation, life, death, resurrection, ascension, and exaltation fulfill Scripture and place one of David's descendants on his throne eternally. This exalted Jesus appears as immanent deity in Acts. "Great David's greater Son reigns, more gloriously than great David himself ever did, as Prophet and Priest and King; but he bears this triple dignity as the Servant of Yahweh who crowned his service by pouring out his soul to death."[7] Like the early church, the contemporary church's conviction about Jesus's Davidic heritage is to be foundational for our interpretation of Old Testament texts, for our interpretation of the meaning of his life, death, and resurrection, and for our appreciation of his divine mission. The church understands Jesus as the legitimate Davidic heir to the throne of Israel, and as the Lord of God's eschatological present-future kingdom, and this gives substance to the church's missional identity and practices—in relationship to Israel, to the other nations and peoples, and within the eschatological history of Jesus Christ.

Luke has a particular preference for using the designation *the Lord* when referring to Jesus. In his gospel, he uses the title seventeen times. In Acts, there are many unambiguous references to Jesus as *Lord*. In Luke's theology, *the Lord* communicates a sentiment of reverence and religious adoration and loyalty toward Jesus. For him the resurrection and outpouring of the Spirit have vindicated the lordship of Jesus. Although Hans Conzelmann reasons that we should not read any cosmological reference into the title *Lord*, some aspects of Lucan theology contradict this assertion.[8] Similar to the Father,

---

7. Bruce, *This Is That*, 82.

8. Conzelmann, *Theology of Luke*, 171.

Jesus gives the Spirit, mediates salvation, and directs his chosen people through his self-manifestation. Strauss writes, "While admitting that Luke 'does not explicitly expound the deity of Christ,' Douglas Buckwalter repeatedly insists that [Lucan theological] features indicate Luke's personal belief or conviction concerning Jesus"—that is, Luke deemed Jesus to be divine.[9] It must be remembered, however, that Luke has no concern in *Luke-Acts* to specify or detail the relation of the divine to the human Jesus, because this is not significant for his aims in writing the two-volume work. Nevertheless, he did consider Jesus to be both human and divine, and this conviction that the divine Lord Jesus mediates salvation was embraced by the earliest Christians, and has influenced the church's awareness of its missional character and objectives ever since. This conviction about the lordship, salvific ministry, substitutionary sacrifice, and unique and historical death and resurrection of Christ is critical not only for the church's missional vocation—it is also indispensible for ecclesiology, since a biblical, missional ecclesiology cannot be developed without these central christological convictions.

Following the Radical Tradition of Jesus

The Waiter's Union, in Brisbane, describes itself as "a network of residents in West End who are committed to developing a sense of community in the locality with our neighbours, including those who are marginalized, in the radical tradition of Jesus of Nazareth . . ." The community "emerged sometime after 1985, when Dave and Ange Andrews returned from India to Australia, and expressed interest in doing the same kind of faith-based community work in West End as they had done in New Delhi . . . They started with two or three households twenty years ago; there have rarely been more than twenty households at any one time during the network's journey." The Waiter's Union cultivates intentional community. "Monday mornings from 6.30 to 7.30am we meet for worship, reflection, and planning for the week. Throughout the week people meet in a range of groups to nurture their souls and sustain their faith and values . . . Sunday night from 6.30 to 8.00pm we meet for public worship with local people in the basement of St Andrew's Anglican Church. Every two weeks we have a community meal, to which everyone is invited. Every six weeks we have a small gathering for fellowship with people in the network and every six weeks we have a large gathering with people in their region who are not in their network but who need continuing support for their faith-based community work. Every six months we have a two-week live-in community orientation program that provides an intensive introduction or re-introduction to the spiritual disciplines that are the foundation for their faith-based community work. Every twelve months we have a camp, to give us the chance to get away and just relax together."

9. Strauss, *Davidic Messiah*, 339–40, referring to Buckwalter's work *Character and Purpose.*

This community life supports the Waiter's Union's mission and faith-based community work. "The most intensive learning experience found within the network is in a household dedicated to formation. Between four and six people live in this house at any one time... It serves as a resource for ongoing training in community development. In 2010, groups helping Waiters explore spirituality, philosophy, politics, lifestyle, and so on, include short-term study groups, a reading group, a documentary group, a men's group, and various groups focused on social justice issues... One group of people the network is involved in has sought to promote the aspirations of the original inhabitants of their neighbourhood by lobbying for permission for them to build the as-yet-unbuilt cultural centre in Musgrave Park, which is in the middle of the neighbourhood. Another group of people the network is involved in has sought to support refugees by sponsoring their settlement and the settlement of their families, working through the anguish we go through as 'strangers in a strange land.' Through a whole range of groups in the network we have sought to relate to the people in their community who have physical, intellectual, and emotional disabilities—not as clients, nor as consumers, still less as users—but as their friends! None of the things that any of us are doing seems that great. However, we constantly encourage one another to remember that true greatness is not in doing big things, but in doing little things with a lot of love over the long haul. And that is exactly what we are trying to do!"[10]

MESSIANIC IMAGES FOR A MISSIONAL PEOPLE

Four other images of Christ are worth noting in Luke-Acts, since they have missional implications for the church—*Servant, Prophet, Savior,* and *Holy and Righteous One.*

1. *Servant:* The concept of the *Servant* is introduced in Isaiah with these words, "Here is my servant, whom I uphold, my chosen one, in whom I delight; I will put my Spirit on him, and he will bring justice to the nations."[11] The Servant's mission, as described by these Scriptures, is to be the Elect One of God, chosen from birth to bear the Spirit, making known the truth of God to the world—bringing justice to God's people. The Servant is portrayed as living in submission to God, and suffering outrageous abuse, shame, and rejection. Luke's theology readily embraces this suffering *Messianic Servant* imagery and applies it to Jesus. God will vindicate him, for the suffering is the path to fulfilling his mission.[12] Looking to its suffering *servant-Messiah,* the church finds inspiration and hope as it seeks to proclaim his message even in the face of persecutions, opposition,

---

10. Andrews and Beazley, *Learnings,* 15–19. See the whole book for a detailed description of the Waiter's Union, its network, training, and lessons. Online: http://www.lastfirst.net and http://www.waitersunion.org. Used with permission.

11. Isa 42:1.

12. Bruce, *This is That,* 86–88.

and suffering. The church adopts the Servant's cosmic message and mission to the nations, as it is invited to participate in his vocation and actions.

2. *Prophet:* Jesus is also depicted as a prophetic figure in *Luke-Acts*. He is the prophet whose coming was foretold by Moses. As a prophet, he engaged in the miraculous, declared God's holy word to the covenant people, and was rejected by the Jews for his admonition of them. As a prophet, he is correlated with the mainstream of Israel's tradition and thus legitimated, even if rejected. In Luke, the authoritative nature of the prophets meant that Jesus's *way* for the people of Israel, and for the church, is legitimized. The church, as a missional people, is to embrace the *way* of Jesus's radical ethic, cosmic mission, prophetic message, counter-cultural lifestyle, and redemptive gospel.

3. *Savior:* Jesus is the *Savior* in Luke's theology. As *Savior,* he offered consolation to Israel, redemption to Jerusalem, light to the nations, healing of illness and disease, forgiveness of sins, and the good news of the gospel of truth. Jesus is the chosen, messianic, and unique *Savior* of the entire world. The church has only ever been effective missionally when this conviction has been clear and "front-and-center," and when its structures and ministries are formed around the mission of its Savior.

4. *Holy and Righteous One:* Another designation used for Jesus is the *Holy and Righteous One.* The sin of those who rejected, abused, and despised him is contrasted with his nature as holy and righteous, and they are made holy and righteous through him alone. God's vindication of his *Holy One* displayed how Jesus's death was in fulfillment of the Father's plan. As the Messiah is holy and righteous, so his gospel, his church, his disciples, and his mission are holy and righteous. The church and its mission will often fall short and miss the mark. However, united with the Holy and Righteous One it participates with a Person and in a mission that is far greater than it is, and which gives its whole nature and work meaning and definition.

As we have seen in our brief survey of Luke-Acts, a revelation of the person and work of Christ must have far-reaching implications for how we minister, engage in mission, live the Christian life, and comprehend the church. This is easily demonstrated throughout Scripture, since all of the christological passages of Scripture have significant ecclesiological implications. An understanding of the saving significance of the sacrificial nature of Jesus's death, and a concept of his roles as ruler, reconciler, and revealer, must produce in us some profound personal responses—reverent awe, overwhelming gratitude, complete dependence, spiritual fervor and devotion, the pursuit of holiness, and the desire to know true Christian community and fellowship, to name a few.

Stuart Murray argues that Christendom placed ecclesial forms at the center of mainstream Christian institutional life. Post-Christendom churches, if they are to engage contemporary western culture, must move Jesus from the margins of their life to the center. For Murray this involves highlighting the implications of Jesus's humanity for discipleship, understanding the death and resurrection of Christ in the context of his life, and "indwelling the gospel narratives in ways that shape our priorities, stir our imagination and train our reflexes."[13] It also involves "reading Scripture from a Jesus-centered perspective," denying systems of interpretation that "muffle" the voice of Christ, and allowing pre-Christendom and dissident movements, such as the Anabaptists, to help us understand what it means to follow Christ in contemporary culture. The Sermon on the Mount and the Lord's Prayer need rediscovery, writes Murray, as passages that offer a form of spirituality, political engagement, marginal discipleship, and resistance to ungodly powers, which are crucial to post-Christendom Christianity. The example of Jesus as a cultural subversive on the margins, an unpredictable evangelist, a storyteller and question-poser, an uncompromising political activist, and as an awkward dinner guest who challenged prevailing powers and perspectives, needs to be rediscovered by congregations. For Stuart Murray and Darrell Guder, Jesus's incarnational life was often misunderstood in Christendom, and is pertinent in post-Christendom discipleship and ecclesial life, since "the essential character of the incarnation as the definition of Christian existence was largely diluted for the majority of Christendom."[14]

A misunderstanding or failure to grasp the person, work, and mission of Christ, may be the single most important reason why many Christians and churches live in spiritual poverty and missional disinterest. Christology is central to any missional ecclesiology, and churches will only achieve their missional potential when they are grounded in the gospel of Jesus Christ, and shaped by a compelling vision of the person and work of Christ—as the Messiah, the Lord, the Holy and Righteous One, the Servant, the Savior, and the Son of David/Son of God/Son of Man.[15] This comprehension is inadequate if it is only conceptual. A true realization of these truths grips the desires and practices of disciples and congregations, revolutionizing their missional commitment and action. Christ-centered churches experience renewed proclamation of Scripture and service in the world. Christ-centered ecclesiology is the only authentic vision of the church offered in Scripture, and a Christ-centered ecclesiology cannot help but be thoroughly missional and gospel-centered. In my opinion, only ministries that endeavor to lead people to the vicarious, sacrificial, atoning, revealing, and reconciling Christ will have any permanent or substantial influence. This is why I affirm that Christology is fundamental to ecclesiology.

HOW DOES THE CENTRALITY OF JESUS
AFFECT A MISSIONAL VIEW OF THE CHURCH?

What are the *implications* of the claims that our understanding of Jesus Christ is crucial to a robust, biblical, missional ecclesiology, and that this understanding and our view of the church are inseparable? How do these claims *concretely influence* our theology and practice of the church?

Before we get on to that, I need to say a word about the relationship between Christology, ecclesiology, and mission. As a systematic and applied theologian, my default position is to locate the development of Christology before an ecclesiology. However, I am acutely aware that this seems, at times, to run in the face of history. My friend and

---

13. Murray, *Post-Christendom*, 311.

14. Ibid., 313. See Guder, *Continuing Conversion*, 110.

15. See the following work for a detailed treatment of these designations: O'Toole, *Luke's Presentation*.

colleague Darrell Jackson, who teaches with me at Morling College, reminds me that, "at the very least, early Christology is an ecclesially forged theology—that is the point of David Bosch, who understood (possibly overstating his position) the various Gospels to contain communally shaped theologies. The Christology—missiology—ecclesiology spectrum (however the three elements are arranged) is *very* linear." This lineal representation can be misleading. I am convinced that the gospel precedes the church—here I am agreeing with John Webster who claims that God's unilateral, asymmetrical, original, and paramount grace, especially in the person and work of Christ, precedes the response of the church, and forms its nature, purpose, and future. However, the development of Christology, missiology, and ecclesiology was, historically, much more integrated than such a linear progression might suggest. The church reflected on the nature of Christ, did its early mission in the name and power of Christ, and the person and work of Christ shaped the mission and nature of the church, and all of these dynamics were integrated and interwoven, in an inextricable way. To overcome the deficits of linear thinking, and the unnecessary duality of ecclesiology/Christology that it undergirds, a reappraisal of the relationship between Christology, missiology, and ecclesiology is in order. "A more integrated reflection on the ecclesial nature of Christology, and on the christological nature of ecclesiology, is in order."[16]

Darrell Jackson's doctoral work, "demonstrated the fact that the church is described as the *body of Christ* with much greater regularity than any alternative (including *family*). On this basis it is possible to argue that ecclesiology is far more than christologically centered; it is possible to describe ecclesiology as christologically composed."[17] A more integrated discussion of the relationship between these theologies is warranted, but beyond the scope of this text. Having said that, recognizing the complex, non-linear, and integrated relationship between Christology, missiology, and ecclesiology, I now briefly describe some of the implications or consequences of the centrality of Jesus Christ for the missional church. I have grouped these under the categories of *ecclesiological foundations* and *ecclesiological results*.

ECCLESIOLOGICAL FOUNDATIONS

Our theology, structures, mission, and practices of the church are to be firmly grounded in our convictions about the person and work of Jesus Christ. Jürgen Moltmann demonstrates this Christ-centered approach to ecclesiology in chapter three of *The Church in the Power of the Spirit*. For Moltmann, "the doctrine of the church, therefore, where it concerns the foundation of the church and the conditions in which it exists, is indissolubly connected with the doctrine of Jesus, the Son of God."[18] In that chapter of his book, Moltmann writes that the church's self-understanding is predicated on its understanding of Christ, and the person and work of Christ form its being. The church is caught up in his mission, passion, future, and hope. It is grounded in his historical incarnation, passion,

16. Quotations are from the correspondence between Darrell Jackson and me on the theology of this book.

17. Jackson, "Discourse of 'Belonging.'"

18. Moltmann, *Church in the Power*, 66.

and resurrection, and oriented toward his eschatological reign. The church's nature, structures, and mission are firmly located within his historical and eschatological messianic mission. All of these dimensions of the church are to be grounded in and oriented toward Christ, as a testimony to his liberation of the oppressed, good news to the poor, lordship over human history, and eschatological reign.[19] This ecclesial focus on Jesus Christ should not be superficial, triumphalist, or aggressive. It must be an ecclesiology constructed upon the Christ of history, the Christ of faith. Moltmann says, "There is no true *theology of hope* which is not first of all a *theology of the cross*."[20] Our ecclesiology is grounded, given form and meaning, in the crucified, suffering, resurrected, and returning God. Human beings can be liberated from poverty, injustice, oppression, and meaninglessness. However, the church should remember that such liberation is not achieved through power and esteem. In the crucified and resurrected Christ we understand that "what public opinion holds to be lowliest, what the state has determined to be disgraceful, is changed into what is supreme . . . The glory of God does not shine on the crowns of the mighty, but on the face of the crucified Christ."[21] Miroslav Volf says that the scandal of the cross is not only its particular affront to the dominant themes of our age (modernity is convinced that all things can be healed or perfected, especially through reason, social control, and human endeavor), but also that the self-donator, the sufferer, the "crucified," may not change the violent aggressor. Volf says that in that scandal, in the "company of the Crucified," the disciples discovered the "promise of the cross," the true hope contained in the authentic gospel of Jesus Christ.[22] And so, John Howard Yoder is right when he declares, "Only at one point, only on one subject—but then consistently, universally—is Jesus our example: in his cross."[23] In his cross he presents the church with a new social order, a way of forgives, sacrifice, suffering, reconciliation, and grace. In Moltmann's words,

> The God of success and the apathetic man of action completely contradict what we find at the core of Christianity: the suffering God and the loving, vulnerable man. On the other hand, the crucified God contradicts the God of success and his idol-worshippers all the more totally. He contradicts the officially optimistic society. He also contradicts the revolutionary activism of the sons of the old establishment. "The old rugged cross" contradicts the old and the new triumphal theology (*theologia gloria*) which we produce in the churches in order to keep pace with the transformations of an activistic and rapidly changing society.[24]

19. Ibid., 68–85.

20. Moltmann, "Crucified God," 8.

21. Moltmann, *Crucified God*, 327.

22. Volf, *Exclusion and Embrace*, 22–28.

23. Yoder, *Politics of Jesus*, 95.

24. Moltmann, "Crucified God," 6. See Moltmann's description of what it means for the church to follow the way of the cross, in: Moltmann, *Crucified God*, 53–75; Moltmann, *Open Church*, 82–94; Moltmann, *Spirit of Life*, 60–71.

Our Theological Themes Are Interdependent and Inseparable

Our theology of the person and work of Jesus Christ, the church, and mission are interdependent. Theologies of mission, the church, and of Christ are interdependent and interwoven, such that it is impossible to adequately describe any one of the three without some reference to the others. While a biblical Christology is indispensible for a missional ecclesiology and a theology of mission, any suggestion that one of these three "precedes" the other two is more than a little misleading, given their theological and historical interdependence. Recognition of this complex and synergistic relationship between our theologies of Christ, church, and mission does not diminish the centrality of Christ and his good news, but it does appreciate their rich and historical connections. Moltmann suggests that we should be continually seeking to discern the "historical conditioning" of our images of Christ, church, and the messianic mission.[25]

Our Perspectives Are Scriptural and Gospel-Centered

Our understandings of Jesus Christ and his church lead to effective mission when they are scriptural, gospel-centered, and enamored with the Messiah's cross, resurrection, return, and reign. In *Confessing God*, John Webster rightly asserts that the norm of all Christology is Scripture, and, in my opinion, it is equally true to say that only a Christology and ecclesiology deeply embedded in Scripture will lead to effective, Christ-honoring mission in and through the church.[26] Webster laments "the negative effects upon Christology" when the union between Christ and his church is exaggerated, when the church is deified, and when the church is seen to do the work that belongs to Christ alone. This results from poor biblical foundations for Christology and ecclesiology, and from "a decidedly thin theology of the cross."[27] In terms of Christian leadership and ecclesial structure, Jesus Christ is the primary overseer and "minister of the church," who guides the church in its corporate mission, its faithfulness to the gospel, its structures, ministries, and practices, and in the application of individual spiritual gifts.[28]

John Webster suggests that an ecclesiology based on Scripture will emphasize the perfection of God and the election of God's people, and will preserve the distinction between Christ and the church, while recognizing the crucial role the church has to play in the mission of Christ.[29] A Christ-centered ecclesiology recognizes that Jesus Christ, his message, person, kingdom, and reign cannot be contained in the church—the church serves its Lord and is scrutinized by his person, work, and Spirit. The church must die to itself continually that it might truly serve, glorify, and witness to Christ. As Webster says,

> The church is not the institutional container of the incarnation; it is, rather, that sphere of human life and fellowship which is besieged by, permanently under attack from, the Word made flesh. One of the most striking features of Bonhoeffer's

25. Moltmann, *Church in the Power*, 66.
26. Webster, *Confessing God*, 146.
27. Ibid., 165–66.
28. Webster, *Word and Church*, 198, 204.
29. Webster, *Confessing God*, 153–74.

Christology fragments is his insistence that Jesus Christ is a question posed *to* the church, that the church is relentlessly interrogated by the fact that at the heart of its life is the presence of the incarnate one who cannot be assimilated into or clothed by a form of religious life.[30]

Missional churches have an absolute dependency on and confidence in the gospel of Jesus Christ, and this trust permeates and forges their leadership and ministry structures, their mission in the world, and their witness to Christ.[31] Hans Küng says that the church is "maintained in truth" when it remains in the particular "*truth of the gospel of Jesus Christ.*" He asserts that all perspectives, reasoning, practices, church leaders and authorities, doctrines, personalities, faiths, and so forth, are ultimately subject to the *Christian message*, the gospel of Jesus Christ as originally recorded in the New Testament . . . and thus *Jesus Christ* himself."[32] Küng makes a strong case for the presence of Christ "in the entire life of the church," and especially in its worship. Christ and the church are not synonymous, and the church cannot contain him. It is through obedience and submission to Christ that the church grows. Küng writes that the church grows: (1) *From its head*, the Lord Jesus Christ; (2) *Towards its head*, who is the goal of all growth; (3) *Inwards*, in love, faith, hope, and so forth, and; (4) *Outwards*, through the proclamation of the gospel and faithful participation in the mission of Jesus Christ. All of these dimensions of growth are enabled by and centered on Christ, so that the church is "the fullness of Christ, who fills all things with his body."[33]

When missional ecclesiology is Christ-centered,[34] it is captivated with the passion of Christ's life, sufferings, and crucifixion, with the astonishing resurrection event, and with an authentic anticipation of Christ's return and reign. John Zizioulas, concerned that Christian theology too often focuses entirely on the cross and Christ's suffering, says that a healthy ecclesiology will emphasize all aspects of Christology—creation, incarnation, suffering, crucifixion, resurrection, parousia, and eschatological reign. "Such an ecclesiology will have profoundly positive consequences for the Christian life, the organization of the Church, the sacraments, and for every aspect of the Church's witness to the world."[35] As the body of Christ, the church embraces the eschatological reign of Christ in history as its hope, and as the context of its missional nature and outward gaze. As Hans Küng affirms, "The reign of God, fulfilled, realized, and personified in Christ, remains the horizon of the Church, and the focal point of its own life which it strives to bring to the world."[36]

Miroslav Volf writes that the church should continue the mission of Jesus, through the proclamation of the scriptural truths of the new creation, forgiveness, reconciliation,

---

30. Webster, *Word and Church*, 120; Bonhoeffer, *Christology*, 30.

31. See Piper, *God Is the Gospel*; Goldsworthy, "Gospel."

32. Küng, *Church—Maintained*, 20, 40.

33. Küng, *Church*, 234–41.

34. Or any form of ecclesiology, for that matter.

35. Zizioulas, *Lectures in Dogmatics*, 132–35. See Moltmann's reflections on "the community of the cross" and "the resurrection and the future of Jesus" and the church: Moltmann, *Church in the Power*, 85–97; Moltmann, *Theology of Hope*, 139–229; Moltmann, *Open Church*, 82–94.

36. Küng, *Church*, 96.

transformation, trinitarian embrace, and rebirth.[37] From the perspective of a missional theology of the church, such proclamation is also, and more importantly, about the church honoring its essential missional nature. It honors this core missional being and its Messiah's mission when it proclaims faithfully the gospel of Jesus Christ, so that individual human beings, people groups, and even entire cultures and societies, might come to a redemptive, personal, salvific faith in him.

In missional ecclesiology, any proclamation of "glad tidings," authentic expression of election, or culturally sensitive offering of the church for "reception," must include an acceptance of the historicity of the crucifixion and resurrection. It must also include the centrality of the person and work of Jesus Christ, his divine/human nature, and his saving and atoning work on the cross, as the only means of salvation and the forgiveness of sins. There is a clear location of missional proclamation, presence, witness, and service in the core commitments and convictions of the gospel of Jesus Christ (this yields the characteristics described by David Bebbington: emphasizing conversion, expressing the gospel through mission and activities of social reform, commitment and obedience to Scripture, and focusing on the person and work of Christ).[38] Missional ecclesiology pursues mission with faithful and confident witness to and proclamation of the historic, orthodox Christian understanding of the gospel of Jesus Christ.

ECCLESIOLOGICAL RESULTS

Our approach to the person and work of Jesus Christ will influence our understanding of the nature and organization of the church. Christology can be constructed using a number of different approaches, and Karl Rahner has described the characteristics of Christology from *above* and *below*.[39] Both of these approaches to Christology are types of *high* Christology. Talking about Christology from *above* and *below* is different from the distinction between *high* and *low* Christology, which respectively place emphasis on Christ's divinity and humanity. Christology from *below* reflects on the human Jesus through the narratives of the Gospels and tends to emphasize his presence in our personal life, missional and ministry efforts, and contemporary experience. This proceeds to "ascend" into reflection on his saving work and divinity, and is the preferred approach of Karl Rahner and Wolfhart Pannenberg (although their approach to such Christology from *below* differs). Christology from *above* is typically dogmatic theological reflection, and "descends" in order to bring such theology to bear on the individual, the church, and the world, and, in doing so, make sense of the human Jesus. According to Roger Haight, the contemporary search for the "authentic" person of Christ and the postmodern quest to apply authentic experience and history to existential questions of meaning and spirituality have called into question and largely abandoned the methodology from *above*.[40]

---

37. Volf, *Exclusion and Embrace*, 13–34.

38. Bebbington, *Evangelicalism*.

39. Rahner, *Concerning Vatican II*, 298.

40. Haight, "Two Types Christology"; Haight, "Towards an Ecclesiology"; Haight, *Future of Christology*.

In *The Shaping of Things to Come*, Michael Frost and Alan Hirsch propose a "Christology from *behind* or *within*, rather than from *above*," which both prioritizes Jesus in ecclesiology, and which views Jesus particularly through his Jewish, cultural, and ideological contexts.[41] In their missional ecclesiology Christology is central, since for them "the person of Jesus stands at the epicenter of what we do" and shapes our ecclesiology when we do church and mission in a biblically faithful way.[42] In their understanding of missional ecclesiology, there is a progression from Christology to missiology to ecclesiology. For these Australian authors, Hellenistic speculative overtones in Christology need to be replaced by what they consider a Hebraic focus on messianic spirituality which is preoccupied with the concrete, historical, practical, and earthy dimensions of Christian discipleship, formed by attention to a Christology from *below*, *behind*, and *within*.

In *The Way of Jesus Christ*, Jürgen Moltmann describes the relationship between christological categories and typologies, the messianic mission of Christ, and the messianic way of the church, especially with regard to the poor, imprisoned, infirm, rejected, dispossessed, and despised. For Moltmann, ancient and modern christological "trends and transmutations" have obscured the vital relationship between our understanding of the nature of Christ and our sense of the messianic mission of the church. He claims that ancient Christologies tended to be too metaphysical, cosmic, and abstract. They were too often dislodged from their historical and eschatological foundations, that is, they evidenced a *Christology from above*. Modern Christologies tend to be too anthropocentric, personal, historical, and demystified, evidencing a *Christology from below*. These unhelpful tendencies and transmutations are corrected by attention to the messianic person and mission of Jesus Christ, especially as described in the Gospels. The church needs to move away from a privatized and anthropocentric Christology and embrace the messianic Christ of the Gospels, and his messianic mission and *way*. As the community of faith practices the *way* of discipleship to Jesus Christ, a *christopraxis* emerges, shaped around the Gospels, and especially the Sermon on the Mount. *Christopraxis* is a "way of life, a way in which people learn who Jesus is" with all of their being, and it shapes the church, its mission, and its christological theory. For Jürgen Moltmann, "The *Sitz im Leben* for Christology—its situation in life—is *the community of Christ*," and its theologizing, witness, and so forth. Authentic Christology, rooted in the Christ of the Gospels, emerges from discipleship, worship, community, and mission, and, inevitably, if it is true and transformational, leads back into discipleship, worship, community, and mission. This mission is especially to the broken, dispossessed, vulnerable, and "the least of these."[43] The church is to demonstrate before the world "the messianic way of life"—the *way* of peace, justice, suffering, martyrdom, righteousness, witness, gospel-embodiment, surrender, compassion, and transformed social and interpersonal relationships. To a world plagued by ecological crisis, war, and social disintegration, this *messianic way* is redemptive and testifies to the church's suffering, historical, resurrected, eschatological, cosmic, and returning Lord (notice that Jürgen Moltmann takes up the best of ancient and modern

41. Frost and Hirsch, *Shaping of Things*, 116 (emphases added).
42. Ibid., 208.
43. Moltmann, *Way of Jesus*, 38–150 (esp. 41–43).

Christologies in this messianic synthesis).[44] Moltmann challenges the church to respond in concrete, missional ways to the historical mission, sufferings, resurrection, and future glorification of Christ. He does this by describing "the historical mission of Christ in the framework of the messianic hope in history; the sufferings of Christ against the horizon of apocalyptic expectation; and the resurrection of Christ in the light of the eschatological vision of the new creation of all things."[45]

In my opinion, Christology from *above* and Christology from *below* both have a role to play in the development of missional ecclesiology. Christology from *above*, as exemplified in the writings of Karl Barth and Emil Brunner, can enrich our theology and missional practice through an immersion in inspirational theology, openness to the supernatural, a reliance on faith, and an assurance in the kerygma. Christology from *below*, as exemplified by Wolfhart Pannenberg and Karl Rahner, can help us form the mission and practices of the church around the witness of the human Jesus, especially through the narratives of the Synoptic Gospels. Such Christology endeavors to substantiate belief through historical inquiry and rational investigation. It facilitates or enables an ecclesiology *for* and *of* the people.[46] Millard Erickson writes that evangelical Protestants tend to value both forms of Christology—worshipping the *kerygmatic* Christ who is both the Christ of faith and of history.[47] I am convinced that only a kerygmatic Christ of faith and history can adequately sustain missional ecclesiology. Jürgen Moltmann has demonstrated how Christology can inform and be informed by the church—can lead to a dynamic christopraxis—when it is rooted in the life, message, ethics, and person of the Messiah of the Gospels. While we may not agree with all of Moltmann's christological conclusions (his concessions on the Virgin Birth, for instance), he has given us an example of a creative synthesis between Christologies from *above* and *below*, and of how to construct Christology with attention to "an eschatological framework of messianic hope and apocalyptic expectations."[48] We may not agree with every dimension of his christological synthesis and novel theological propositions, but he does give us an example of how to engage ancient and modern, and *above* and *below*, Christologies afresh. On some occasions, the various types of Christology sustain different dimensions of the church's faith and witness, and offer the church on mission the necessary theological resources and direction.

Our Christology Is Life-Giving

Our Christology is life-giving when it is deeply rooted in the messianic mission of Jesus Christ and the fellowship of the church. All theology can become lifeless or life-draining doctrine when removed from relationship to Jesus, his mission, and his church—but the doctrine of Christ is especially empty in this case. John Zizioulas writes that Christology must be "translated and lived in an ecclesial way . . . The experience of the Church is the

44. Ibid., 151–341.

45. Ibid., xv.

46. Moltmann, *Open Church*, 120–26.

47. Erickson, *Christian Theology*, 673.

48. Moltmann, *Way of Jesus*, xv.

only way in which the existential meaning of Christology becomes a reality."[49] I would go further and suggest that our doctrine of Christ is at its most life-giving when it is being explored and experienced in the context of a community that is pursuing the mission and fellowship of Christ.

Our Ecclesial Ethics Have Christological Dimensions

Our churches are to pursue the messianic values, instructions, and ethics of Jesus Christ. Missional churches come into being through submission to the values, instructions, ethics, and mission of Jesus Christ, and are therefore radically counter-cultural. John Howard Yoder writes, "The church precedes the world . . . axiologically, in that the lordship of Christ is the center which must guide critical value choices, so that we may be called to subordinate or even to reject those values which contradict Jesus."[50] The church is called to follow and participate in the radical missional ethic of Jesus Christ, and such an ethic is essential to missional ecclesiology—Yoder calls this *"a missionary ethic of incarnation,"* a "messianic ethic" in which "Jesus is the norm."[51] Jürgen Moltmann asserts that the church is present where Christ is present, "in the mission of the believers *and* the suffering of *the least of these."*[52]

Vigen Guroian sees the church as a peculiar, ethical community, whose ethics, values, and social life are shaped around the message, person, and actions of Jesus Christ, especially as presented in the Gospels. Guroian's political, social, and applied ethics are ecclesially based, Christ-centered, liturgical, and missiological.[53] He is rightly convinced that there is an inseparable relationship between the church's ethics, its understanding of the person and work of Christ, its missiological practices, and its ecclesiological dynamism and health.[54] There is an interconnection between the "crisis of mission," the "dereliction of Christian ethics," and the loss of the centrality of Jesus Christ in the life of the church.[55] The church's mission is to embody the ethics of Jesus Christ in its political, social, missional, and liturgical life, and to see the world transformed by the gospel of Christ and the kingdom of God. As the church goes about this mission, it remains centered on the person of Jesus Christ, and his eschatological reign and kingdom. As we saw in the chapter on Guroian's ecclesiology, he believes that the role of the church, through brotherly and sisterly love, missiological passion, and liturgical worship, is to show the world what it really is, and to participate with Jesus as he transfigures the world. The church invites the world into obedience and submission to the Lord Jesus Christ.[56]

---

49. Zizioulas, *Being as Communion*, 261–62. Zizioulas goes on to describe his theory of the union between redeemed hypostasis and Christ in the church. Whether or not one is convinced by this theology, the point he makes about Christology's vitality in the ecclesial setting is valid.

50. Yoder, *Priestly Kingdom*, 11.

51. Ibid., 44; Yoder, *Politics of Jesus*, 1–20.

52. Moltmann, *Open Church*, 105.

53. Guroian, *Ethics after Christendom*, 1–80.

54. Guroian, *Faith, Church, Mission*, 40–42.

55. Ibid., 42.

56. Guroian, *Incarnate Love*, 132–39, 155–59.

Our Mission Is Inculturational and Contextual

Our mission is to be inculturational, as we participate in the mission of the Messiah. There has been ongoing debate about the appropriateness of the "incarnation" as a model for the church's mission, with some recommending that the terms contextual, representational, or inculturational be used instead of incarnational. I am convinced that the concept of "incarnational mission" has some merit, and I appreciate the arguments made for its use. However, given its theological difficulties, I prefer not to use the terminology. Even when "incarnational mission" is used in a qualified way that, firstly, upholds the biblical portrait of the mission of the church, and, secondly, does not dilute the unique nature of Christ's incarnation, it still has the following problems—it runs the risk of diminishing the value and biblical appreciation of Christ's incarnation; it fails to see that the doctrine of the incarnation is as much about the union of the divine Jesus with human nature as it is about the mission of the Son; it does little more than the words contextual or inculturational but is more theologically fraught; it is sometimes used as a rhetorical device to suggest that people are doing mission "in the way of Jesus" when they may well not be; and it underestimates the vast limitations to the analogy being drawn.[57] Whichever term we choose, missional ecclesiology appreciates the value of contextual mission and ministry, and understands that the church participates in the mission of Christ. The "messianic mission of Jesus" is basic to the nature, structures, ministries, and mission of the church, and in each generation it must find ways to contextualize the gospel and pursue the mission of Christ in transformative ways.

Cheers: Christ-centered and Community-sent

On the northern outskirts of Perth, an inculturational community is thriving. For Geoff and Sally Westlake, the journey to Banksia Grove happened after eight years in pastoral ministry and a formative trip in 1998 where Geoff saw many examples of alternative styles of ministry. He experimented with some alternative models when he got back to Perth, finally concluding that most still had a consumerist mentality, a poor theology of mission, and little focus on community.

Cheers is an extraordinary "community development movement, from a Christian base." Cheers has two orientations: it is "Christ-centered and Community-sent." The community focus gives credibility and integrity to relationships. "We focus on relationships over programs. A health indicator is relationship, measured by the content of the conversation." Those involved in the Cheers community do not describe it as a church but as an ecclesia. *Discovering some of the layers of meaning behind this Greek word has been important for their thinking, as well as thinking through the relationship between a theology of mission and the gathered people of God. An* ecclesia *includes the idea of being an assembly that is called together to*

57. Guder provides a balanced analysis of the discussion in: Guder, *Incarnation*.

attend to public affairs. While the word has often been made synonymous with "church" separate from the community, Cheers maintains the "small-p" political orientation that is part of the rich theological meaning of an ecclesia.

Cheers began over a BBQ—a gathering where what was good about the community was noticed and celebrated. This has grown into a fortnightly meeting. What is going on in the local community is recorded in an exercise book. What is good and seen as in the image of God is identified. What is not good is also listed. These items are prayed for and the question "what can we do" is asked. Those meetings decide who will do "the cheering," which may simply be to let someone know that their action has been noticed. They also follow up answers to prayer from previous gatherings. "This meeting keeps our focus on the community." Cheers participants include many people who would not profess to be Christian, and come from local residents groups, playgroups, and school connections. "If a person feels part of Cheers, then they are a participant . . . The more that worship, mission, and discipleship overlap, the more they are each enhanced."[58]

Our Desire Is for Jesus's Eschatological Kingdom

Our vision and efforts are to be directed toward Jesus's eschatological mission, kingdom, and reign. In other words, missional ecclesiology is kingdom-oriented, and focused on God's eschatological mission, purposes, and reign in history. I dedicate more space to this point, largely because one of the pivotal themes in the teaching of Jesus was the kingdom of God, and the presence of God's eschatological reign.[59] The kingdom of God is the scope of God's rule, and more particularly the place in which, at any particular time, his rule is recognized and accepted. The kingdom of God has a place in human history and in eschatology. It has substantial implications for our understanding of the missional nature of the church, and of how we should live and hope as the people of God. Jesus's teaching on the kingdom of God, its mystery, scope, righteousness, and requirements, must affect not only our daily lives but also our understanding of the nature, institutions, and eschatological purpose of the church.[60]

This kingdom is counter-cultural, or antithetical, to many of the values, structures, and ethical systems of the kingdoms of this world. This has radical implications for our lifestyles, churches, and practice of mission. While recognizing and celebrating the presence of the kingdom of God in this world (courageously pointing out where the kingdom

---

58. Powell, "Cheers," 18. (This story was used with permission. It is one of the stories found in the article by Ruth Powell on twenty-two innovative missional communities. For excellent descriptions of these pioneering communities, see http://www.ncls.org.au/download/doc4264/NOVUSMagazine.pdf). See the Cheers website at http://geoffwestlake.com/cheers/.

59. "The phrase occurs fourteen times in Mark, thirty-two times in Luke, but only four times in Matthew." Bromiley, *ISBE*, 24. It also occurs twice in John's Gospel, six times in Acts, eight times in the Pauline epistles, and once in Revelation. A variant of this phrase, "the kingdom of the heavens", occurs thirty-three times in Matthew, and once in a variant reading in John. Elwell, *Evangelical Dictionary*, 607.

60. Harvey, *Another City*, 57–63.

is present), we must also renounce all that is not of the kingdom of God. We are to pursue the righteousness, peace, and joy that are some of the crowning characteristics of the kingdom. We must be prepared to be misunderstood, persecuted, and even disowned at times, as a counter-cultural messianic movement. The Messiah requires all that a person has and is. Obedience to the Messiah, and participation in his counter-cultural, messianic, kingdom-proclaiming mission, may not immediately demand that we give up all that we have, but it certainly requires that we be willing to do this. Sacrifice is one of the hallmarks of the kingdom—"Whoever wants to be my disciple must deny themselves and take up their cross daily and follow me."[61] Such denial of self is complete dedication to Christ, an act of self-surrender to his lordship, eschatological purposes in human history, and messianic mission. Grace is a gift from God—and yet it costs us all that we have, and all that we are.

In the midst of the incredible demands that are presented by the kingdom of God, we are given hope by its eschatological nature. This current age is at times characterized by grief, sinfulness, struggle, and evil, but the age to come will be one of joy, holiness, peace, rest, and comfort. The whole created order will be transformed so that it reflects its original glory. We will live a transformed existence characterized by resurrection life, fellowship will be restored with God, and this restoration is likened in Matthew to a wedding feast.[62] Such descriptions of the future kingdom of God nourish our hope and encourage us to continue proclaiming the good news of the kingdom.

"Today the church faces two big challenges: (1) how to make the kingdom of God understood in the different cultures of the world; and (2) how to live Jesus's own life principles of love, justice, and compassion in a world where the poor are getting poorer and the rich few are getting richer."[63] For John Fuellenbach, the kingdom of God is a broader and more central theme in the teaching of Jesus than that of the church, and represents the way God is working in the world and redeeming all of humankind. While the church is important, an instrument of the kingdom, and a proclaimer of the gospel of Jesus Christ, the kingdom of God transcends the concerns, limitations, and experience of the church.

It is my conviction that, on the one hand, and in view of the kingdom, the church should cultivate an awareness of God's sovereign, eschatological work in the world and the church, and, on the other hand, a sense of urgency about the need for the church to reform its self-understanding, ecclesial structures, and ministry practices. Without such reform, the church will miss opportunities for renewal and mission.[64] Eddie Gibbs is right to say that sluggishness in the forms of inertia, over-analyzing the cultural challenges, or indecision, must be replaced by an eschatological urgency that inspires true mission in the western world.[65] Michael Moynagh claims that the choice the churches in western cultures have to make is between "three futures"—a "slide into oblivion," a series of isolated

---

61. Luke 9:23.

62 Matt 22:1–14 and 25:1–12.

63. Fuellenbach, *Church*, xiii.

64. Frost and Hirsch, *Shaping of Things*, 17–18.

65. Gibbs, *Church Next*, 37–38.

and uncoordinated missional experiments, or the coordinated and strategic establishment of fresh missional communities and approaches to church development.[66] To the later, I would add the intentional re-missionalization of established churches, movements, and denominations.

In *Another City*, Barry Harvey emphasizes decisive mission, on the one hand, and God's providence, mystery, and eschatological actions, on the other. He writes that the modern impulse is to seek to colonize the future, to manage risk, and to render external realities predictable. These "technical mechanisms" have so risen to ascendency in the modern mind that "human moral imperatives, natural causes, and chance reign, in place of religious cosmologies." The "reflexive organization of the self around knowledge environments" moves spirituality, awareness of the presence of God, and theology to the peripheries, both in the private and the public domains.[67] Harvey argues that the church cannot embrace a Constantinian theological triumphalism that equates the eschatological redemptive story with the dominant story of the prevailing culture. Nor can it develop a despairing, disillusioned picture of the present. Instead, a middle-distance approach needs to be upheld. This approach maintains neither a triumphalist optimism nor a "near-sighted" despair. Instead, it is rooted in Christian narrative memory and its associated eschatological and kingdom-oriented hope.[68]

We see a variety of theological responses to the decline and marginality of the churches in western cultures. Michael Jinkins notes that these kind of responses range "from Stanley Hauerwas's acerbic comment, 'God is killing mainline Protestantism in America, and we goddam well deserve it,' to Lorean Mead's more sanguine spin, 'God is always calling us to be more than we have been.'"[69] Jinkins goes on to reflect on the anxiety, rationalism, entrepreneurial orientation, and humanism of much of the literature addressing the decline of the church in the West. He rightly proposes that a robust ecclesiology for "the church facing death" must recover the notion of resurrection. Such an ecclesiology appreciates death as a gift that leads to resurrection, and to the rediscovery of the divine vocation of the church. It is an ecclesiology immersed in a revelation of God's sovereignty, and a certainty about God's eschatological control over human history. Instead of having our ecclesiological imaginations shaped by either thanatophobia or triumphalism, they should be shaped by attention to the Christian narrative, which is one of death and resurrection.[70] As Erwin McManus puts it, "I am convinced and inspired that God would not allow us to live in a time of such great opportunity if he did not have on his heart the desire to pour out the greatest movement of his Spirit in human history."[71]

It is my contention that the church can only make sense of the issues related to its decline, marginality, liminality, and post-Christendom reorientation in western contexts, through the theological grids of the *kingdom of God* and *eschatology*. The church is faith-

---

66. Moynagh, *Emergingchurch.Intro*, 237–41.

67. Harvey, *Another City*, 125–26.

68. Ibid., 142–44.

69. Jinkins, *Church Faces Death*, 12.

70. Ibid., 12–13, 27–32.

71. McManus, *Unstoppable Force*, 48.

ful to the messianic mission of Christ and to its missional nature when it is about the establishment of the kingdom of God on this earth. This involves, of course, not only the redemption and reconciliation of individuals, but also of entire peoples, systems, societies, and cultures.

> The objective of the mission is the establishment of the kingdom of God which is the reign of God over all the forces of death, the triumph of love over all the forces of hatred, the triumph of peace over all the forces of violence and warfare . . . the kingdom of God is the object of the mission, and the life of Jesus Christ continues to be manifest through the church as it witnesses to, embodies and proclaims the kingdom.[72]

In this regard, missional ecclesiology resonates with Miroslav Volf's ecclesiology. Volf's writings have rich social dimensions, which are demonstrated in his treatment of such themes as reconciliation, embrace, cultural identity and conflict, social ethics and responsibility, interfaith and ecumenical dialogue, and a theology of work.[73] Volf asserts that the church is to be both a "prophetic community and a sign of hope,"[74] which serves as a sign and instrument of salvation while conducting a prophetic role in the world in which it resides. It is not enough for churches to be places where Christians worship, gather, pursue discipleship and spirituality, and celebrate the sacraments, since "only prophetic communities can truly worship, and only worshipping communities can truly be prophetic."[75] The church needs to discover its liberation and distinction in the new creation, which set it apart as a sign, foretaste, herald, and witness to the kingdom (even in its frailties and weaknesses). In doing so it can provide a prophetic voice that is far more than a mere social critique (or a reflection of other secular critiques).[76]

The ecclesiological realities of the church as both a prophetic voice and a sign of hope, according to Volf, are directly related to its eschatological vision, trinitarian theology, and pneumatological empowerment. An eschatological vision of the mutual personal indwelling of the Trinity, in the glorification that awaits the church in the new heavens and the new earth, shapes the historical life of the church, so that it behaves prophetically—in such activities as reconciliation, forgiveness, and embrace of the "other."[77] This behavior is empowered by the indwelling Holy Spirit who enlivens and releases the church to be an expression of the new creation.[78] The church as *sign* anticipates the new creation, while not being totally equated with it, and mediates the new creation in the present age. This is true even when the church is being renewed in its frailty. Ideally, the

---

72. Hull, *Mission-Shaped Church*, 5.

73. See Volf, *Exclusion and Embrace*; Volf, "Exclusion and Embrace"; Volf, "Truth, Freedom"; Volf, *The Role of the 'Other'*; Volf, *Christianity and Violence*; Volf, "Distance and Belonging"; Volf, *Forgiveness, Reconciliation and Justice*.

74. Volf, "Church as Prophetic Community."

75. Ibid., 9.

76. Ibid., 16–18.

77. Volf writes that this embrace has four distinct dimensions: "(1) the will to embrace the other, (2) inverting perspectives, (3) engagement with the other, and (4) embracing the other." Volf, "Living with the Other," 16.

78. Volf, "Church as Prophetic Community," 9.

church embodies what it means to be the sign of the new creation more than it speaks of this role. Nevertheless, there is an ontological unity between the church's nature and voice.[79] This prophetic role is pluriform and includes the many dimensions of the church's witness—calling people to discipleship, participating in social action, ministries of justice and reconciliation, embracing difference and diversity, and so forth. "There is a need for dynamic relation to God and sympathy with people; for a revival of a *tearful tradition—orthopathy*."[80] Therefore, the church's prophecy is both to the world and to itself. Through prayer it is to hear the message of Christ anew.[81]

The church's vision of the kingdom of God and anticipation of the new creation have social dimensions. It is compelled to work toward the final, eschatological reconciliation. The "eschatological transition" of final reconciliation has social dimensions, and implications for present social ethics, a theology of work, justice, and the church's conscious participation in social reconciliation and compassion.[82] The church is called to collaborate in the "ushering in" of the new creation.[83] Miroslav Volf proposes, "It is both possible and theologically wise to construct Christian social ethics within the framework of belief in the eschatological continuity between present and future creation."[84] He writes of the implications of this theological framework for the church's social and ecological involvement. Such activities are a necessary way of loving one's neighbor and embracing the "other"—especially the "other" of a different cultural identity than our own.[85] Practices of compassion, forgiveness, grace, and agapic love are to be grounded in eschatological hope.[86] Self-centeredness should be relinquished for generosity and forgiveness, as churches and individuals seek to demonstrate the values and vision of the kingdom of God.[87]

According to Darrell Guder, modern ecclesiological grammar and metaphors that associate the reign or kingdom of God with spreading, building, or extending are culture-bound and unbiblical. "The New Testament employs the words *receive* and *enter* . . . Taken together they indicate the appropriate way for a community to live when it is captured by the presence of God's reign."[88] As a gift received, and a realm entered, the kingdom and reign of God are not to be equated with the church. However, no one should suggest that the kingdom is completely distinct from the church. The church is part of God's kingdom, but not the sum-total of it. The kingdom is present wherever God rules—in the church, in the life of the individual, in nations and cultures, and wherever God's word is planted and growing. It is a now-and-not-yet kingdom, to use the terms of an *inaugurated eschatology*.

79. Ibid., 19–20.

80. Ibid., 10.

81. Ibid., 11, 26.

82. For Volf's theology of work see Volf, "Eschaton, Creation," 130–43; Volf, *Work in the Spirit*; Volf, "Arbeit Und Charisma"; Volf, *Zukunft Der Arbeit*.

83. Volf, "Final Reconciliation," 106–7.

84. Volf, "Loving with Hope," 28.

85. Volf, "Vision of Embrace," 195–205.

86. Volf, "Against a Pretentious Church," 284.

87. Volf, *Free of Charge*.

88. Guder, *Missional Church*, 93–94.

As mentioned earlier in this book, Hans Küng argues that presentist-*futurist* eschatology is essential for understanding Jesus's purposes for the church. He describes the church as the *eschatological community of salvation*, ushered into existence through the eschatological event of the life, message, death, resurrection, and reign of Jesus Christ.[89] As the *eschatological community of salvation* the church is an *anticipatory sign* of the final and already present reign of God; and all dimensions of its nature, structures, and mission in the world are shaped by the eschatological reign. As we have noted, Küng says that this has concrete implications for the church as it lives in the service of the kingdom and reign of God—its whole life must be formed around an eschatological self-consciousness, it does not exist for itself, it trusts in God's purposes and power, and it takes on the counter-cultural form of a servant. As a servant of the eschatological reign of God it directs its whole being toward the kingdom and messianic mission of the Lord Jesus Christ.[90] As Jürgen Moltmann puts it, the church has a missiological nature that is directed toward God's transfiguration of the world—"the church takes up the society in which it lives into its own horizon of expectation," and this guides its efforts toward changing individuals, advocating for justice, performing compassionate actions, humanizing and socializing people, and seeking peace for creation.[91]

John Zizioulas believes that confessional pluralism presents obstacles to the church's witness to the kingdom of God. For the sake of mission, and in spite of the difficulties involved, Zizioulas urges the many Christian confessions to seek reconciliation and relationship, instead of confessional division.[92] He is not proposing an amalgamation of confessions here, but a more effective ecumenical cooperation and dialogue. Zizioulas is right to argue that a return to authentic ecumenical relationship and conversation—one that respects difference but seeks practical cooperation—can enhance the mission of the church and its witness to the kingdom of God. The "church represents the divine reign as its *sign* and *foretaste*," its "*agent* and *instrument*," "its community, its servant, and its messenger."[93] A "vision of the reign of God" nurtures the church's missional character and practices:

> Testing and revising our [ecclesiological] assumptions and practices against a vision of the reign of God promises the deep renewal of the missionary soul of the church that we need. By daily receiving and entering the reign of God, through corporate praying for its coming, and longing for its appearance, and in public living under its mantle, this missionary character will be nourished and revived.[94]

Missional ecclesiology is shaped by a theology of the kingdom of God, a clear understanding of the relationship between the kingdom and the church, and an anticipation of God's eschatological reign. The missional church is passionately convinced that "the

89. Küng, *Church*, 81.

90. Ibid., 96–103.

91. Moltmann, *Theology of Hope*, 329.

92. Zizioulas, *Being as Communion*, 259–60.

93. Guder, *Missional Church*, 77–109.

94. Ibid., 109.

church is an instrument or agent of the mission of God, the outcome of which is to be the kingdom of God."[95] It follows the Messiah and his messianic mission, proclaiming the kingdom that was so central to his gospel message and his eschatological actions.

Our Mission Is Unified and Collaborative

In 1999, a group of pastors met at Reservoir Garden Baptist Church, Penang, Malaysia, to consider how the churches of Penang might join together for mission and ministry in the new millennium, to glorify and witness to Jesus Christ. There was a consensus that the churches should join together to do three citywide events to celebrate the year 2000. The three events were a prayer conference, an evangelistic rally, and a charity event. The events were very successful and spurred the pastors to plan for a Penang Pastor's Prayer Summit, the first of its kind in Penang. At the Prayer Summit in 2001, Lawrence Khong of Faith Community Baptist Church, Singapore joined the Summit for one afternoon to share the vision of the Love Singapore Network. Inspired by the unity of the Singapore churches to work together to transform their city, a few Malaysian pastors gathered in Sungai Petani to brainstorm what a similar network in Penang might look like. The Love Penang Network was formed in 2001 out of the desire to impact the city of Penang with the love of Jesus Christ, through the unity of the churches. The network is convinced that mission in Penang can be enhanced as churches come together to glorify Jesus Christ and express his love in a unified, collaborative way. Seven churches finally formed the Love Penang Network and together they were involved in the following activities for a decade until 2010.

Citywide Prayer Meetings:

The churches come together once a month for a combined prayer meeting. This is open to all churches in the network and all other churches in Penang as well. The prayer meetings are held in different churches each month, and members of all the eleven churches are encouraged to participate.

Serving Migrant Workers and Refugees, and Planting Congregations:

The network's Migrant Workers Ministry has planted congregations among the Indonesian, Vietnamese, Myanmarese, and Nepalese workers in Penang. Many have come to Christ and been discipled. In 2010, the network assisted in the establishment of a school for the urban poor, catering mainly to the children of the Rohingya refugees in Butterworth and Seberang Jaya. The eleven churches partnered together to share facilities and resources to serve and reach out to migrant workers and refugees in Penang.

---

95. Hull, *Mission-Shaped Church*, 5.

Fund Raising for Charities and Other Projects:

The network raises funds for orphanages, schools, charities, and other projects. It has also been instrumental in the launch of the Charis Hospice, a palliative care center for terminally ill people.

The Love Penang Network has now discontinued the citywide events but has launched a grassroots movement networking its members to engage with seven spheres of influence—education, religion, family, government, media, celebration, and economics.[96]

QUESTIONS FOR REFLECTION

1. Which image or story about Jesus captures your imagination, and why?

2. Are you comfortable with this list of seven implications and applications (the seven sections under Foundations and Results)? Would you modify the list in some way?

3. In your own words, what does it mean for a local church to be truly: (1) Christ-centered, (2) missional, and (3) a servant of the kingdom of God?

---

96. Online: http://thelpn.blogspot.com.au. Used with permission.

16

The Spirit-Empowered Church:
Responding to the Spirit's Power and Presence

*The Spirit is not something that "animates" a Church which already some-
how exists. The Spirit makes the Church be. Pneumatology does not refer
to the well-being but to the very being of the Church. It is not about a
dynamism which is added to the essence of the Church. It is the very essence of the Church. The Church is constituted in and through eschatology
and communion. Pneumatology is an ontological category in ecclesiology.*[1]

—JOHN ZIZIOULAS

*You show that you are a letter from Christ, the result of our ministry, writ-
ten not with ink but with the Spirit of the living God, not on tablets of stone
but on tablets of human hearts.*

—2 CORINTHIANS 3:3

THE SPIRIT CREATES AND FILLS THE CHURCH

A MISSIONAL THEOLOGY OF the church requires a substantial theology of the Spirit.
Missional ecclesiology is only as good as its theology of the Spirit (its *missional pneumatology* and its *pneumatological mission*). Craig Van Gelder, a thinker who writes much
on the missional nature of the church, writes that a missional theology of the church
needs to take pneumatological considerations seriously, since the church "are a people of
God who are created by the Spirit to live as a missionary community."[2] According to Van
Gelder, our missiological and ecclesiological rethinking of the church in western culture
begins with the recognition that the church is created and empowered by the Spirit as a
unique, spiritual community. It is the Spirit who "creates, leads, and teaches the church to

---

1. Zizioulas, *Being as Communion*, 132.
2. Van Gelder, *Essence of the Church*, 25.

live as the distinctive people of God,"[3] who develops and renews the church as his ongoing and dynamic creation, and who forms the community of faith into a counter-cultural community embodying the reign of God. The Spirit is the advocate-helper of the church who helps it be faithful to the redemptive reign of God and indwells it with his power and presence. The Spirit works in the church so that it is holy. The Spirit also establishes the marks of the true church, which Van Gelder suggests are established and taught by the Spirit himself.[4]

This emphasis on the work of the Spirit in shaping missional communities and in forming individual disciples who are dedicated to personal mission is crucial to the formation of missional ecclesiology. As John Zizioulas says, pneumatology is about "the very essence of the Church" and "is an ontological category in ecclesiology."[5] Hans Küng puts it this way: "For Paul there can be no new eschatological existence at all without the Spirit. If there is no Spirit, it does not mean that the community lacks its missionary commission, but that there is no community at all."[6]

> The Spirit of God communicated through the glorified Lord is thus seen to be, in various ways, the basis of the church's existence, its source of life and controlling power. The church is filled and vivified, sustained and guided by his Spirit, the power and strength of God. The church owes to the Spirit its origin, existence, and continued life, and in this sense the church is a *creation of the Spirit*.[7]

Of the twelve ecclesiologists presented in the first half of this book, Jürgen Moltmann paints the clearest portrait of the church created, filled, and empowered by the Spirit. The church enjoys "fellowship with Christ" as the Spirit reveals Christ, unites the church with Christ, glorifies Christ, and forms the church for the sake of Christ's messianic mission. "Faith in Christ and hope for the kingdom are due to the presence of God in the Spirit." The presence of the Spirit not only forms the church as the "messianic fellowship of service for the kingdom of God," but also helps the church understand itself "as the messianic fellowship in the world and for the world."[8] The Spirit creates the church, fills it with his grace and gifts, and empowers it for the service of the messianic mission and the coming kingdom of God. The Spirit is not merely present in the church's sacraments, ministries, missions, and structures—instead, all of these dimensions of the church are "conceived in the movement and presence of the Spirit." The Spirit shapes all aspects of the church for the glory and mission of the triune God—its "ministries and functions, its gifts and the tasks assigned to it" are taken up in the person of the Spirit, as the Spirit empowers and fills the church for the sake of the messianic mission and the eschatological kingdom.[9]

---

3. Ibid., 31.

4. Ibid., 42–44, 78–81, 86, 112–18, 142–62, 180.

5. Zizioulas, *Being as Communion*, 132.

6. Küng, *Church*, 165.

7. Ibid., 172.

8. Moltmann, *Church in the Power*, 197–98.

9. Ibid., 289.

The church is one, holy, catholic, and apostolic in the power of the Spirit, and the Spirit uses these four attributes for the glory of Christ and the extension of his coming kingdom.[10] As I noted in the chapter on Jürgen Moltmann's ecclesiology, Moltmann writes that these four attributes and the *notae ecclesiae* are not merely self-referential or internal. Instead, the Spirit uses them for the sake of the *missio Dei*, to usher in the kingdom of God, to witness to God's eschatological and trinitarian history, and to bring liberation, healing, justice, mercy, and hope to a wounded and sinful world.[11] In other words, the Spirit fills and uses the following *for the glory and eschatological mission of the Messiah*— the unity, holiness, catholicity, and apostolicity of the church, the faithful preaching of the Scriptures, the proper administration of the sacraments, and, as Menno Simons proposed, holy living, brotherly love, unreserved testimony, and suffering.[12] The church in the power and presence of the Spirit exists for the mission of Christ, and is empowered by the Spirit for the sake of Christ's mission and glory. The Spirit creates the church, fills and animates the church. The Spirit empowers the church for Christ-honoring mission, service, love, and compassion. The Spirit is concurrently forming the nature of the church, filling it with his presence and power, and propelling it forward into the messianic mission and eschatological kingdom of Jesus Christ.[13]

INTEGRATING OUR UNDERSTANDINGS OF CHRIST, MISSION, CHURCH, AND SPIRIT

John Zizioulas believes that western theology has neglected of a theology of the Spirit in its treatment of the nature, structures, and mission of the church. He is also concerned that western ecclesiology too often separates a theology of the Spirit from a theology of Christ in its efforts to describe the church.[14] Such a neglect and separation have had negative consequences for western ecclesiology, writes Zizioulas, and a similar problem has occurred in Orthodox theology—he believes that the problem is not as pronounced in Orthodox ecclesiology as it is in its western counterparts. As I noted in the chapter on Zizioulas, he is convinced that only a genuine dialogue between the various theological traditions can help solve this issue, and arrest what he considers its harmful ecclesiological results.[15]

A worthwhile ecclesiology must integrate a theology of Christ and a theology of the Spirit.[16] This is an important corrective for missional ecclesiology, which often fails to

10. Ibid., 337–38.

11. Ibid., 361.

12. Krauth et al., *Book of Concord*, art. 7; McNeill, *Calvin: Institutes*, IV, 1, 9; Yoder, *Royal Priesthood*, 77–89; Simons, *Works of Menno Simons*, 83–88.

13. Moltmann, *Source of Life*, 55–69. Oden suggests that the emerging church movement in western culture is attractive to many people because it presents a vitality of community and mission, soaked in pneumatological themes. This "emerging pneumatology," writes Oden, is very similar to Moltmann's pneumatological principles. Oden, "Emerging Pneumatology," 267–84.

14. Zizioulas, "Mystery of the Church," 295.

15. Zizioulas, *Being as Communion*, 123–26.

16. Zizioulas, "Die Pneumatologische," 133–47; Zizioulas, *Being as Communion*, 126–42.

systematically integrate christological and pneumatological notions in its theology of the church and its mission. Ecclesiological conceptions of the church's community and mission must be shaped in the light of a theology of the Spirit. This is because all trinitarian, human, and ecclesial communion and mission *require* the activity and presence of the Spirit.[17] "Pneumatology is an ontological category in ecclesiology," and is constitutive of all of our understandings of Christology, missiology, and ecclesiology.[18] Therefore, while pneumatology tends to be sporadic in much of the literature addressing the missional nature of the church, a robust missional ecclesiology recognizes the activity of the Spirit in creating and remissionalizing the church. The work and presence of the Spirit is at the very essence of the church and of its mission. The Spirit leads her into distinctive witness, so that she might faithfully proclaim the reign of God, and the person and work of Jesus Christ.[19]

John Zizioulas writes much on ontology in his work—ontology is about the nature of *being*, and Zizioulas is greatly concerned with the *being* of God, humans, and the church. He says that Christians are ontologically united with the church—our *being* is united with the church's *being* through the work of the Spirit. The church, therefore, is not to be considered as a mere institution that is separate from us, or that we should seek to control or resist. We are one with the church. As the familiar phrase goes, "we are the church." So rather than standing at a distance from the church and criticizing its institutions and practices, we are to understand ourselves as deeply connected with the church and its mission, presence, and being in the world.

As we have seen, Zizioulas believes that integrating Christology and pneumatology in our theology of the church will help ward off some of the negative expressions of church life, including clericalism and anti-institutionalism. He is convinced that making pneumatology "*constitutive* of Christology and ecclesiology" in this way—especially if the eschatological and communion aspects of our theology of the Spirit are used to form our theology of Christ and the church—will lead to positive consequences for ecclesiology:[20]

- *The removal of "all pyramidal notions" in ecclesiology* so that the ministries of the church practice mutual submission and dependency.

- *The reshaping of ecclesial identity* so that it is eschatological, and not merely historical.

- *The reorientation of "the notion of institution"* so that the church wrestles with what it means to be *in-stituted* by Jesus Christ and *con-stituted* by the Spirit. "If pneumatology is assigned a constitutive role in ecclesiology, the entire issue of *Amt und Geist*, or of "institutionalism," is affected. The notion of communion must be made

---

17. Zizioulas, "Mystery of the Church," 299.

18. Zizioulas, *Being as Communion*, 132.

19. Van Gelder, *Essence of the Church*, 31, 42–44.

20. "The important thing about this synthesis is that Pneumatology must be made *constitutive* of Christology and ecclesiology, i.e. condition the very being of Christ and the Church, and that this can happen only if two particular ingredients of pneumatology are introduced into the ontology of Christ and the Church. These ingredients are: eschatology and communion." Zizioulas, *Being as Communion*, 139.

to apply to the very ontology of the ecclesial institutions, not to their dynamism and efficacy alone."[21]

As the church faces global challenges, including pluralism, relativism, and anti-institutionalism, it should seek to renew its mission and community life, pursuing ecclesial renewal and ecumenical cooperation. John Zizioulas challenges us to find hopeful solutions and ecclesiological renewal in the dialogue between Christology, missiology, ecclesiology, and pneumatology—that is putting a theology of Christ, mission, church, and Spirit into a creative and mutually enriching conversation.

SPIRITUAL GIFTS, MINISTRY, AND THE CHURCH'S MISSION

Since theological perspectives and presuppositions shape treatments on spiritual gifts, this area of church life has often been a locus of controversy and contention. It would be either arrogant or naive of me to suggest that I am free from such undergirding perspectives, as I approach this theme of spiritual gifts and their relationship to the mission of the church. However, it is my aim here to arrive at honest explanations of the Pauline texts relating to spiritual gifts, in order to understand their original meaning and intention, and to reflect, briefly, on their implications for the church's mission. Texts in Romans, 1 Corinthians, and 1 and 2 Timothy set the scene for a Pauline theology of spiritual gifts. I will also briefly consider what actions local churches can take to pursue these gifts, as they seek to enhance their mission and ministry.

Spiritual gifts assume an important role in Pauline theology. Therefore such a study of the biblical texts and consideration of their application in the life and mission of the local church are of great significance. Miroslav Volf writes, "The *pneumatological structure* of the church follows from the sovereignty of the Spirit in the bestowal of charismata."[22] The *charismata* are important for both the *charismatic/pneumatological structure* of the church and its continuation of the mission of Jesus Christ.

At this stage, it is appropriate to make some preliminary observations on the way Paul uses the words *pneuma, pneumatikos, charisma,* and *charismata* (meaning, respectively, *spirit, spiritual, free gifts of grace,* and *gifts of the Spirit*).[23] The verbal noun *pneuma* (*spirit*) "means the elemental natural and vital force which, matter and process in one, acts as a stream of air in the blowing of the wind and the inhaling and exhaling of breath, and hence [transferred] as the breath of the spirit which, in a way which may be detected both outwardly and inwardly, fills with inspiration and grips with enthusiasm."[24] While *pneuma* may take on the meanings of *wind* and *breath*, it may also take on the sense of *life*, and it may often take on the meaning and function of *psuche* (*soul*). Hermann Kleinknecht

---

21. Ibid., 139–42.

22. Volf, *After Our Likeness,* 232.

23. The main Greek words used in the section are (1) *pneuma* (meaning *spirit*), (2) *pneumatikos* (meaning *spiritual*), (3) *pneumatikoi* (same word, just the plural, and meaning *spiritual ones*), (4) *charis* (meaning *grace*), (5) *charisma* (meaning *free gift of grace* or *expressions of grace*), (6) *charismata* (again, the plural, meaning *free gifts of grace,* or *gifts of the Spirit*), (7) *charizomai* (*to give freely, bestow graciously*), and (8) *psuche* or *psyche* (meaning *soul*).

24. Kittel et al., *Theological Dictionary,* 334–35.

writes that *pneuma* is largely "coterminous" with *psuche* and may be used interchangeably with it.[25] The transferred meaning of *pneuma* is *spirit*, meaning that breath or spirit which blows from the invisible world of the divine. The verbal noun *pneuma* occurs 145 times in Pauline literature, usually referring to the Holy Spirit, although the full title occurs only sixteen or seventeen times. The flexibility of Paul's use of the definite article with *pneuma* has caused some debate as to the meaning of *pneuma* in Pauline texts. Gordon Fee deals thoroughly with this issue in his work *God's Empowering Presence*.[26] The fundamental meaning of the associated adjective *pneumatikos* (*spiritual*) is that which belongs to, or pertains to, spirit. Thus when Paul uses the adjective in 1 Corinthians it usually refers to God's people as *pneumatikoi* (*spiritual ones*), or to a number of activities or realities belonging especially to the realm of the Spirit.

The term *charisma* denotes a *free gift of grace*, involving God as the divine giver.[27] It is a verbal noun of *charizomai* (*to give freely, bestow graciously*), and it occurs almost exclusively in the Pauline writings. The term is always found within a soteriological framework and is often concretely portrayed in specific gifts, such as in Romans 12:6 and 1 Corinthians 12:11. *Charis* (*grace*) is the source of *charisma* (the *free gift of grace*), while *charisma* is the concrete expression of *charis*. Often *charisma* is used without any reference whatsoever to the Spirit, but "simply designates a variety of ways God's grace is evidenced in the midst of, or in the lives of, his people."[28] However, manifestations of the Spirit are frequently the defining characteristic of the usage of the word. Thus, God graciously bestows a variety of *charismata* on his people, as seen in 1 Corinthians 1:4–7. This leads to *charismata* being understood as *gifts of the Spirit*, and the Pauline emphasis on grace-relatedness is pronounced. A number of lists of *charismata* can be found in 1 Corinthians 12–14.

It is important to note that Paul seemed dissatisfied with the Corinthian under-standing of *pneumatika* to mean *ecstatic religious experiences*, and thus he seemed to have preferred the term *charismata*, in which he focused on grace-relatedness and Christ. Siegfried Schatzmann writes on this issue, "the spiritual elitists in Corinth, who were acquainted with [*pneumatika*] as a technical term from their pre-Christian expe-riences, imposed their category on the community's understanding of charismata."[29] Thus, Paul's presentation of *charismata* as having an orientation in the grace of God is significant in the light of the Corinthian dilemma. Don Carson notes, "The quest for an individualizing and self-centered form of 'spirituality' was in danger of denying the source of all true spiritual gifts, the unbounded grace of God."[30] Therefore, Paul switches from *pneumatikon* (expressions of *spirit*) to *charisma* (expressions of *grace*) to place the emphasis on divine grace. Carson notes that the term *charisma* is not merely a technical Pauline term referring exclusively to a number of supranormal gifts, for it

25. Ibid., 336.

26. Fee, *God's Empowering Presence*, 14–32.

27. Vine et al., *Vine's Expository Dictionary*, 487.

28. Fee, *God's Empowering Presence*, 33.

29. Schatzmann, *Pauline Theology*, 32.

30. Krauth et al., *Book of Concord*, 23.

can embrace gifts such as generosity and salvation itself.[31] Similarly, *charisma* should not be understood as a technical term simply referring to the gift of salvation, for this would be reductionistic. A Pauline understanding encompasses manifold expressions of gifts of God's grace.

In Romans 1:11 Paul expresses his desire to impart a spiritual gift that the Roman Christians might be strengthened. Such spiritual gifts are the result of the activity of the Holy Spirit, and since elsewhere Paul emphasizes the variety and profitability of the gifts, it is unnecessary here to speculate about the precise nature of the gift mentioned in this passage.[32] Charles Cranfield notes that the word "represented by *gift* here" is used in Romans in a few different ways. Pauline writings, however, use this noun largely "to denote a special gift or endowment bestowed on a member of the church by God in order that it may be used by that member in his service" and in the service of God's people.[33] This is Paul's basic understanding of the purpose and nature of the spiritual gifts.

The contrast between Adam and Christ is the purpose of Romans 5:15–17. This contrast is made specific by the apostle's reference to Adam's trespass and Christ's free gift. Paul probably meant that this gracious gift is Christ himself and his work for humankind, and in the context of verses 17–21, this must include the undeserved gift of a status of righteousness before God. The supreme spiritual gift is manifest because of grace and is specifically the atonement, forgiveness, Spirit, and eternal life given by God in Christ Jesus our Lord—through his life, death, resurrection, and glorification. Paul drives home this point in his antithetical statement in Romans 6:23. Pauline theology presents a God who graciously gives his Son and his Spirit, and these then proceed to distribute other gifts of a spiritual nature to the church. Siegfried Schatzmann's conclusion is lucid when he writes "in the statement 'the gift of God is eternal life in Jesus Christ our Lord,' the apostle established the foundational charisma without which all or any charismata cannot be received."[34] Ernst Käsemann asserts, "Other charismata only exist because of the existence of this one charism to which they are all related, and they only exist where the gift of eternal life is manifest in the eschatologically inaugurated dominion of Christ."[35] Such theological foundations must be considered as fundamental to a correct understanding of the nature of spiritual gifts and to an appropriate application of these gifts in the life and mission of the local church. The spiritual gifts are grounded in the supreme gift of Jesus Christ for the salvation and redemption of the world, and are therefore framed within a missiological context from their outset. Christians use the spiritual gifts in the service of Christ and his mission, and while they are undeniably important for the edification and building up of the church, they have an outward, missiological dimension—especially as we consider their foundation in the redemptive mission of Jesus Christ and in the eschatological inauguration of his messianic kingdom.

31. Ibid., 20–21.

32. Barrett, *Epistle to the Romans*, 25.

33. Cranfield, *Epistle to the Romans*, 79.

34. Schatzmann, *Pauline Theology*, 17.

35. Käsemann and Bromiley, *Commentary on Romans*, 64.

In Romans 12:6–8 Paul provides an ethical exhortation regarding each believer's place as a member of the "one body in Christ," and their relationships with their fellow-members. The apostle deals with a list of spiritual gifts here, which differ from those given in 1 Corinthians 12:8–10, 28–30, and Ephesians 4:11, using the analogy of a body. The thrust of this ethical exhortation is that the Roman Christians must not boast about their use of the spiritual gifts, or allow the recognition of their giftedness to cause them to be proud. Rather, they should think of themselves "with sober judgment, in accordance with the faith God has distributed to each of you." This "measure of faith" is not based on emotion or personal opinion, but is established in an individual's God-given relationship with Christ, which all Christians equally share. Such exhortation is central to a Pauline concept of spiritual giftedness. Those who have been entrusted with spiritual gifts have ethical boundaries, according to the apostle, and are therefore accountable in the application of those gifts. They must learn the value of mutual submission and edification.

Prophecy, service, teaching, exhorting, giving, leadership, and mercy are named as spiritual gifts in this passage. The text does not suggest "an already developing or existing ministerial order," or a trend to "institutionalize ministries, offices, or gifts."[36] Paul's aim was to ensure that those who were spiritually gifted would function in such a manner that the church would be edified and built-up. No spiritual gifting should cause individuals to regard themselves, or to be regarded by others, as personally superior to the other members of the "one body in Christ." The spiritual gifts are freely given and are in no way earned or merited by the recipient—therefore any personal elevation or pride is unjustified. The community of faith should not unduly hinder people from exercising their gifts. In order to witness to the person and work of Christ, life in the body of Christ is to be a witness to the world, as the church serves him and his mission. The spiritual gifts, like so much of the church's behavior, ethics, relationship to governing powers, and life in community, are to witness to Christ in a way that glorifies him and serves his mission and purposes in the world (Romans 12–16). This and other dimensions of our life in Christian community are to witness to Jesus Christ, so that everyone "might come to faith and obedience—to the only wise God be glory forever through Jesus Christ!"[37]

From Paul's epistle to the Romans we move to his first epistle to the Corinthians. In 1 Corinthians 1:7, he expresses gratitude for their spiritual gifts, which are a confirmation of the gospel and of Paul's ministry in Corinth. The TNIV rendering of this text suggests that the Corinthians potentially have all the gifts of God at their disposal; however, a study of the grammar may suggest, "that they do not come short, either in comparison with others or with normal expectations of Christians who have the Spirit, in any of the gifts that they do possess."[38] A crucial point to note is that Paul puts the gifts in their eschatological context—"as you eagerly wait for our Lord Jesus Christ to be revealed." Paul's pneumatological perspective here is eschatologically shaped—that is, it is directed toward Jesus Christ and his eschatological mission and glorification—and this has significant

---

36. Schatzmann, *Pauline Theology*, 21.

37. Rom 16:26–27.

38. Fee, *First Epistle to the Corinthians*, 41.

bearing on our perspective of the nature and function of spiritual gifts. Paul is grateful for the Corinthian's spiritual giftedness; however, he reminds them that even these are not the final glory and that they should await the coming of Christ with eager expectation. There are varieties of gifts, and the implication is that God gives spiritual gifts that are uniquely harmonious with individual callings and ecclesial needs. Hans Conzelmann encapsulates the idea in this verse well when he writes that Paul "differs both from the Gnostics and also from the legalists in holding not that everyone's gifts are the same, but that each has their own, particular gift."[39] Too often, the church has emphasized gifts that serve its present institutional shape, rather than serving the mission of God or the urgent needs of the church. Spiritual gifts are uniquely distributed, and it is time for the church to create a spirit of freedom and permission-giving, so that gifts of the Spirit might emerge that are vital for the present ecclesiological and missional challenges and opportunities.

The most substantial Pauline treatise on spiritual gifts occurs in 1 Corinthians 12–14. Gordon Fee summarizes these chapters with this sentence: "Being 'spiritual' in the present means to edify the community in worship."[40] This Pauline treatment of spiritual gifts was intended to be corrective before it was intended to be instructional. The apostle develops a general and theological response to the Corinthians' understanding of worship and spiritual gifts in chapters 12 and 13, and then specifically addresses the primary issue in chapter 14. This primary issue is the abuse of the spiritual gift of tongues in corporate worship—and associated matters of ecclesial order and the community's public witness to Jesus Christ.

In 1 Corinthians 12:4–30 Paul emphasizes the multiplicity and unity of spiritual gifts and, as in Romans 12:6–8, he uses the analogy of a body. However, the Corinthians seem to practice the corporate use of tongues in a disorderly manner, undermining the unity and purpose of the spiritual gifts. This is why Paul argues for "the absolute need for intelligibility in the assembly" in chapter 14:1–25. He also argues for "the absolute need for order in the assembly" in chapter 14:26–40.[41] Thus, spiritual gifts are again understood to be for the edification and building up of the church. In the passage 13:1 to 14:1 the gifts are not contrasted with love, rather love is held up as the crucial ingredient for the expression of all spiritual gifts. Paul expounds the nature of this love which seeks the benefit and nourishment of the church. The reader can feel the Corinthians squirming in their seats as they hear this corrective passage read, for they would have realized that such self-sacrificial love was not underpinning their use of the spiritual gifts. Paul's understanding of love as the foundation for any acceptable expression of spiritual gifts is why he writes "Make love your aim, and eagerly desire the spiritual gifts, especially that you may prophecy" in chapter 14:1. All corporate expressions of the spiritual gifts must be for mutual edification, not for increased individual spirituality.

The Pauline emphasis in these chapters is not on the number and kinds of spiritual gifts, for the list in chapter 12:8–10 is not systematic, hierarchical, nor exhaustive.

---

39. Conzelmann, *1 Corinthians*, 118.

40. Fee, *First Epistle to the Corinthians*, 570.

41. Ibid., 571.

Frederick Bruce notes that "the list is not intended to be exhaustive . . . and the possibility is not excluded that new gifts might subsequently be bestowed to meet changing needs for which some of the gifts mentioned here made no adequate provision."[42] Again, Paul's primary concern is that the Corinthians express these diverse spiritual gifts in their corporate worship with a motivation of love and a desire for mutual edification. Thus in chapter 14:40 Paul concludes by saying: "everything should be done in a fitting and orderly way." While mutual edification, God-honoring order, and Christ-like love are key concerns for Paul when he describes the appropriate use of the spiritual gifts, we should not miss, however, his concern for the church's mission and public witness in 1 Corinthians 12–14. Paul's missional spirit comes through in his description of how the spiritual gifts should be used, since he is concerned that all aspects of the church testify to Jesus Christ, his gospel, and his eschatological mission.[43]

There are two references to spiritual gifts in the Pastoral Epistles, which are especially worth noting. These are 1 Timothy 4:14 and 2 Timothy 1:6. Timothy's giftedness seems to be of a permanent status in order to complement his particular calling, as was Paul's gift of celibacy. Hence the gift was received through prophecy and the laying on of hands by the presbytery (1 Timothy 4:14), and/or by Paul (2 Timothy 1:6). Guthrie writes, "The endowment is connected with the laying on of hands, and must be understood in the light of the special tasks to which Timothy was commissioned on that important occasion."[44] Timothy is exhorted, "do not neglect your gift," and even to "fan into flame the gift of God." A Pauline theology of the spiritual gifts exhorts recipients to treasure and utilize their gifts for the good of the Christian community, for the extension of the gospel, and for the sake of the messianic mission of Jesus Christ. God remains the giver of the gifts, equipping believers to minister with and to his church, and equipping believers to follow Christ's eschatological mission in the world and in human history.

Unfortunately, many churches are guilty of neglecting the spiritual gifts and of losing their ministry and missional consequence. Churches need "to fan them into flame." Missional churches need to seriously consider how the spiritual gifts mentioned by Paul in 1 Corinthians 12:4–11, and in other passages, are used in corporate worship for the edification and building-up of the assembly, and for the equipping of the people of God for mission and service. Many spiritual gifts are in serious neglect in evangelical and other Protestant congregations. The spiritual gifts that are used in abundance are the gifts of service, teaching, exhorting, and leadership—and these are used by a small handful of mostly professional ministers. Without wanting to minimize the importance of those gifts, this narrowing expression of giftedness is an indictment on our churches, and a significant hindrance to the church if it is to participate in Christ's mission in the world, in the power of the Spirit.

Those few who do utilize their spiritual gifts in our churches should be commended for their humility, accountability in the application of their gifts, and value of mutual

42. Bruce, *1 and 2 Corinthians*, 119.

43. See 1 Cor 14:13–25.

44. Guthrie, *Pastoral Epistles*, 126.

submission and edification. However, although the Pauline texts on spiritual gifts do not attempt to institutionalize ministries, offices, or gifts, it is evident in many our churches that this has occurred (to a greater or lesser degree). Our institutional, professional ministers are the ones who are predominantly functioning in their spiritual gifts, and few lay people are given the encouragement or opportunity to develop or use their spiritual gifts in the service of the messianic kingdom, in the edification of the church, or in the pursuit of the mission of God.

Churches need to find ways to help Christians discover, develop, and utilize their spiritual gifts. This is important for the edification and building up of the congregation, and for the discovery and release of authentic expressions of the *missio Dei*. Christians in leadership roles must make a genuine commitment to search for and recognize people's spiritual gifts; then to develop those gifts and give people opportunities to function in those gifts in mission and ministry. Thus, the clergy should see themselves as equippers and facilitators, rather than as doers. Ephesians 4:11–16 is the biblical model. People should be discipled by mentors—mentors who are committed to helping people discover their spiritual gifts, assisting them develop in maturity as they use these gifts, and exhorting them to fan their gifts into flame. These mentors should be passionately committed to mission, and would walk alongside people as they explore their gifts in the ministry contexts of the church and in the church's missional activities.

More opportunities to minister *and* be involved in mission should be made available to the members and attendees of churches—drama groups, sharing times, service involvement, participation in missional experiments, church planting, and so forth. The more people who get involved in the running of church services the better and the more people involved in all of the ministries and missional life of the church the better. Once people have been exposed to a variety of ministry and mission opportunities, they should be encouraged to find their spiritual gifts with guidance from mentors. They should then concentrate on those ministries and missional opportunities that develop and utilize the gifts given them by the Spirit. Services and meetings should have times available for people to deliver a word of prophecy, exhortation, comfort, or edification. Churches should seek to include their whole congregation in the missional life of the church. Naturally, the church leadership will keep each person accountable for their service and missional experimentation, as the congregation likewise keeps the leadership accountable. However, freedom of expression, encouragement of creativity, missional experimentation, and open exploration of spiritual giftedness should characterize the churches. The people of God are to pursue what the Spirit is doing in both the church and the world.

PRACTICAL CONSEQUENCES OF A THEOLOGY OF THE SPIRIT FOR THE MISSIONAL CHURCH

What are some of the consequences of a theology of the Spirit for a missional theology of the church? What happens to our understanding and practice of church when it is attentive to a theology of mission, Christ, and the Spirit?

Here I briefly outline some of the implications or consequences of pneumatology for the missional church, under the headings *being, structures, community, theology, world,* and *mission.*

SPIRIT-CONSTITUTED BEING

Hans Küng writes that Christian theology must preserve the distinction between the church and the Spirit. While they are unified they remain distinct, since the Spirit of Jesus Christ *reigns* over the church, is *distinct* from the church, *precedes* the church, and works *where* and *when* he wills. Küng is concerned that the church, while enjoying the presence, vivification, and guidance of the Spirit, does not make the mistake of assuming that it is the same as the Spirit, or that it can control the Spirit. The church and its structures, decrees, doctrines, offices, and so forth, remain at all times in submission to the sovereignty and will of the Father, Son, and Holy Spirit.[45] The church "cannot 'possess' him, cannot control, restrain, direct, or master him," since in the church "the Spirit breathes, not when he must but when he wills."[46] Missional churches cultivate an ecclesial life that is open to change and critical examination, open to the power and will of the Spirit of Jesus Christ. They recognize that the church is in submission to the Spirit of Christ, and must remain in a process of critical examination and renewal as it seeks the kingdom and will of its Lord.

The Spirit animates the church's worship, ministries, structures, missional initiatives, and so forth, "so that they indicate the presence of God." In this way, asserts John Webster, the church's forms are "indications of the presence of the Spirit who bears Christ to the church and the world and so fulfills the Father's purpose."[47] The Spirit also creates the church—he causes it to come into being. Pneumatology is essential to the *very being* of the church. "The Spirit's life-giving and revelatory agency is fundamental to the church's being, including its visibility in creaturely time and space. The church is and is visible because God the Holy Spirit is and acts."[48] Recognizing the presence of the Spirit as he animates ecclesial forms, makes the church visible to the world, and creates the *being* of the church, should compel us to submit our churches to his "life-giving and revelatory agency."

SPIRIT-FILLED STRUCTURES

The church's structure is essentially *charismatic* and emerges as it is filled and empowered by the Spirit of Jesus Christ. The charismatic structure of the church is demonstrated in the gifts and ministries freely given by the Spirit. While there is a variety of ministry functions and charisms, and some of them lead to formal offices in the church, every Christian has been gifted by the Spirit of Christ for service and mission. Unpacking Pauline theology, Hans Küng asserts that gifts for ministry are not normally exceptional. Instead, the Spirit of God distributes his gifts for the edification and benefit of the church, and for the sake of the messianic mission of Jesus Christ. The church, then, has both a formal

---

45. Küng, *Church*, 172–78.

46. Küng, *Church—Maintained*, 24.

47. Webster, "Visible Attests," 102.

48. Ibid., 104.

structure *and* a charismatic structure, and both have an important role to play in the life of the church—but the foundational structure is the charismatic one. "One can speak of a *charismatic structure of the Church*, which *includes but goes far beyond the hierarchical* structure of the church."[49] The church discovers fresh missional movement and zeal when the charismatic structure is cultivated and released. "If the charisms of individual Christians were discovered and furthered and developed, what dynamic power, what life and movement there would be in such a community, such a church."[50]

Miroslav Volf writes that the Spirit orchestrates the life and structure of the church. The Spirit shapes the church's *"pneumatological structure"* through his sovereign distribution of the *charismata*, for the sake of the glory of God and the eschatological mission of the Messiah.[51] As a Free Church missiologist, I agree with Volf's basic outline of the Free Church, charismatic, locally assembled nature of the church. Volf proposes that a local gathering of believers is constituted as a church when there is a biblical adherence to Scripture, a confession of Christ, a biblical participation in the sacraments, and a group of believers gathered in the name of Christ—he calls this last one "the presence of the people of God" and "the church as assembly."[52] Building his ecclesiology on Matthew 18:20, Volf says, "*Where two or three are gathered in Christ's name, not only is Christ present among them, but a Christian church is there as well.*"[53] Such a church seeks to obediently structure and organize itself around biblical guidelines and to follow the commands of Christ. When a faith community is constituted as a church, it demonstrates the following characteristics: (1) *Cognitive specification* and *confessional affirmation* of the person and work of Christ; (2) "The public confession of faith in Christ through the pluriform speaking of the Word"; (3) The preservation of historic Christian doctrines (especially, for Volf, in their Reformation, Protestant, Free Church forms); (4) Obedience to Scripture; (5) The biblical practice of the sacraments; (6) Ministries of social concern and compassion, and; (7) Participation in the missional purposes and history of the triune God. The truest expression of the church is found in the gathered and concrete assembly that meets to read the Scriptures and celebrate the sacraments of baptism and the Lord's Supper.[54] Jaroslav Skira notes that for Volf, "These elements belong to the *esse* of the church, while institutional aspects belong to the *bene esse* of the church."[55] Biblically faithful actions and institutional forms must never be separated from the subjective freedoms associated with Free Church congregational ecclesiology; especially since the church's primary structure is the Spirit-constituted, charismatic, assembled one.[56]

Along with Miroslav Volf, I am convinced that the local gathering of the people of God is the authentic constitution of the church and the witness to the universal church's

49. Küng, *Church*, 188.

50. Ibid., 191.

51. Volf, *After Our Likeness*, 232.

52. Ibid., 131–37.

53. Ibid., 136.

54. Ibid., 130–54.

55. Skira, "After Our Likeness," 376.

56. Volf, *After Our Likeness*, 135.

eschatological gathering.[57] Therefore, the form that the local church takes is significant and should be approached soberly, prayerfully, and with adequate theological and biblical consideration. Biblically faithful congregations are organized around the sacraments of baptism and the Lord's Supper, around the public profession of the Lordship of Jesus Christ, around the mission of God, and around ecumenical cooperation and communion. Such churches "grow in unity, sanctity, catholicity, and apostolicity" because of the "constitutive presence of Christ."[58] Such considerations have important implications for missional ecclesiology and the way it approaches the questions of "What constitutes a local church?" and "What is important for its essence, governance, structure, mission, and community life?" It is not enough to allow a leadership or governance structure to emerge unreflectively in a missional church setting. Nor is it healthy for a local congregation to be blasé about such structures or about what constitutes worship when the people of God gather. Missional ecclesiology's emphasis on contextualization might sometimes lead to inattention to those things that are essential to the *esse* of a local church. Additionally, in practice, the egalitarian models of church that are planted by missional ecclesiologists (missional church planters) are often too cautious about asserting that there are "non-negotiables" in ecclesial life, practice, and structure. While the charismatic structure of the church is foundational, and missional churches are wise to embrace a contextual and flexible institutional life that enables mission, the church still has both a formal structure *and* a charismatic structure—both are important and deserve adequate consideration.

Miroslav Volf's "participatory ecclesiology" focuses on the active priesthood of all believers. His "polycentric community" is about leadership and mission being demonstrated by the whole community of believers. These two notions resonate with missional ecclesiology. The Holy Spirit generously distributes the charismata for the sake of participatory and polycentric community, service, and mission.[59] All members of congregations should be encouraged to use their gifts for ministry and to participate in ecclesial decision-making. Grass-root, local, polycentric, and participatory leadership and governance structures are most effective for local church mission. "The polycentric character of the church has a twofold theological grounding, namely, in the Christian call to faith and in the charismata."[60] Volf goes on to describe how such charismata, multiplicity of gifting, Spirit-empowerment, and "polycentric-participative models of church life" might release local churches to maturity, service, and mission.[61] On the other hand, ecclesial institutions have an important role to play, especially when they correspond to the nature of the Trinity, are inspired by grace and love, are viewed as provisional, and are responsive to the church's broad mission in the world.[62] Institutional forms, formalized leadership, and pastoral offices need "the vivifying presence of the Spirit," even more than they need decentralization or egalitarian reformulation. A rejection of institutions and structures in

57. Ibid., 128.
58. Ibid., 158.
59. Ibid., 228–33.
60. Ibid., 225.
61. Ibid., 227–33.
62. Ibid., 234–41.

ecclesial life is simply not possible.[63] I am concerned that some missional ecclesiologists tend to reject or dismiss established ecclesial forms or the important role of ecclesial institutions and procedures. Volf does not permit such sentiment. The aim should not be to simply replace established forms of church with newer, more relevant, or dynamic forms; rather, "the vivifying presence of the Spirit" and polycentric-participative expressions of charismata are to be fostered in all congregations, whether "established" or "missional."[64]

In addition, fellowship with other churches and acknowledging their important place in relationship to one's own church are an "ecclesial minimum."[65] In anticipation of the eschaton, all churches are required to genuinely fellowship with other churches and share their confession of faith in Jesus Christ. This might be a challenge for missional ecclesiology. Some missional church plants are too isolated, too disconnected from established forms of church, and too narrowly located within particular sub-cultures and generational groups. An authentic missional ecclesiology respects the role of other congregations in missional endeavor, in faithful biblical witness, and in expressing the unity, catholicity, holiness, and apostolicity of the church.[66] Christ acts sovereignly within a local congregation through the charismata, which are distributed universally and graciously for the sake of the mission of God and for the benefit of the entire, universal church.[67] The charismatic giftings of all believers in a congregation should be exercised and nurtured. Miroslav Volf's ecclesiology is pneumatological—characterized by inclusion, participation, mutuality, and polycentricity.[68]

Leonard Sweet laments that modernity resisted the notion of "the priesthood of all believers," since modernity was an "age of representation." Postmodern culture, however, is an "age of participation" and access—a "karaoke world."[69] A missional pneumatology affirms, in theology and practice, that all believers are gifted for service, ministry, and mission, and must be empowered to participate in, and contribute fully to, meaningful expressions of Christian worship. Missionary witness is more credible and effective if it comes from the whole body of believers and not merely a professional guild or "outreach program." Bosch says that the division between the sacred and the secular in western culture might be diminished when it is not just a "religious class" that does ministry but, instead, the entire local faith community. Bosch writes, "Newbigin suggests that the only hermeneutic of the gospel is a congregation of men and women who believe it and live by it."[70] Jesus's model of servant leadership involved setting aside ultimate divine authority for service, which is symbolized "by the throne and the towel"—this is an inspiring im-

---

63. Ibid., 257.

64. Ibid., 227, 257. I am not trying to set up an artificial distinction between *established* and *missional* here, but make a point about prior ecclesial and pneumatological considerations.

65. Ibid., 157.

66. Guder, *Missional Church*, 75.

67. Volf, *After Our Likeness*, 228–33.

68. Ibid., 221–57.

69. Sweet, *Soultsunami*, 216.

70. Bosch, *Believing in the Future*, 59, quoting Newbigin, *Gospel in a Pluralist Society*, 222–33.

age for Christian leaders.[71] Stuart Murray claims that the Constantinian division between clergy and laity has had at least six unfortunate consequences: (1) Hierarchical structures and patriarchal ethos that compromise mission; (2) Poor recognition of ministry in broader society; (3) A back-to-front emphasis on clergy rather than lay ministry; (4) The dominance of worship styles and contributions by a small, elite group; (5) Unrealistic expectations on leaders, and; (6) Ethical inconsistencies. For Murray, these are only solved by these four practices: (1) Developing indigenous leaders within congregations; (2) Elevating bivocationalism; (3) Training leaders to prioritize lay leadership development and release, and; (4) Restoring the concept of "the priesthood of all believers" in shared mission. This fourth point involves making worship services serve this end and recognizing believers' baptism as ordination for ministry.[72] This affirmation of mutual giftedness and shared ministry does not mean that the gift of leadership is unimportant in Christian communities. It does mean that such Christian leadership facilitates, equips, and empowers such shared priesthood, as it responds to what the Spirit of Jesus Christ is doing in and through the church. Responding to God's empowering Spirit, the church discerns together "God's specific missionary vocation for the entire community, and for all of its members."[73]

SPIRIT-FORMED COMMUNITIES

There should be inward and outward expressions of the Spirit in missional communities and individual believers, since the Spirit fills with inspiration and grips with enthusiasm. The work of the Spirit is usually evidenced by its transformational effect on the recipient and on the community of faith, and in the realms of ethical living, boldness in witness, passion for God, a renewed enthusiasm, and the like. The Spirit is concerned with the transformation of the whole person and the whole church into the likeness and image of Christ.[74] The activity of the Spirit should have a noticeable impact on the life of the Christian and consequently on the community of believers when gathered for worship and when engaged in mission. Missional communities place an emphasis on the transformational work of the Spirit, on his empowering presence, and on his missional efficacy and impetus. The Spirit testifies to Christ and enables the church to do likewise as it pursues *his redemptive mission* and as it seeks faithful witness to *his truth*. The Spirit calls the church to a continuing process of repentance and renewal.

> The church has continually every reason for . . . conversion, reform, and renewal . . . The church, believing in the Spirit of Christ who guides it continually into truth, knows that the Spirit again and again confronts it also with its own sin, with the justice of Christ, and with judgment. It knows that in this very way the Spirit demands of it once more a new faith in Christ, a greater fidelity to the gospel, and a life lived more seriously according to his message . . . The church under the Spirit may never simple leave things as they are, but must continually allow all

71. Webber, *Younger Evangelicals*, 120–21, 150–53.

72. Murray, *Post-Christendom*, 261–64, 307, 326, 332.

73. Barrett, *Treasure in Clay Jars*, 85, 165–67.

74. 2 Cor 3:17–18.

things to become new in this Spirit who renews the face of the earth and also of the church.[75]

Receiving and Extending God's Extravagant Grace

Christ pours out his Spirit upon the church according to his extravagant grace. The church exists by grace, and its mission and purpose are shaped by its reception and extension of that grace. God's redemptive mission to humankind reveals his grace, and his church is called to announce and embody that grace. Furthermore, grace is the source of the gifts of the Spirit and this should influence our understanding of the nature of the *charismata* in our missional ecclesiology. These gifts are a gift of grace, and thus should not be a source of pride, self-exaltation, or elitism in the life of the individual Christian, nor in the assembly of believers. God has given a variety of gifts according to his abundant mercy and graciousness, and all recognition must go to him alone. The Pauline emphasis on grace as the foundation for all the spiritual gifts is profound and may not be ignored. In addition, there are numerous ways in which God's grace is evident in the midst and lives of his people. Narrow definitions or understandings of the gifts and evidences of the Spirit must be avoided. Pressure for Christians to conform to certain expressions or manifestations of the gifts of the Spirit must also be avoided, since the gifts are varied, present in forms that edify the community at their point of need, and divinely originated. Spiritual gifts should be used in a way that is permeated by grace, Christocentric, and missionally oriented. They are to be characterized by a form of spirituality that is self-giving, rather than individualizing or self-centered, since all spiritual gifts have their origin in divine grace and serve to edify the community of believers. Leaving aside the grand dreams of Christendom and modern culture, our churches are called to be places of grace, Christocentric mission, humility, self-sacrifice, and "littleness," as these are the constraints of the Spirit.[76]

Glorifying Jesus Christ and Depending on the Holy Spirit

Various Christian groups have proposed particular measuring sticks for determining whether the Spirit is active in the life of the believer or in the Christian community. However, the main evidence of the Spirit's activity is the glorification of Jesus Christ. The holistic exaltation of Christ as Lord, that is, the testimony to this truth in every aspect of the believer's private and public life, is the primary evidence of the activity of the Spirit in the believer. I am not talking about perfection here but submission of one's whole life to Christ. This is also the evidence of the activity of the Spirit in the faith community and, particularly, in the community gathered for worship. Within the scope of this unwavering commitment to the Lordship of Christ, "the missionary community confesses its dependence upon the Holy Spirit, shown in particular in its practices of corporate prayer."[77] Christ gives his authority to the church for mission, according to Lesslie Newbigin, in the form of "a living community, a tradition of teaching, and the continuing work of

75. Küng, *Church—Maintained*, 26–27.
76. Hall, *End of Christendom*, 65–66.
77. Barrett, *Treasure in Clay Jars*, 117–25.

the divine Spirit illuminating the tradition in each new generation."[78] Missional churches remain attentive to their dependency on the Spirit and their glorification of Christ, since without this dependency and witness there can be no authentic mission.

Celebrating Diversity as an Opportunity for a Missional Imagination

The Apostle Paul's analogy of the body focuses on the edification of the community through diverse manifestations of the Spirit, as opposed to individual indulgence. Diversity in the church is essential to true unity and to mutual edification. The diverse manifestations of the Spirit are valuable as they contribute to the edification of the community and the exaltation of the body's Head. Therefore, when the people of God gather for public worship or seek fresh expressions in the missional dimensions of their existence, conformity should not be imposed nor diversity suppressed. This is because God gives diverse manifestations of the Spirit for the edification of the body and to empower the church to carry on the messianic mission of Christ. The variety of spiritual gifts is evidence of the unifying activity and presence of the Spirit, and each Christian should seek to contribute, as the Spirit moves and leads them.

This contribution occurs both in the public gathering of the people of God for worship and in the missional life of the congregation. The Spirit has both outward and homeward movements that are expressed in diverse ways by the people of God, and communities should celebrate and encourage such double movements, which are at the heart of missional communities. Some have called this the centripetal and centrifugal dimensions of the mission of the church, and the Spirit of God is active in both: that is, outward in a variety of missional endeavors, and homeward in community formation and in "drawing the church toward its destination, unity with Christ in heaven."[79] The image of the church as a body should shape the missional imagination of the people of God as they seek together to be faithful to the gospel. The diversity of the body of Christ provides opportunities for creative, inculturational mission, and should shape our missional imagination, strategies, and spirit. As Robert Webber puts it, "The church as the 'body' participates in the incarnation as 'an extension of God's presence in the world' . . . The church is the presence of the eschatological future in the world. In this sense, the church does not 'have' a mission; it is mission, by its existence in the world as 'an extension of God's presence in the world.'"[80] The church is remarkably diverse—in giftings, temperaments, cultures, ages, socio-economic backgrounds, political persuasions, and ethnicities. Yet the Spirit unifies the church in all its remarkable diversity, guiding it into unified worship, mission, and glorification of Christ.

78. Newbigin is quoted in ibid., 141.

79. Moynagh, *Emergingchurch.Intro*, 143–50.

80. Webber, *Younger Evangelicals*, 112–13.

Gathering the Nations

In the southwestern area of Sydney is one of Australia's most rapidly growing and ethnically diverse churches. Parkside Church consists of people from over fifty different linguistic, cultural, and ethnic backgrounds, who gather as one family for worship and mission, reflecting a united, diverse congregation of evangelical faith. Their dream is to become a vibrant congregation from more than one hundred different ethnic backgrounds, worshipping together as one family, affecting Australia and beyond— "to be a Christian community committed to bringing Christ to people of all nations." Surrounding the walls of the church are the flags of these fifty nations. True to their God-given mission, 30 percent of Parkside's congregation are from an Anglo-Celtic background, 40 percent are first generation migrants to Australia, and the other 30 percent are second or third generation Australians from migrant families.

Parkside's mission in southwestern Sydney includes a program called Just Care. This is a community outreach of Parkside, which has been providing practical help and support to disadvantaged youth, children, and families from all diverse ethnicities and religions in their area. Since its inception, Just Care has provided emergency food parcels, financial assistance, and job training to people in the local community. A Just Care trailer equipped with BBQ facilities has been visiting local parks in order to make contact with youth and families and to share the gospel. Aside from its mission within Sydney, Parkside has international mission teams serving among the world's poorest, especially in Asia and the Indian subcontinent. The church's passion for mission among all the nations and ethnicities of Australia and beyond is becoming truly global, as they seek to reflect the Messiah's heart for the nations and demonstrate genuine unity in extraordinary diversity.[81]

Witnessing through Disciplined and Holistic Worship

Order and missional attentiveness must be preserved in the public assembly of believers. This spiritual discipline is not an inhibiting restraint, but rather order for the sake of edification and witness, which is applied in all situations where the people of God are gathered together. This is especially the case in public worship, so that such gatherings might be missionally fruitful and credible. The individual Christian is responsible for cultivating a lifestyle of godliness, self-control, and love, which is a life of godly orderliness enabled by the Spirit.

Such Spirit-enabled personal discipline contributes to the edification of the body and to the church's witness in a post-Christendom, secular society. An orderly, biblically attentive, Spirit-enabled, and missionally sensitive balance of "word, emotion, and will" in public

81. Online: http://www.parksidechurch.com.au. Used with permission.

worship is necessary, writes Eddie Gibbs. He suggests that this is because "postmodern people will not tolerate any separation of the body, mind, and will."[82] He may idealize postmodern conviction here. Nevertheless, it is true to say that missional ecclesiology, shaped by an attention to the power and presence of the Spirit, emphasizes "word, emotion, and will" in worship. Moreover, it understands the importance of these interwoven and inseparable dimensions of the human person, in its theology and practice of mission.

Ministering in the Spirit of Christ

Christian leadership must be characterized by humility and service, and by willingness to recognize and honor those who serve in less visible or seemly roles. This also carries over to the public assembling of the people of God for worship and in to the church's mission in the world. Those members of the body who are "weaker" and have less seemly gifts should not be treated with dishonor, neglect, or contempt when God's people gather; rather they should be honored and allowed to give expression to their necessary and vital spiritual gifts, and natural talents. No spiritual gifts, regardless of their form or manifestation, are expressed in the community apart from persons who are made in the image of God and are consequently of great value to him. They are first of all gracious endowments of the Spirit, given to individuals within the body for its mutual edification, and in the service of the mission and person of the Messiah. Philippians 1:27 to 2:18 and 3:7–16 show us what it looks like to be a disciple and a servant leader fashioned after the Spirit of Jesus Christ. Christian leadership that is empowered by the Spirit and imitative of Christ's humility only enhances the church's mission.

Pursuing Love and Eagerly Desiring Spiritual Gifts

Love must never be set over against the spiritual gifts, for this was not Paul's point in 1 Corinthians 12. Instead, love is the manner in which all gifts are to function—it transcends and embraces all spiritual gifts and acts of service, for it is the overarching source of these. The logical conclusion, therefore, is that Christians should pursue love and eagerly desire spiritual gifts. Christians must allow the characteristics of *agape*, as described by Paul in 1 Corinthians 13, to permeate every aspect of their public and inner lives. This *love* must be evident in the community of believers when gathered for worship, especially in the way in which spiritual gifts function. In the community the operation of the spiritual gifts must be with patience, kindness, humility, consideration, selflessness, rejoicing with the truth, always protecting, always trusting, always hoping, and always persevering. The Christian's life is to be a tangible expression of such love, and his or her use of the spiritual gifts should be evidence that such magnificent love does indeed exist, and is indeed edifying for the whole community when gathered together to worship their precious and holy Lord and Savior.

This love should characterize all Christian mission, so that this mission is an expression of the divine love revealed in the *missio Dei*. As love shapes the form and use of the spiritual gifts, these gifts are used in the service of the mission of God, as he builds his

82. Gibbs, *Church Next*, 165.

church and reveals his redemptive purposes for humanity and creation. Spiritual gifts must not be quenched or despised. Rather, these spiritual gifts should be fanned into flame and encouraged, in the effort to edify, exhort, console, and instruct the church, and in the church's continuation of the eschatological, messianic mission of Jesus Christ. The spiritual gifts and graces bestowed by Christ on the church are not only for the edification of the gathered community, but also for the sake of mission, witness, and service. The Spirit makes the whole of a person's life a charismatic offering to God, as she or he embraces Christ and is filled with his Spirit. Jürgen Moltmann puts it this way,

> The charismata are by no means to be seen merely in the 'special ministries' of the gathered community. Every member of the messianic community is a charismatic, not only in the community's solemn assemblies but every day, when members are scattered and isolated in the world . . . The call to the fellowship of Christ and the gift of the Holy Spirit make a charisma out of bondage and freedom, marriage and celibacy, manhood and womanhood, Jewish and Gentile existence. For the call puts the person's particular situation at the service of the new creation. The Spirit makes the whole biological, cultural, and religious life history of a person charismatically alive.[83]

SPIRIT-SHAPED THEOLOGY

A missional theology of the church is inadequate without a robust theology of the Spirit. This is because the church does not have a mission without the presence, power, and enabling of the Spirit. Moreover, there is no church without the Spirit. The Spirit enables the church to be a missional community. Stephen Bevans puts it this way:

> I propose that the church will live out its mission worthily only to the extent that it allies itself with and is transformed by the Spirit. Only in this way can it live in fidelity to its Lord, who himself was allied to the Spirit in his mission and was transformed by the Spirit's power. If the Spirit is the first way that God sends and is sent, the Spirit's activity becomes the foundation of the church's own missionary nature. If the church is to express its nature, therefore, it needs first to look to the Spirit's activity.[84]

As we will see, Stephen Bevans describes how the Spirit *calls*, *equips*, and *challenges* the church to be a *missional church*. The church cannot understand its missional nature without a theology of the Spirit. To separate missional ecclesiology from its grounding in a robust theology of the Spirit is to make an unbiblical and ultimately enervating move. The Spirit forms the church as a missional community, and, consequently, missional ecclesiology is dependent on a theology of the Spirit, that is, a Spirit-shaped missional theology.[85] Taking up John Zizioulas's challenge, missional ecclesiology needs to construct a theology of the church that is attentive to both Christ and the Spirit. A missional theology of the church must seek a critical conversation between the various theological streams associated with the doctrines of God, Christ, mission, the church, the gospel, and the Spirit.

83. Moltmann, *Church in the Power*, 296.

84. Bevans, "God inside Out," 102.

85. Bevans, "Church as Creation."

Church renewal, adequate ecclesiological foundations, and sustainable missional activity, are dependent on such a conversation. Hans Küng reminds his readers that the Spirit is an "eschatological gift" to the church, precisely because the Spirit was given to the church at the eschatological "turning point" in human history—"the death and resurrection of Christ."[86]

Pauline theology is a missional theology. David Bosch makes a forceful case for Paul writing as a missionary, pastoral theologian.[87] In his missional theology, Paul forms an inseparable connection between a theology of Christ, the Spirit, the church, the church's mission, and the eschatological reign and action of God in human history. The Spirit of Jesus Christ reveals the church to be the "eschatological people of God," the alternative city, the counter-cultural society called to witness to God's final and cosmic reign in Christ Jesus. The church needs a theology of the Spirit that helps it understand how the Spirit of Jesus Christ is "present and efficient in the ecclesia," and how the Spirit guides and equips the church for obedience and passion for God's mission.[88]

SPIRIT-INFUSED WORLD

The Holy Spirit is present in creation, cultures, and the world. The Spirit moves in these spheres of life, in these realms of the created order. The Spirit is present there because of God's sovereignty, his eschatological purposes, his in-breaking kingdom, his restorative and salvific mission, and in order to convict the world of sin, righteousness, and judgment. The Spirit bears witness to Jesus Christ in the world and in human history, in surprising, scandalous ways and places—one only has to think of the scandal presented in the Gospels, of the presence of God among prostitutes, tax collectors, lepers, and the like, and extrapolate that out to the "untouchables" or despised in our context. Citing Jürgen Moltmann and Jonathan Edwards, Pete Ward suggests that missional communities are not merely attentive to the work of the Spirit in their midst when they are gathered for worship. They are also aware of the presence of the Spirit in popular spirituality and contemporary spiritual quests, in postmodern and consumer culture, in discipleship expressed and experienced in the world, in God's mission to humankind, and, ultimately, in creation as a whole.[89] In other words, their pneumatology affects not only their worship gatherings and their core ecclesiology, but also their understanding of the mission of Christ and his presence in the world, and their response to that mission. I consider these themes in a little more detail in the chapter on the mission of the Trinity.

SPIRIT-EMPOWERED MISSION

How does the Spirit empower the church for the mission of the triune God? A missional theology of the Spirit emphasizes the way in which the Spirit constitutes, empowers, animates, and fills the church's being, community witness, and missional life. The church's mission is dependent on the Spirit's presence. The Spirit *precedes* the church's mission.

86. Küng, *Church*, 166.

87. Bosch, *Transforming Mission*, 124.

88. Küng, *Church*, 166–68.

89. Ward, *Liquid Church*, 78–86.

He is active and present in the cultures and peoples of the world, preparing the soil for the missional efforts and gospel proclamation of the church. The Spirit is *present* in the mission of the church, animating the church's passion, and enlivening and filling its participation in the *missio Dei*. The Spirit *prevails* even where the church can no longer be present, when the church has had to withdraw from a culture or people, or when the church is simply not present anymore. The Spirit continues to outwork God's sovereign, eschatological purposes in the history of the world. The Spirit *persists* in convicting hearts, transforming lives, confronting principalities and powers, and leading toward repentance and discipleship to Jesus Christ, *before* the church arrives, *while* the church is on mission, and even *after* the church has, if necessary, and for whatever reason, withdrawn. Such a missional theology of the Spirit does not minimize the importance of the church in the economy of the triune God's mission, but it does frame it pneumatologically, with attention to the prevenient grace and sovereign work of the Spirit. The Spirit is the fulfillment of God's promise, his life-giving breath, power-in-weakness, personal presence, and assurance of what is to come. Through the Spirit, God empowers the church's proclamation and embodiment of the gospel, and obedience to all that this gospel entails. The Spirit guides the church into the kind of witness that is only possible through authentic holiness, unity, catholicity, and apostolicity. The Spirit enables faith, assures us of adoption into God's family, is present in our baptism, communion, worship, and prayers, and enables people to hear the liberating truth of the gospel. The Spirit distributes the charismata for the edification and maturity of the church, for the glorification of Christ, and for bold, passionate, effective witness. The church and its mission are utterly dependent on the Spirit, who creates, fills, and empowers it.

In *The Church as Creation of the Spirit*, Stephen Bevans unpacks Martin Luther's declaration that "it is the proper work of the Holy Spirit to make the church," to demonstrate how the Spirit creates the church by calling, equipping, and challenging the church "to be a missionary church."[90] Bevans writes that as we look across history—the history of the universe, the people of Israel, the person and work of Jesus Christ, and the church—we see the Spirit *calling* the church to be missional. The Spirit also *equips* the church to be missional, through its charismatic structures, spiritual gifts, depth of community, and its nature as a community-in-mission. Finally, the Spirit *challenges* the church to be missional, through such things as Pentecostalism, the growth of the church in Majority World settings, globalization, migration, contextualization, inter-religious dialogue, gender-issues, and contemporary discussions about human sexuality. To Bevan's list, we might add things such as terrorism, global financial crises, religious fundamentalism, ecological concerns, poverty, human trafficking, and energy and food security. These are some of the contexts within which the Spirit is challenging the church to embrace its missional nature and purpose. "We are not created for ourselves; we are created for mission. *Veni, Creator Spiritus!* Come, Creator Spirit!"[91]

90. Bevans, "Church as Creation," 5.
91. Ibid., 6–18.

I teach at Morling Theological Seminary in Sydney. At Morling, one way we talk about our mission is "*equipping the whole believer to take the whole gospel to the whole world.*" Karl Rahner insists that the Spirit meets the Christian and empowers them for mission, not just in explicit missional endeavors—such as proclaiming the gospel, living in holiness and unity as a form of witness, engaging in ministries of mercy and justice, and so forth—but also in the Spirit-infused experiences of everyday life. One of these everyday forums is our work. Miroslav Volf says that the church needs a pneumatological theology of work, in which *charisma* is the foundation for our work, and which helps us see how the Spirit of God fills our working lives that they might cooperate with God in his preservation, salvation, and transformation of the world.[92] The Spirit empowers our daily lives of work, play, rest, parenting, commuting, relating, and so on, for the sake of the glory of the Father and the mission of Jesus Christ. We encounter the Spirit in our human relationships, in our duties fulfilled, in our bitterness and enmities relinquished, in our ethics upheld, in our failings and weaknesses, in our human sexuality, and in our attention to the Spirit in the ordinary, mundane, and everyday experiences.[93] In those ordinary moments and experiences of the Spirit (if one might consider them "ordinary" given their depth of meaning), the Spirit shows us not only how to love, obey, and worship Christ, but also how to witness to him in every dimension of our lives. We discover in these ordinary, daily settings, *and* in our explicit, intentional mission, the way in which the Spirit is shaping our whole lives to be a living testimony to Jesus Christ. The Spirit empowers and equips the whole Christian to take the whole gospel to the whole world.

Jürgen Moltmann has written two important works on pneumatology, in which he outlines the implications of the Spirit as the "source of life" for a contemporary "theology of life."[94] In that work, he wrote that the mission of the Spirit is to empower the church to proclaim the gospel, that women and men might come to a personal faith redemption and discipleship, and to lead people into Christian community and a Christian social ethic. Moltmann claims, however, that while these things are important, the mission of God is not limited to them. He blames the *filioque* for limiting western theological thought to the Spirit of redemptive activity, instead of opening it up to an expansive theology of the Spirit in creation and the world.[95] The Spirit has a "mission of life" in the world, which the church is caught up in, including ministry in the darkest, loneliest, most fraught spheres of human culture and society. This "mission of life" is about the spread of the kingdom of God and the advancement of the *missio Dei*—not the mere expansion of the church. The church is important in God's eschatological purposes and is shaped as a missional community because of, and for the sake of, the mission of God. However, the church does not exist for the sake of its own expansion or glory. It exists for the gospel of Jesus Christ, the advancement of God's kingdom, and the glorification of the triune God. The church participates in the "mission of life," as the Holy Spirit, who is the "source of life,"

92. Volf, *Work in the Spirit*, 88–122.

93. Rahner et al., *Content of Faith*, 367–74; Rahner, *Spirit in the Church*, 1–31.

94. Moltmann, *Source of Life*; Moltmann, *Spirit of Life*. He also deals with the relationship between pneumatology and ecclesiology in: Moltmann, *Church in the Power*, 197–336; Moltmann, *Trinity*.

95. Moltmann, *Spirit of Life*, 306–9.

"goes ahead of the church's mission to the world."[96] According to Moltmann, the mission of the triune God is to renew and restore human beings, peoples, cultures, the church, and creation—the mission of God is to *bring life*. Wherever passion, hope, love, and effort for life exist, the Spirit of God is present, ministering in those places for the sake of God's eschatological, cosmic purposes.

A robust missional ecclesiology must have solid pneumatological foundations. The Spirit creates, fills, sustains, chastens, baptizes, comforts, and empowers the church. The Spirit enables the church to follow the messianic mission of Jesus Christ, to be his body and bride, and to participate in the *missio Dei* in human history. The charismatic structure and missiological expressions of the church are the result of God's empowering presence in its nature, structures, ministries, and mission. However, the Spirit does not just enable, empower, or vivify the church—he constitutes the church, creating its very being. In John Zizioulas's words, "The Spirit makes the Church be . . . Pneumatology does not refer to the well-being but to the very being of the Church . . . Pneumatology is an ontological category in ecclesiology."[97] Or, as John Webster puts it, "The Spirit's life-giving and revelatory agency is fundamental to the church's being, including its visibility in creaturely time and space. The church is and is visible because God the Holy Spirit is and acts."[98]

QUESTIONS FOR REFLECTION

1. How can the *spiritual gifts* be used as *missional gifts and graces* in your church?

2. How do we recognize the presence of the Spirit beyond the walls of the church—in popular spirituality, contemporary spiritual quests, postmodern and consumer culture, film and media, sports and recreation, etc.? How do we collaborate with the Spirit and participate in what God is already doing in those places?

3. What practical things can your church do to align its *formal leadership structures* with its *charismatic/pneumatological structure*?

96. Moltmann, *Source of Life*, 10–25.
97. Zizioulas, *Being as Communion*, 132.
98. Webster, "Visible Attests," 104.

17

The Trinity-Imaging Church:
Reflecting Trinitarian Communion and Mission

The theology of the missio Dei defines the church within the framework of the doctrine of the Triune God. David Bosch has described this theological consensus succinctly, explaining that mission "is understood as being derived from the very nature of God. It was thus put in the context of the doctrine of the Trinity" . . . To be authentically evangelical, I repeat, our ecclesiology must be missional . . . Rooted in the trinitarian nature and action of God, this ecclesiology derives its purpose from God's mission.[1]

—DARRELL GUDER

Based on the premise that nature and action are inextricably linked . . . any construal of missional theology as the church's participation in the missio Dei, cannot disregard the doctrine of the immanent Trinity . . . The perichoretic model of the Trinity points to the inseparability of the missio Dei and the imago Dei, being and doing, the self and the Other. The oneness of the divine mission implies an integral missionary praxis that is rooted in the worship of this Triune God.[2]

—SENG-KONG TAN

TRINITARIAN THEOLOGY IS INDISPENSIBLE for a meaningful understanding of the missional church. All missional ecclesiology is located in the context of the redemptive, eschatological mission of the triune God. Each member of the Trinity is involved in the triune God's missional action and nature. We observe this throughout salvation history and in God's redemptive purposes for all creation. The Spirit empowers the church to pursue, faithfully and passionately, the mission of the triune God.[3]

---

1. Husbands and Treir, *Community of the Word*, 124–26.
2. Tan, "Trinitarian Ontology," 279.
3. Van Gelder, *Essence of the Church*, 33.

To construct a trinitarian understanding of the missional church, we need to consider the *correspondence* and *difference* between the trinitarian nature of God and the communing, missional nature of the church. We also need to reflect on the missional implications of *both* the economic and the immanent Trinity on our ecclesiology.[4] As Karl Rahner's famous axiom asserts, "The *economic* Trinity is the *immanent* Trinity and the *immanent* Trinity is the *economic* Trinity."[5] Put simply, the *immanent Trinity* describes the nature or essence of God—who God *is in himself*—his ontological, eternal, social being. The *economic Trinity* describes "how God is *known to us*" or "how God is *for us*"—how each person of the Trinity has characteristics, roles, and functions in human history and in the economy of salvation.[6] The immanent Trinity and the economic Trinity are, of course, the same Trinity. Therefore, it is misleading to talk about either of these two dimensions of our understanding of the Trinity in isolation from each other—both dimensions have implications for a missional ecclesiology. The immanent Trinity and economic Trinity are, however, distinguishable, and are useful ideas for understanding the nature, functions, and relations of the trinitarian persons, and the corresponding realities of the church.

Missional ecclesiology is shaped with attention to the interior life of the Trinity (the social or immanent Trinity) *and* the acts, roles, and functions of the trinitarian persons in history and in the economy of salvation (the economic Trinity). The social reality of the Trinity, especially as revealed in a theology of the immanent Trinity, has potential for helping us appreciate the social community of the church (the correspondence is important but, as Miroslav Volf reminds us, there are limitations to the analogy).[7] Likewise, the functions of each member of the Trinity in the mission of God help us understand the missional nature of the church "within creation, re-creation, and the final consummation."[8] The sending activity and the missional nature of the triune God are the source of the church's mission. The Father sends the Son, the Father and Son send the Spirit, and the Trinity sends the church missionally into the world. "This perspective helps us understand the creation of a church in light of God's being, God's social reality as a Trinity, and the work of all three persons. The ministry of the church, in turn, must reflect all three aspects of the Godhead."[9]

Trinitarian themes are not as prevalent in the missional church literature as the themes dealt with in the previous three chapters of this book. I am concerned that trinitarian thought is alarmingly absent in missional ecclesiology. When considering missional ecclesiology as a theological discipline, we might lament with Karl Rahner that,

4. The *immanent* Trinity is sometimes called the *ontological, eternal,* or *social* Trinity, depending on the author.

5. Rahner, *Trinity,* 22. Rahner means that *in the economy of salvation* we understand and experience *who God eternally, ontologically, and really is.* Therefore, the economic Trinity is the immanent Trinity, and vice versa. For explorations of the possibilities, limits, and theological implications of Karl Rahner's rule, including descriptions of those theologians that extend or restrict this rule, see Sanders, *Image of the Immanent Trinity.* Jürgen Moltmann extends Karl Rahner's rule in: Moltmann, *Trinity,* 154, 160.

6. Zizioulas, *Lectures in Dogmatics,* 69; McGrath, *Christian Theology,* 296.

7. Volf, *After Our Likeness,* 198–200.

8. Van Gelder, *Essence of the Church,* 35, 97.

9. Ibid., 130.

"Should the doctrine of the Trinity have to be dropped as false, the major part of religious [missional] literature could well remain virtually unchanged."[10]

Trinitarian perspectives are now widely discussed in the broader ecclesiological literature, since in the last four decades there has been a resurgence of interest in trinitarian theology (thanks, largely, to the groundbreaking work of Karl Barth and Karl Rahner which inspired this trinitarian doctrinal renaissance). Many of the twelve comparative ecclesiologists in this book have important things to say about the relationship between trinitarian theology and the church. It is my contention that trinitarian considerations can no longer remain sparse in missional ecclesiology. David Bosch, Stephen Bevans, Roger Schroeder, and Lesslie Newbigin have of course dealt with trinitarian themes and the mission of the church. Their explicit work on the relationship between trinitarian theology and the mission of the church is introductory, however, and there is a real need for others to continue the work they began. Trinitarian perspectives are central to many contemporary understandings of the nature and expressions of the church, and it is time that they were more fully explored for the missional nature, purpose, and activities of the church.

Pete Ward is an example of a theologian who has taken up this challenge. He uses the notion of *perichoresis* to describe how the relationships in the Trinity draw our mission and worship into "the divine trinitarian dance of God." These divine relations shape our understanding of the "dancing flow of relationship" in our Christian communities and lead us away from individualism and monolithic institutionalism. "The static monolith of the congregation is replaced by a dynamic, inclusive, and fluid dance of intimate communication."[11] While space does not allow me to provide a thorough trinitarian theology for the missional church in this book, my hope is that this chapter will contribute to an ongoing conversation, which others will take further.

Trinitarian themes can too often be abstract and removed from the concrete realities of the church. The abstraction that accompanies trinitarian theology can sometimes be unhelpful for ecclesiology. It would seem that other biblical and theological notions have more immediate and obvious relevance for ecclesiology, ministry, and mission. However, we should not discount the relevance or implications of trinitarian theology for our understanding of the church. Karl Rahner laments that, despite the importance of the doctrine of the Trinity for a distinctively Christian faith and theology, "Christians are, in their practical life, almost mere 'monotheists.'"[12] The communion and mission of the Trinity can shape a fuller understanding of the communion and mission of the church. However, these trinitarian reflections must remain in critical dialogue with other biblical and theological understandings—especially those that have immediate and explicit implications for the nature, structure, purpose, and mission of the church.

It is possible to come up with many examples of how "a trinitarian understanding is now the common starting point for thinking about God's people in the world, about the

---

10. Rahner, *Trinity*, 10–11. The word *missional* is added here to emphasize my point.

11. Ward, *Liquid Church*, 49–55.

12. Rahner, *Trinity*, 10.

church, and about how the church participates in God's mission in the world."[13] I agree with Craig Van Gelder when he asserts that ecclesiology and missiology are not only "interrelated and complementary"; they are both grounded in the doctrine of the Trinity, "the Triune God in mission to all creation."[14] In this chapter, therefore, I consider some of the implications of trinitarian theology for missional ecclesiology.

THE COMMUNION AND MISSION OF THE TRINITY

The doctrine of the Trinity declares that although God is *one substance*, he exists in three *persons*, being Father, Son, and Holy Spirit—these persons *exist in and for* each other, in a relationship of intersubjectivity, "mutuality, and reciprocity."[15] This Trinity, although each maintains concrete *persona*, exist in *perichoresis*. *Perichoresis* is a Greek word indicating "reciprocation, interpenetration, mutual inexistence."[16] The German phrase *nebenein-ander, ineinander, miteinander* describes the three divine persons as being, "next to one another, in one another, and with one another." The Athanasian Creed proclaims that in the Christian faith "we worship one God in Trinity and Trinity in unity, without either confusing the persons or dividing the substance."[17] All that God is, in the essence of his divine nature, is wholly in each of the three persons, for God is one being but not one person. In the Trinity we see three persons in one being, who are unified in harmonious, eternal relations. Perfect intimacy exists between the persons of the Godhead. The immersion within the Godhead is one of ultimate and reciprocal dedication, respect, and love. The idea of *perichoresis* illustrates this well—the Trinity exists in mutual interpenetration, mutual inexistence, reciprocation, love, purpose, and harmony.[18] John of Damascus declared "each person has being in each other without any coalescence."[19]

Unity and oneness permeate the Trinity. The triune God *is* relations.[20] The people of God are the beneficiaries of the relationship of love, intimacy, and communion between the persons of the Godhead. The redemptive mission of Jesus Christ is connected with his deep love for the Father, and with his longing to fulfill his Father's purposes. In the Godhead, we see the highest example of self-sacrifice and mutual dedication, as three

13. Van Gelder, *Essence of the Church*, 11.

14. Ibid., 31.

15. Pinnock, *Flame of Love*, 36.

16. Fortman, *The Triune God*, 363.

17. Zwiefalten version.

18. "The oneness of God is not the oneness of a distinct, self-contained individual; it is the unity of a *community* of persons who love each other and live together in harmony . . . They are what they are only in relation with one another. Each only exists in this relationship and would not exist apart from it. Father, Son, and Holy Spirit live only in and with and through each other, eternally united in mutual love and shared purpose. Behind this understanding of the Trinity lies . . . the *perichoresis* doctrine." Guthrie, *Christian Doctrine*, 92–3. Jürgen Moltmann puts it this way, "The unity of the triunity lies in the eternal perichoresis of the trinitarian persons. Interpreted perichoretically, the trinitarian persons form their own unity by themselves in the circulation of the divine life." Moltmann, *Trinity*, 175.

19. Elwell, *Concise Evangelical Dictionary*, 381.

20. Cunningham, *These Three*, 71.

divine persons exist in perfect harmony and unity, sharing the same divine faculties and power. John Zizioulas says,

> The phrase 'God is love' means that God is constituted by these personal rela-
> tionships. God is communion: love is fundamental to his being, not an addition
> to it . . . That 'God is love' means that God is the communion of this Holy Trinity
> . . . If we took away the communion of the Trinity to make God a unit, God
> would not be communion and therefore would not be love.[21]

The interior life of the Trinity can help us understand the nature and potential of communion among God's people. The love, intimacy, unity, and embrace of the members of the Trinity provide a model or analogy for the church—here I am referring to the notion of the immanent (ontological) Trinity. As Miroslav Volf reminds his readers, there are ways in which ecclesial communion corresponds to trinitarian communion, and there are limitations to the analogy. Volf's trinitarian ecclesiology affects his understanding of communion within local churches, the nature of human personhood, and the structure of ecclesial relationships. The Trinity is his determining analogy for the nature of the church. I believe that Volf is right when he says that the trinitarian analogy should shape the church's self-understanding, ecclesial life, and depth of love, *and* help her navigate the complexities and paradoxes of unity and multiplicity, as she *images the Trinity*.[22] The love and communion between Christians and churches should correspond, as far as creaturely possible, to the trinitarian relations.

John Webster is critical of some aspects of communion ecclesiology. He rightly demonstrates how the communing nature of the church is a direct result of the gospel, and that this gospel precedes the church's essential nature, its interpersonal and divine-human communion, and its ecclesial forms, structures, practices, and mission. This is the gospel of the triune God, "out of the plenitude and limitless perfection of his own self-originating life as Father, Son, and Spirit," reaching out in history to redeem humanity. Because of God's grace and perfection, he directs human beings to "attain their end, which is fellowship with the Father, through the Son, and in the Spirit." The church's communion and its ecclesial nature are a direct result of the gospel. Therefore, while we consider the joy of communion with each other and with God, we must never forget the correct progression. The perfect, triune God reaches out to humanity according to his grace and purpose, in the historical movements of the Father, Son, and Spirit, and especially in the historical life, death, resurrection, and final glorification of Jesus Christ. Because of the triune God's actions in history, and of his willingness to invite us into his "own self-originating life," human beings can be redeemed and sanctified, enjoying communion with each other and with God. "A theology of the church needs to be undergirded by a theology of divine perfection; this is accomplished by tying ecclesiology to election, thus generating an account

---

21. Zizioulas, *Lectures in Dogmatics*, 53. He goes on to write, "God is love in his very being. It is not however himself that he loves, so this is not self-love. The Father loves the Son, the Son loves the Father and the Spirit, the Spirit loves the Father and the Son: it is another person that each loves. It is the person, not the nature or essence, who loves, and the one he loves is also a person. Because divine love is a matter of personal communion this love is free: each person loved is free to respond to this love with love." Ibid., 53–54.

22. Volf, *After Our Likeness*, 194–97.

of the church as differentiated, asymmetrical fellowship with God." It is my contention here that John Webster's correction of some of the excesses and theological orientations of communion ecclesiology is a sound one, which challenges us to put communion in its rightful context in relation to God's perfection, divine election and the gospel of salvation, and other evangelical commitments.[23]

This leads us to the trinitarian ground of mission and the trinitarian foundations of the missional life of the church. The communion and mission of the Trinity are inextricably linked. We cannot afford to consider them as separate dimensions of God, or as separate realities shaping disconnected dimensions of ecclesiology or the church's mission. This is because the mission of the triune God is to bring humanity back into communion with the Father, Son, and Holy Spirit. Moreover, the communion within the triune God is the source or wellspring of his divine mission, and the mission of the triune God is directed toward his divine communion. In other words, *the communion of the triune God is the mission of the triune God, and the mission of the triune God is the communion of the triune God.* Again, God's being-in-communion is God's being-on-mission, and God's being-on-mission is God's being-in-communion.

Missional ecclesiology claims that this trinitarian dynamic is reflected in the church—the church's being-in-communion is the church's being-on-mission, and vice versa. For the church, *there is no true communion without mission, and no true mission without communion.* Put simply, Scripture does not allow for a mission that is separate from a community-on-mission, or for a community that is separate from a missional community. To separate or juxtapose communion and mission is a grave error.

We could demonstrate and defend the claim that the communion of the triune God is the mission of the triune God, and vice versa, in a number of ways. One approach—and I am not suggesting that this is the only approach—is to look at the passages of Scripture that indicate the trinitarian nature of God (or at least the distinct persons within the Godhead and their relations with each other), and notice how the communion and mission of God are interconnected. Take a few select passages from the Gospel of John, for example.[24] This gospel has noteworthy passages that support the doctrine of the Trinity. They provide insight into the relationships between the Father, Son, and Holy Spirit, and how this divine trinitarian communion is deeply and inseparably connected to the divine trinitarian mission:

- John 1:1–5: Deity, involvement in creation, eternal existence, distinction from God (*the Word was with God*), and oneness with God (*the Word was God*), are all attributed to Jesus Christ in this passage. Notice how John quickly moves from a description of the deity of Jesus Christ and his unity with the Father, to the missional, redemptive nature and ministry of Jesus: "In him was life, and that life was the light of all people. The light shines in the darkness, and the darkness has not overcome it."

23. Webster, *Confessing God*, 153–93, 197–201.

24. I could have chosen other books of the Bible (and their applicable passages) to demonstrate this point, of course, but the Gospel of John will have to suffice at this time, given the limitations of space. All quotations are from Today's New International Version.

- John 1:14, 18: The Incarnation illustrates Christ's distinction from the Father (*who came from the Father*), and his oneness with the Father (*God the one and only Son*). Jesus's oneness with the Father is directly linked with his incarnational mission, his demonstration of "truth and grace," and his revelation of both the nature and mission of God.

- John 5:17–30: The deity of the Son and the unity of the Father and the Son are clear in this passage. Notice that this unity and the mission of God are woven together. The Son relies on the Father, only doing what the Father does. Amidst this extraordinary description of the communion between the Father and the Son are descriptions of the life-giving, judging, incarnational, redemptive, eschatological mission of God. The gospel of Jesus Christ is embedded in the intimate, reciprocal union of the Father and the Son.

- John 14:6–11: The unity of the Father and Son is evident in this passage (*anyone who has seen me has seen the Father*), and yet their distinctive persons are still maintained (*no one comes to the Father except through me*). Verses 6 and 7 show the deep connection between the mission of God and the communion between the Father and the Son—and they reveal how the mission of the triune God is to bring women and men back into communion with God himself. The communion of the triune God is the source of the mission of the triune God, and the mission of the Son is to bring women and men into restored communion with the Father. The gospel of salvation is richly embedded in the union of the Father and the Son—in fact, the gospel is presented to humanity through the movements or processions of the trinitarian persons, so that human beings might believe and obey that gospel and, thereby, enter into restored communion with the eternally communing Father, Son, and Holy Spirit.

- John 14:15–21: "If you love me, keep my commands [*the Son*]. And I will ask the Father, and he [*the Father*] will give you another advocate [*the Holy Spirit*] to help you and be with you forever—the Spirit of truth." Together the Father, Son, and Holy Spirit give the disciple and the church the power to obey "what I command." As the church continues the mission of Jesus Christ, the Father sends his empowering Presence, the Holy Spirit, and the church's mission and unity are caught up in the mission and unity of the triune God. "On that day you will realize that I am in my Father, and you are in me, and I am in you."

- John 15:26: The Father, Son, and Holy Spirit are portrayed as one in purpose and mission in this verse, as the missional processions within the triune God are a testimony to Jesus. The church is caught up in the loving relations and missional intent and actions of the Trinity and, like the Spirit, testifies to the saving person and work of Jesus Christ.

- John 16:5–16: In this passage, we see a remarkable inter-relation, intimacy, and communion between the Father, Son, and Holy Spirit (especially verses 13–15). This communion of love is generously extended toward Christian believers and the church, drawing them up into the trinitarian communion. Notice, however, that we learn of this trinitarian communion in its inseparable connection with the trinitarian mission. Each member of the Trinity has a role to play in the economy of salvation, in the eschatological mission of the triune God—as humanity is confronted with sin, righteousness, and judgment, and a choice whether to accept the saving truth of the gospel of Jesus Christ. From the communion of God emerges the mission of God, and the mission of God leads women and men toward the communion of God. The two are so deeply connected as to be inextricable. Trinitarian *communion is mission*, and trinitarian *mission is communion*.

• John 17: In this chapter we again see the divine love, common purpose, and astonishing unity of the members of the Trinity. The church is embraced by this loving Trinity as through the ministry of the Trinity they become one, "just as you are in me and I am in you. May they also be in us *so that the world may believe that you have sent me*." The unity within the church and the union between the church and the Trinity are for the sake of *communion* and for the sake of *mission*. Both themes are present in this passage because they are inseparable. The love, intimacy, and embrace of the members of the Trinity are directed, by God's grace, toward the church, especially in the context of his eschatological mission in human history. "As you have sent me into the world, I have sent them into the world . . . I have given them the glory that you gave me, that they may be one as we are one—I in them and you in me—so that they may be brought to complete unity. Then the world will know that you sent me and have loved them even as you have loved me."[25]

• John 20:21–22: Father, Son, and Holy Spirit are *united* in a process of *missional sending*—the Father sending the Son, the Father and Son sending the Spirit, and the Son sending the church into the world. In Newbigin's words, mission can be understood "as proclaiming the kingdom of the Father, as sharing the life of the Son, and as bearing the witness of the Spirit."[26]

After considering the "priority of relationality" in contemporary trinitarian thought, John Franke concludes that, "God is missional by nature. The love of God lived out and expressed in the context of the eternal community of love gives rise to the missional character of God, who seeks to extend the love shared by Father, Son, and Holy Spirit into the created order."[27] This divine community of love is also a community of mission, and these two dimensions of the triune God shape the church's nature, structure, and actions.

25. John 17:18, 22–23. Moltmann writes on John 17, "The unity of the community is in truth the trinitarian fellowship of God himself, of which it is a reflection and in which it participates . . . The community is the 'lived out' Trinity. In the community, that mutual love is practiced which corresponds to the eternal love of the Trinity." Moltmann, *History and the Triune*, 63–64.

26. Newbigin, *Open Secret*, 29. Newbigin's treatment of a trinitarian theology of mission can be found in: Newbigin, *Trinitarian Doctrine*; Newbigin, *Open Secret*.

27. Franke, "God Is Love," 113, 119.

APPLYING TRINITARIAN THOUGHT TO MISSIONAL ECCLESIOLOGY

What are the implications of the trinitarian mission and communion for missional eccle-siology? I apply trinitarian theology here to the nature and mission of the church in the following progression: *Personhood, Community, Theology, World,* and *Mission*.

REVEALING AUTHENTIC PERSONHOOD

Trinitarian perspectives help reveal the true nature of human personhood. They enrich missional ecclesiology's understandings of the essence of human nature and the role of the church in faith, discipleship, and human flourishing. Miroslav Volf's Free Church ecclesiology, for instance, is centered on trinitarian theology. This trinitarian thought influences his theology of personhood. Volf critiques Free Church and Episcopal ecclesi-ology in a way that elevates his own particular ecclesiological conclusions when he sug-gests, "both models underestimate the enormous ecclesiological significance of concrete relations with other Christians."[28]

According to Volf, these two dynamics are inseparably interrelated and interwo-ven—individual faith in and relationship with Jesus Christ, and interpersonal, eccle-sial mediation of that faith through authentic immersion in Christian community.[29] Individual acceptance of salvation and faith through the person and work of Jesus Christ is not diminished in Volf's theological anthropology. However, he also emphasizes: (1) The impossibility of authentic faith outside the interpersonal communion, discipleship, and accountability experienced in a concrete Christian community; (2) The transmission of faith "through interpersonal ecclesial interaction," and; (3) The necessity of the local church community for nurturing a full and rich faith and personhood.[30]

The ecclesiological and anthropological insights developed by Volf in these perspec-tives can inform missional ecclesiology. Missional ecclesiology is inadequate unless it de-velops a theology of human personhood, and connects such a theological anthropology to its perspectives on the nurturing of faith in concrete Christian communities. A lot of the missional literature deals with the nature of Christian communities, including their missionality, ecclesial structures, multiplication, forms of worship, and the like. However, missional ecclesiology cannot afford to ignore such matters as theological anthropology, the development of faith through participation in local worshipping faith communities, or the connection between theological anthropology and missional ecclesiology.

When one reads Miroslav Volf, it becomes clear that it is not enough to suggest that all believers are gifted for ministry and should be equipped for mission. Missional ecclesiol-ogy must seriously consider the relationship between individual faith and the interpersonal, ecclesial mediation of faith. "In the complex ecclesial reality of *all* churches, the relation of individuals to the church depends on their relation to Christ, just as their relation to Christ

---

28. Volf, *After Our Likeness*, 134.

29. Ibid., 159.

30. Ibid., 172.

depends on their relation to the church; the two relations are mutually determinative."[31] Volf's perspectives on these matters enrich a missional theology of the church.

Human beings, in Christian theology, are created, relational beings. The Genesis account describes human beings as being created by God in his relational image—not self-sufficient, but relational and interdependent. We are formed from "dust," not as a closed historical event, but as process. Not only are we fashioned from "clay" by our Creator at our conception—our entire lives are a testimony to the process of renewal and divine creativity. To be a creature is to be shaped by God from nothing, and to be birthed into a process of being called and created, so that we might fulfill our God-ordained purpose, to glorify and praise God. We are continually being created and, of course, are firmly located within the created order. God continually forms and sustains creation parentally, and human beings are a part of creation, enjoying the filial care and concern of the Creator Father. Humanity, though at times deluded by visions of grandeur, self-sufficiency, or transcendence, is not self-made, but is continually created out of the abundance of God's immeasurable love, sovereignty, and grace. Humanity, formed by God and located within the world, is interdependent, not merely sharing the origins of other created things, but being woven into the fabric of the created order in mysterious and inexplicable ways— there is no room for Gnostic-like disembodied spirituality in Christian theology. Human sexuality evidences this. We share the realities of gender, reproduction, sexual appetite, and sexual differentiation with other living creatures, and, like other living things, these elements of sexuality are highly prone to abuse, environmental factors, power and gender relationships, genetic influences, time and space, socialization, fear and intimidation, pleasure and freewill, individuality, ambiguity, fluidity, and mystery. Our sexuality testifies to our location within the created order. This embodiment witnesses to the web of relationships that all created things share in, and so the pathological urge to live as disembodied, spiritual beings or, conversely, to indulge in animalistic, impersonal sexual practices or other forms of hedonism and self-indulgence, is to deny our Trinity-reflecting relationality, and to live without communication, communion, or genuine life. Both ends of the spectrum are dualistic, failing to appreciate humanity's relational embedding in creation, failing to appreciate our creation in the image of the Trinity, and failing to appreciate how the movements of the Trinity value our embodiment and physicality.

As created beings the created order, or the "world," is the theatre in which our lives unfold—sexuality, work, family, commitments, spirituality, politics, society, suffering, ecology, achievement, failure, creative arts, and the like—even though throughout history the human response to this reality has been mixed, hostile, ambiguous, and sometimes gnostically oriented. Religious and spiritual movements have fluctuated between the poles of the deification of the sensual and the repulsion of all things "unspiritual," and have often sought to enable adherents to escape the worldly realities of birth, death, sexuality, and human society. In the historical and eschatological significance of the movements and actions of the persons of the Trinity, we are affirmed as created beings, and the created order is itself honored, as the triune God comes into our created context to redeem, sanctify, save, and heal.

---

31. Ibid., 159.

In the Incarnation, for instance, Christ reveals his ongoing relationship to creation, which includes humankind, and his willingness to purposefully engage with (or use) the contours of creation—being, time, space, and matter. Human nature, essence, and being are radically liberated and graced by the immanence (and transcendence) of the historical actions of the persons of the Trinity, and by the in-breaking work of Christ in the Incarnation, crucifixion, and resurrection. In assuming human form, God unambiguously and forcefully declared creation to be good, humanity to be of incredible value, and salvation to be located in our humanity, as all of creation is redeemed without altering its essence (I am not diminishing the realities of humanity's sin, rebellion, and brokenness here).

Glorification of the triune God is the creation's ultimate purpose—along with relational, non-subsumed union with the same. Creation's future is to be revealed as the kingdom of glory, praise, and exaltation of the Trinity. The history of humanity and creation, past, present, and future, is the history of the triune God demonstrating his grace and glory among us. Humanity, as part of creation, is compelled to glorify God along with the rest of creation. The church desperately needs a trinitarian theology of the human person (that is, a trinitarian anthropology that informs that church's fellowship, mission, structure, and engagement with sexuality, institutions, systems, cultures, and societies), if it is to cultivate communities of mission and rich human fellowship, and if it is to nurture disciples.

ENRICHING CHRISTIAN COMMUNITY

Ecclesiology is conceived relationally, rather than hierarchically, in the light of trinitarian considerations. Such ecclesiology becomes attentive to the restoration of human community and divine-human communion. Rather than reflecting "a monarchical view of the Trinity that is monotheistic, modalistic, and subordinate"[32] in its ecclesial institutions, missional ecclesiology calls the church to displays of love, mutuality, and non-hierarchical expressions of leadership and governance, which image the Trinity.

According to Jürgen Moltmann, the Social Trinity emphasizes unity through relationship and has real implications for ecclesial community. He writes,

> By virtue of their eternal love they live in one another to such an extent, and dwell in one another to such an extent, that they are one. It is a process of most perfect and intense empathy . . . The doctrine of the perichoresis links together in a brilliant way the threeness and the unity, without reducing their threeness to the unity, or dissolving the unity in the threeness. The unity of the triunity lies in the eternal perichoresis of the trinitarian persons. Interpreted perichoretically, the trinitarian persons form their own unity by themselves in the circulation of the divine life.[33]

> True human fellowship is to correspond to the Triune God and be his image on earth. True human fellowship will participate in the inner life of the Triune God.[34]

32. Spence, *Trinity: Part One*, 8.

33. Moltmann, *The Trinity*, 175.

34. Moltmann, *History and the Triune*, 60. Moltmann claims that western trinitarian thought is too often a form of "monotheistic monarchianism." He singles out the theology of Tertullian, Barth, and Rahner for examination. Moltmann then attempts to construct an alternative approach around the Social Trinity, in-

Mutual submission and servant leadership are preferable to forms of ecclesial institutionalism or hierarchy that express themselves oppressively—whether they are episcopal, presbyterian, congregational, or another form of governance. Mutual giving and receiving, framed within a spirit of humility and self-sacrifice, characterizes missional communities that evidence trinitarian values. Miroslav Volf puts it this way,

> When we give, we often engage in rivalries and set up hierarchies. But when gifts circulate within the Godhead, no rivalry happens; and hierarchy is not reaffirmed. The one who gives is not greater than the one who receives, for all give and all receive. Each gives glory to the other with each gift given . . . Like gifts among divine persons, human gifts should express and foster equality.[35]

Not all hierarchy or institution is necessarily oppressive or constraining. Within every form of church polity there are those who seek a trinitarian balance between functional and institutional authority on the one hand, and genuine collegiality, mutuality, and equality on the other. Following the biblical pattern, missional ecclesiology challenges the whole congregation to explore their diversity and multiplicity of gifting and contributions, while maintaining unity. Worship should be conducted through a trinitarian paradigm, "power must be seen as a flowing perichoretically through the community," and both "unity and multiplicity" are to be embraced.[36] However, mutuality and deep relationship do not diminish the need for mutual obligations and ministerial functions in the church.

As human beings we are "called into community" and "this is understandable if relationships are what ultimately matter, and the Triune God who creates the community is himself communal. Here, the social analogy of the Trinity is stimulating. In our church life, this must be a dominant value. True spirituality is expressed in Triune-Godlike relationships."[37] Cornelius Plantinga notes that the implications are far reaching for human relationships in the church if we are to image God in our relationships and be baptized into the family of the triune God.

> In our fellowship and *koinonia*, in such homely endeavors as telling one another the truth or in doing such honest work as will help those in need—above all in that love which "binds everything together in perfect harmony"—we show not only that we have become members one of another, but also that we are restored community, we-in-the-plural, have become a remarkable image of God . . . Race, class, sex, and other alienations are transformed into delightful complementaries, so that we may know and respect the other as other, but as co-other, loved other, fellow family members . . . Baptism in the threefold name marks the adoption of human beings into the joy and warmth of the family of God . . . If some member should be abused or

---

cluding its implications for Christian faith and the church. Cunningham is critical of Moltmann's high levels of trinitarian abstraction, however, and is unconvinced that Moltmann has demonstrated the relevance of his approach for the church. Moltmann, *Trinity*, 129–90; Cunningham, *These Three*, 42–43. For a considered response to Moltmann's critics, and to those who are critical of social trinitarian thought, see McDougall, "Return of Trinitarian Praxis?"

35. Volf, "Being as God Is," 10–11. See Volf, *After Our Likeness*, 214–17.

36. Spence, *Trinity: Part Two*, 13; Volf, *After Our Likeness*, 193.

37. Davidson, *Living as Trinitarian*, 4.

diminished by other Christians, we oppose this injustice . . . because it a desecration of the communal sacrament.[38]

Miroslav Volf says that the correspondence between the ecclesial and trinitarian communions can be seen in the following dimensions of the church's life together:

- Trinitarian theology does away with the "dichotomy between univer-salization and pluralization," since it embraces "unity and multiplicity" at once. Our churches and ecclesial institutions struggle to keep up with this reality. Nevertheless, we should consistently think in such trinitarian terms, because of the biblical witness. This is a helpful challenge to missional ecclesiology, as it seeks to minister to and through largely post-denominational persons, and to do mission in a pluralistic and multicultural society.[39]

- Missional communities seeking to form rich interpersonal relation-ships within their own churches, and between themselves and other groups, can pursue "ecclesial correspondence to the Trinity" as "an object of hope and thus also a task for human beings."[40] Human beings (interpersonally) and churches as gatherings of persons (inter-ecclesially) cannot be internal to one another in the same way the divine persons are internal to each other (perichoretically). However, in "mutual giving and receiving, we give to others not only something, but also a piece of ourselves, something of that which we have made of ourselves in communion with others; and from others we take not only something, but also a piece of them."[41]

- According to Volf, Free Church polity and ecclesiology tend to move away from trinitarian thought due to innate individualism, volunteerism, and emphasis on Christology.[42] This can be seen, at times, in the contemporary litera-ture on missional ecclesiology, and especially that work written by Free Church authors. However, "a trinitarian reshaping of Free Church ecclesiology" has worthwhile implications and enhancements for missional ecclesiology, as this chapter demonstrates.[43]

- The correspondence between ecclesial and trinitarian relations should be manifest in such things as valuing of the gifts and ministries of others, unity of heart and mind, and gracious, non-hierarchical forms of leadership and gov-ernance. Catholic, Orthodox, and Magisterial ecclesiologists might disagree with Volf on this point, since it implies that non-Free Church forms of leadership and governance do not manifest the communion and unity of trinitarian relations. That is true if those forms of governance and ministry are seen solely as *power over*, but if they are seen as nourishing and deepening the life of the community,

38. Plantinga, "Perfect Family," 27. See Plantinga, "Social Trinity."

39. Volf, *After Our Likeness*, 193.

40. Ibid., 195.

41. Ibid., 211.

42. Ibid., 196.

43. Ibid., 197.

namely *power for and with*, they can also share in trinitarian love and relatedness. Volf's understandings illustrate the convictions of his Free Church ecclesiology.

It is clear that the connections one makes between trinitarian theology and ecclesiology depend on theological tradition, personal preference, and the era in which one is writing. Miroslav Volf, of course, makes much of the correspondence (and limitations) of the trinitarian analogy. Addressing the limitations, he cautions his readers not to "*overestimate* the influence of trinitarian thinking on political and ecclesial reality."[44] For Volf, while trinitarian thinking holds great promise for understanding the nature of the church and of human relationships, the "conceptualization process" does not simply proceed "in a straight line from above (Trinity) to below (church and society)" or that "social reality is shaped in this way."[45] One has to be aware of the limitations of the trinitarian analogy, of the frailties of real people and their churches, and, yet, in the presence of these realities, reflect theologically on the implications of the Trinity for mission, faith, human community and personhood, and church.[46]

Understanding and Celebrating People as Humans-in-Community

The doctrine of the Trinity encourages Christians to think theologically about God as dynamic and relational, rather than static and individual.[47] This is because "the oneness of God is not the oneness of a distinct, self-contained individual; it is the unity of a *community* of persons who love each other and live together in harmony . . . They are what they are only in relation with one another."[48] God is "wholly constituted by relationality, in other words, God is not (first) three independent entities who (then) decide to come into relation with one another; God, is, rather, 'relationship without remainder' . . . Three participate in one another in a profound way, undermining any attempt to understand them independently of one another."[49]

From this emerges the notion of *perichoresis*—as each person of the Trinity exists *in* and *for* the other they are in perfect relationship, and must be worshipped and approached as One.[50] Each member of the trinitarian persons has "their Being in each other and reciprocally contains one another, without any coalescing or commingling with one another and yet without any separation from one another . . . God is known only in a circle of reciprocal

---

44. Ibid., 194.

45. Ibid. For Volf, while the church should be modeled on the trinitarian relations, the two limitations on the church's ability to image the Trinity are: (1) the church is not divine, and our understanding of the nature of God is limited; (2) the church on earth suffers from the realities of sin, brokenness, and so forth. Volf, "Trinity Is Our Social Program," 405–7.

46. Volf, *After Our Likeness*, 198–200.

47. Spence, *Trinity: Part One*, 2. Stephen Spence is Deputy Principal (Academic) and Professor of New Testament and Theology, at Tabor College in Adelaide, Australia. I am quoting some of his excellent lecture notes here.

48. Giles, *Trinity and Subordinationism*, 11.

49. Cunningham, *These Three*, 165.

50. *Perichoresis* means *mutual interpenetration, co-inherence,* and *enveloping.* See Torrance, *Doctrine of God*, 170.

relations."[51] John Zizioulas and Joseph Ratzinger agree—Zizioulas writing that God is essentially "a relational being" who has "no ontological content, no true being, apart from communion,"[52] and Ratzinger suggesting that "the Church's action and behavior must correspond to the 'we' of God by following the pattern of this relationship."[53]

Understanding God in this way, writes Miroslav Volf, has real implications for our understanding of the nature of the church, human personhood, and relations in church life. This is because,

> As baptism *into* the Triune name attests, beginning the Christian pilgrimage does not mean simply to respond to God's summons but to enter into communion with the Triune God; to end the Christian pilgrimage does not mean simply to have accomplished an earthly task but to enter into perfect communion with the Triune God.[54]

Much has been written recently about the need for postmodern and missional churches to enjoy meaningful fellowship and community. Understanding God as relational and dynamic in his trinitarian communion and appreciating the way in which the church corresponds to this communion help missional ecclesiology form a theological basis for life-changing, intimate Christian community. Human beings are relational at their core and experience this relationality at its best in communion with the Trinity, and in immersion in a community of faith that is shaped after the likeness of the triune God.

The *communitas* that missional communities experience—that is, the acute, deep sense of community they experience while going through a chaotic, unpredictable, liminal period of change and transformation—is evidence of the formation of a distinct, ecclesial culture during those times. *Communitas* can be the fruit of the liminal process that all cultural groups go through when they experience significant social change, transition, and upheaval.[55] However, *communitas* is also much more than that—it is the creaturely reflection of the intimate community and agapic love within the Trinity. *Missional communitas is trinitarian* because the acute experience of community, which occurs when a church is going through chaotic, transformative, missional change, is an expression of the communion within the Trinity. God uses these times to deepen a church's communion and forge its missional identity. He uses these periods of upheaval to shape a people in the image of the Trinity. Trinitarian theology must cause missional churches to reject the most individualistic dimensions of modernity, if we truly believe that there is a correspondence between the trinitarian and ecclesial natures. A trinitarian outlook also gives

---

51. Ibid. Pinnock writes, "God is not an isolated individual but a loving interpersonal communion, to whom we owe our very existence . . . If God is a loving relationality, grace is primary because it is rooted in the loving divine communion . . . Relationality features also in the understanding of salvation as union with God . . . The social Trinity depicts God as beautiful and supremely lovable. God is not a featureless monad, isolated and motionless, but a dynamic event of loving actions and personal relationality." Pinnock, *Flame of Love*. These are select phrases taken from pages 23–42, without, I believe, any injustice done to their context.

52. Zizioulas, *Being as Communion*, 17.

53. Ratzinger, *Church, Ecumenism*, 31.

54. Volf, "Being as God Is," 3.

55. Roxburgh, *Missionary Congregation*, 49–56; Turner, *Ritual Process*, 132.

the church the courage to embrace the community- and identity-forming potential of periods of significant ecclesial self-examination, upheaval, and reformation.[56]

Theological anthropology, shaped by trinitarian thought, moves beyond individualism toward the notion of *humans-in-community*; a fuller understanding of what it means to be human, and of the nature of human community, is embraced and celebrated. "Individualism and hierarchy are seriously challenged by trinitarianism" and "the social Trinity is the paradigm not only for the church but for human society. A monotheistic conception of God leads to individualism . . . Jürgen Moltmann is right in his perception that social and political views follow from particular conceptions of God and especially the Trinity."[57] An adequate missional ecclesiology needs a clearly articulated theological anthropology that emerges out of trinitarian perspectives on faith, community, and human nature. Such a trinitarian understanding of human nature and of humans-in-community helps congregations build theological foundations and practical approaches to discipleship and mission. Missional ecclesiology emphasizes persons-in-relationship as fundamental to authentic spirituality and discipleship.[58] This is supported by a theological anthropology and appreciation of human community that is shaped by trinitarian considerations.

Perceiving Human, Ecclesial, and Divine Being as Communion

John Zizioulas reminds us that human, ecclesial, and trinitarian *being* all are essentially *communion*. This communion forms human identity and makes human freedom possible. All communion finds its origin in the triune God, who graciously shares his communion with human beings and the church, and who offers this communion to the world in human history. Douglas Knight summarizes Zizioulas's theology this way:

> Zizioulas's central concern is human freedom and the relation of freedom and otherness. Freedom is not restricted, but enabled, by our relationships with other persons, Zizioulas argues, for the community in which God includes us is the place in which our personal identity and freedom come into being. God is intrinsically communion and free, and his communion and freedom he shares with us. The Father, Son, and Holy Spirit are the source of the communion of the universal church, and the promise of real freedom for the world. This communion is being actualized by God in the world in the community of the church. The persons gathered into this communion will come to participate in the freedom of God, and through them the world will participate in this freedom too.[59]

It is clear that the idea of communion is at the heart of Zizioulas's trinitarian theology.[60] He writes much on the notion of *hypostasis*—the essential substance and nature of a thing, and especially of the church, the human person, and the triune God.[61] For

56. Hiebert, *Missiological Implications*, 68–116.

57. Spence, *Trinity: Part One*, 8; Johnson, *She Who Is*, 361.

58. Frost and Hirsch, *Shaping of Things*, 111–12.

59. Knight, *Theology of Zizioulas*, 1.

60. Kärkkäinen, *Introduction to Ecclesiology*, 95.

61. Zizioulas, "Contribution of Cappadocia," 23–25.

Zizioulas, the concrete and practical communion of persons in the church is fundamentally sourced in the *being* or *communal hypostasis* of God.[62] God's trinitarian nature is essentially relational and communal. When the church experiences real communion it *images* God, and reflects or embodies his trinitarian "way of being."[63] The church only knows such free communion because of the trinitarian *being* of God.

This communion is at once intimacy, freedom, and otherness. True ecclesial communion is conformity to the being of God, in the church's essence and life together, since the God it worships and images is "intrinsically communion and free." Communion is equally about "unity and otherness, difference as well as togetherness," since neither of these realities precedes nor is more fundamental than the other is. Oneness is no more important than freedom, and plurality is no more important than unity. "*Being* (which we may equally call 'substance' or 'nature') does not precede *relation* . . . (Since) *being* and *relationship* are simultaneous."[64]

John Zizioulas's theology challenges missional ecclesiology toward an understanding of community that is shaped by trinitarian relations because, in Zizioulas's theology, an ecclesiology of communion can only be established upon trinitarian foundations.[65] Our understanding of the communion, freedom, and otherness present within the Trinity should lead us to relinquish ecclesiologies that are individualistic or conforming. We should also abandon attempts to enable people to become disciples in isolation, that is, apart from community. Conversely, we reject forms of church that diminish freedom and otherness.[66] True being is only possible through and in communion, since "communion is an ontological category." Such communion, however, must be genuinely free—an expression of a free and concrete personhood and Christian community that images the nature of God. Otherwise, it is fatally flawed.[67]

The people of God are united in human freedom and ecclesial communion when they enter into a communion that embraces love, grace, forgiveness, faith, and hope, as well as the presence of the other and of the divine.[68] Zizioulas, true to his sacramental ecclesiology, even suggests that the Eucharist bonds biological and ecclesial hypostasis through its sacramental nature. He believes that it is in the Eucharist that the people of God assume their regenerated personhood that is made in the image of Christ, and are immersed in ecclesial communion. In the Eucharist, Christians join freely in love, communion, and faith, rather than individuality, separateness, exclusivity, and egocentricity.[69] Zizioulas attempts to develop both a communion ecclesiology and a eucharistic ecclesiology, identifying truth with communion.[70] For Zizioulas, the Eucharist is the locus of truth in the community of faith.

62. Zizioulas, *Being as Communion*, 15.

63. Ibid.

64. Knight, *Theology of Zizioulas*, 1–2.

65. Zizioulas, "Mystery of the Church," 295; Zizioulas, *Church as Communion*, 104–5.

66. Zizioulas, *Communion and Otherness*, 4; Zizioulas, "Constantine Scouteris," 5.

67. Melissaris, "Challenge of Patristic Ontology," 473; Melissaris, "Orthodox Anthropology"; Zizioulas, *Being as Communion*, 18.

68. Ibid., 19, 50–53; Zizioulas, "On Being," 45.

69. Zizioulas, *Being as Communion*, 53–65.

70. Ibid., 101.

In addition, ecclesial communion is displayed in the Eucharist, which is the principal and crucial location of all interconnected and authentic personhood. The Eucharist is the place in which Christ constitutes the church (in a pneumatically mediated way), and the event in which the church can be discovered in all its fullness.

Enjoying Communion and Cherishing the Church

It is my firm belief that the church cannot be truly missional, and cannot genuinely reform, until women and men *enjoy trinitarian communion* with each other and with God, until they *cherish the church*, and until they *practice rigorous ecclesiological reflection* before and within the process of reform. In other words, ecclesial communion and love, theological reflection, missional being and practice, and reforming effort, are best when they occur concurrently. These are interdependent, determining the quality and substance of each other. We too often emphasize one at the expense of the others. As we enjoy communion with each other and with the triune God, we are drawn into a deeper love for his church, and an appreciation of how the church's communion and mission correspond to the communing and missional movements of the Trinity. Missional ecclesiology cannot afford to be rigorously missiological and only superficially or sporadically ecclesiological, in its outlook and theologizing. Joseph Ratzinger asserts that rigorous ecclesiological reflection *before* undertaking ecclesial reform will ensure that any reform that is pursued will be constructive, biblically and theologically sound, genuinely healing, and "illuminated and led by the logos of faith."[71] Missional ecclesiology must seek to do careful theological reflection *before* undertaking missional reform, *during* the process of ecclesial change, and *after* the missional transformation process, in order to gain the most from an action-reflection learning approach to missional renewal. This is "building the bridge while one walks on it," as Alan Roxburgh puts it.[72]

The biblical narrative and mandate, the example of Jesus Christ, the witness of the Spirit, and the communing love of the Trinity which embraces the people of God compel Christians to cherish the church. We are not presented with an alternative. The church is the holy, precious Bride and the mystical body of Christ. Jesus's presence resides in and with it, and he witnesses most clearly to the world through its love. Since this is the case, and since *we are the church* and are called to be the presence of Christ in the world, both individually and communally, it is vital for Christians to elevate, cherish, and honor the church of which we are a part. Therefore, while some missional ecclesiologists might wish to abandon the established church, pursue new initiatives without any accountability or reference to the broader church both present and past, and dismiss the established church as irrelevant, we should remember that all Christians are corporately the church. We all have co-responsibility for its particular and universal health, mission, development, and broader renewal.[73]

71. Ratzinger, *Called to Communion*, 9.
72. Roxburgh, *Crossing the Bridge*.
73. Ratzinger, *Called to Communion*, section 5.

I have already noted that the primary notion in Joseph Ratzinger's ecclesiology is *communion*. Miroslav Volf's critique of Ratzinger's ecclesiology concentrates on Ratzinger's communion ecclesiology and his notion of *corporate personality*. Volf considers this notion to prioritize the universal church over the local, particular church, affording the universal church greater priority and higher honor. For Ratzinger, the universal church is "*ontologically and temporally* prior to every *individual* particular church . . . since every local community of faith exists through a '*mutual interiority*' with the whole, and receives its ecclesiality joined with it and out of it."[74] The communion between the churches is given substance and is sustained through the Eucharist and the episcopate. This *communion* between the multiple persons, congregations, and universal whole, is given expression through the multiplicity of liturgies, ministries, communities, societies, and charisms in the manifold churches. For Ratzinger, *communion* is about identity and ministry to the communion, and mission is the outward movement from communion— just as the Trinity is both communion and outward movement in mission.

Missional ecclesiology, if it is not wedded to episcopal notions, will inevitably reject the prioritizing of the universal in Joseph Ratzinger's theology of communion, and the hierarchical overtones in his notion of the *communion hierarchica*.[75] Ratzinger's prioritization of the universal church over the local church, however, is not necessarily representative of Catholic ecclesiology, especially since *Lumen Gentium*. There has been a recent shift in Catholic ecclesiology toward an emphasis on the importance of the local church and on the whole people of God as the church. This is illustrated by the following quotation from a work on Catholic systematic theology.

> The church is one because of the indwelling of the one Holy Spirit in all the baptized; it is holy because it is set apart by God's graciousness for the reception of a mysterious love of predilection; it is catholic in the original sense of the word, meaning that it is whole and entire, possessing all the parts needed to make it integral; and it is apostolic because it remains in continuity in essentials with the original witnessing of the first-century apostles . . . Catholics are often inclined to apply these descriptive characteristics only to the worldwide, universal church, yet they are beginning to learn from the eastern Orthodox Churches and others that these characteristics are meant to apply just as truly to the local church.[76]

It is my conviction that *communion* is a theologically rich concept, deeply rooted in trinitarian theology, which helps us understand the dynamic relationship between particular churches and the universal church, between the self and the whole, and "between the human 'I' and the divine 'Thou' in a universally communal 'We.'"[77] A theology of *communion* compels missional ecclesiology to consider its approaches to missional leadership, ministry, movements, and structures, in the light of the trinitarian relations. One cannot profitably ignore the pressing implications of trinitarian theology on such missional church impulses and expressions. The communion between individual Christians, the

74. Ratzinger, *Some Aspects of Church*, 5; Ratzinger, "Local Church," 8.
75. Ratzinger writes, for example, that the church's "deep and permanent structure is not democratic but sacramental, consequently hierarchical." Ratzinger and Messori, *Ratzinger Report*, 49.
76. Fahey, "Church," 43. Quoted in Kärkkäinen, *Introduction to Ecclesiology*, 29.
77. Volf, *After Our Likeness*, 29–30.

local congregation, the broader church, and the triune God calls us to put the immediate concerns of the local congregation into trinitarian context.

Communion has its grounding in trinitarian theology. The love, self-giving, mutuality, and being *from* and *toward* that are evidenced in the communion of the Trinity are also, ideally, characteristic of the communion found among the people of God.[78] Yet Miroslav Volf cautions against grounding ecclesial communion in trinitarian terms if "such a union, emerging from *pure* relationality, results, however, in dissolution of the respective individual identities of the various local churches."[79] Volf suggests that emphasizing complementarity, rather than pure relationality, would allow the trinitarian dimensions of communion to richly inform ecclesial communities "as independent and yet mutually related entities affirming one another in mutual giving and receiving."[80] The trinitarian notion of *communion*, therefore, helps missional churches embrace a deeper love for the church and a respect for the way the church is called to reflect the trinitarian relations. It should also lead to a richer understanding of the intimate connections between personhood, faith, church, and mission, as these reflect the inner life and outward movements of the Trinity.

Renewing Ecclesial Life and Practices

Stephen Spence rightly asserts that trinitarian thought becomes meaningful especially "in the context of Christian practices," so Christians and churches need to be attentive not just to the theory "but also to the *practice*, of trinitarian theology."[81] The practice of trinitarian theology is about the concrete implications of trinitarian thought for our understanding and practice of church, discipleship, mission, ecclesial unity, spiritual gifts, ministry office, and worship.[82] John Thompson suggests, "It is generally agreed that many older statements of the Trinity, while true, failed to give more than a static conception of God and were not integrated in any real way either with experience, worship or the whole context of theological thought and action."[83] Any missional theology of the church that is rooted in trinitarian thought must buck this trend, so to speak. In Miroslav Volf's words,

> Conceiving the structure of the church in a consistently trinitarian fashion means conceiving not only the institution of office as such, but also the *entire (local) church* itself in correspondence to the Trinity . . . The various gifts, services, and activities that all Christians have correspond to the divine multiplicity. The symmetrical reciprocity of the relations of the trinitarian persons finds its correspondence in the image of the church in which *all* members serve one another with their specific gifts of the Spirit in imitation of the Lord and through the power of the Father. Like the divine persons, they all stand in a relation of mutual giving and receiving.[84]

78. Ratzinger, *Introduction to Christianity*, 134–35.

79. Volf, *After Our Likeness*, 207.

80. Ibid.

81. Spence, *Trinity: Part One*, 5.

82. Volf, *After Our Likeness*, 214–20.

83. Thompson, *Modern Trinitarian Perspectives*, 352, quoted in Spence, *Trinity: Part One*, 6.

84. Volf, *After Our Likeness*, 218–19.

Similarly, David Cunningham calls for a theological discussion on the Trinity that:

• Brings the doctrine out of dry academic or dogmatic speculation, releasing it to dynamic conversations among the people of God in the churches in our present context;

• Shapes trinitarian thought in such a way that it is more intelligible to both Christians and to non-Christians;

• Demonstrates how trinitarian considerations influence the shape of Christian discipleship and ecclesiology;

• Moves beyond mere systematic and theologizing language, since, "despite the abstract language which it often must employ—[the Trinity] is not just something that Christians think, it is something that they do. It should thus be more than just a device for arranging the Table of Contents in volume after volume of systematic theology. Our belief in the Triune God shapes us in profound ways—affecting what we believe, what we say, how we think, and how we live."[85]

Missional communities must not only consider the correspondence between their community life and the nature of the Trinity—they must also reflect that divine nature in their renewed ecclesial practices, structures, and leadership. Missional churches are committed to equipping and releasing people to mission, to the participatory nature of Christian worship, and to the priesthood of all believers.[86] "The various gifts, services, and activities that all Christians have correspond to the divine multiplicity," so the congregation's practical missional life, experience of community, and opportunities for service are to reflect this trinitarian multiplicity. These practical dimensions of the church's life find renewal and fresh meaning in the light of the trinitarian mission and community.[87]

Soma Communities

Soma Communities are an innovative group of churches engaging in mission in the city of Tacoma, Washington, reflecting both the communion and mission of the triune God. On their website, they tell their remarkable story in this way.[88]

"Soma began as a small group of people asking the question, 'What would it look like if the people who call themselves followers of Jesus began to live out their identity of BEING the church instead of merely ATTENDING a church?' As they looked at the story of God's people, they saw that they were called by him to be his

85. Cunningham, *These Three*, ix.

86. Murray, *Post-Christendom*, 261–64.

87. Volf, *After Our Likeness*, 219.

88. This material comes from Soma Communities's website and information brochure (with only slight modification), and is used with permission. Online: http://tacoma.somacommunities.org/family/our-story and http://tacoma.somacommunities.org/family/gatherings

own special family and then sent by him to be on his mission. Soma determined to live their lives as 'called' and 'sent' ones who express, through actions and words, the good news of God among the people and city of Tacoma.

After about a year of learning, listening, and preparation Soma sent several of their people out to start the first four Missional Communities in their own neighborhoods. Along the way they continued to ask the question, 'What does the good news of Jesus Christ look like to the people we live with and love?' And, 'How should we live so they can also experience God's love?' This has led them to serve their community in ways that show what God is really like—to display his image and love to everyone. Soma wanted to make sure their DOING comes out of their BEING, not the other way around. They also realized that many people, rightly or wrongly motivated, also did not know how to live out the mission of the gospel in the everyday stuff of life. This led them to work out what they call the Rhythms: Storyformed, Listen, Celebrate, Bless, Eat, and ReCreate. They began training people in how their new identity informs how they work out the gospel in these everyday rhythms. This led to a greater effectiveness in their Missional Communities' ministry and mission as they continued to reach more people and multiply . . . 4 to 8 . . . 8 to 16...16 to 24... 24 to 40... and to the formation of new churches. God drew other churches to join Soma (Pneuma, The Sound, and Harambee) and eventually they changed the name from Soma Church to Soma Communities to demonstrate that they are no longer just one expression of the church in Tacoma, but many expressions of the church spread throughout the Greater Puget Sound.

Soma's Missional Community Gatherings live life together as a family on God's mission, seeing each other often, and gathering together in homes at least weekly. Their Expression Gatherings are groups of missional communities working together to uniquely express the gospel in their area, gathering at different times and in different ways for equipping, worship, training, and to serve together in their area."

RENEWING CHRISTIAN THEOLOGY

Trinitarian thought in the life of a community of faith can help Christians explore theology in fresh ways. It can help renew Christian theology around life-giving perspectives and themes, around the concrete experience of theologizing in Christian community, and around the importance of human connection in shaping theological thought. Renewed theological activity can occur as Christians are encouraged to explore the implications of trinitarian thought for their participation in Christian community, their everyday Christian practices, and their missional lives. Ellen Charry argues that "under the influence of modern notions of truth, theology became more interested in the coherence of Christian doctrine than in the ability of those doctrines to sponsor a godly life . . .

Classical theology was an exercise in Christian *paideia* (helping people know, love, and enjoy God) an intellectual and spiritual undertaking—helping people both to understand and to be formed by loving the God they confess."[89] Charry goes on to suggest, "Baptism into the Triune life is the foundation of Christian theological identity."[90] She proposes that living in the Trinity leads to a life of humility and community, and to the discovery that knowledge is not about mastery of concepts and information, but about spiritual growth and "knowing."[91]

Some established forms of theological and ministerial education are overly rooted in the downsides of the rationalisms and dualisms of modernity. Such theological education is too often removed from embodied spiritual practices, Christian community, and formation of character, missional faithfulness, "wisdom, spiritual sensitivity, and servant leadership."[92] Trinitarian thought is fundamental to genuine Christian theologizing. Trinitarian theology, when it is at its best, demands a reconceptualization of theological and ministerial education. It demands a fresh approach to theology. All Christians should learn to understand their faith in the light of trinitarian thought, in an integrated, systematic, holistic, and interdisciplinary fashion. Churches should help Christians to integrate their theology with their Christian practices, spirituality, and life in the world. Miroslav Volf puts it this way, "because Christian beliefs relate to everyday practices as a fitted set of beliefs with a claim to express truth about God and God's relation to the world, theologians must be concerned with just how beliefs relate to everyday practices—and must be so concerned precisely for the sake of everyday practices."[93]

Experiencing the Trinity

Created for communion with God and others, Christians need to feel free to experience God as Trinity, whether they can come to terms with trinitarian theological and philosophical abstraction or not. The Trinity, for many, becomes real to them through their experiences of God—as they experience a sense of connection with the Father, Son, and Holy Spirit, not as separate beings, but in their trinitarian unity. David Wright suggests, for instance, that early trinitarianism was,

> an area in which the axiom *lex orandi, lex credendi* (literally, "the law of praying (determines) the law of believing") was most evidently operative. From the outset, Father, Son, and Spirit were named together in baptism and in benediction. Christians at worship regularly expressed what theologians struggled to articulate satisfactorily. Believers "lived" tensions and animosities that reasoned faith found hard to resolve.[94]

Missional ecclesiology emphasizes experiential worship, liturgy, and communion with God, which are important for contemporary expressions of faith and for mission

---

89. Charry, "Spiritual Formation," 367–68.
90. Ibid., 371.
91. Ibid., 373–77.
92. Webber, *Younger Evangelicals*, 168–71.
93. Volf, "Theology," 260–61.
94. Wright, "Trinity," 1147.

to postmodern people.[95] Trinitarian theology contributes to such themes. Trinitarian theology is more than philosophical speculation—it is a response to the complex human experience of redemption in Christ, and is often concerned with explaining the human experience of the triune God. It is the lived experience of sharing in the divine, loving trinitarian community—of being brought through the will of the Father, the sacrifice of the Son, and the power of the Spirit into communion with the divine persons. Miroslav Volf explains this experience of communion, and it is one that people often feel when they become aware of God's delight in them.

> When God turns toward the world, the circle of exchanges within the divine communion begins its outbound flow. God gives to creatures because God delights in them and because they are needy. That delight is part of God's more encompassing relation with human beings, and the name of that relation is communion. It is a different sort of communion than communion among diving persons. Still, it is a communion across the chasm that divides humanity from divinity.[96]

Considering Embodiment, Communion, and the Past

While John Zizioulas's Eastern Orthodox sacramental ecclesiology is at odds with many Protestant, evangelical ecclesiological perspectives, it is worth detailing here some of the challenges Zizioulas's ecclesiology presents for missional ecclesiology.[97] These challenges are especially located in his views on *being as communion*, eucharistic community, and the nature of the Christian's connectedness to the church.[98] Douglas Knight suggests that Zizioulas's ecclesiology poses four important questions to western theology. In the following few paragraphs, I frame a series of challenges to missional ecclesiology around Knight's four questions, suggesting that they are as important to missional ecclesiology as they are to western theology.[99]

1. *Is Gnosticism deeply rooted in western theology and in its soteriological themes of escape from the flesh into disembodiedness?*[100]

John Zizioulas's trinitarian ecclesiology suggests that *the nature of being is communion*. Missional ecclesiology is at its best when it emphasizes spirituality, mission, and discipleship with attention to persons-in-relationship and to the communion between the Trinity, individual human beings, and the gathered church. This is expressed through a rejection of individualism, disembodied spirituality, privatized faith, and system-justifying forms

---

95. Moynagh, *Emergingchurch.Intro*, 123–24, 166; Kimball, *Emerging Church*, 105–96.

96. Volf, "Being as God Is," 11.

97. If not at odds, it is at least different given its Episcopal rather than Free Church foundations.

98. Patricia Fox writes that John Zizioulas's communion ecclesiology has four distinctive features. She dedicates a chapter to these features. I list these four here verbatim: (1) Trinitarian theology as the essential context for ecclesiology; (2) Ecclesiology requires a synthesis between Christology and pneumatology; (3) The eschaton enters history: The Eucharist "makes the church"; (4) Ecclesiology has a cosmic dimension. Fox, *God as Communion*, 71–98.

99. Knight, *Theology of Zizioulas*, 5–6.

100. Zizioulas, *Eucharist, Bishop, Church*, 131; Zizioulas, "Early Christian Community," 35–39.

of spirituality and the like, as well as a desire for the reconciliation of human beings in their inner, interpersonal, structural, and environmental dimensions. Missional ecclesiology rejects otherworldly spirituality and calls for an earthy, missional, and holistic engagement with the world.[101] In the missional and incarnational movements of the triune God we perceive his love for the entire created, physical order; and the valuing (rather than rejection) of embodiment, in the trinitarian actions. An authentic missional ecclesiology is concerned for the whole person, the reclaiming of bodiliness and embodiment, the "hallowing of the everyday," the presence of God in the ordinary, and the desire to see such down-to-earth matters as sacramental and holy.[102] Dan Kimball, for instance, advocates an approach to spiritual formation that is holistic, experiential, and communal, which draws from ancient spiritual disciplines, and which releases people to social engagement.[103]

While experimentation in worship and spiritual formation is to be encouraged—especially if a community attentive to the Spirit and the Scriptures shapes and scrutinizes such experimentation—we should avoid any experimentation that has Gnostic-like qualities. I do not want to overstate this point but some approaches to alternative worship lean toward otherworldliness and disembodiment. There is something stimulating and potentially mission empowering about innovative, mystical, liturgically experiential, narrative-shaped, participatory, and multisensory worship experiences. However, the goal must remain the glorification of Christ, the proclamation of the gospel in word and deed, the faithful pursuit of the *missio Dei*, and participation in biblically faithful, embodied, authentic worship. It must not degenerate into the pursuit of Gnostic-like experiences (thankfully, this does not happen often).[104] Zizioulas's caution about western theology, whether one accepts its premise or not, is worth heeding for those involved in the alternative worship dimensions of missional ecclesiology. It also challenges missional churches to ground their ecclesial life in the concrete realities of good works, missional endeavors, community practices, and acts of justice, service, mercy, and peace.

2. *Is the West gripped by soteriological and broader theological notions that inevitably result in an "evasion of communion and manyness," since they prioritize individualism, "freedom from other people," and the concerns for otherness that are grounded in the western intellectual traditions and modernity?*[105]

---

101. Frost and Hirsch, *Shaping of Things*, 111–12.

102. Ibid., 109–62.

103. Kimball, *Emerging Church*, 213–25 and his list of resources for spiritual formation on 258–59.

104. See http://www.alternativeworship.org; http://www.emergingworship.org; Baker and Gay, *Alternative Worship*. For Generation X and Y statistics, information, and approaches to faith see Rabey, *Search of Authentic Faith*.

105. Zizioulas, *Being as Communion*, 65, 104–5, 216. Both Melissaris and Jesson note this theme in Zizioulas's writings: Jesson, "Orthodox Contributions," 12; Melissaris, "Challenge of Patristic Ontology," 479–80.

John Zizioulas emphasizes communion and multiplicity and the interdependence of unity and otherness, communion and freedom, and difference and togetherness.[106] A missional theology of the church should support such assertions, grounding them in the biblical material and a trinitarian theology, and rejecting any kind of "evasion of *communion* and manyness." For example, inculturational mission in secular, postmodern, post-Christendom cultures must occur in the context of relationships. Inculturational forms of mission and church are characterized by empathetic and vulnerable connectedness with non-Christians. People are often converted into Christian community before they decide to become disciples of Jesus Christ.[107]

Missional ecclesiology is grounded in local, worshipping communities—it must never forget its trinitarian rootedness in *communion* and *otherness*. The local church is the locus of mission and communion. Douglas John Hall and Robert Webber suggest that through genuine *koinonia*, these Christian communities might contrast with and heal the fragmentation, disconnectedness, and social disintegration experienced by many people in western cultures. Churches can help remedy the diminishing social cohesion in western cultures.[108] Simple forms of church are often needed to recover deeper expressions of community. A simple ecclesiality can aid in the rediscovery of friendship "as our relational paradigm . . . (which is) non-hierarchical, holistic, relaxed, and dynamic."[109] Such *koinonia* is cultivated by the presence of the Spirit and by attention to the "practices by which [we] are formed, trained, equipped, and motivated as missionary communities."[110] Our churches are to be places of hospitality, justice, peace, and reconciliation. Through such demonstrations of love and trinitarian communion, they reflect the eschatological reign of God and the messianic mission of our Lord Jesus Christ.[111] Authentic witness is only possible where there is authentic community.[112]

3. Is the individuality and emphasis on rationality in the western theological tradition an avoidance of the communal "practices and disciplines of the Christian life"?[113]

In the chapter on John Zizioulas, I briefly mentioned that not all evangelical thinkers would be comfortable with Zizioulas's understandings of the nature of truth. For Zizioulas, truth is essentially relational and communal, rather than *merely* grounded in cognitive, propositional, or kerygmatic statements. While I have some serious reservations about Zizioulas's ontological and communal understanding of the nature of truth, I do think that his attempt to show the connection between relationality, ontology, kerygma, and

---

106. Knight, *Theology of Zizioulas*, 1–2.

107. *Hunter III, How to Reach*, 59, 65.

108. Hall, *End of Christendom*, 59–61. See Webber, *Younger Evangelicals*, 51–52, 101–6.

109. Murray, *Post-Christendom*, 275.

110. Guder, *Missional Church*, chapter 6. Written by Inagrace T. Dietterich, "Missional Community: Cultivating Communities of the Holy Spirit," 142–82.

111. Ibid., 153–82.

112. Kraus, *Authentic Witness*, 156. Quoted in Guder, *Missional Church*, 182.

113. Zizioulas, *Being as Communion*, 131, 213; Zizioulas, "Human Capacity," 406; Zizioulas, "Early Christian Community," 23–42; Zizioulas, *Communion and Otherness*, 286–307.

truth is admirable. Without accepting all of Zizioulas's theological constructs, missional ecclesiology can pay heed to his concerns and strive to avoid an approach to theology or faith that is individualistic, rigid, rationalistic, (hyper) textual, and (merely) propositional. A trinitarian theology, which emphasizes communion, dynamic mission, embodiment, and interdependent discipleship, will not permit such approaches to theology or faith. Neither Gnostic-like mysticism nor inflexible intellectualism serves faith, mission, church, or theology well. Many people in western cultures are engaged by experiential and holistic expressions of truth, and the church should keep this in mind as it develops contemporary missional activities, worship experiences, and discipling approaches. Missional ecclesiology agrees with Zizioulas that the spiritual life is formed communally and by spiritual practices and disciplines that are discovered in authentic Christian community. Zizioulas's views on the communal and relational nature of truth have something to teach us—even if we choose to qualify them in evangelical ways. His views might help missional ecclesiology think through a richer theological framework for communal approaches to mission, apologetics, and gospel proclamation. This is preferable to justifying what we are doing by a simple appeal to the changes in western culture. As we consider how the trinitarian nature of God affects our understanding of human nature, the church and its mission, and the dynamics of spiritual formation, we appreciate the need to embrace the communal "*practices* and *disciplines* of the Christian life."

> 4. *Is western theology concerned for the present (as is true of many of the intellectual traditions shaped by modernity and western philosophical history) without enough reference to the past (the history and tradition of the entire church, as an ongoing "manifestation of the eschata")?*[114]

Missional ecclesiology must embrace history and tradition as a corrective to the overt pragmatism and historical amnesia of some contemporary expressions of western Protestantism. The triune God speaks to his church through his presence in its leadership, Scriptures, history, tradition, reasoning, experiences, and context. It makes no sense to minimize or ignore the presence or voice of the Trinity to the church within its traditions and history. But such a reflection on what God is saying in these things must be critical. This critical exploration of the entire history and diverse traditions of the Christian church can happen in a variety of ways. This includes engagement in ecumenical dialogue, examination of pre- and post-Reformation eastern and western theological and liturgical traditions, creative exploration of worship styles, and innovative use of liturgy, sacred space, prayer, contemplation, music, symbols, rituals, creative arts, and sacraments.[115] Naturally, those of us with evangelical convictions will bring these to the table in our dialogue with others, and in our critical exploration of the resources, themes, and voices of the church's traditions and historical movements. We will not abandon our biblical convictions and commitment to evangelical beliefs and practices. Yet we will shape a movement of missional churches that values tradition as a resource, an expression of God's eschatological dealings with humanity and the church, and a source of inspiration

114. Zizioulas, *Being as Communion*, 19–26; Zizioulas, "Early Christian Community," 23.

115. Webber, *Younger Evangelicals*, 173–227.

and ecclesiological formation. Ancient and traditional forms of worship, mission, liturgy, and prayer can be mined for resources as we develop churches and practice mission in contemporary cultures. This includes the early church, the eastern and western church Fathers, and the historical and contemporary theological traditions spanning Europe, Asia, Africa, Oceania, and North and South America. All of these can offer apologetic, spiritual, missiological, and ecclesiological insight, and we need to be careful not to have our imaginations restricted to a single tradition within a few cultures (or a single one).[116] Robert Webber writes that there is a renewed interest in Celtic spirituality and missiology, in medieval approaches to epistemology, and in the catholicity of people like John Wesley. Within all traditions of the church and throughout its entire history we see God sovereignly working out his eschatological purposes, and can discern the church's vocation, nature, and purpose.[117]

Along with open and critical engagement with diverse traditions, missional ecclesiology must analyze the traditions and history of the church. Good examples of this are the works of Stuart Murray Williams and of John Howard Yoder. Both have written extensively on the Constantinian and post-Constantinian eras of western church history. While not everyone agrees with their respective treatments of Constantinianism or Christendom, their work demonstrates the nature of a genuine scholarly attempt to learn from history. Unfortunately, less scholarly authors have provided treatments of the topic that are not nuanced or well researched—these writers have too often ignored the complex societal, ecclesiological, and political challenges that faced the churches of Christendom. A similar error is made in superficial critiques of the theology and practice of Evangelicalism and the Reformers, or of the theology and practice of the Emerging-Missional Church Movement. Such superficial interpretations of church history and tradition and of the complex theological, cultural, and ecclesiological realities faced by the churches at the time are too often poorly considered and researched. They result in an interpretation of history and tradition that is questionable (whether they are commenting on the church in Christendom, the Reformers, the evangelical churches, or the Emerging-Missional Church Movement).

John Zizioulas's view that the history and traditions of the entire church are ongoing manifestations of the *eschaton* is a helpful corrective to these tendencies. His view also helps remedy the habit some are in of overstating the problems facing the current churches of the West, since we are called to see the church in the light of God's ongoing and eternal eschatological purpose. The trinitarian actions in salvation history provide us with immediate, sure, and eschatological hope.

SEEING GOD'S GRACE AND MISSION IN THE WORLD

Along with the rest of creation, humanity shares the history of the triune God's salvific, redeeming relationship to the world. As creatures made in the image of God, uniquely charged with the care of creation, we are to treat the rest of creation with the deep honor that reflects the way in which our identity, heredity, and destiny are enmeshed with it

116. Ibid., 82.

117. Ibid., 71–82. I am not excluding or ignoring the dark times in the church's history in this statement.

(and redeemed along with it). Human beings do not exist in transcendent, subduing, monarchical relationship to the rest of creation. The connectedness and interpenetration within the trinitarian Godhead are reflected in our relationships to creation and the world. Humanity, as part of creation, participates, communes, communicates, loves, and breathes in the mysterious interrelationships of the created order, finding salvation and divine life through the incarnational presence of God in this physical theatre. A dualistic, utilitarian, and subjugating understanding of creation is nonsense, and ultimately self-destructive. Human history testifies to this—nuclear proliferation, ecological genocide, unconscionable genetic experimentation, loss of biodiversity, global warming, viral metamorphoses, and the like. We cannot escape the consequences of our actions toward the rest of the created order, precisely because humanity is a fundamental part of creation, and because God freely engages in a loving relationship with his creation.

Since humanity is part of creation, the dimensions of world, body, culture, and history are closely related in a Christian understanding of humanity. As created beings, humans are embodied in skeletal, muscular, respiratory, nervous, and cardiovascular systems (to name a few). This embodiment is in the world (we are immersed in structural and systemic realities—political, economic, social, religious, and the like), and the theatre within which this drama is played is human history (time, space, matter, the realm of the spirit, and living organisms existing interdependently since the creation of the world). As inextricably part of creation, human beings are soul and body, within history and society. This existential and fleshly unity is consubstantial in nature, an active rather than passive dynamic. Spirit and flesh enrich, complement, and complete each other in the stage-show of the past being made present (human history).

Human beings do not naturally see themselves as conflicted beings, living with an intolerable kind of multi-personality disorder, but as ordinary people located within body, world, and history. They normally reconceive the abstract notions of body, world, and history in more concrete ideas of family, sexuality, politics, disease, war, terrorism, suffering, love, imagination, work, equality, finances, and the like. While humanity's divine purpose to glorify God and experience union with God is, in one sense, beyond the world, human beings and the church are essentially and actually in the world—the world of body, society, and history. So being human means that our individual and ecclesial life (bodiliness) find expression and a call to responsible care in the present realities of the world—that is why we are so acutely responsible for and influenced by ecology, social systems, structures, institutions, and the rest of creation. Humanity, body, world, church, culture, and history are then, relational concepts, knit together in the interdependent web of all created things. This interpersonal and mutually responsible relatedness means that human beings are not only located in body, world, and history, but have a unique ability to shape their physical realities, cultures, and histories, for the glorification of the Trinity. This is the hopeful expectation of human existence—not that human beings do this in self-sufficient isolation from their Creator; but that we are invited to participate in the embrace of the triune God, and in the Trinity's redeeming and restoring activity in individual lives, social systems, the world in general, human history, and the eschatological age to come. As Miroslav Volf puts it,

> When the Trinity turns toward the world, the Son and the Spirit become, in Irenaeus's beautiful image, the two arms of God by which humanity was made and taken into God's embrace (see *Against Heresies* 5,6,1). That same love that sustains nonself-enclosed identities in the Trinity seeks to make space "in God" for humanity.[118]

God's extravagant, irrationally broad, and unmerited grace is poured out upon humankind in the movements of the trinitarian persons and manifested in our bodies, in the world, in the church, and in history. This grace is most marvelously demonstrated in the redemptive work and sacrifice of Jesus Christ. Human beings are incomplete, fractured, and destitute without radical grace. Creation, humanity, culture, church, bodies, and world are the theatres in which the triune God's love, forgiveness, and liberation are revealed. The triune God reaches out his arms to humanity in those theatres. Grace presupposes and extols human nature and bodiliness, is always prior and subversive in the world, and orientates human history toward eschatological redemption through the cross and resurrection of Jesus Christ. The seemingly darkest and apparently least honorable elements of creation, the body, the world, and human history—those places where we are confronted by ambiguity, incomprehensibility, human frailty and suffering, terrifying mystery, and brutal inhumanity—may be the very locations where we discover the redemptive, prevenient activity of the Father, Son, and Holy Spirit. These may also be the places where we discover the church. As disciples of Jesus are empowered by the Spirit to glorify the Father in these difficult places, we learn, often, what it means to be truly human, and truly the church, created in the image of the relational, triune, loving God.

A trinitarian orientation leads to a fresh perspective on the nature of, and connections between, the church, humanity, creation, cultures, bodies, and world. God has a particular kind of relationship with the world, as we have seen, and the church needs to reflect this in its mission, service, and communion. Colin Gunton suggests that God's relationship with the created order is "personal, not logical, the product of the free and personal action of the Triune God."[119] Missional ecclesiology claims that Christians are called to love the world and to love human beings as God's beloved creation, his precious children. I do not mean "love the *spirit* or the *ways* of the world," but love the world as Christ loves it; so that, through the person and work of Jesus Christ, it might know the redemption and transformation that only God offers. Christians are also called to demonstrate appropriate stewardship, to avoid Gnostic dualisms, to reject cultural exclusion, and to participate in God's redemptive activities in creation and society. We do this as we anticipate the new heaven and earth.[120] Miroslav Volf proposes that an adequate and "genuinely Christian reflection" on such issues is only formed in the light of the actions and nature of the trinitarian God, and such trinitarian theological moorings only serve to enrich missional ecclesiology. In *Exclusion and Embrace*, for instance, Volf claims that,

---

118. Volf, *Exclusion and Embrace*, 128.

119. Gunton, *Promise of Trinitarian*, 72. As Jürgen Moltmann is one of the ecclesiologists studied in this book, it is worth noting the controversy surrounding his theology of the *openness* of the economic Trinity to the world. This shapes his views on the social, immanent, and doxological Trinity. For a good discussion of the implications of Moltmann's trinitarian conceptions for missional theology, see Daugherty, "Missio Dei: The Trinity."

120. See Bosch, *Believing in the Future*, 39.

"A genuinely Christian reflection on social issues must be rooted in the self-giving love of the divine Trinity as manifested on the cross of Christ; all the central themes of such reflection will have to be thought through from the perspective of the self-giving love of God."[121]

REFLECTING THE TRINITARIAN MISSION

How can the church reflect the mission of the Trinity in its structures, life together, and actions? In addition to the suggestions I have already made in this chapter, I would like to answer this question with proposals that surface from the writings of some of the ecclesiologists studied in this book.

1.   Thomas Hopko asserts, "Everything which is authentically of the Church is trinitarian in its essence and existence, in its content and life."[122] The church that is missional, if it is to reflect the missional nature of the Trinity, must be trinitarian, in its "content and life." Its missional endeavors, charismatic expressions, ecclesial structures, ministry forms and practices, scriptural interpretation and application, liturgy and worship, and depth of community must be shaped around trinitarian themes—if these dimensions of the church are to be authentically missional, reflecting the passion of the Father, Son, and Holy Spirit. The clearest illustrations of this point can be found in the church's fellowship or communion, and in its mission. As we have seen, mission and communion are inseparable in the triune God and in his church. To be trinitarian, the church's fellowship must reflect the trinitarian relations—loving, unified, reciprocal, mutual, free, and interdependent. To be trinitarian, the church's mission must be fashioned after, and solidly located within, the mission of the triune God. Lesslie Newbigin says that such trinitarian mission can be understood "as proclaiming the kingdom of the Father, as sharing the life of the Son, and as bearing the witness of the Spirit."[123]

2.   After conducting an excellent study of the narratives and cultures of Australian churches that have gone through change and renewal, Jeffrey Pugh asks about the criteria for assessing the health and "godliness" of this change. To do this he turns to the trinitarian ecclesiologies of Jürgen Moltmann and Miroslav Volf for answers. Pugh suggests that healthy church cultures evidence the following trinitarian features: (1) Polycentric church life with "participative consensual decision-making"; (2) Unity of heart and purpose; (3) Multiplicity of gifts and service; (4) Fluid structures and institutions; (5) Reciprocity of charismata; (6) Generative leadership that develops the whole church for maturity, service, and mission; (7) Mutual sharing, recognition, and honor; (8) Witness to the world; (9) Collegial ministry relationships and release of the priesthood of all believers;

---

121. Volf, *Exclusion and Embrace*, 25.

122. Hopko, *All the Fulness*, 66–67 (see 22–29, 91–93).

123. Newbigin, *Open Secret*, 29.

and (10) Freedom for relationship and from regulation.[124] After considering the trinitarian ecclesiologies of Jürgen Moltmann and Miroslav Volf, and after examining the cultures of churches that have gone through significant change and renewal, Jeffrey Pugh rightly comes to a strong conclusion—leading churches into the health that is associated with trinitarian ecclesial culture is a prerequisite in any effort to cultivate a trinitarian, missional ecclesiology. Trinitarian health leads to sustainable missional passion and action.[125]

3.   The church is the "presence of God's truth and love," says Karl Rahner, when it reflects and expresses the fellowship and eschatological mission of "the inner-trinitarian processions. *The duality of the inner-trinitarian processions forms the basis of the presence of God in the Church and is therefore the basis of the nature of the Church.* If the nature of the Church is to be elucidated, nothing more 'intelligible' or simpler will suffice."[126] The church is the presence of the triune God's self-communicative truth as it receives and proclaims the gospel of Jesus Christ, confesses and lives out scriptural truth, participates in God's mission in the world, and refuses to accept anything less than truth-filled worship, fellowship, mission, and ecclesial structures. It is the presence of the triune God's inner-trinitarian and outwardly expressed love when it demonstrates this divine love in hospitality, care for "the least of these," holiness, love of neighbor, passion for justice and mercy, and the like. We have seen that Karl Rahner avoids differentiating between the activities that are the presence of God's truth and those that are the presence of God's love. This is because these two are complex and interdependent, taking various forms in church history. "The Trinity of the economy of redemption is the immanent Trinity" and, similarly, the triune God's self-communicative truth and love are meant to interdependently, inseparably permeate all aspects of the church's nature, structures, mission, and fellowship.[127]

4.   John Webster reminds us that Christian hope is not only eschatological hope; it is grounded in the perfection and self-originating historical actions of the Trinity. Our hope is grounded in "the fact that all occasions of human history, including its future, are caught up within the economy of the Triune God's mercy."[128] So our hope is based on the perfect nature of the triune God, as self-communicated in Scripture. It is also based on the triune God's historical actions, especially in the life, death, and resurrection of Jesus Christ. Moreover, it is based in God's ultimate, eschatological purpose and plan, and in our deep, rich, and real communion with the perfect (self-originating and complete) inner trinitarian life of God.[129]

---

124. These features emerge directly from the trinitarian ecclesiologies of Moltmann and Volf.

125. Pugh, "Symbols of Dysfunction," 457–58.

126. Rahner, *Theology of Pastoral Action*, 29, 33–34. Italics are in the original quotation.

127. Ibid., 33–43.

128. Webster, *Confessing God*, 199.

129. Ibid., 195–214.

5. Jürgen Moltmann's ecclesiology centers on the trinitarian mission of God. He demonstrates how the church defines its ecclesial life and mission by the trinitarian interior life and eschatological mission. As we have seen, Moltmann writes that the church has a mission in the world but it is not its mission—it is the mission of the Trinity, revealed in human history, breaking into the present and awaiting fulfillment in the future. The Spirit empowers the church for mission. The Spirit does this by being present in the church's proclamation, sacraments, offices, acts of justice, compassion, and mercy, liturgy and worship, and witness in the world, for the sake of the gospel of Jesus Christ.[130] This mission is trinitarian and fruitful when it is framed within a charismatic ecclesial life, agapic fellowship, and dynamic ministries and structures. Such mission is characterized by: (1) the sharing of possessions; (2) hospitality and the welcome of the stranger; (3) pastoral compassion and care; and (4) the cultivation of the "new sociality" of trinitarian community.[131] Grass-roots ecclesial renewal and reformation, worship services led by the whole congregation, voluntary church membership, and the fostering of small, fellowshipping, missional communities characterize missional communities. Such missional congregations reflect the trinitarian unity and mission.[132]

Missional ecclesiology has trinitarian foundations. This trinitarian thought shapes its ecclesiological content, missiological convictions, and congregational expressions. Trinitarian theology is fundamental to missional ecclesiology's vision for humans-in-community and communities-on-mission.

QUESTIONS FOR REFLECTION

1. Do you agree that in the church *there is no true communion without mission, and no true mission without communion*? If this is the case, what does it mean practically for the fellowship and mission of your church in the coming year?

2. Consider taking time over the next few months to read Lesslie Newbigin's *The Open Secret*. Under three headings, list practical ways that your church can do the following: (1) Proclaim the kingdom of the Father ("mission as faith in action"); (2) Share the life of the Son ("mission as love in action"); (3) Bear the witness of the Spirit ("mission as hope in action").[133]

3. Look at Jeffrey Pugh's list of the ten features of churches that reflect the trinitarian life (poly-centricity, unity, multiplicity, fluidity, reciprocity, generativity, interpenetration, witness, collegiality, and freedom).[134] How are your congregation and leadership team doing in these areas, and how could you grow into these?

130. Moltmann, *Church in the Power*, 53–65.

131. Moltmann, *Sun of Righteousness*, 164.

132. Moltmann, *The Passion*, 120–26.

133. Newbigin, *Open Secret*.

134. Pugh, "Symbols of Dysfunction," 457–58. Explanations for each of these ten features can be found in Jeffrey Pugh's PhD thesis online: http://theses.flinders.edu.au/public (by searching under his surname).

18

The Courageous and Future Church: Being Salt, Light, and a City

This, I believe, is the primary task of the church after Christendom—to offer hope humbly, graciously, gently, and winsomely. Hope must be realistic, not triumphalistic. It must be sensitive to the pain and disorientation of the present as well as confident in God's future. It is hope rooted in the story of Israel and culminating in the story of Jesus—a story that the Christendom shift transmuted into just another imperial epic, but a story that marginal churches might just be able to recover and commend with sensitivity and integrity.[1]

—STUART MURRAY

WHAT ARE THE CONSEQUENCES for the church if it truly embraces a missional ecclesiology? I'd like to offer several propositions.

FROM DEFENDING THE STATUS QUO TO ALLOWING CONFRONTING QUESTIONS

In 1969, David Gleicher came up with a formula for explaining resistance to organizational change and for describing the factors required for overcoming this resistance—these included dissatisfaction with the status quo, realignment of vision and values, and concrete steps taken toward the achievement of the fresh vision. This formula has been presented in a variety of ways over the years and took its most popular form under the refinement of Kathleen Dannemiller, who presented it as Dissatisfaction + Vision + Feasibility *must be greater than* Resistance, if an organization is to go through substantial and ongoing cultural change.[2]

Resistance to change can, of course, be active or passive. Such resistance builds in organizations where there is lack of conviction about the need for change, there is change fatigue, there is a clash of values or priorities, there is uncertainty about whether change

---

1. Murray, *Church after Christendom*, 232.
2. Beckhard, *Organization Development*; Dannemiller and Jacobs, "Changing the Way."

can really occur, there are deeply embedded and conserving power structures, there is too much invested in the status quo, and when security, authority, status, meaning, privilege, and so forth are threatened by the proposed change.[3] In other words, people's anticipation of the consequences of the change combine with their values, experiences, and institutional position, and with their grief and anxiety as a result of the concrete transitions that happen in the process of change. This perfect storm of resistance can only be overcome if the forces on the other side of the ledger are greater: dissatisfaction with the way things are, the realignment of values, the embrace of fresh vision, the sense that the proposed change is indeed feasible, the ability to successfully navigate the change grief cycle, the skill and empathy of the leader of change and especially his or her ability to manage transitions, and the life-giving, status-quo-confronting presence and power of the Holy Spirit.[4] Leading change and transition is not easy! Those who lead radical, thoroughgoing change—change that leads a community into unknown and threatening territory—require courage, skill, empathy, character, vision, and willingness to sacrifice self for the good of the community.[5]

Leading change is not for the faint hearted—it is for the faith hearted. A genuine re-missionalization of the church will never happen until Christian leaders stop defending the status quo, examine the source of their own resistance, and start allowing, encouraging, wrestling with, and responding to confronting questions. The Arab Spring, which has recently spread through Tunisia, Egypt, Libya, Bahrain, Syria, Yemen, and other parts of the Arab world, shows us what can happen when people feel disenfranchised with governments and institutions that becoming self-serving, silencing, and resistant to change. These governments refused to allow or listen to confronting questions, or calls for democratic reform. Similarly, the Occupy Movement, which has sparked protests over social and economic inequality in Kuala Lumpur, New York, San Francisco, London, Sydney, and close to one hundred cities in eighty-two countries, demonstrates the passion people feel about being heard, and their alienation from government, secular, and religious institutions that become monolithic, self-preserving, oppressive, and silencing. The Arab Spring and the Occupy Movement are only two recent examples of resistance to change triggering momentum for renewed, participatory organizational cultures. The Christian church has a long tradition of silencing and resisting critique and change, or, when it is at its best, listening, responding, and reforming. If the church is going to truly reform, to become genuinely missional, kingdom-of-God-focused, and gospel-honoring, then it must allow confronting, uncomfortable questions and have the courage to respond and change. Not all questions are the right questions. Not all questions are gospel-centered, Christ honoring, formed with the right motives, or biblically faithful. Having said that, there is too much defensiveness by church leaders to missional, reforming, prophetic voices, and to calls for a "missional renaissance."[6] It has to stop. We have to listen. We have to question what we are doing and why we are doing it. We have to allow others to question us and our

3. Palmer et al., *Managing Organizational Change.*

4. Bridges, *Managing Transitions.*

5. Bate, *Strategies for Cultural Change*, 218.

6. McNeal, *Missional Renaissance.*

ecclesial practices and structures. We must embrace the questions, respond with courage, let go of institutional inertia and personal pride, and pursue the mission of God.

FROM MISSIONAL PRAGMATISM TO MISSIONAL ECCLESIOLOGY

Western culture is steeped in pragmatism and some would say this spirit is becoming prevalent in our globalized culture. The church has not been immune to the effects of such pragmatism. The most well known example of this is church growth theory. This theory claimed that churches must adopt certain practices if they are going to grow—dynamic leadership, effective structures, mobilized laity, appropriate facilities, targeted outreach, homogeneous attention, excellent preaching and public worship, integration of newcomers, clever use of finances and other resources, responsiveness to people's felt needs, systematic relationships between large celebrations, congregational gatherings, and small groups, and other such practical principles.[7] The influence of such thinking on the worldwide Protestant church cannot be overstated. I do not want to suggest that all church growth theories or pragmatic approaches to church life are to be rejected as necessarily corrupted or corrupting. That is clearly not the case. Such pragmatism, however, is dangerous if it becomes an end in itself, if it is divorced from sound biblical and theological convictions and footings, if its motivations, wisdom, and epistemological foundations remain unexamined, and if the effectiveness of a practice becomes the measurement of its worth, morality, and appropriateness in the church.

Missional ecclesiology is not immune to such temptations. Even a casual reader of the missional literature of the last decade would notice how deeply pragmatic it can be, and the affinities it often shares with church growth theory. Some of the missional literature decries church growth on the one hand while embracing its epistemologies and predilections with the other. This should not come as a surprise, given the prevalent place of pragmatism in the church and culture. The antidote is not to pursue the impractical or the abstract, but to ground missional ecclesiology in sure theological foundations and in the biblical text—especially the biblical narrative of the eschatological, messianic mission of God in human history. As I lamented earlier in this book, the missional literature is long on missiology and church practice, but short on theology and ecclesiology. There are hopeful movements in the right direction—the recent works of people like Michael Frost, Craig Van Gelder, Andrew Kirk, and Christopher Wright are examples of this—but this is just a starting point. It is my contention that one of the major tasks of the next couple of decades is the construction of a missional ecclesiology that is robust, systematic, biblically grounded, ecumenical, and substantial. Individual Christians, pastors, churches, and denominations must move from missional pragmatism to a genuine missional theology and ecclesiology.

7. Yamamori and Lawson, *Introducing Church Growth*; Wagner, *Your Church Can Grow*; McGavran and Arn, *Ten Steps for Church Growth*; Moyes, *How to Grow*; Cho and Hostetler, *Successful Home Cell Groups*; Stetzer and Dodson, *Comeback Churches*; Olson, *The Amercian Church*.

FROM THE DOMESTICATION OF MISSIONAL LANGUAGE TO THE RELEASE OF MISSIONAL VITALITY

The language of *missional* is rapidly becoming domesticated. We now have missional clothing, accessories, and wall art, a burgeoning body of missional literature, and an ever-growing number of pastors and Christian leaders willing to baptize almost everything they do in the word *missional*. While seeking a publisher for this book I was told by a couple of publishers that they are no longer publishing in this area because the missional church has become passé. Good grief! It should be clear to us all that the explosion of interest in all things *missional* has not yet resulted in a church that is completely shaped around the *missio Dei*. It has not yet resulted in a church that understands its nature, structures, theology, and ministries in the light of the eschatological mission of the Messiah. My good friend and colleague Michael Frost puts it this way,

> If the missional conversation is over, it occurs to me that it probably hasn't really ever been had. That's because "missional" is not a style or a fad. It's not an add-on, the latest church accessory, the newest cool idea for church leaders. *The fact that some are suggesting the conversation is over leads me to think that they weren't listening in the first place.* My call—and the call of many other missional thinkers and practitioners—was not for a new approach to *doing* church or a new technique for church growth. I thought I was calling the church to revolution, to a whole new way of thinking about and seeing and being the followers of Jesus today. I now find myself in a place where I fear those robust and excited calls for a radical transformation of our ecclesiology have fallen on deaf ears.[8]

We cannot acquiesce to the domestication or commercialization of the *missional* concept! The church desperately needs a robust missional ecclesiology and the release of genuine missional vitality. So what would it mean for the church to be truly missional? How do we know whether something is missional or not? Let me make some suggestions about what missional really means, in an attempt to define and reclaim the concept. I will do so by going back to some claims that I have already made in this book.

Truly missional churches, leaders, denominations, programs, and so on, are shaped around the following central, determining convictions:

1. *The Church Is to Pursue the Notae Missionis:* Missional churches pursue and integrate the four missional marks (*notae missionis*) in their ecclesial life and relationship with the world—missional *foundations, ecclesiology, contrast,* and *outlook*. These churches then express these *notae missionis* through missional *practices* and *characteristics*. I've detailed these missional marks and practices in chapter 14, so I won't go over them again, but these provide a useful and accurate lens by which to determine whether something is actually *missional*.

2. *The Church Is Essentially Missional:* The relationship between the missional nature of God and the missional essence of the church is such that mission is "a permanent and

---

8. Frost, *The Road to Missional*, 16.

intrinsic dimension of the church's life."[9] Mission is central, pivotal, and constitutive of its nature, not a contingent, peripheral, optional activity of the church. The church "is missionary by its nature" and "exists by mission, just as fire exists by burning."[10] The church is "a communion-*in-mission* . . . missional by its very nature."[11] This is a radical vision of the church, which is rooted in Scripture and in God's redemptive mission in human history.

3. *The Church Exists for, and as a Result of, Mission:* The church serves the mission of Christ and is caught up in the missional purposes and "movements" of the triune God. The church exists because of that mission—the eschatological mission of God's redemptive reign over all creation and history. The church exists to glorify and worship God, in all dimensions of its being, including its faithfulness to his cosmic, redemptive, eschatological mission.

4. *The Church Is Given Form and Substance by God's Mission:* "Mission is not just the conversion of the individual, nor just obedience to the word of the Lord, nor just the obligation to gather the church. It is the taking part in the sending of the Son, the *missio Dei,* with the holistic aim of establishing Christ's rule over all redeemed creation."[12] The church's nature, structures, ministries, and programs are given form and substance by the mission of God, for the glory of God the Father, and are evaluated in the light of that mission. We do not produce these things, and then baptize them in the language of mission. We must not adopt the language of "missional," applying it to programs and structures that are not wholeheartedly shaped around the eschatological mission of God, and then consider our job done or the language of "missional" passé! Mission precedes, permeates, defines, confronts, evaluates, and produces the church's nature, structures, and entire ecclesial life, as the church seeks to participate with the triune God in his sovereign mission in redemptive history.

5. *The Missio Dei Determines and Precedes the Missiones Ecclesiae:* The *missio Dei* has "important consequences" for "the *missiones ecclesiae* [the missional activities of the church]."[13] This includes the need for the church to cease focusing merely on the *activities* of mission. Instead, it should recognize that gospel proclamation, works of justice and compassion, church health, growth, and planting, and so on, are all grounded in and directed toward the *missio Dei.* They are not so much missional activities as expressions of the essential missional nature of the church.

6. *Missiology and Ecclesiology Are Inseparable:* Ecclesiology is inconceivable without a Christ-centered missiology, and vice versa. Biblical ecclesiology places mission at the center of the church's being and ministries, and develops a biblically faithful, community formed, missional hermeneutic and theology of the church. Our

---

9. Bosch, *Believing in the Future*, 27–32.

10. Ibid., 31–32.

11. Bevans and Schroeder, *Constants in Context*, 298 (quoting Flannery, *Ad Gentes*, 2).

12. Hartenstein, "Theologische Besinnung," 54 (quoted in Engelsviken, "Missio Dei," 482).

13. Bosch, *Transforming Mission*, 391.

understanding of the missional nature and activities of the church must be trinitarian, biblically shaped, historically informed, contextually relevant, ecumenically
attentive, eschatologically oriented, and practically applied in ordinary, concrete,
local church settings. Our gaze is primarily toward the messianic mission of Christ
and the trinitarian *missio Dei*—as well as the consequences of this Christ-centered
missiology for the communion, nature, organization, mission, and ministries of the
church.[14]

7. *Christian Leadership Exists for the Glory and Mission of God*: Missional leaders approach their leadership roles as missiologists, developing the outlook, skills, and
practices associated with that discipline. This is true whether they are local church,
denominational, or para-church leaders. They are constantly asking these questions
of their leadership posture and practices, and about the direction in which they are
leading their churches:

   a. "Is this leading the church toward faithful obedience to, and expression of,
   the mission of God?"

   b. "Will this give glory to Jesus Christ and serve his eschatological mission?"

   c. "How can I continue to shape my pastoral and leadership practices around
   the insights of missiology and around a missional theology of the church?"

8. *A Worthwhile Missional Ecclesiology Is Theologically Reflective*: A missional ecclesiology is dependent on a dynamic Christology, a life-giving theology of the Spirit,
and a trinitarian understanding of ecclesial communion and mission. In other
words, a substantial missional ecclesiology is impossible without robust attention to
Christology, pneumatology, missiology, trinitarian theology, and issues surrounding the gospel-culture relationship. Missional churches practice a missional hermeneutic, since, as Christopher Wright asserts, it is "not just that the Bible contains a
number of texts that happen to provide a rationale for missionary endeavour, but
that the whole Bible is itself a 'missional' phenomenon."[15]

9. *Missional Churches "Change the Scorecard"*: Reggie McNeal writes that the following shifts are necessary for a church to become missional and, thereby, "change the
scorecard" for church leadership (i.e., how church leaders measure their church's
health, spirituality, growth, and missional life):[16]

   a. "The shift from internal to external focus for churches."

   b. "The shift from program development to people development."

   c. "The shift from church-based to kingdom-based leadership."

14. Guder, *Missional Church*, 11–12.

15. Wright, "Mission as a Matrix," 103.

16. "The missional expression of the church will require new metrics to measure its vitality. The current
scorecard for the North American church is tied to the definitions of church as a place and church as a
vendor of religious goods and services." McNeal, *Missional Renaissance*, 37–38.

10. *Missional Churches Make Clear, Practical Commitments to Local and Global Mission:* Let me illustrate this by providing the *Mission Covenant* of the Baptist Churches of NSW/ACT, Australia (the family of churches of which I am a member). I am a part of the group who designed this *Mission Covenant*, to help churches understand what mission-shaped churches look like and how they practice missional vitality.[17]

Mission Covenant

"Christian mission is the announcement and demonstration of the Lordship of Jesus Christ, in the way of Jesus, to our world, both locally and globally.

We acknowledge the Lordship of Jesus Christ and recognize that it extends over all creation and all aspects of human life and society. We believe that through his death and resurrection, Jesus is the Saviour of all those who accept him as such by faith through grace. It is as our resurrected Saviour that we acknowledge him as our Lord. We believe his Lordship extends to all people, and therefore it is his Lordship that gives us our mission. We embrace our calling to be committed to both its verbal announcement and its demonstration through acts of compassion, generosity, hospitality and justice.

As a community of faith within the union of Baptist Churches of NSW and ACT, we therefore commit to live out the following marks of a mission-shaped church:

1. A mission-shaped church *announces* the Lordship of Jesus locally and globally.[18] This will be evidenced by:

   a. Regular opportunity for response to the gospel within the life and mission of the church;

   b. Regular opportunities for members to hear of evangelistic projects and needs they might commit to;

   c. A regular assessment of the needs of our immediate neighbourhood/locality to determine whether certain ethnic, demographic or sub-cultural groups are not hearing the announcement of the Lordship of Jesus;

   d. A corporate commitment to at least one local and one global evangelistic focus;

   e. Active and prayerful consideration as to how we can be involved with planting a new congregation;

   f. A commitment to regularly pray as a whole church for non-Christians to turn to Jesus whether they are found locally or globally.

---

17. Michael Frost also helped design this *Mission Covenant*. He quotes this document here: Frost, *Road to Missional*, 61–62.

18. The covenant has the following footnotes in this sentence: "As stated in the preamble, we understand the Lordship of Jesus to include his salvific work on the cross and through his resurrection. He is both Lord and Saviour." "The 'local and global' focus is understood to embrace regional and national horizons—i.e., the mission commitment is both to the community local to the church, and beyond."

2. A mission-shaped church *demonstrates* the Lordship of Jesus locally and globally. This will be evidenced by:

   a. The fostering of a community life that models compassion, generosity, hospitality and justice as expressions of the love of Jesus;

   b. Regular opportunities for members to hear of effective community development projects and needs they might commit to;

   c. A regular assessment of the needs of our immediate neighbourhood/locality to determine whether certain ethnic, demographic or sub-cultural groups are not benefiting from the demonstration of the Lordship of Jesus;

   d. A corporate commitment to at least one local and one global initiative aimed at addressing injustice, alleviating suffering or showing practical love in Jesus's name;

   e. An annual review of our budget and the degree to which our missional priorities are reflected in our financial commitments;

   f. A commitment to regularly pray as a whole church for the needs of our world, locally, regionally, nationally and globally.

3. A mission-shaped church does mission *in the way of Jesus.*
   This will be evidenced by:

   a. Regular teaching from the Gospels about the missional priorities, lifestyle and message of Jesus, and the fostering of a faith community that reflects this;

   b. Regular opportunities for members to discern their own missional vocation;

   c. Regular training and resourcing for members to be able to inculturationally develop friendships and share their faith in culturally and relationally effective ways;

   d. Active reliance on the empowering Spirit in the announcement and demonstration of Jesus's Lordship;[19]

   e. Regular assessment of the time commitments of pastoral staff and lay leaders to determine that too much of their time is not spent on "in-house" church activities and that they are freed to engage regularly with unchurched people;

   f. Regular teaching on the needs of our world and ways members can become actively involved."[20]

19. It is striking that this is the first and only mention in the *Mission Covenant* of a person of the triune God other than Jesus. This matter will need to be addressed by NSW/ACT Baptists in future rewrites of this *Mission Covenant.*

20. This *Mission Covenant* and its associated footnotes can be found online: http://www.missionone. com.au/various/covenant.html. The Baptist Union of NSW and ACT also offers churches practical resources, listed under each point and sub-point of the covenant, to assist them in their missional efforts. Used by permission.

Are my church, my leadership, my theology, and my denomination genuinely missional? Our attention to these nine broad principles, including the *Mission Covenant*—imperfect as our efforts might be—will help us answer this question.

FROM WESTERN VOICES TO ECCLESIOLOGIES FROM THE MAJORITY WORLD

The missional conversation in western contexts continues to be dominated by white (Caucasian), middle-class, Euro-American, tertiary educated, males (I know I fit that profile!). The following voices are mostly absent or, at the very least, get very little attention: females, minority groups, the economically disadvantaged, and missional leaders from the Majority World. For example, missional church conferences and seminars are still dominated by the former group, to a degree that should cause some shame. The missional conversation cannot be truly attentive to the Spirit and to God's redemptive mission in the church and the world if it continues to ignore the voices and missiological perspectives of women, the marginal, the impoverished, and the extraordinary missionary vitality and important theological voices of Majority World contexts. This correction needs to happen soon, if the missional conversation is to mature and reflect God's missional purposes for the church and humanity.

Philip Jenkins describes how Christianity has moved from the West into Africa, Asia, and Latin America, and he predicts that by the year 2050 only about one-fifth of the world's three billion Christians will be non-Hispanic Caucasian. Jenkins believes that this will result in religious, political, and social transformation and struggle, especially with the corresponding growth in Islam. The Christendom that is forming in the developing world is not middle class; it is the faith of poor non-whites living south of Europe, North America, and Russia. This new Christendom will be shaped by the concerns, values, spiritualities, and social and religious concerns of those outside the wealthy global north.[21]

Stephen Bevans speaks of the global shift in this way,

> A major area in which missiology has developed since *Transforming Mission* is the emergence of the "new church history." As Karl Rahner and Walbert Bühlmann pointed out decades ago, we are now living in a "world church" where the vast majority of Christians are members coming from the "third church" of the South, or the "Two-Thirds World." David Barrett's statistical studies have basically confirmed this shift, and Philip Jenkins has predicted that by 2025 fully two-thirds of Christians will live in Africa, Latin America, and Asia. One may not agree, as Peter Phan emphatically does not (nor do we), with all of Jenkins's interpretations of the implications of this epochal demographic shift, but scholars are fairly unanimous in acknowledging the accuracy of the facts. The "average Christian" today is female, black, and lives in a Brazilian *favela* or an African village.[22]

As I noted in my introduction to this book, I hope, in a companion volume to this work, to examine the ecclesiologies of a group of important female and male thinkers

---

21. Jenkins, *Next Christendom*.
22. Bevans et al., "Missiology after Bosch," 70.

from Africa, Latin America, Asia, and other parts of the Majority World, in order to more fully understand the missional nature and practices of the church. The quality and quantity of ecclesiological works coming out of the Majority World are so considerable that they merit a separate volume.

FROM PAROCHIALISM TO AUTHENTIC ECCLESIOLOGICAL DIALOGUE

Missional ecclesiology will only take root in the churches when denominational or theological parochialism is replaced by critical yet authentic ecclesiological dialogue. It is time to rethink our theology and practice of denominationalism, ecumenism, catholicity, and unity, through the lens of a missional understanding of the church. This book has explored the ecclesiological insights of twelve thinkers from four theological traditions in order to construct an initial missional ecclesiology because of a pivotal conviction—that missional ecclesiology is best developed with attention to the theological and missiological insights of a wide range of Christian traditions and voices. The missional God has been (and continues to be) pursuing his redemptive mission through his church and in the world and, sometimes, *through his church in spite of his church*, in all its ecclesiological, socio-cultural, historical, geographic, structural, and other forms. The church can hear from the missional Spirit of God in the traditions and histories of the church, if it will only take time to listen. A parochial approach to the Christian faith may serve our short-term or vested interests, but it does not serve the mission of Christ, the church of Christ, or the work of Christ in the world, the church, and human history. I am advocating a critical ecclesiological dialogue here, one that listens and learns, but which is also certain of its own negotiable and non-negotiable convictions—this is the only honest approach to ecumenical dialogue that I am aware of, as I appreciate my own biblical, Reformed evangelical, Christ-centered, Free Church, charismatic, trinitarian, ecumenical, and missional convictions. In my case, then, I want to learn from the missiological and ecclesiological insights of other theological traditions, while holding them up to the scrutiny of my own theological convictions. Conversely, if I am honest in this process, my theological convictions will be enriched and scrutinized by the insights of my dialogue partners, so that my evangelical beliefs take on a depth and breadth not possible within a more parochial posture.

What role do denominations have to play in cultivating the missional imagination of churches and leaders and in fostering an environment of ecclesiological dialogue? Both Michael Moynagh and the *Mission-Shaped Church Report* are right to suggest that while much ecumenical and denominational activity "can seem life-emptying, dull, and bureaucratic,"[23] denominations and broader-church gatherings are useful as long as they serve particular functions. These functions include gracious accountability, the encouragement present in broader-church participation in regional gatherings and worship events, genuine support and resourcing, encouragement and care (especially in difficult times), networking of pioneers and missionary initiatives, and coaching and mentoring. At the same time as funding fresh initiatives and serving as permission-givers, denomina-

23. Moynagh, *Emergingchurch.Intro*, 158.

tions can also fund approaches to selecting and training pioneers, partner with missional churches in planting, advocate for missional churches and their leaders, research fresh approaches to church and distribute their findings, facilitate learning networks, create space for theological and ecclesiological reflection, and actively sustain these innovative churches.[24]

In *Church Next*, Eddie Gibbs calls this the movement "from bureaucratic hierarchies to apostolic networks," and many of these networks are crossing theological and denominational divides, as churches seek genuine missional cooperation and ecclesiological dialogue. Beginning with the institutional and cultural problems of mainline denominations in the West, the shift in western Protestantism toward "super-churches" and "new apostolic networks," and the emergence of "dynamic churches in the majority world," Gibbs goes on to propose the implications for local churches, regional networks of churches, and denominational and ecumenical institutions. His implications and proposals revolve around notions of relationships, ecumenical cooperation and dialogue, flattened organizational structures, permission giving, resourcing and equipping, diversification and decentralization, healthy accountability, the potential of networks, and missional courage.[25]

From the perspective of missional ecclesiology, ecumenical cooperation is critical to missional effectiveness in contemporary culture—hence the approach taken in this book. Globalization, multiculturalism, intellectual pluralism, and the burgeoning dialogue between evangelicals, mainline churches, Free Churches, Pentecostalism, Catholicism, and Eastern Orthodoxy have facilitated such ecumenical openness among younger evangelicals—not a naïve, ill-informed openness, but a respectful and critical openness.[26] It is time that we examined our denominational and ecumenical structures for their "cultural captivity," so that authentic "structures of connectedness" are developed that facilitate the church's mission.[27]

The unity of the church has an internal and external character. Historically, evangelicals have emphasized the notion that the unity of the church is primarily of an internal, spiritual character, rather than an external one. This unity is through being joined in the mystical body of Christ. Whether or not there is visible fruit to such unity, and without denying the visible existence of the catholic and local church, this unity is an invisible bond that is forged by the Spirit of Christ and by our common profession of his resurrection and lordship. All such unity must manifest itself in the local community of believers. Any unity of the church universal is objectified and outlived in the unity of the local church. Similarly, the catholicity of the church includes all true believers and is predominantly applied to the invisible church. In my theological tradition, evangelicalism, emphasis is usually placed on the spiritual dimensions of catholicity—all genuine believers are part of one mystical catholic church and this is concretely expressed in their participation in the local congregation.[28]

---

24. Ibid., 158–65, 210–42; Williams, *Mission-Shaped Church*, 125–49.

25. Gibbs, *Church Next*, 69–92.

26. Webber, *Younger Evangelicals*, 37–38, 110–12.

27. Guder, *Missional Church*, 248–68.

28. Berkhof, *Systematic Theology*, 572.

This emphasis on internal cohesion must be complemented by genuine efforts toward visible and concrete expressions of unity and catholicity—by the movement from theological parochialism to ecclesiological dialogue and missiological learning and cooperation. Jesus Christ does not give us any other option. We are his one, holy, catholic, and apostolic church, and must express a unity in diversity that is a beacon to the world and a living testimony to the redemptive, unifying, eschatological gospel of Jesus Christ. Robert Webber notes the wide range of sources for the recovered emphasis on the visible unity and catholicity of the church—secularism, pluralism, globalization, the communication revolution, inter-Christian dialogue, the demise of denominationalism, the worship movement, missional theology, and so on. There is a growing intentionality about ecumenical cooperation and networking between diverse communities of faith, which reflects a genuine desire for practical expressions of catholicity and unity.[29] This is not about flattening out or ignoring difference, or relinquishing theological distinctives or biblical and evangelical convictions. My core evangelical, Free Church ecclesiological convictions, which I outlined in the introductory chapter of this book, shape and inform my ecumenical engagement, for instance. However, such ecumenical dialogue is about genuine attention to the Spirit and to the redemptive activity of Christ in the church and the world, and about cooperation with the triune God and each other in his restoration of all things in Christ Jesus.

I began by telling three stories of contemporary churches confronting new missional challenges and opportunities. The church, especially in western cultures, has reached the point of no return. It is time for us to commit together to a missiological vision for the church, like the one articulated in this book—theologically reflective, mission-forged, Christ-centered, Spirit-empowered, Trinity-imaging, gospel-shaped, cooperative, and dialogical—for the glory of Christ Jesus our Lord. It is time for the church to be what the Spirit of Jesus Christ has already made it—salt, light, and a city set on a hill.

QUESTIONS FOR REFLECTION

1. Is your church resisting change? Does it allow confronting questions? How do you experience change and uncomfortable questions about your ministry?

2. Consider your church in the light of the *Mission Covenant*. How can your church more fully announce and demonstrate the lordship of Jesus locally and globally, doing mission in the way of Jesus?

3. How do you feel about dialogue with other theological traditions? How do we ensure that this dialogue is genuine while critical? How can it be informed by attention to Scripture, church history, and our tradition's theological distinctives?

29. Webber, *Younger Evangelicals*, 107–23.

Resources: Practicing Missional Ecclesiology

THIS BOOK HAS MAINLY focused on theological principles undergirding missional ecclesiology, developed in ecumenical conversation. It has focused more on missional theology than missional practice. Some will ask, "But what does this look like in practice?" "How can these theological themes be practically applied in Christian communities and leadership?"

The following books, articles, and websites provide additional and practical resources, supplementing the theology in this book. They have been chosen because of their practical nature—I could have added further theological works but have chosen to focus on more practical resources. They will help you reflect on how to establish the theological themes articulated in this book in your own ministry and missional context.

ON THE THINKING-IN-COMMUNITY CHURCH

Branson, Mark Lau. *Memories, Hopes, and Conversations: Appreciative Inquiry and Congregational Change.* Herndon, VA: Alban, 2004.

Chester, Tim, and Steve Timmis. *Total Church: A Radical Reshaping around Gospel and Community.* Wheaton, IL: Crossway, 2008.

Cronshaw, Darren. "Re-envisioning Theological Education, Mission, and the Local Church." *Mission Studies* 22, no.1 (2011) 91–115.

Harper, Brad, and Paul Louis Metzger. *Exploring Ecclesiology: An Evangelical and Ecumenical Introduction.* Grand Rapids, MI: Brazos, 2009.

Sedmak, Clemens. *Doing Local Theology: A Guide for Artisans of a New Humanity.* Maryknoll, NY: Orbis, 2006.

Webber, Robert E. *Younger Evangelicals: Facing the Challenges of the New World.* Grand Rapids, MI: Baker, 2003.

ON THE MISSION-FORGED CHURCH

Barrett, Lois Y. *Treasure in Clay Jars: Patterns in Missional Faithfulness.* Grand Rapids, MI: Eerdmans, 2004.

Breen, Mike, and Alex Absalom. *Launching Missional Communities: A Field Guide.* Pawleys Island, SC: 3DM, 2010.

Cole, Neil. *Organic Church: Growing Faith Where Life Happens*. San Francisco, CA: Jossey-Bass, 2005.

Driver, John. *Images of the Church in Mission*. Waterloo, ON: Herald, 1997.

Frost, Michael. *Exiles: Living Missionally in a Post-Christian Culture*. Peabody, MA: Hendrickson, 2006.

Frost, Michael. *The Road to Missional: Journey to the Center of the Church*. Grand Rapids, MI: Baker, 2011.

Frost, Michael, and Alan Hirsch. *The Shaping of Things to Come: Innovation and Mission for the 21st Century Church*. Peabody, MA: Hendrickson, 2003.

Gibbs, Eddie. *Church Next: Quantum Changes in How We Do Ministry*. Downers Grove, IL: IVP, 2000.

Guder, Darrell L., ed. *Missional Church: A Vision for the Sending of the Church in North America*. Grand Rapids, MI: Eerdmans, 1998.

Hirsch, Alan. *The Forgotten Ways: Reactivating the Missional Church*. Grand Rapids, MI: Brazos, 2006.

Holt, Simon Carey. *God Next Door: Spirituality and Mission in the Neighbourhood*. Melbourne, Vic: Acorn, 2007.

McManus, Erwin Raphael. *An Unstoppable Force: Daring to Become the Church God Had in Mind*. Boulder, CO: Group, 2001.

McNeal, Reggie. *Missional Renaissance: Changing the Scorecard for the Church*. San Francisco, CA: Jossey-Bass, 2009.

Nessan, Craig L. *Beyond Maintenance to Mission: A Theology of the Congregation*. Nashville, TN: Fortress, 2010.

Roxburgh, Alan J., and Fred Romanuk. *The Missional Leader: Equipping Your Church to Reach a Changing World*. San Francisco, CA: Jossey-Bass, 2006.

Stetzer, Ed, and David Putman. *Breaking the Missional Code: Your Church Can Become a Missionary in Your Community*. Nashville, TN: Broadman & Holman, 2006.

Van Gelder, Craig, and Dwight J. Zscheile. *The Missioal Church in Perspective: Mapping Trends and Shaping the Conversation*. Grand Rapids, MI: Baker Academic, 2011.

Williams, Rowan, et al. *Mission-Shaped Church: Church Planting and Fresh Expressions of Church in a Changing Context*. London: Church House, 2004.

ON THE CHRIST-CENTERED CHURCH

Frost, Michael, and Alan Hirsch. *ReJesus: A Wild Messiah for a Missional Church*. Peabody, MA: Hendrickson, 2009.

Gushee, David P. *Kingdom Ethics: Following Jesus in Contemporary Context*. Downers Grove, IL: IVP, 2003.

McKnight, Scot. *A Community Called Atonement: Living Theology.* Nashville, TN: Abingdon, 2007.

Moltmann, Jürgen. *The Open Church: Invitation to a Messianic Lifestyle.* London: SCM, 1978.

Moltmann, Jürgen. *The Way of Jesus Christ: Christology in Messianic Dimensions.* San Francisco, CA: HarperSanFrancisco, 1990.

Roberts, Dave. *Following Jesus: A Non-Religious Guidebook for the Spiritually Hungry.* Lake Mary, FL: Relevant, 2004.

Yancey, Philip. *The Jesus I Never Knew.* Grand Rapids, MI: Zondervan, 1995.

ON THE SPIRIT-EMPOWERED CHURCH

Bevans, Stephen B. "God Inside Out: Toward a Missionary Theology of the Holy Spirit." *International Bulletin of Missionary Research* 22, no. 3 (1998) 102–5.

Bevans, Stephen B. "The Church as Creation of the Spirit: Unpacking a Missionary Image." *Missiology* 35, no.1 (2007) 5–21.

Fee, Gordon D. *Paul, the Spirit, and the People of God.* Peabody, MA: Hendrickson, 1996.

Lord, Andrew. *Spirit-Shaped Mission: A Holistic Charismatic Missiology.* Carlisle: Paternoster, 2005.

Tyra, Gary. *The Holy Spirit in Mission: Prophetic Speech and Action in Christian Witness.* Downers Grove, IL: IVP Academic, 2011.

Van Gelder, Craig. *The Essence of the Church: A Community Created by the Spirit.* Grand Rapids, MI: Baker, 2000.

ON THE TRINITY-IMAGING CHURCH

Cunningham, David S. *These Three Are One: The Practice of Trinitarian Theology.* Maiden, MA: Basil Blackwell, 1998.

Fiddes, Paul S. *Participating in God: A Pastoral Doctrine of the Trinity.* London: Darton, Longman & Todd, 2000.

Pembroke, Neil. *Renewing Pastoral Practice: Trinitarian Perspectives on Pastoral Care and Counselling.* Aldershot: Ashgate, 2006.

Seamands, Stephen A. *Ministry in the Image of God.* Downers Grove, IL: IVP, 2005.

Tennent, Timothy C. *Invitation to World Missions: A Trinitarian Missiology for the Twenty-First Century.* Grand Rapids, MI: Kregel, 2010.

Chester, Tim. *Delighting in the Trinity: Just Why are Father, Son, and Spirit Such Good News?* Saint Clair Shores, MI: Monarch, 2005.

ON THE COURAGEOUS AND FUTURE CHURCH

Boff, Leonardo. *Ecclesiogenesis: The Base Communities Reinvent the Church.* Maryknoll, NY: Orbis, 1986.[1]

Branson, Mark Lau, and Juan F. Martinez. *Churches, Cultures, and Leadership: A Practical Theology of Congregations and Ethnicities.* Downers Grove, IL: IVP Academic, 2011.

Clapp, Rodney A. *Peculiar People: The Church as Culture in a Post-Christian Society.* Downers Grove, IL: IVP, 1996.

Drane, John W. *The McDonaldization of the Church: Consumer Culture and the Church's Future.* London: Darton, Longman & Todd, 2000.

Escobar, Samuel. *The New Global Mission: The Gospel from Everywhere to Everyone.* Downers Grove, IL: IVP Academic, 2003.

Gaillardetz, Richard R. *Ecclesiology for a Global Church: A People Called and Sent.* Maryknoll, NY: Orbis, 2008.

Gibbs, Eddie, and Ryan K. Bolger. *Emerging Churches: Creating Christian Community in Postmodern Cultures.* Grand Rapids, MI: Baker, 2005.

Jenkins, Philip. *The Next Christendom: The Coming of Global Christianity.* Oxford: Oxford University Press, 2011.

Kenneson, Philip D. *Beyond Sectarianism: Re-Imagining Church and World.* New York, NY: Trinity, 1999.

Murray, Stuart. *Church After Christendom.* Milton Keynes: Paternoster, 2004.

Onwubiko, Oliver A. *The Church in Mission in the Light of Ecclesia in Africa: A Trilogy.* Nairobi: Paulines, 2001.

Phan, Peter C. *In Our Own Tongues: Perspectives from Asia on Mission and Inculturation.* Maryknoll, NY: Orbis, 2003.

Segundo, Juan L. *The Community Called Church.* Maryknoll, NY: Orbis, 1973.

Shenk, Wilbert R. *Write the Vision: The Church Renewed.* New York, NY: Trinity, 1995.

Sine, Tom. *The New Conspirators: Creating the Future One Mustard Seed at a Time.* Downers Grove, IL: IVP, 2008.

Sobrino, Jon. *The True Church and the Poor.* Eugene, OR: Wipf & Stock, 2004.

Taylor, Steve. *The Out of Bounds Church: Learning to Create a Community of Faith in a Culture of Change.* Grand Rapids, MI: Zondervan, 2005.

Wan, Enoch, and Michael Pocock, eds. *Missions from the Majority World: Progress, Challenges, and Case Studies.* Pasadena, CA: William Carey, 2009.

---

1. This list *On the Courageous and Future Church* includes, but is obviously not limited to, works on the church in mission from the Majority World.

BLOGS AND WEBSITES

Alban Institute: http://www.alban.org/

Anabaptist after Christendom Material: http://www.anabaptistnetwork.com/After Christendom

Center for Parish Development: http://www.missionalchurch.org/resources/essays. html

Church Multiplication Associates: http://www.cmaresources.org/

Ekklesia Project: http://www.ekklesiaproject.org/

Emergent Village: http://www.emergentvillage.com/

Friend of Missional: http://friendofmissional.org/

Gospel and Our Culture Network in the UK: http://www.gospel-culture.org.uk/

Gospel and Our Culture Network in the US: http://www.gocn.org/

KC Sentral: http://kcsentral.com/

Lifeway Research: http://www.edstetzer.com/

Mission One Covenant: http://www.missionone.com.au/various/covenant.html

Missional Church Network: http://missionalchurchnetwork.com/

Missional Network: http://www.roxburghmissionalnet.com/

Missional Primer: http://jrwoodward.net/2008/11/a-primer-on-todays-missional-church/

New Monasticism: http://www.newmonasticism.org/

Newbigin.Net: http://www.newbigin.net/

Next Reformation: http://nextreformation.com/

Resurgence: http://theresurgence.com/

Tall Skinny Kiwi: http://tallskinnykiwi.typepad.com/tallskinnykiwi/

Tinsley Institute: http://www.morling.nsw.edu.au/tinsley_institute/

Vintage Faith: http://www.vintagechurch.org/

Bibliography

Andrews, Dave, and Helen Beazley, eds. *Learnings: Lessons We Are Learning about Living Together*. Woolloongabba, Qld: Frank Communications, 2010.

Avis, Paul D. L. *The Church in the Theology of the Reformers*. London: Marshall, Morgan & Scott, 1981.

Baker, Jonny, and Doug Gay. *Alternative Worship*. London: SPCK, 2003.

Barrett, C. Kingsley. *A Commentary on the Epistle to the Romans*. Black's New Testament Commentaries. London: Black, 1971.

Barrett, Lois Y. *Treasure in Clay Jars: Patterns in Missional Faithfulness*. Grand Rapids, MI: Eerdmans, 2004.

Bate, Paul. *Strategies for Cultural Change*. Oxford: Butterworth-Heinemann, 1994.

Baum, Gregory. "The Church We Love: A Conversation with Miroslav Volf." *The Ecumenist* 37 (2000) 13–16.

Bauman, Zygmunt. *Liquid Modernity*. Cambridge: Polity, 2000.

Bebbington, David W. *Evangelicalism in Modern Britain: A History from the 1730s to the 1980s*. London: Unwin Hyman, 1989.

Beckhard, Richard. *Organization Development: Strategies and Models*. Reading, MA: Addison-Wesley, 1969.

Beilby, James K., and Paul R. Eddy, eds. *The Nature of the Atonement: Four Views*. Downers Grove, IL: IVP Academic, 2006.

Berkhof, Louis. *Systematic Theology*. Edinburgh: Banner of Truth, 1979.

Bevans, Stephen B. "The Church as Creation of the Spirit: Unpacking a Missionary Image." *Missiology* 35, no. 1 (2007) 5–21.

———. "God Inside Out: Toward a Missionary Theology of the Holy Spirit." *International Bulletin of Missionary Research* 22, no. 3 (1998) 102–5.

———. "Models of Contextual Theology." *Missiology* 13, no. 2 (1985) 185–202.

Bevans, Stephen B., and Roger P. Schroeder. *Constants in Context: A Theology of Mission for Today*. American Society of Missiology Series. Maryknoll, NY: Orbis, 2004.

Bevans, Stephen B., et al. "Missiology after Bosch: Reverencing a Classic by Moving Beyond." *International Bulletin of Missionary Research* 29, no. 2 (2005) 69–72.

Boersma, Hans. Review of *Can These Bones Live? A Catholic Baptist Engagement with Ecclesiology, Hermeneutics, and Social Theory*, by Barry A. Harvey. *Religious Studies Review* 35, no. 2 (2009) 427–29.

Bonhoeffer, Dietrich. *Christology*. London: Collins, 1966.

Bonk, Jonathan J. *Missions and Money: Affluence as a Missionary Problem*. Revised and expanded edition, American Society of Missiology Series. Maryknoll, NY: Orbis, 2007.

Bosch, David J. *Believing in the Future: Toward a Missiology of Western Culture*. New York, NY: Trinity, 1995.

———. *Transforming Mission: Paradigm Shifts in Theology of Mission*. Maryknoll, NY: Orbis, 1991.

Boutin, Maurice. "Anonymous Christianity: A Paradigm for Inter-Religious Encounter?" *Journal of Ecumenical Studies* 20, no. 4 (1983) 602–29.

Bridges, William. *Managing Transitions: Making the Most of Change*. 3rd ed. Philadelphia, PA: Da Capo, 2009.

Bromiley, Geoffrey W., ed. *The International Standard Bible Encyclopedia*. Vol. 3. Grand Rapids, MI: Eerdmans, 1979.

———, ed. *The Library of Christian Classics—Zwingli & Bullinger*. Santa Ana, CA: Westminster, 1979.

Bruce, Frederick F. *1 and 2 Corinthians*. New Century Bible Commentary. Grand Rapids, MI: Eerdmans, 1980.

———. *This Is That: The New Testament Development of Some Old Testament Themes*. Exeter: Paternoster, 1968.

Buckwalter, Douglas. *The Character and Purpose of Luke's Christology*. Society for New Testament Studies

Monograph Series. Cambridge: Cambridge University Press, 2005.

Buttrey, Michael. "Twelve Ways to Prematurely Write Off Yoder." *On the Road*, no. 47 (December 2010) 8–11.

Cardoza-Orlandi, Carlos F. *Mission: An Essential Guide*. Nashville, TN: Abingdon, 2002.

Carter, Craig A. "Beyond Theocracy and Individualism: The Significance of John Howard Yoder's Ecclesiology for Evangelicalism." In *The Community of the Word: Toward an Evangelical Ecclesiology*, edited by Mark Husbands and Daniel J. Treier, 173–87. Downers Grove, IL: IVP, 2005.

———. "The Legacy of an Inadequate Christology: Yoder's Critique of Niebuhr's Christ and Culture." *Mennonite Quarterly Review* 77, no. 3 (2003) 387–401.

———. *The Politics of the Cross: The Theology and Social Ethics of John Howard Yoder*. Grand Rapids, MI: Brazos, 2001.

Cartwright, Michael G., ed. *The Royal Priesthood: Essays Ecclesiological and Ecumenical—John Howard Yoder*. Grand Rapids, MI: Eerdmans, 1994.

Castells, Manuel. *The Rise of the Network Society*. Vol. 1, The Information Age: Economy, Society and Culture. Oxford: Blackwell, 2000.

Charry, Ellen T. "Spiritual Formation by the Doctrine of the Trinity." *Theology Today* 54 (1997) 367–80.

Cho, David Yonggi, and Harold Hostetler. *Successful Home Cell Groups*. Plainfield, NJ: Logos, 1981.

Clapp, Rodney A. *A Peculiar People: The Church as Culture in a Post-Christian Society*. Downers Grove, IL: IVP, 1996.

Conzelmann, Hans. *1 Corinthians: A Commentary on the First Epistle to the Corinthians*. Hermeneia: A Critical and Historical Commentary on the Bible. Philadelphia, PA: Fortress, 1975.

———. *The Theology of St. Luke*. 1st Fortress ed. Philadelphia, PA: Fortress, 1982.

Coulter, Dale M. Review of *Another City: An Ecclesiological Primer for a Post-Christian World*, by Barry A. Harvey. *Pneuma* 22, no. 2 (2000) 333–36.

Cranfield, Charles E. B. *A Critical and Exegetical Commentary on the Epistle to the Romans*. The International Critical Commentary. London: T & T Clark, 2004.

Cunningham, David S. *These Three Are One: The Practice of Trinitarian Theology*. London: Blackwell, 1997.

D'Costa, Gavin. "Karl Rahner's Anonymous Christian—A Reappraisal." *Modern Theology* 1, no. 2 (1985) 131–48.

Dannemiller, Kathleen D., and Robert W. Jacobs. "Changing the Way Organizations Change: A Revolution of Common Sense." *The Journal of Applied Behavioral Science* 28, no. 4 (1992) 480–98.

Daugherty, Kevin. "Missio Dei: The Trinity and Christian Missions." *Evangelical Review of Theology* 31, no. 2 (2007) 151–68.

Davidson, Max. *Living as Trinitarian Christians*. Macquarie Park, NSW: Morling College, 2005.

———. *Marks of the True Church, and the Visible and Invisible Church*. Macquarie Park, NSW: Morling College, 2005.

Drane, John W., and Olive F. Drane. "Breaking into Dynamic Ways of Being Church." In *Breaking New Ground: The First Scottish Ecumenical Assembly 2001*, edited by Action of Churches Together in Scotland, 138–54. Dunblane: Action of Churches Together in Scotland, 2001.

Draper, Jonathan. Review of *Being as Communion: Studies in Personhood and the Church*, by John D. Zizioulas. *Modern Theology* 5, no. 4 (1989) 400–1.

Driver, John. *Images of the Church in Mission*. Scottdale, PA: Herald, 1997.

Dulles, Avery R. *Models of the Church*. New York, NY: Doubleday, 1987.

Dych, William V. *Karl Rahner*. Outstanding Christian Thinkers. London: Geoffrey Chapman, 1992.

Elwell, Walter A., ed. *The Concise Evangelical Dictionary of Theology*. London: HarperCollins, 1991.

———, ed. *Evangelical Dictionary of Theology*, Baker Reference Library. Grand Rapids, MI: Baker, 1984.

Engelsviken, Tormod. "Missio Dei: The Understanding and Misunderstanding of a Theological Concept in European Churches and Missiology." *International Review of Mission* 92, no. 367 (2003) 481–97.

Erickson, Millard J. *Christian Theology*. Grand Rapids, MI: Baker, 1994.

Fahey, Michael A. "Church." In *Systematic Theology: Roman Catholic Perspectives*, edited by Francis Schüssler Fiorenza and John P. Galvin, 315–74. Minneapolis, MN: Fortress, 1991.

Fee, Gordon D. *The First Epistle to the Corinthians*. The New International Commentary on the New Testament. Grand Rapids, MI: Eerdmans, 1987.

———. *God's Empowering Presence: The Holy Spirit in the Letters of Paul*. Peabody, MA: Hendrickson, 1994.

Flannery, Austin P., ed. *Ad Gentes: Decree on the Church's Missionary Activity*. Vatican Council II: The Conciliar and Post Conciliar Documents. Collegeville, MN: Liturgical, 1992.

Fortman, Edmund J. *The Triune God: A Historical Study of the Doctrine of the Trinity*. Theological Resources. Philadelphia, PA: Westminster, 1972.

Fox, Patricia. *God as Communion: John Zizioulas, Elizabeth Johnson, and the Retrieval of the Symbol of the Triune God*. Collegeville, MN: Liturgical, 2001.

Franke, John R. "God Is Love." In *Trinitarian Theology for the Church: Scripture, Community, Worship*, edited by Daniel J. Treier and David Lauber, 105–19. Downers Grove, IL: IVP Academic, 2009.

Fries, Heinrich, and Karl Rahner. *Unity of the Churches: An Actual Possibility*. New York, NY: Fortress, 1985.

Frost, Michael. *Exiles: Living Missionally in a Post-Christian Culture*. Peabody, MA: Hendrickson, 2006.

———. *The Road to Missional: Journey to the Center of the Church*. Grand Rapids, MI: Baker, 2011.

Frost, Michael, and Alan Hirsch. *ReJesus: A Wild Messiah for a Missional Church*. Peabody, MA: Hendrickson, 2008.

———. *The Shaping of Things to Come: Innovation and Mission for the 21st Century Church*. Peabody, MA: Hendrickson, 2003.

Fuellenbach, John. *Church: Community for the Kingdom*. London: Orbis, 2002.

George, Timothy. *Theology of the Reformers*. Nashville, TN: Broadman, 1988.

Gibbs, Eddie. *Church Next: Quantum Changes in How We Do Ministry*. Downers Grove, IL: IVP, 2000.

Gibbs, Eddie, and Ryan K. Bolger. *Emerging Churches: Creating Christian Community in Postmodern Cultures*. Grand Rapids, MI: Baker, 2005.

Giles, Kevin. *The Trinity and Subordinationism: The Doctrine of God and the Contemporary Gender Debate*. Downers Grove, IL: IVP, 2002.

Goldsworthy, Graeme. "Gospel." In *New Dictionary of Biblical Theology*, edited by T. Desmond Alexander and Brian S. Rosner, 523. Leicester: IVP, 2000.

Guder, Darrell L. *The Continuing Conversion of the Church*. Grand Rapids, MI: Eerdmans, 2000.

———. *The Incarnation and the Church's Witness*. Christian Mission and Modern Culture. New York, NY: Trinity, 2000.

———. *Missional Church: A Vision for the Sending of the Church in North America*. Grand Rapids, MI: Eerdmans, 1998.

Gunton, Colin E. *The Promise of Trinitarian Theology*. Edinburgh: T&T Clark, 1991.

Guroian, Vigen. "Bible and Ethics: An Ecclesial and Liturgical Interpretation." *Journal of Religious Ethics* 18, no. 1 (1990) 129–57.

———. "The Christian Gardener: An Orthodox Meditation." *Christian Century* 113, no. 7 (1996) 228–31.

———. "'Cleansers of the Whole Earth': The Ecological Spirituality of the Armenian Church." *Greek Othodox Theological Review* 36, no. 3–4 (1991) 263–76.

———. *Ethics after Christendom: Toward an Ecclesial Christian Ethic*. Grand Rapids, MI: Eerdmans, 1994.

———. *Faith, Church, Mission: Essays for Renewal in the Armenian Church*. New York, NY: Armenian Prelacy, 1995.

———. "Family and Christian Virtue in a Post-Christendom World: Reflections on the Ecclesial Vision of John Chrysostom." *St Vladimir's Theological Quarterly* 35, no. 4 (1991) 327–50.

———. "'I Confess the Cross Because I Know of the Resurrection.'" *St Vladimir's Theological Quarterly* 50, no. 4 (2006) 339–55.

———. *Incarnate Love: Essays in Orthodox Ethics*. Notre Dame, IN: University of Notre Dame Press, 1987.

———. "Let No Man Join Together." *Touchstone: A Journal of Mere Christianity* 24, no. 1 (2011) 28–32.

———. "Liturgy and the Lost Eschatological Vision of Christian Ethics." *Annual of the Society of Christian Ethics* 20 (2000) 227–38.

———. "Love in Orthodox Ethics: Trinitarian and Christological Reflections." *Cross Currents* 33, no. 2 (1983) 181–97.

———. "Moral Formation and Christian Worship." *Ecumenical Review* 49, no. 3 (1997) 372–78.

———. "The Moral Imagination in an Age of Sentiments." *The Intercollegiate Review* 34, no. 1 (1998) 10–19.

———. "Notes Toward an Eastern Orthodox Ethic." *Journal of Religious Ethics* 9, no. 2 (1981) 228–44.

———. "The Problem of an Orthodox Social Ethic: Diaspora Reflections." *Journal of Ecumenical Studies* 21, no. 4 (1984) 709–29.

———. *Rallying the Really Human Things: The Moral Imagination in Politics, Literature, and Everyday Life*.

Wilmington, NC: ISI, 2005.

———. "Salvation: Divine Therapy." *Theology Today* 61, no. 3 (2004) 309–21.

———. "Seeing Worship as Ethics: An Orthodox Perspective." *Journal of Religious Ethics* 13, no. 2 (1985) 332–59.

———. "Tradition and Ethics: Prospects in a Liberal Society." *Modern Theology* 7, no. 3 (1991) 205–24.

Guthrie, Donald. *The Pastoral Epistles: An Introduction and Commentary*. Tyndale New Testament Commentaries. Nottingham: IVP, 2009.

Guthrie, Shirley C. *Christian Doctrine*. Louisville, KY: Westminster, 1994.

Haight, Roger. *The Future of Christology*. New York, NY: Continuum, 2007.

———. "Towards an Ecclesiology from Below." In *Imaginer La Theologie Catholique*, edited by Jeremy Driscoll, 413–36. Rome: Studia Anselmiana, 2000.

———. "Two Types of Christology." *Chicago Studies* 38 (1999) 117–27.

Hall, Douglas John. *The End of Christendom and the Future of Christianity*. New York, NY: Trinity, 2002.

Hartenstein, Karl. "Theologische Besinnung." In *Mission zwischen Gestern und Morgen*, edited by Walter Freytag, 54. Stuttgart: Evang. Missionsverlag, 1952.

Harvey, Barry A. *Another City: An Ecclesiological Primer for a Post-Christian World*. New York, NY: Trinity, 1999.

———. "The Body Politic of Christ: Theology, Social Analysis, and Bonhoeffer's Arcane Discipline." *Modern Theology* 13, no. 3 (1997) 319.

———. *Can These Bones Live? A Catholic Baptist Engagement with Ecclesiology, Hermeneutics, and Social Theory*. Grand Rapids, MI: Brazos, 2008.

———. "The Eucharistic Idiom of the Gospel." *Pro Ecclesia* 9, no. 3 (2000) 297–318.

———. "From the Heart of the Storm: Ecclesial Performance between Pentecost and Parousia." *Review & Expositor* 97, no. 3 (2000) 315–38.

———. "God: An Open Question." *Theology Today* 60, no. 4 (2004) 574–76.

———. "Insanity, Theocracy, and the Public Realm: Public Theology, the Church, and the Politics of Liberal Democracy." *Modern Theology* 10, no. 1 (1994) 27–57.

———. *Politics of the Theological: Beyond the Piety and Power of a World Come of Age*, American University Studies Series VII: Theology and Religion. New York, NY: P. Lang, 1995.

———. "A Post-Critical Approach to 'Religionless Christianity.'" *Union Seminary Quarterly Review* 46, no. 1–4 (1992) 39–58.

———. "Re-Membering the Body: Baptism, Eucharist and the Politics of Disestablishment." In *Baptist Sacramentalism*, edited by Anthony R. Cross and Philip E. Thompson, 96–116. Carlisle: Paternoster, 2003.

———. "Round and Round About the Town: The Ecclesial Dimensions of Living in the Truth." *Perspectives in Religious Studies* 25, no. 1 (1998) 105–14.

———. "Where, Then, Do We Stand?: Baptists, History, and Authority." *Perspectives in Religious Studies* 29, no. 4 (2002) 359–80.

Harvey, Barry A., et al. *Stormfront: The Good News of God*. Grand Rapids, MI: Eerdmans, 2003.

Hauerwas, Stanley M., and L. Gregory Jones, eds. *Why Narrative? Readings in Narrative Theology*. Eugene, OR: Wipf & Stock, 1989.

Hauerwas, Stanley M., and William H. Willimon. *Resident Aliens: Life in the Christian Colony—A Provocative Christian Assessment of Culture and Ministry for People Who Know That Something Is Wrong*. Nashville, TN: Abingdon, 1989.

Heifetz, Ronald A. *Leadership without Easy Answers*. Harvard, MA: Belknap, 1998.

Henson, N. Christine. "Letty Russell: Contributions toward a Holistic Ecclesial Vision." *Religious Education* 92, no. 1 (1997) 107–18.

Hiebert, Paul G. *Missiological Implications of Epistemological Shifts*. New York, NY: Trinity, 1999.

Hill, Graham J. G. "Emerging-Missional Ecclesiology and the Future of Denominational Leadership and Affiliation." In *Beyond 400: Exploring Baptist Futures*, edited by Michael Parsons and David J. Cohen, 86–100. Eugene, OR: Wipf & Stock, 2011.

———. "An Examination of Emerging-Missional Ecclesiological Conceptions: Missional Ecclesiology and the Ecclesiologies of Miroslav Volf, Joseph Ratzinger, and John Zizioulas." PhD diss., Flinders University of South Australia, 2009.

Hirsch, Alan, and Debra Hirsch. *Untamed: Reactivating a Missional Form of Discipleship*. Grand Rapids, MI:

Baker, 2010.

Hopko, Thomas. *All the Fulness of God: Essays on Orthodoxy, Ecumenism and Modern Society*. Crestwood, NY: St. Vladimir's Seminary, 1982.

———. "The Lima Statement and the Orthodox." *St Vladimir's Theological Quarterly* 27, no. 4 (1983) 281–90.

———. "Ministry and the Unity of the Church: An Eastern Orthodox View." *St Vladimir's Theological Quarterly* 34, no. 4 (1990) 269–79.

———. "The Narrow Way of Orthodoxy." *St Vladimir's Theological Quarterly* 40, no. 1–2 (1996) 3–15.

———. "The Narrow Way of Orthodoxy: A Message from Orthodoxy in America to Eastern Europe." *Christian Century* 112, no. 9 (1995) 296–99.

———. *The Orthodox Faith: Volume 1—Doctrine*. New York, NY: Orthodox Church in America, 1971.

———. *The Orthodox Faith: Volume 2—Worship*. New York, NY: Orthodox Church in America, 1972.

———. *The Orthodox Faith: Volume 3—Bible and Church History*. New York, NY: Orthodox Church in America, 1979.

———. *The Orthodox Faith: Volume 4—Spirituality*. New York, NY: Orthodox Church in America, 1984.

———. "The Orthodox Parish in America." *Greek Orthodox Theological Review* 48, no. 1–4 (2003) 1–10.

———. *Speaking the Truth in Love: Education, Mission, and Witness in Contemporary Orthodoxy*. Crestwood, NY: St. Vladimir's Seminary, 2004.

———. "Tasks Facing the Orthodox in the 'Reception' Process of BEM." *Greek Orthodox Theological Review* 30, no. 2 (1985) 235–47.

Horton, Michael. "Evangelical Arminians." *Modern Reformation* 1, no. 3 (1992) 15–19.

Hull, John M. *Mission-Shaped Church: A Theological Response*. London: SCM, 2006.

Hunsberger, George R., and Craig Van Gelder, eds. *The Church between Gospel and Culture: The Emerging Mission in North America*. Grand Rapids, MI: Eerdmans, 1996.

Hunter III, George G. *How to Reach Secular People*. Nashville, TN: Abingdon, 1992.

Husbands, Mark, and Daniel J. Treier, eds. *The Community of the Word: Toward an Evangelical Ecclesiology*. Downers Grove, IL: IVP, 2005.

Jackson, Darrell R. "The Discourse of 'Belonging' and Baptist Church Membership in Contemporary Britain: Historical, Theological, and Demotic Elements of a Post-Foundational Theological Proposal." ThD, Birmingham University, 2009.

Jenkins, Philip. *The Next Christendom: The Coming of Global Christianity*. 3rd ed. Oxford: Oxford University Press, 2011.

Jennings, J. Nelson. "Another City: An Ecclesiological Primer for a Post-Christian World." *Mission Studies* 17, no. 1–2 (2000) 304–5.

Jesson, Nicholas A. "Orthodox Contributions to Ecumenical Ecclesiology." Toronto: University of St. Michael's College. No pages. Online: http://www.ecumenism.net/archive/jesson_orthodox.pdf.

———. "Where Two or Three Are Gathered: Miroslav Volf's Free Church Ecclesiology." Toronto, Ontario: University of St. Michael's College. No pages. Online: http://www.ecumenism.net/archive/jesson_volf.pdf.

Jethani, Skye. "Special Needs Boy Removed from Church: Can the Values of Entertainment and Hospitality Coexist?" No pages. Online: http://www.skyejethani.com/special-needs-boy-removed-from-church/762/.

Jinkins, Michael. *The Church Faces Death: Ecclesiology in a Post-Modern Context*. Oxford: Oxford University Press, 1999.

Johnson, Elizabeth A. *She Who Is*. New York, NY: Herder & Herder, 2002.

Kärkkäinen, Veli-Matti. *An Introduction to Ecclesiology: Ecumenical, Historical and Global Perspectives*. Downers Grove, IL: IVP, 2002.

———. "Miroslav Volf: Participatory Ecclesiology." In *An Introduction to Ecclesiology: Ecumenical, Historical and Global Perspectives*, 134–41. Downers Grove, IL: IVP, 2002.

Käsemann, Ernst, and Geoffrey W. Bromiley. *Commentary on Romans*. Grand Rapids, MI: Eerdmans, 1980.

Kee, Howard C. *Good News to the Ends of the Earth: The Theology of Acts*. London: SCM, 1990.

Kelly, Geoffrey B., and John W. de Gruchy. *Karl Rahner: Theologian of the Graced Search for Meaning*. Edinburgh: T&T Clark, 1992.

Kimball, Dan. *The Emerging Church: Vintage Christianity for New Generations*. Grand Rapids, MI: Zondervan, 2003.

Kirk, J. Andrew. *The Mission of Theology and Theology as Mission*. Valley Forge, PA: Trinity, 1997.

———. *What Is Mission?: Theological Explorations*. Minneapolis, MN: Fortress, 2000.

Kittel, Gerhard, et al. *Theological Dictionary of the New Testament*. Grand Rapids: Eerdmans, 1985.

Klug, Eugene F. A. "Luther's Understanding of 'Church' in His Treatise on the Councils and the Church of 1539." *Concordia Theological Quarterly* 44, no. 1 (1980) 27–38.

Knight, Douglas H. *The Theology of John Zizioulas: Personhood and Church*. Aldershot: Ashgate, 2007.

Köstenberger, Margaret E. *Jesus and the Feminists: Who Do They Say That He Is?* Wheaton, IL: Crossway, 2008.

Kraus, C. Norman. *The Authentic Witness: Credibility and Authority*. Grand Rapids, MI: Eerdmans, 1978.

Krauth, Charles P., et al. *The Book of Concord: Or the Symbolical Books of the Evangelical Lutheran Church*. 2 vols. Philadelphia, PA: Frederick, 1882.

Kreider, Alan. *The Change of Conversion and the Origin of Christendom*. New York, NY: Trinity, 1999.

Küng, Hans. "Abuse Rooted in Clerical Celibacy." *National Catholic Reporter* 46, no. 11 (2010) 14–20.

———. "A Christian Scholar's Dialogue with Muslims." *Christian Century* 102, no. 30 (1985) 890–94.

———. "Christianity and World Religions: The Dialogue with Islam as One Model." *Muslim World* 77, no. 2 (1987) 80–95.

———. *The Church*. London: Search, 1968.

———. *The Church—Maintained in Truth: A Theological Meditation*. New York, NY: Vintage, 1982.

———. *Disputed Truth: Memoirs*. New York, NY: Continuum, 2008.

———. "Global Ethics and Education in Tolerance." *Diogenes*, (1996), 137.

———. *Global Responsibility: In Search of a New World Ethic*. New York, NY: Crossroad, 1991.

———. *On Being a Christian*. Garden City, NY: Image, 1984.

———. "Participation of the Laity in Church Leadership and in Church Elections." *Journal of Ecumenical Studies* 6, no. 4 (1969) 511–33.

———. *Reforming the Church Today: Keeping Hope Alive*. New York, NY: Crossroad, 1990.

———. *Structures of the Church*. New York, NY: Crossroad, 1982.

———. "Towards a Universal Civilization." *Islam and Christian-Muslim Relations* 11, no. 2 (2000) 229–34.

———. "What Is the True Religion?: Toward an Ecumenical Criteriology." *Journal of Theology for Southern Africa*, no. 56 (1986) 4–23.

———. "Why I Remain a Catholic." *Journal of Ecumenical Studies* 17, no. 1 (1980) 141–47.

———. *Yes to a Global Ethic*. New York, NY: Continuum, 1996.

Küng, Hans, and Jürgen Moltmann. *The Ethics of World Religions and Human Rights*, Concilium. London: SCM, 1990.

Ladd, George E. *A Theology of the New Testament*. Grand Rapids, MI: Eerdmans, 1993.

Leithart, Peter J. *Defending Constantine: The Twilight of an Empire and the Dawn of Christendom*. Downers Grove, IL: IVP, 2010.

Lindbeck, George A. "The Church." In *Keeping the Faith*, edited by Geoffrey Wainwright, 179–208. Philadelphia, PA: Fortress, 1988.

Littell, Franklin H. "Church and Sect." *The Ecumenical Review* 6, no. 3 (1954) 262–76.

Luther, Martin. *Martin Luther's Werke: Kritische Gesamtausgabe, Tischreden (Table Talk)* 1–6 vols. Weimar: Hermann Böhlaus Nachfolger, 2009.

Masters, Peter. *The Baptist Confession of Faith 1689: Or the Second London Confession with Scripture Proofs*. London: Wakeman Trust, 1989.

McClendon, James W., and John Howard Yoder. "Christian Identity in Ecumenical Perspective: A Response to David Wayne Layman." *Journal of Ecumenical Studies* 27, no. 3 (1990) 561–80.

McDougall, Joy A. "The Return of Trinitarian Praxis? Moltmann on the Trinity and the Christian Life." *The Journal of Religion* 83, no. 2 (2003) 177–203.

McGavran, Donald A., and Winfield C. Arn. *Ten Steps for Church Growth*. San Francisco, CA: Harper & Row, 1977.

McGrath, Alister E. *Christian Theology: An Introduction*. 4th ed. Malden, MA: Blackwell, 2007.

———. *Christianity's Dangerous Idea: The Protestant Revolution—A History from the Sixteenth Century to the Twenty-First*. New York, NY: HarperOne, 2007.

———. *"I Believe": Exploring the Apostles' Creed*. Downers Grove, IL: IVP, 1998.

McKnight, Scot. "Five Streams of the Emerging Church." *Christianity Today* February (2007).

McLaren, Brian D. *The Church on the Other Side: Doing Ministry in the Postmodern Matrix.* Grand Rapids, MI: Zondervan, 2000.

McManus, Erwin R. *An Unstoppable Force: Daring to Become the Church God Had in Mind.* Loveland, CO: Group, 2001.

McNeal, Reggie. *Missional Renaissance: Changing the Scorecard for the Church.* 1st ed. San Francisco, CA: Jossey-Bass, 2009.

McNeill, John T., ed. *Calvin: Institutes of the Christian Religion.* Vol. 1 and 2. Philadelphia, PA: Westminster, 1960.

Meilaender, Gilbert. *Faith and Faithfulness: Basic Themes in Christian Ethics.* Notre Dame, IN: University of Notre Dame Press, 1991.

Melissaris, Athanasios G. "The Challenge of Patristic Ontology in the Theology of Metropolitan John (Zizioulas) of Pergamon." *Greek Orthodox Theological Review* 44, no. 1–4 (1999) 467.

———. "Orthodox Anthropology and Archetypal Psychology: Comparing John Zizioulas and James Hillman on Personhood." ThD diss., Boston University School of Theology, 1997.

Milbank, John, et al., eds. *Radical Orthodoxy: A New Theology.* London: Routledge, 1999.

Moltmann, Jürgen. *The Church in the Power of the Spirit: A Contribution to Messianic Ecclesiology.* 2nd ed. London: SCM, 1992.

———. "The Crucified God: Perspectives on a Theology of the Cross for Today." *Journal of Theology for Southern Africa*, no. 9 (1974) 9–27.

———. *The Crucified God: The Cross of Christ as the Foundation and Criticism of Christian Theology.* London: SCM, 1974.

———. "The 'Crucified God': A Trinitarian Theology of the Cross." *Interpretation* 26, no. 3 (1972) 278–99.

———. "Ecumenism beneath the Cross: Part I." *AFER* 18, no. 6 (1976) 314–19.

———. "Ecumenism beneath the Cross: Part II." *AFER* 19, no. 1 (1977) 2–9.

———. *Experiences in Theology: Ways and Forms of Christian Theology.* Minneapolis, MN: Fortress, 2000.

———. *The Future of Creation: Collected Essays.* Philadelphia, PA: Fortress, 1979.

———. *History and the Triune God: Contributions to Trinitarian Theology.* New York, NY: Crossroad, 1992.

———. *Jesus Christ for Today's World.* Minneapolis, MN: Fortress, 1994.

———. *The Open Church: Invitation to a Messianic Lifestyle.* London: SCM, 1978.

———. *The Passion for Life: A Messianic Lifestyle.* Philadelphia: Fortress Press, 1978.

———. *The Source of Life: The Holy Spirit and the Theology of Life.* Minneapolis, MN: Fortress, 1997.

———. *The Spirit of Life: A Universal Affirmation.* Minneapolis, MN: Fortress, 1992.

———. *Sun of Righteousness, Arise!: God's Future for Humanity and the Earth.* Minneapolis, MN: Augsburg Fortress, 2010.

———. *Theology of Hope: On the Ground and the Implications of a Christian Eschatology.* New York, NY: Harper & Row, 1967.

———. *The Trinity and the Kingdom: The Doctrine of God.* 1st US ed. San Francisco, CA: Harper & Row, 1981.

———. *The Trinity and the Kingdom: The Doctrine of God.* Minneapolis: Fortress, 1993.

———. "The Triune God: Rich in Relationships." *Living Pulpit* 8, no. 2 (1999) 4–5.

———. *The Way of Jesus Christ: Christology in Messianic Dimensions.* San Francisco, CA: HarperSanFrancisco, 1990.

Moltmann, Jürgen, and Karl-Josef Kuschel. *Pentecostal Movements as an Ecumenical Challenge*, Concilium. London: SCM, 1996.

Moltmann, Jürgen, and Elisabeth Moltmann-Wendel. "Becoming Human in New Community." *Ecumenical Review* 33, no. 4 (1981) 354–65.

———. *Humanity in God.* New York, NY: Pilgrim, 1983.

Moore, Mary E. "Inclusive Language and Power: A Response." *Religious Education* 80, no. 4 (1985) 603–14.

Moyes, Gordon. *How to Grow an Australian Church: A Practical Guide for Church Growth*, Glen Iris: Vital, 1975.

Moynagh, Michael. *Emergingchurch.Intro.* Oxford: Monarch, 2004.

Murray, Stuart. *Church after Christendom.* Milton Keynes: Paternoster, 2004.

———. *Post-Christendom: Church and Mission in a Strange New World.* Carlisle: Paternoster, 2004.

Nation, Mark T. *John Howard Yoder: Mennonite Patience, Evangelical Witness, Catholic Convictions.* Grand

Rapids, MI: Eerdmans, 2006.

Neill, Stephen. *The Unfinished Task*. Edinburgh: Edinburgh House, 1957.

Newbigin, Lesslie. *The Gospel in a Pluralist Society*. London: SPCK, 2004.

——. "One Body, One Gospel, One World." *The Ecumenical Review* 11, no. 2 (1959) 143–56.

——. *The Open Secret: An Introduction to the Theology of Mission*. Rev. ed. Grand Rapids, MI: Eerdmans, 1995.

——. *Trinitarian Doctrine for Today's Mission*. Richmond, VA: John Knox, 1964.

O'Donovan, Leo J. "A Changing Ecclesiology in a Changing Church: A Symposium on Development in the Ecclesiology of Karl Rahner." *Theological Studies* 38, no. 4 (1977) 736–62.

——. "A Final Harvest: Karl Rahner's Last Theological Writings." *Religious Studies Review* 11, no. 4 (1985) 357–61.

——. "A Journey into Time: The Legacy of Karl Rahner's Last Years." *Theological Studies* 46, no. 4 (1985) 621–46.

——. "Karl Rahner and Ignatian Spirituality." *Journal of Religion* 83, no. 1 (2003) 146–48.

——. "Karl Rahner, SJ (1904–84): A Theologian for the Twenty-First Century." *Theology Today* 62, no. 3 (2005) 352–63.

——. "On Reading Rahner in a New Century." In *Finding God in All Things*, edited by Mark Bosco and David J. Stagaman, 125–42. New York, NY: Fordham University Press, 2007.

——. "(Rahner, K., SJ, 1904–1984) in Memoriam." *Journal of the American Academy of Religion* 53, no. 1 (1985) 129–31.

——. *A World of Grace: An Introduction to the Themes and Foundations of Karl Rahner's Theology*. Washington, DC: Georgetown University Press, 1995.

O'Toole, Robert F. *Luke's Presentation of Jesus: A Christology*. Subsidia Biblica. Roma: Editrice Pontificio Istituto Biblico, 2004.

Oakes, Edward T. Review of *Can These Bones Live? A Catholic Baptist Engagement with Ecclesiology, Hermeneutics, and Social Theory*, by Barry A. Harvey. *First Things*, no. 189 (2009) 56–58.

Oborji, Francis A. *Concepts of Missio: The Evolution of Contemporary Missiology*. Maryknoll, NY: Orbis, 2006.

Oden, Patrick. "An Emerging Pneumatology: Jürgen Moltmann and the Emerging Church in Conversation." *Journal of Pentecostal Theology* 18, no. 2 (2009) 263–84.

Oden, Thomas C. "The Church." *Journal of Ecumenical Studies* 7, no. 1 (1970) 117–19.

Olin, John C, ed. *A Reformation Debate: Sadoleto's Letter to the Genevans and Calvin's Reply*. New York, NY: Fordham University Press, 2000.

Olson, David T. *The American Church in Crisis: Groundbreaking Research Based on a National Database of over 200,000 Churches*. Grand Rapids, MI: Zondervan, 2008.

Palmer, Ian, et al. *Managing Organizational Change: A Multi-Perspective Approach*. 2nd ed. New York, NY: McGraw-Hill, 2009.

Park, Joon-Sik. *Missional Ecclesiologies in Creative Tension: H. Richard Niebuhr and John Howard Yoder*. American University Studies, Series VII, Theology and Religion. New York, NY: Peter Lang, 2007.

Peters, Ted. *God as Trinity: Relationality and Temporality in Divine Life*. 1st ed. Louisville, KY: Westminster, 1993.

Pinnock, Clark H. *Flame of Love: A Theology of the Holy Spirit*. Downers Grove, IL: IVP, 1996.

Piper, John. *God Is the Gospel: Meditations on God's Love as the Gift of Himself*. Wheaton, IL: Crossway, 2005.

Plantinga, Cornelius. "The Perfect Family." *Christianity Today* 28, March 4 (1988) 27.

——. "Social Trinity and Theism." In *Trinity, Incarnation, and Atonement: Philosophical and Theological Essays*, edited by Ronald J. Feenstra and Cornelius Plantinga, 21–47. Notre Dame, IN: University of Notre Dame Press, 1989.

Powell, Ruth. "Cheers." *Novus: Innovations in Australian Church Life* (2006). No pages. Online: http://www.ncls.org.au/download/doc4264/NOVUSMagazine.pdf.

Pugh, Jeffrey R. "Symbols of Dysfunction, Strategies for Renewal." PhD diss., Flinders University, 2006.

Putman, David, and Ed Stetzer. *Breaking the Discipleship Code: Becoming a Missional Follower of Jesus*. Nashville, TN: B&H, 2008.

Rabey, Steve. *In Search of Authentic Faith: How Emerging Generations Are Transforming the Church*. Colorado Springs, CO: Waterbrook, 2000.

Radmacher, Earl D. *The Nature of the Church*. Lafayette, IN: Schoettle, 1996.

Rahner, Karl. *Anonymous Christianity and the Missionary Task of the Church*. Vol. 12, Theological Investigations. London: Darton, Longman & Todd, 1970.

———. "The Church of Sinners." *Cross Currents*, no. 3 (1951) 64–74.

———. *Concern for the Church*. Vol. 20, Theological Investigations. London: Darton, Longman & Todd, 1981.

———. *Concerning Vatican Council II*. Vol. 6, Theological Investigations. London: Darton, Longman & Todd, 1974.

———. *Confrontations 1*. Vol. 11, Theological Investigations. London: Darton, Longman & Todd, 1974.

———. *Ecclesiology, Questions in the Church, the Church in the World*. Vol. 14, Theological Investigations. London: Darton, Longman & Todd, 1976.

———. *Foundations of Christian Faith: An Introduction to the Idea of Christianity*. New York, NY: Seabury, 1978.

———. *Nature and Grace: Dilemmas in the Modern Church*. New York, NY: Sheed & Ward, 1964.

———. "New Image of the Church." In *Theological Investigations, Vol. 10: Writings of 1965–7*, 3–29. London: Darton, Longman & Todd, 1973.

———. *Servants of the Lord*. New York, NY: Herder & Herder, 1968.

———. *The Shape of the Church to Come*. London: SPCK, 1974.

———. *The Spirit in the Church*. New York, NY: Seabury, 1979.

———. *Theology of Pastoral Action*. Studies in Pastoral Theology, Vol. 1. New York, NY: Herder & Herder, 1968.

———. *The Trinity*. New York, NY: Herder & Herder, 1970.

Rahner, Karl, et al., eds. *The Content of Faith: The Best of Karl Rahner's Theological Writings*. New York, NY: Crossroad, 1993.

Ratzinger, Joseph. *Called to Communion: Understanding the Church Today*. San Francisco, CA: Ignatius, 1996.

———. *Church, Ecumenism, and Politics: New Essays in Ecclesiology*. New York, NY: Crossroad, 1988.

———. *Das Neue Volk Gottes: Entwürfe zur Ekklesiologie*. Düsseldorf: Patmos, 1969.

———. "The Ecclesiology of Vatican II." *Osservatore Romano* 1727 (2002) 5–7.

———. *The Feast of Faith: Approaches to a Theology of the Liturgy*. San Francisco, CA: Ignatius, 1986.

———. *God Is Near Us: The Eucharist, the Heart of Life*. Fort Collins, CO: Ignatius, 2003.

———. *The God of Jesus Christ: Meditations on the Triune God*. Quincy, IL: Franciscan, 1978.

———. *Gospel, Catechesis, Catechism: Sidelights on the Catechism of the Catholic Church*. Fort Collins, CO: Ignatius, 1997.

———. *Introduction to Christianity*. London: Burns & Oates, 1969.

———. *Jesus of Nazareth*. New York, NY: Doubleday, 2007.

———. "Letter to the Bishops of the Catholic Church on Some Aspects of the Church Understood as Communion." *Document of the Congregation for the Doctrine of the Faith* art. 4. (1992).

———. "The Local Church and the Universal Church." *America* 185, no. 16 (2001) 7–11.

———. *Pilgrim Fellowship of Faith: The Church as Communion*. Fort Collins, CO: Ignatius, 2005.

———. *Principles of Catholic Theology: Building Stones for a Fundamental Theology*. San Francisco, CA: Ignatius, 1987.

———. "The Proper Meaning of 'Sister Churches.'" *The Pope Speaks* 46, no. 3 (2005) 136–41.

———. *Some Aspects of the Church Understood as Communion*. Rome: Congregation for the Doctrine of the Faith, 1992.

———. *The Spirit of the Liturgy*. Fort Collins, CO: Ignatius, 2000.

Ratzinger, Joseph, and Vittorio Messori. *The Ratzinger Report: An Exclusive Interview on the State of the Church*. San Francisco, CA: Ignatius, 1985.

Ratzinger, Joseph, and Karl Rahner. *The Episcopate and the Primacy*. Freiburg: Herder, 1962.

Reimer, A. James. "Miroslav Volf: One of the New Theologians." *The Conrad Grebel Review* 18, no. 3 (2000) 3–19.

Richard, Earl. *Jesus: One and Many—The Christological Concepts of New Testament Authors*. Wilmington, NC: Michael Glazier, 1988.

Rowland, Tracey. *Ratzinger's Faith: The Theology of Pope Benedict XVI*. Oxford: Oxford University Press,

2008.

Roxburgh, Alan J. *Crossing the Bridge: Church Leadership in a Time of Change*. Costa Mesa, CA: Percept, 2000.

———. *The Missionary Congregation, Leadership, and Liminality*. New York, NY: Trinity, 1997.

———. *What Is Missional Church? An Introduction to the Missional Church Conversation*. Eagle, ID: Allelon, 2007.

Roxburgh, Alan J., and Fred Romanuk. *The Missional Leader: Equipping Your Church to Reach a Changing World*. San Francisco, CA: Jossey-Bass, 2006.

Russell, Letty M. "Affirming Cross-Cultural Diversity: A Missiological Issue in Feminist Perspective." *International Review of Mission* 81, no. 322 (1992) 253–58.

———. *Becoming Human*. Library of Living Faith. Philadelphia, PA: Westminster, 1982.

———. "Beginning from the Other End." *Duke Divinity School Review* 45, no. 2 (1980) 98–106.

———. *Church in the Round: Feminist Interpretation of the Church*. Louisville, KY: Westminster, 1993.

———. *The Church with Aids: Renewal in the Midst of Crisis*. Louisville, KY: Westminster, 1990.

———. "Clerical Ministry as a Female Profession." *Christian Century* 96, no. 5 (1979) 125–26.

———. "Cultural Hermeneutics: A Postcolonial Look at Mission." *Journal of Feminist Studies in Religion* 20, no. 1 (2004) 23–40.

———. "Feminist Critique: Opportunity for Cooperation." *Journal for the Study of the Old Testament*, no. 22 (1982) 67–71.

———, ed. *Feminist Interpretation of the Bible*. Oxford: Blackwell, 1985.

———. *The Future of Partnership*. Philadelphia, PA: Westminster, 1979.

———. "God, Gold, Glory, and Gender: A Postcolonial View of Mission." *International Review of Mission* 93, no. 368 (2004) 39–49.

———. "Good Housekeeping." In *Feminist Theology: A Reader*, edited by Ann Loades, 225–37. Louisville, KY: Westminster, 1990.

———. *Growth in Partnership*. 1st ed. Philadelphia, PA: Westminster, 1981.

———. "Hot-House Ecclesiology: A Feminist Interpretation of the Church." *Ecumenical Review* 53, no. 1 (2001) 48–56.

———. *Household of Freedom: Authority in Feminist Theology*. Philadelphia, PA: Westminster, 1987.

———. *Human Liberation in a Feminist Perspective—A Theology*. Philadelphia, PA: Westminster, 1974.

———. *Imitators of God: A Study Book on Ephesians*. New York, NY: United Methodist Church, 1984.

———. "Impossible-Possibility." *Duke Divinity School Review* 39, no. 2 (1974) 73–78.

———. "Inclusive Language and Power." *Religious Education* 80, no. 4 (1985) 582–602.

———. *Inheriting Our Mothers' Gardens: Feminist Theology in Third World Perspective*. 1st ed. Philadelphia, PA: Westminster, 1988.

———. "Justice and the Double Sin of the Church." *Living Pulpit* 2, no. 1 (1993) 18–19.

———, ed. *The Liberating Word: A Guide to Nonsexist Interpretation of the Bible*. Philadelphia, PA: Westminster, 1976.

———. "Liberation and Evangelization: A Feminist Perspective." *Occasional Bulletin of Missionary Research* 2, no. 4 (1978) 128–30.

———. "Moving from 'Can't Do' to 'Can Do.'" *Union Seminary Quarterly Review* 58, no. 3–4 (2004) 221–25.

———. "Practicing Hospitality in a Time of Backlash." *Theology Today* 52, no. 4 (1996) 476–84.

———. "Renewal in the Churches: Changing Structures in the East Harlem Protestant Parish." *Union Seminary Quarterly Review* 21, no. 3 (1966) 333–38.

———. "Toward a Trinitarian Language of Hospitality." *Living Pulpit* 8, no. 2 (1999) 26–27.

Russell, Letty M., et al. *Just Hospitality: God's Welcome in a World of Difference*. Louisville, KY: Westminster, 2009.

Sanders, Fred R. *The Image of the Immanent Trinity: Rahner's Rule and the Theological Interpretation of Scripture*. Issues in Systematic Theology. New York, NY: Peter Lang, 2005.

Schatzmann, Siegfried S. *A Pauline Theology of Charismata*. Peabody, MA: Hendrickson, 1987.

Schillebeeckx, Edward H. *Church: The Human Story of God*. Translated by J. Bowden. London: SCM, 1990.

Schindler, David L. "Introduction: Grace and the Form of Nature and Culture." In *Catholicism and Secularization in America*, 10–30. Notre Dame, IL: Notre Dame University Press, 1990.

Schweizer, Eduard. *The Good News According to Luke*. Atlanta, GA: John Knox, 1984.

Shenk, Wilbert R. *The Transfiguration of Mission: Biblical, Theological & Historical Foundations.* Missionary Studies. Scottdale, PA: Herald, 1993.

——. *Write the Vision: The Church Renewed.* New York, NY: Trinity, 1995.

Simons, Menno. *Complete Works of Menno Simons.* 2 vols. Ann Arbor, MI: University of Michigan Library, 2005.

——. "Reply to Gellius Faber, 1554." In *The Complete Writings of Menno Simons* 1561, no. 3, 625–781.

Simson, Wolfgang. *Houses That Change the World: The Return of the House Churches.* Waynesboro, GA: Authentic, 1998.

Skira, Jaroslav Z. Review of *After Our Likeness: The Church as the Image of the Trinity*, by Miroslav Volf. *Theological Studies* 60, no. 2 (1999) 376–77.

Spence, Stephen. *The Trinity: Part One.* Unley: South Australian Baptist Union, 2006.

——. *The Trinity: Part Two.* Unley: South Australian Baptist Union, 2006.

Stetzer, Ed, and Mike Dodson. *Comeback Churches: How 300 Churches Turned Around and Yours Can Too.* Nashville, TN: B&H, 2007.

Stewart, John W. "The Shape of the Church: Congregational and Trinitarian." *The Christian Century* 115, no. 16 (1998) 541.

Strauss, Mark L. *The Davidic Messiah in Luke-Acts: The Promise and Its Fulfillment in Lukan Christology.* Sheffield: Sheffield Academic, 1995.

Sweet, Leonard, ed. *The Church in Emerging Culture: Five Perspectives.* Grand Rapids, MI: Zondervan, 2003.

——. *Soultsunami: Sink or Swim in New Millennium Culture.* Grand Rapids, MI: Zondervan, 1999.

Tan, Seng-Kong. "A Trinitarian Ontology of Missions." *International Review of Mission* 93, no. 369 (2004) 279.

Tavard, George H. "The Church." *Continuum* 6, no. 1 (1968) 106–11.

Thielicke, Helmut. *A Little Exercise for Young Theologians.* Grand Rapids, MI: Eerdmans, 1962.

Thiselton, Anthony C. *New Horizons in Hermeneutics.* Grand Rapids, MI: Zondervan, 1992.

Thompson, John. *Modern Trinitarian Perspectives.* New York, NY: Oxford University Press, 1994.

Thornhill, John. *Sign and Promise: A Theology of the Church for a Changing World.* London: Collins, 1988.

Tidball, Derek, et al., eds. *The Atonement Debate: Papers from the London Symposium on the Theology of Atonement.* Grand Rapids, MI: Zondervan, 2008.

Tizon, Albert. *Transformation after Lausanne: Radical Evangelical Mission in Global-Local Perspective.* Eugene, OR: Wipf & Stock, 2008.

Torrance, Thomas F. *The Christian Doctrine of God: One Being Three Persons.* London: T&T Clark, 2002.

Tripole, Martin R. "A Church for the Poor and the World: At Issue with Moltmann's Ecclesiology." *Theological Studies* 42, no. 4 (1981) 645–59.

Turner, Victor W. *Dramas, Fields, and Metaphors.* Ithaca, NY: Cornell University Press, 1974.

——. *The Ritual Process.* Ithaca, NY: Cornell University Press, 1969.

Van Gelder, Craig. *The Essence of the Church: A Community Created by the Spirit.* Grand Rapids, MI: Baker, 2000.

Vine, William E., et al. *Vine's Expository Dictionary of Old and New Testament Words.* New Precept Study ed. Old Tappan, NJ: F. H. Revell, 1985.

Visser 't Hooft, Willem A. *The Pressure of Our Common Calling.* New York, NY: Doubleday, 1959.

Volf, Miroslav. *After Our Likeness: The Church as the Image of the Trinity.* Grand Rapids, MI: Eerdmans, 1998.

——. "Against a Pretentious Church: A Rejoinder to Bell's Response." *Modern Theology* 19, no. 2 (2003) 281–85.

——. "Arbeit und Charisma: Zu einer Theologie der Arbeit." *Zeitschrift für Evangelische Ethik* 31 (1987) 411–33.

——. "Being as God Is: Trinity and Generosity." In *God's Life in Trinity*, edited by Miroslav Volf and Michael Welker, 3–12. Minneapolis, MN: Fortress, 2006.

——. "Catholicity of 'Two or Three': A Free Church Reflection on the Catholicity of the Local Church." *The Jurist* (1992) 525–46.

——. "Changing and Changeless." *Christian Century* 122, no. 10 (2005) 8.

——. *Christianity and Violence.* Presented October 2003 at the Tools for Peace Conference. No pages. Online: http://repository.upenn.edu/cgi/viewcontent.cgi?article=1001&context=boardman.

———. "The Church as a Prophetic Community and a Sign of Hope." *European Journal of Theology*, no. 2 (1993) 9–30.

———. "Community Formation as an Image of the Triune God: A Congregational Model of Church Order and Life." In *Community Formation: In the Early Church and in the Church Today*, edited by Richard N. Longenecker, 213–37. Peabody, MA: Hendrickson, 2002.

———. "Democracy and Charisma: Reflections on the Democratization of the Church." *Concilium* 28 (1992) 430–34.

———. "Distance and Belonging." In *Abrahamic Faiths, Ethnicity and Ethnic Conflicts*, edited by Paul Peachey, et al., 213–36. Washington, DC: Council for Research in Values & Philosophy, 1997.

———. "Ecumenical Quandary." *Christian Century* 117, no. 7 (2000) 248.

———. "Eschaton, Creation and Social Ethics." *Calvin Journal of Theology* 30, no. 1 (1995) 130–43.

———. *Exclusion and Embrace: A Theological Exploration of Identity, Otherness, and Reconciliation*. Nashville, TN: Abingdon, 1996.

———. "Exclusion and Embrace: Theological Reflections in the Wake of 'Ethnic Cleansing'." *Journal of Ecumenical Studies* 29, no. 2 (1992) 230.

———. "The Final Reconciliation: Reflections on a Social Dimension of the Eschatological Transition." *Modern Theology* 16 (2000) 91–113.

———. *Forgiveness, Reconciliation and Justice: A Christian Contribution to More Peaceful Social Environments*. Presented February 2001 at the Capps Lecture. No pages. Online: http://livedtheology.org/pdfs/Volf.pdf.

———. *Free of Charge: Giving and Forgiving in a Culture Stripped of Grace: The Archbishop's Official 2006 Lent Book*. Grand Rapids, MI: Zondervan, 2006.

———. "'It Is Like Yeast': How the Gospel Should Relate to Culture." *Theology, News and Notes* 41, no. 3 (1994) 12–15.

———. "Kirche Als Gemeinschaft: Ekklesiologische Überlegungen aus Freikirchlicher Perspektive." *Evangelische Theologie* 49 (1989) 52–76.

———. "Living with the Other." *Journal of Ecumenical Studies* 39 (2002) 8–25.

———. "The Nature of the Church." *Evangelical Review of Theology* 26, no. 1 (2002) 68.

———. "New Congregationalism: A Protestant Response." *Concilium* (1996) 232–37.

———. "On Loving with Hope: Eschatology and Social Responsibility." *Transformation* 7, no. 3 (1990) 28–31.

———. *The Role of the 'Other'*. Presented in 2001 at the Brandywine Forum in St David's, Pennsylvania. No pages. Online: http://www.globalengagement.org/issues/2001/09/mvolf-bwf-other-p.htm.

———. "Theology for a Way of Life." In *Practicing Theology: Beliefs and Practices in Christian Life*, edited by Miroslav Volf and Dorothy C. Bass, 245–63. Grand Rapids, MI: Eerdmans, 2002.

———. "Theology, Meaning, and Power." In *The Future of Theology: Essays in Honor of Jürgen Moltmann*, edited by Miroslav Volf, et al., 98–113. Grand Rapids, MI: Eerdmans, 1996.

———. "'The Trinity Is Our Social Program': The Doctrine of the Trinity and the Shape of Social Engagement." *Modern Theology* 3, no. 14 (1998) 403–24.

———. "Truth, Freedom, and Violence." In *Christianity and Culture in the Crossfire*, edited by David A. Hoekema and Bobby Fong, 28–50. Grand Rapids, MI: Eerdmans, 1997.

———. "A Vision of Embrace: Theological Perspectives on Cultural Identity and Conflict." *Ecumenical Review* 48, no. 2 (1995) 195–205.

———. "Way of Life." *Christian Century* 119, no. 24 (2002) 35.

———. *Work in the Spirit: Toward a Theology of Work*. New York, NY: Oxford University Press, 1991.

———. *Zukunft der Arbeit—Arbeit der Zukunft: Das Marxsche Verständnis der Arbeit und Seine Theologische Wertung*. Munich: Kaiser, 1987.

Volf, Miroslav, and Maurice Lee. "The Spirit and the Church." *The Conrad Grebel Review* (Special Issue: Miroslav Volf) 18, no. 3 (2000) 20–45.

Wagner, C. Peter. *Your Church Can Grow*. Ventura, CA: Regal, 1984.

Ward, Pete. *Liquid Church*. Peabody, MA: Hendrickson, 2002.

Weaver, J. Denny. "The John Howard Yoder Legacy: Whither the Second Generation?" *Mennonite Quarterly Review* 77, no. 3 (2003) 451–71.

Webber, Robert E. *The Younger Evangelicals: Facing the Challenges of the New World*. Grand Rapids, MI: Baker, 2003.

Webster, John B. "Biblical Reasoning." *Anglican Theological Review* 90, no. 4 (2008) 733–51.

———. "The Church and the Perfection of God." In *The Community of the Word: Toward an Evangelical Ecclesiology*, edited by Mark Husbands and Daniel J. Treier, 75–95. Leicester: Apollos, 2005.

———. *Confessing God: Essays in Christian Dogmatics II*. London: T&T Clark, 2005.

———. *Holy Scripture: A Dogmatic Sketch*, Current Issues in Theology. Cambridge: Cambridge University Press, 2003.

———. "Justification, Analogy and Action: Passivity and Activity in Jüngel's Anthropology." In *The Possibilities of Theology: Studies in the Theology of Eberhard Jüngel in His Sixtieth Year*, 106–42. Edinburgh: T&T Clark, 1994.

———. "Principles of Systematic Theology." *International Journal of Systematic Theology* 11, no. 1 (2009) 56–71.

———. "The Self-Organizing Power of the Gospel of Christ: Episcopacy and Community Formation." *International Journal of Systematic Theology* 3, no. 1 (2001) 179–93.

———. "The Visible Attests the Invisible." In *The Community of the Word: Toward an Evangelical Ecclesiology*, edited by Mark Husbands and Daniel J. Treier, 96–113. Leicester: Apollos, 2005.

———. *Word and Church: Essays in Christian Dogmatics*. Edinburgh: T&T Clark, 2001.

Willard, Dallas. *The Divine Conspiracy: Rediscovering Our Hidden Life in God*. San Francisco, CA: HarperSanFrancisco, 1998.

———. *The Great Omission: Reclaiming Jesus's Essential Teachings on Discipleship*. San Francisco, CA: HarperSanFrancisco, 2006.

———. *Renovation of the Heart: Putting on the Character of Christ*. Colorado Springs, CO: NavPress, 2002.

———. *Revolution of Character: Discovering Christ's Pattern for Spiritual Transformation*. Colorado Springs, CO: NavPress, 2005.

———. *The Spirit of the Disciplines: Understanding How God Changes Lives*. San Francisco, CA: HarperSanFrancisco, 1990.

Williams, Rowan, et al. *Mission-Shaped Church: Church Planting and Fresh Expressions of Church in a Changing Context*. London: Church House, 2004.

Winter, Ralph D., et al. *Perspectives on the World Christian Movement: A Reader*. 4th ed. Pasadena, CA: William Carey, 2009.

Wright, Christopher J. H. "Mission as a Matrix for Hermeneutics and Biblical Theology." In *Out of Egypt: Biblical Theology and Biblical Interpretation*, edited by Craig Bartholomew, et al., 102–43. Grand Rapids, MI: Zondervan, 2004.

———. *The Mission of God: Unlocking the Bible's Grand Narrative*. Downers Grove, IL: IVP Academic, 2006.

———. *The Mission of God's People: A Biblical Theology of the Church's Mission*. Grand Rapids, MI: Zondervan, 2010.

Wright, David F. "Trinity." In *Encyclopedia of Early Christianity*, edited by Everett Ferguson, 1142–47. New York, NY: Garland, 1999.

Wright, Nicholas T. *The New Testament and the People of God*. Christian Origins and the Question of God. Minneapolis, MN: Augsburg Fortress, 1996.

Yamamori, Tetsunao, and E. LeRoy Lawson. *Introducing Church Growth: A Textbook in Missions*. Cincinnati, OH: New Life, 1975.

Yoder, John Howard. "Binding and Loosing." In *The Royal Priesthood*, edited by Michael G. Cartwright, 323–58. Grand Rapids, MI: Eerdmans, 1994.

———. *Body Politics: Five Practices of the Christian Community before the Watching World*. Nashville, TN: Discipleship Resources, 1992.

———. *The Christian Witness to the State*. Institute of Mennonite Studies Series. Newton, KS: Faith & Life, 1964.

———. "The Disavowal of Constantine: An Alternative Perspective in Interfaith Dialogue." In *The Royal Priesthood*, edited by Michael G. Cartwright, 242–61. Grand Rapids, MI: Eerdmans, 1994.

———. *For the Nations: Essays Evangelical and Public*. Grand Rapids, MI: Eerdmans, 1997.

———. "The Free Church Ecumenical Style." In *The Royal Priesthood*, edited by Michael G. Cartwright, 231–41. Grand Rapids, MI: Eerdmans, 1994.

———. "The Nature of the Unity We Seek: A Historic Free Church View." In *The Royal Priesthood*, edited by Michael G. Cartwright, 221–32. Grand Rapids, MI: Eerdmans, 1994.

——. "The Otherness of the Church." In *The Royal Priesthood*, edited by Michael G. Cartwright, 53–66. Grand Rapids, MI: Eerdmans, 1994.

——. "A People in the World." In *The Royal Priesthood*, edited by Michael G. Cartwright, 66–101. Grand Rapids, MI: Eerdmans, 1994.

——. *The Politics of Jesus: Vicit Agnus Noster*. Grand Rapids, MI: Eerdmans, 1994.

——. *The Priestly Kingdom: Social Ethics as Gospel*. Notre Dame, IN: University of Notre Dame Press, 1985.

——. *The Royal Priesthood: Essays Ecclesiological and Ecumenical*. Grand Rapids, MI: Eerdmans, 1994.

——. "Sacrament as Social Process: Christ the Transformer of Culture." *Theology Today* 48, no. 1 (1991) 33–44.

——. "To Serve Our God and to Rule the World." In *The Royal Priesthood*, edited by Michael G. Cartwright, 128–40. Grand Rapids, MI: Eerdmans, 1994.

——. "Why Ecclesiology Is Social Ethics: Gospel Ethics Versus the Wider Wisdom." In *The Royal Priesthood*, edited by Michael G. Cartwright, 102–26. Grand Rapids, MI: Eerdmans, 1994.

Yoder, John Howard, et al. *A Declaration on Peace: In God's People the World's Renewal Has Begun*. Scottdale, PA: Herald, 1991.

Yoder, John Howard, et al. *The War of the Lamb: The Ethics of Nonviolence and Peacemaking*. Grand Rapids, MI: Brazos, 2009.

Zizioulas, John D. *Being as Communion: Studies in Personhood and the Church*. Crestwood, NY: St. Vladimir's Seminary, 1985.

——. "The Bishop in the Theological Doctrine of the Orthodox Church." *Kanon* 7 (1985) 23–35.

——. *The Church as Communion: A Presentation on the World Conference Theme*. Geneva: WCC, 1994.

——. *Communion and Otherness*. Orthodox Peace Fellowship's Occasional Paper 19: Andreas, 1994.

——. *Communion and Otherness: Further Studies in Personhood and the Church*. London: T&T Clark, 2007.

——. "Constantine Scouteris: The People of God—Its Unity and Its Glory: A Discussion of John 17:17–24 in the Light of the Patristic Thought." *The Greek Orthodox Theological Review* 30, no. 4 (1983) 399–420.

——. "The Contribution of Cappadocia to Christian Thought." In *Sinasos in Cappadocia*, edited by Frosso Pimenides and Stelios Roades, 23–37. London: Ekdoseis Agra, 1985.

——. "Die Pneumatologische Dimension Der Kirche." *Internationale Katholische Zeitschrift "Communio"* 2 (1973) 133–47.

——. "The Early Christian Community." In *Christian Spirituality: Origins to the Twelfth Century*, edited by Bernard McGinn and John Meyendorff, 23–43. New York, NY: Crossroad, 1985.

——. "The Ecclesiological Presuppositions of the Holy Eucharist." *Nicolaus* 10 (1982) 333–49.

——. "Episkope and Episkopos in the Early Church: A Brief Survey of the Evidence." In *Episcopé and Episcopate in Ecumenical Perspective*. Faith and Order Paper 102. Geneva: WCC, 1980.

——. *Eucharist, Bishop, Church: The Unity of the Church in the Divine Eucharist and the Bishop During the First Three Centuries*. Brookline, MA: Holy Cross Orthodox, 2001.

——. "Human Capacity and Human Incapacity: A Theological Exploration of Personhood." *Scottish Journal of Theology* 28 (1975) 401–47.

——. "Implications ecclésiologiques de deux types de Pneumatologie." In *Communio Sanctorum*, edited by Jean-Jacques von Allmen and Boris Bobrinskoy, 141–54. Geneva: Labor et fides, 1982.

——. *Lectures in Christian Dogmatics*. London: T&T Clark, 2008.

——. "The Mystery of the Church in Orthodox Tradition." *One in Christ* 24, no. 4 (1988) 294–303.

——. "The Nature of the Unity We Seek: Response of the Orthodox Observer." *One in Christ* 24, no. 4 (1988) 342–48.

——. "On Being a Person: Towards an Ontology of Personhood." In *Persons, Divine and Human: King's College Essays in Theological Anthropology*, edited by Christoph Schwobel and Colin E. Gunton, 33–46. Edinburgh: Clark, 1991.

——. "The Theological Problem of 'Reception.'" *Bulletin of the Centro pro Unione* 26 (1984) 3–6.